£1.99

HARRY PARTCH, HOBO COMPOSER

Eastman Studies in Music

Ralph P. Locke, Senior Editor
Eastman School of Music

Additional Titles of Interest

Claude Vivier: A Composer's Life
Bob Gilmore

Composing for Japanese Instruments
Minoru Miki
Translated by Marty Regan
Edited by Philip Flavin

Dane Rudhyar: His Music, Thought, and Art
Deniz Ertan

*Dear Dorothy:
Letters from Nicolas Slonimsky to Dorothy Adlow*
Nicolas Slonimsky
Edited by Electra Slonimsky Yourke

*Elliott Carter's "What Next?"
Communication, Cooperation, and Separation*
Guy Capuzzo

John Kirkpatrick, American Music, and the Printed Page
Drew Massey

Leon Kirchner: Composer, Performer, and Teacher
Robert Riggs

Narratives of Identity in Alban Berg's "Lulu"
Silvio J. dos Santos

Portrait of Percy Grainger
Edited by Malcolm Gillies and David Pear

The Sea on Fire: Jean Barraqué
Paul Griffiths

A complete list of titles in the Eastman Studies in Music series
may be found on our website, www.urpress.com.

S. ANDREW GRANADE

HARRY PARTCH
HOBO COMPOSER

UNIVERSITY OF ROCHESTER PRESS

The University of Rochester Press gratefully acknowledges the following for their generous support of this publication: the Howard Hanson Institute for American Music at the Eastman School of Music, University of Rochester; the University of Missouri Research Board; and the AMS 75 PAYS Endowment of the American Musicological Society, funded in part by the National Endowment for the Humanities and the Andrew W. Mellon Foundation.

Copyright © 2014 by S. Andrew Granade

All rights reserved. Except as permitted under current legislation, no part of this work may be photocopied, stored in a retrieval system, published, performed in public, adapted, broadcast, transmitted, recorded, or reproduced in any form or by any means, without the prior permission of the copyright owner.

First published 2014

University of Rochester Press
668 Mt. Hope Avenue, Rochester, NY 14620, USA
www.urpress.com
and Boydell & Brewer Limited
PO Box 9, Woodbridge, Suffolk IP12 3DF, UK
www.boydellandbrewer.com

ISBN-13: 978-1-58046-495-6
ISSN: 1071-9989

Library of Congress Cataloging-in-Publication Data

Granade, S. Andrew, author.
  Harry Partch, hobo composer / S. Andrew Granade.
    pages cm — (Eastman studies in music, ISSN 1071-9989 ; v. 120)
  Includes bibliographical references and index.
  ISBN 978-1-58046-495-6 (hardcover : alkaline paper)—ISBN 1-58046-495-5 (hardcover : alkaline paper) 1. Partch, Harry, 1901–1974. 2. Composers—United States—Biography. 3. Hobo songs—History and criticism. I. Title. II. Series: Eastman studies in music ; v. 120.
  ML410.P176G73 2014
  780.92—dc23
  [B]   2014029786

A catalogue record for this title is available from the British Library.

This publication is printed on acid-free paper.
Printed and bound by CPI Group (UK) Ltd, Croydon, CR0 4YY

For Joy

CONTENTS

List of Illustrations	ix
Acknowledgments	xi
Prologue: To Sound American	1
1 The Hobo in Partch's Early Life and Aesthetic	23
Interlude 1: Transients and Migrants	46
2 The Transient Journey	63
3 *Bitter Music*	88
4 A Knight of the Road	110
Interlude 2: Hoboes	129
5 *U.S. Highball:* Becoming a Musical Hobo	144
6 A Newsboy Letter	198
7 Trading on a Hobo Image	219
8 The Strangest Kind of Hobo	252
Epilogue: To Be American	278
Glossary of Instruments and Hobo Slang	285
Notes	289
Bibliography	327
Index	343

ILLUSTRATIONS

Figures

1.1	Photograph of Harry Partch, August 1931	39
I.1	Veterans in the Bonus Expeditionary Force, 1932	50
2.1	Dust Bowl migrants from Missouri on US Highway 99, California, 1937	70
2.2	Dorothea Lange, "Migrant Mother," 1936	74
2.3	Line drawings by Partch (*Bitter Music*) and Woody Guthrie (*Bound for Glory*)	80
3.1	Dorothea Lange, "Toward Los Angeles, California. 1937"	89
3.2	Dorothea Lange, "Hobo wakes up early in the morning," 1939	91
3.3	Partch's opening drawing for his August 28, 1935, entry in his journal *Bitter Music*	93
4.1	Photograph by Partch of hoboes near Fort Yuma, Arizona, February 1940	112
4.2	Partch, hobo song "While My Heart Keeps Beating Time"	115
5.1	Partch on top of a boxcar, riding as a hobo	146
5.2	Pages 9–10 of Partch's composition notebook, 1941	155
5.3	Partch's first draft libretto of *U.S. Highball*	160

5.4	First page of Partch's sketches for the variations on the word "Chicago" (*U.S. Highball*)	168
5.5	First page of version B of *U.S. Highball* for voice, Adapted Guitar, Kithara, and Chromelodeon	172
6.1	Henry Inman, *News Boy*, 1841	202
6.2	James Henry Cafferty, *Newsboy Selling New-York Herald*, 1857	203
6.3	Partch's tonality diamond	215
7.1	Harry Partch, Ethel Luening, and Alix Maruchess, April 1944	245
E.1	Columbia Records, advertisement for *The World of Harry Partch*	284

Tables

1.1	Partch's movements and life as a hobo	33
3.1	Songs and musical citations in *Bitter Music*	102
5.1	Versions of *U.S. Highball*	159

ACKNOWLEDGMENTS

There is an old maxim that holds that the best writing is never accomplished alone. Although I occasionally felt as though I were going alone, especially after long days spent staring at the screen willing the words to appear, in reality I was aided and abetted by more people than I can possibly thank in this short space. What follows is a small payment on a large debt of gratitude.

When I initially began studying Harry Partch, I was fortunate to find a welcoming community of scholars, artists, and musicians who were selfless in their desire to spread information about the composer they universally call Harry, and to engender the love they hold for him and his music. From the earliest stages of this project Danlee Mitchell provided council, support, and direction, answering my constant stream of questions and even reading over sections of the manuscript. Dean Drummond and the faculty, staff, and students at Montclair State University welcomed me to New Jersey and made my stay there studying Partch's instruments both productive and pleasant. Dean, in particular, provided wonderful context for Partch's music and generously allowed me complete access to the instruments. Many of the insights I gained would not have been possible without his help. His recent passing was a blow to all of us who work on Partch's music. Philip Blackburn of the American Composers Forum opened his treasure trove of Partch materials to me over a long weekend in St. Paul, Minnesota. His enthusiasm for Partch is boundless. Jon Szanto answered numerous queries about the collections of Partch's music released on CRI. Jon Roy, currently working on a new documentary on Partch, provided a listening ear and access to the multitude of scanned documents he collected for his film. Finally, Bob Gilmore and Thomas McGeary, two men whose writings have had a great impact on our understanding of Partch, graciously pointed me in the right direction time and again.

Every scholar quickly finds that librarians and archivists are key to any successful research project, and I was fortunate in the men and women who opened their holdings to me and even suggested areas I had not thought of exploring. David Null, University Archivist at the University of Wisconsin, Madison, located numerous documents from Partch's time in Madison. Bernard R. Crystal at Columbia University granted full access to the Douglas S. Moore Papers. Suzanne Eggleston Lovejoy at Yale University tracked down a stray letter from Partch to Quincy Porter. Thomas Tanselle at the John Simon Guggenheim Memorial Foundation sent pages upon pages of documents concerning Partch's numerous applications to that institution. George Boziwick at the Music Division of the New York Public Library for the Performing Arts aided in my study of the Otto Luening, Henry Cowell, and League of Composers collections. First Marlys Scarborough at the University of Illinois Music Library, and then Adriana Cuervo at the Sousa Archives and Center for American Music of the University of Illinois at Urbana-Champaign, were tireless in retrieving documents from the Harry Partch Estate Archive. Finally, Laura Gayle Green, fearless librarian at my home institution of the University of Missouri–Kansas City throughout most of this writing, hunted down countless obscure records and was a constant source of friendship and encouragement as well.

The students and faculty at the UMKC Conservatory of Music and Dance have been welcome sources of support. My gracious colleagues Olga Ackerly, Bill Everett, Sarah Tyrrell, and Erika Honisch have listened to various presentations on this material over the years and always have had keen insights to share. Bill, in particular, was a willing audience for my ideas and expert editor in the sections he read; he even suggested a key organizational design. Many of my sources were gathered and organized by my outstanding GTAs, particularly David McIntire, Melinda Lein, Jessica Horner, and Nathinee Chucherdwatanasak, and I am grateful for their enthusiasm for the topic. Many colleagues have offered sources and guidance at the perfect moment. Michael Hicks generously shared his work on Columbia's marketing of the avant-garde, Denise Von Glahn enthusiastically discussed her work on Thomas Whitney Surette and the Guggenheim Foundation music awards, Mark Davidson offered up Partch's Alan Lomax connection, and Graham Raulerson supplied his dissertation on the hobo in American music and acted as a sounding board for my exploration of Partch's hobo output. Brett Boutwell and Sara Haefeli read chapters and offered critiques that made the book better in all ways. George Keck first encouraged me into the field and not only listened generously to my ramblings on Partch, but modeled how to be a musicologist. David Patterson, my dissertation advisor, who shepherded me through my early explorations into Partch's life and work, has continued to offer keen criticisms that seem to find the heart of the problem. His example of how to do good work while enjoying the process continues to inspire me.

Finally, thanks are due to my family. Large sections of this book were written at my in-laws' house on Greer's Ferry Lake in Arkansas, where they allowed my family to camp for weeks at a time, even hanging the "Chimes of Partch" on the back deck, where they serenaded my morning writing sessions. Phil and Pat Shupe are second parents and their family is my own in every way. My brother and sister-in-law, Stephen and Misty Granade, read sections and listened to my long discussions of Partch and the hobo. My parents, Ray and Ronnie Granade, have particularly supported my work. My father read every word of this manuscript and offered his historian's eye for detail and his expert editing at crucial moments. My sons, Sam and Noah, have known when to give me space to write and when to pull me away for play-time outdoors. They both enrich my life in ways I cannot begin to articulate. And my wife, Joy, regularly listened to my ideas, my frustrations, and my triumphs, and cared equally about all three. Stephen King wrote in *On Writing: A Memoir of the Craft*: "And whenever I see a first novel dedicated to a wife (or a husband), I smile and think, There's someone who knows. Writing is a lonely job. Having someone who believes in you makes a lot of difference. They don't have to make speeches. Just believing is usually enough." Joy, thanks for believing.

PROLOGUE

To Sound American

This is the story of a man who became a hobo out of necessity and remained one for its freedoms. It is the story of a composer who rejected the tenets of music as he found them and sought to return music to its roots. It is the story of American music, and how music reflects and reacts with the culture in which it lives. It is the story of Harry Partch and his music.

Two important questions frame this story: "Why Harry Partch?" and "Why hoboes?" Those questions entwine in all the scholarship and literature on this uniquely American composer. They inform reviews like Alex Ross's, of a production of Partch's version of *Oedipus*, where he proclaimed: "Of all the triumphantly weird characters who have roamed the frontiers of American art, none ever went quite as far out as the composer Harry Partch. His exit from civilization has assumed the status of legend, and it's all true."[1] And they stretch back to 1949, where, in his preface to the first edition of Partch's formative book *Genesis of a Music*, Otto Luening eloquently pinpointed why the hobo was crucial to any approach to the composer's music:

> For long periods he withdrew from a society which seemed indifferent to the lonely searchings of a creative man. At one time, for a period of eight years, he drifted around the country, riding the rails and hitchhiking, in company with the wanderers and hoboes of the lumber camps, the harvest fields, the sea, and the vineyards, and came to know the souls of these people.
> In certain of his compositions, *U.S. Highball, Barstow, San Francisco, Letter from Hobo Pablo, Bitter Music*, for example, he has given voice to their life, and has become in a moving way a poet and singer of these wandering Americans—perhaps of all wanderers and of all the spiritually isolated.[2]

Luening highlighted Partch's compositions of the early 1940s featuring the hobo (later collected by Partch as *The Wayward*, and now known as his Americana works), as having special relevance to both the composer's output and to American music. Indeed, Luening asserted specifically that these works and Partch's personal hobo experiences mark him as a uniquely American composer. Paul Earls, writing at the end of Partch's life about *Delusion of the Fury*, agreed with Luening, going so far as to note, "An entire study could be done on his preoccupation with 'bums'; they form the core of *The Wayward* series and touches of this source are apt to crop up in any of Partch's works."[3]

Harry Partch certainly encouraged the connection between his music and the hobo as he roamed the country, composing, performing, writing essays and manuscripts, taking up residencies, and granting interviews. He extolled the liberties and virtues of hobo life and the threads of that life woven through his compositions. He downplayed the struggles inherent to hoboing, though he hated the hardships associated with homelessness and poverty and was happy to give them up and never be hungry again. He was careful to use the aura granted by his hoboing to construct his image as an outsider correcting societal and musical ills.

This hobo preoccupation lasted his entire life and colored impressions from his earliest to his last years. When he recounted childhood memories in interview or in print, he often recalled coming in from a day of play and sitting down at the dinner table only to find that his father had brought home hoboes to give them food and a place to sleep in return for a bit of work.[4] On the other end of the scale, in an interview he gave in March 1974, five months before his death, he likewise touted his fascination with hoboes and their lifestyle:

> Harry Partch: I would have gotten a taste of a truer life, a more down-to-earth life, a life of sleeping out on a riverbank, cooking my own food. And, ohhh, what a relief that was. Because I'd done a lot of camping as a child, and this was getting back to that. And then I experienced flophouses for twenty-five cents a night, even less sometimes. It was all so clean and beautiful to be close to nature. And the food I got was just infinitely better for a small fraction of the price.
>
> Vivian Perlis: It wasn't strictly a matter of the Depression, an economic matter; it was a way of life that you knew you wanted, you wanted it in a way, didn't you?
>
> Harry Partch: Yes, I wanted it. But it finally became very onerous.[5]

From the beginning to the end of his life, Partch clothed himself with the hobo's lore.

We may wonder why Partch would wish to ally himself with the hobo, often understood today to be a dirty, poor, good-for-nothing, begging vagrant. It is a strange mantle for a man to assume while attempting to make inroads into the musical community, one then as now concerned with appearances and perceptions. But popular mythology and early twentieth-century literature portrayed the hobo differently. To that age, the hobo was a distinctly American figure along the lines of the frontiersman and cowboy. He was an iconoclast, defying traditional ways of life to cling to rugged American individualism.[6] He was idolized as an idealistic dreamer, a man driven by wanderlust.[7]

Small wonder that Partch wished to adopt this image and that it remained with him throughout his life. Even today, writers describe Partch as an iconoclast and link him with that strain of American experimental and idealistic composers that began with Charles Ives and continued through Henry Cowell and John Cage. Michael Nyman, in one of the first books on the experimental tradition in music, connected Partch with Varèse and Alois Hába as a composer interested in striking off on his own by moving beyond the system of equal temperament.[8] David Nicholls, focusing exclusively on the American experimental scene, listed Partch as one of thirteen composers in the first part of the twentieth century who formed a distinctly American music by staying true to their individual ideals and looking away from Europe. He found Partch's importance in his assimilation of ideas from around the globe and use of them in startling new ways.[9] Michael Broyles placed Partch in relation to Frank Zappa, arguing that Partch represented the maverick tradition at its purest and Zappa at its most visible.[10] And finally, the publicity surrounding Michael Tilson Thomas's "American Mavericks" series has linked Partch with composers from William Billings to Charles Ives, Steve Reich, and Laurie Anderson, in concerts, digital media, and publications that praise them all as "the voices who created a new American sound for the twentieth century and beyond."[11]

However, beyond the broad category of experimental composers, the one area where Partch has perhaps cast the longest iconoclastic shadow is among microtonalists. Lou Harrison, who followed Partch into microtonality, famously quipped, "To Harry, who told us the truth about tune, as Kinsey did about sex."[12] Although few use Partch's idiosyncratic form of just intonation today, many have been inspired by his search outside equal temperament to play with intonation in their compositions. Both Ben Johnston and James Tenney studied with Partch and subsequently began using intonation as a compositional variable, influencing a succeeding generation of composers from Kyle Gann to Manfred Stahnke and John Luther Adams through their long and influential teaching careers. MicroFest, the largest concert series devoted to microtonal music, features a resident ensemble of Partch's instruments and regularly commissions new works for them. In the summer of 2013, Ensemble musikFabrik decided to open the annual Ruhrtriennale Music and Arts Festival with a new production of Partch's *Delusion of the Fury* played on newly created replicas of his instruments, because Partch was "a man who was ahead of his time when he began to engage with microtonality."[13] And throughout Europe, from Paris to Darmstadt to Donaueschingen, young composers revel in minute gradations of pitch and point to Harry Partch as a guiding star.[14]

Collectively, these composers and scholars hold up Partch as the consummate musical outsider, a man finding his way beyond the Western musical system, much as hoboes went outside American society to find their own community. But this focus on Partch as an experimenter also obscures Partch as an American composer, using American folklore as the basis for his music. The depth to which Partch absorbed and used his experiences and the hobo traditions he encountered are fundamental to comprehending his aesthetic and compositional output. This book confronts the received wisdom of Partch as experimenter and attempts to enrich our view of his accomplishments by explaining how the hobo experience is woven through Partch's life, especially during the 1930s and 1940s; how the hobo image shaped his music and its ultimate reception; and how American culture of the Depression and World War II eras holds the key to untangling the meanings and structure of some of Harry Partch's most celebrated compositions in *The Wayward*.

Underlying all of Partch's music in this period was his desire to sound "American." Writing in 1940, Partch declared that his adoption of microtonality and his decision to become a hobo came from the same impulse: "Now, however, my 'evolution' seemed to demand a sudden descent into hobo jungles." Why? Because "The nuance of inflection and thought of the lowest of our social order was a new experience in tone, and I found myself at its fountainhead—a fountainhead of pure musical Americana."[15] In order to sound authentically "American," Partch felt that he needed microtones to capture the subtle gradations of expression and hobo speech. His was not an isolated search. For decades prior to the Depression, American composers had been caught between the desire to sound American, and to respect their European musical training, always attempting to define America's folk music and the role it could play for American composers. As Henry Gilbert put it in 1915, American music "has this problem to face: that it can only become ultimately distinctive by leaving the paths of imitation, and that by leaving the paths of imitation it must temporarily sacrifice both immediate success and the respect ... of both public and academician."[16] Before addressing Partch specifically, I want to look beyond his time and broadly paint the history of this study in order to highlight how Partch's music merges with its dominant trends and the significant ways in which it differs: there was a line between *sounding* American and *being* American, which composers caught up in the search shied from crossing.

Defining an American Sound

For our purposes, the impetus to define America in music goes back forty years before Partch walked into the hobo jungle. It is framed by what I call decorative exoticism.[17] Trained in the harmony-based forms of Western music, composers throughout the early twentieth century adapted melodies, rhythms, and timbres from music they found in the United States but did not alter the European-derived structure of their music. They would not sublimate "American" music through Western European musical form: rather, they wanted an American national music. Through trial and error they found that this music was necessarily exotic, but its growth was a strange blend of the American pioneering spirit in discovering new, uncharted music, and a capitulation to European practices.

This reluctance to shed European influence rested on several factors, most notably reliance on European training. Early in the century, few composers eschewed training overseas. Like most students, composers of the era were products of their educations and adopted wholesale the European attitudes toward the nature and role of music. The assumption of European music's superiority was so prevalent that, in June of 1891, when Jeannette Thurber began looking for a new director for her fledgling National Conservatory of Music, she looked for a European. Surprisingly, though, critics and scholars alike often cite Antonin Dvořák's acceptance of that post, and his subsequent arrival in America in September the following year, as the catalyst for the search for an American national music. While that claim overstates Dvořák's influence, it does point to the widespread discussion that his music and writings initiated among American composers. Thurber had instituted a policy that all talented students, regardless of race or social standing, were to be admitted to the National Conservatory of Music, an undertaking that exposed Dvořák to the range of nationalities that had settled in the United States. Already known for incorporating Bohemian folksongs into his music, Dvořák was impressed by the students, finding their diversity a rich musical trove to mine. Through a series of controversial newspaper articles, he began a debate about the place of those musics in American composition. He summarized his slightly tempered views in his 1895 article "Music in America": "It matters little whether the inspiration for the coming folk songs of America is derived from the negro melodies, the songs of the creoles, the red man's chant, or the plaintive ditties of the homesick German or Norwegian. Undoubtedly the germs for the best of music lie hidden among all the races that are commingled in this great country."[18] Dvořák was not concerned with which type of music became the basis for American art music, only that it be an American vernacular tradition rather than a European art tradition.

Dvořák's suggestions sparked a fire of controversy as composers and critics argued the merits of incorporating folk traditions from people not normally considered genteel enough for high society. The debate continued long after Dvořák left the country in 1895, and a small number of composers began striving to define an American image in music, following Dvořák's ideas. Arthur Farwell was among the first of these composers: returning to Boston in 1899 after a two-year sojourn in Germany, he was eager to draw inspiration from American myths and legends, and gravitated toward the music of Native Americans as the logical first place to find the basis of true American music.[19] Late in his life, Farwell looked back on this period, remarking, "I had taken Dvořák's challenge deeply to heart, and worked in the field of Indian music, not with the idea that this or any other non-Caucasian folk music existing in America was the foundation of a national art, but because it existed only in America and its development was part of my program to further all unique and characteristic musical expressions that could come only from this country."[20] Farwell's adoption of Native American music was part of a self-conscious attempt to foster an American music that would be unique, and free from German musical influence. He began his own publishing house, the Wa-Wan Press, to issue the music of young American composers, wrote and spoke tirelessly on the importance of an American musical identity, and composed works based on Native American melodies.[21]

Farwell's 1901 *American Indian Melodies* was among the Wa-Wan Press's first publications, and one of his first compositions to incorporate Native American themes. He drew these "melodies" from songs collected and catalogued by Alice Fletcher and harmonized by John Comfort Fillmore in *Indian Story and Song from North America*, a work that provided melodies for many composers looking for Native American music.[22] Knowing the prejudices against the use of Native American music, Farwell used the publication to argue for that genre's musical worth by writing in the "Introduction" that the "Approach of the Thunder God" could readily be rendered in a manner to make it appear trivial, (as, for that matter could Beethoven), did we not infuse into its rendition the weightiness, the dignity, the awe, the steady and irresistible on-coming of the Thunder God wrapped in the ominous black cloud. Thus it will be seen that a seriousness no less than that which we accord the works of the masters, must be brought to the interpretation of these songs, the spontaneous utterance of a people whose every word, action or tone invariably bears a deeply vital significance.[23]

This overt exoticization of Native Americans as a proud, noble people, a constant thread in the music and writings of the "Indianist" composers, is especially pronounced in Farwell's works.[24] He feared that his music would be judged as trivial because of its incorporation of non-Western sources and went to great lengths to ensure that his music was taken as seriously as Beethoven's.

Looking at these early works, it is quite easy to see the basis of Farwell's fear. He was composing during the heyday of the Reservation Boarding School System, in which young Native Americans were indoctrinated into European culture in an attempt to "kill the Indian, save the man."[25] Because of this dominant view, Farwell approached his chosen melodies—from a "savage people"—in a blatantly Romantic manner, in order to make them more palatable. Not only did he rhetorically tie Native American music to Germany, he used the melodies as a decorative ornament upon European musical structures and harmonies. He recast them with new harmonizations based on his understanding of religious ceremonies and his knowledge of European musical practices, and published them, hoping to convince other composers that his was the way to an American musical identity.[26]

Dvořák's and Farwell's arguments persuaded Charles Wakefield Cadman, but his notions of how to use Native American melodies differed significantly from Farwell's. Although Cadman also used songs collected by Alice Fletcher, he was more flexible in his approach and often modified the melodies extensively. While Farwell romanticized Native Americans in an attempt to persuade skeptical Americans of the validity of using those melodies, Cadman accepted them as compositional fodder without much comment. He was more interested in the creative application of melodies than in simply reharmonizing them. Besides, he argued, "only one-fifth of all Indian thematic material is valuable in the hands of a composer—is suitable for harmonic investment."[27] As a result of his selectivity, Cadman had perhaps the greatest success among these composers when, in 1918, the Metropolitan Opera House in New York premiered his opera *Shanewis*, *the Robin Woman*: the Met stopped producing German operas during that season, in deference to World War I–inspired patriotic sentiment, leaving a slot available for Cadman's work.²⁸

Shanewis's success cemented in Cadman's mind the idea that Native American music represented America. He went on to write two more operas on the subject and a host of songs and instrumental works, but in a sense it was the genre's swan song; many composers were already looking elsewhere for a response to Dvořák's challenge. For twenty years, composers had experimented with Native American melodies, imagining in the pounding open fourths and fifths that peppered their piano works a kind of primitivism that matched their notions of Native American rituals. The music of composers such as Farwell and Cadman lacked any resemblance to actual Native American practices, but in its historical context, it was a trembling first step toward an indigenous American music. By the 1920s, musical thought on both sides of the Atlantic had changed. The primitivism that buoyed many explorations into tribal musics had subsided, and American composers had lost interest in evocations of Native Americans. Following World War I, musicians throughout the Western world began listening intently to the recordings and concerts of the music of African Americans that were flooding the market, the emerging genre of jazz.

American composers still wanted to define America in music, and as the 1920s dawned it was logical that American composers would be attracted to the music that famously led F. Scott Fitzgerald to christen the decade "The Jazz Age." It was a period of vast economic growth, of questioning America's role in the world after the Great War, and of advances in radio and recording technology that transformed music into a consumer good. In the angular melodies, syncopated rhythms, and expanded harmonies of Louis Armstrong's hot jazz and Paul Whiteman's danceable sweet jazz, Americans found music that matched their attitudes.²⁹

Aaron Copland was among the first European-trained American composers to use jazz in his music. While studying in Paris, Copland attended a jazz concert and later remembered that "it was like hearing it for the first time. It was then that I first began to realize the potentiality of jazz material for use in serious music."³⁰ Back home in New York City in 1924, he traveled to jazz clubs in the West Fifties and to the Cotton Club in Harlem, trying to hear the best in modern jazz. He encouraged friends and fellow composers to tap into this bounty and, on several occasions, even took Boston Symphony conductor Serge Koussevitzky with him to the clubs. His proselytizing paid off, and the frequency of these jaunts increased, after the League of Composers commissioned a new work from the young composer, to be premiered by the maestro in New York. The resulting piece, *Music for the Theatre* (1925), was the first in which Copland attempted, through the incorporation of jazz elements, to be self-consciously American. He emulated the genre's instrumentation by writing for a chamber orchestra of as few as eighteen musicians, he saturated the piece with various forms of syncopation, he added subtle colors of pitch bending, and he even adopted Louis Armstrong's sly sense of humor by quoting a popular tune during the "Dance" with his tongue firmly in his cheek.[31]

But even with this careful attention to integrating jazz elements into many levels of a composition, Copland's work, and that of many other Parisian-trained composers, was still more related to the decorative exoticism of Farwell and Cadman than to the work of Louis Armstrong. Throughout the 1920s, composers from George Antheil to John Alden Carpenter to Louis Gruenberg experimented with the angular melodies, syncopated rhythms, and expanded harmonies inherent in jazz music. While these elements were layered through their music, they were still basically writing piano character pieces, symphonies, and concertos complete with all the European trappings. They may have selected different effects and methods in their compositions inspired by jazz, but they used them to achieve the same goal. All wanted their compositions to sound American and, for most of them, jazz was the most American music of the time.[32] It was a different decorative element than Native American music, but still one that rarely penetrated to the music's structural level.

The use of jazz syncopations and dance band ensembles—techniques that had epitomised the image of America as brimming with fast-paced promise—dissipated with the Great Depression. As Americans began to question whether the United States was still a land of opportunity, or whether the American dream was only a fantasy, some composers began reevaluating their ideas about the relation between art and society, and the aims of modern music[33] Since many Americans did not support modern music, they reasoned, it was their responsibility to find a new medium through which to speak. Along with the rest of the country, American composers began to search for their roots. This did not necessitate a renunciation of compositional techniques, but rather a simplification of their use. It became modern to simplify.[34]

Composers soon decided that one of the best ways to simplify their style, and directly communicate with their audience, was to become even more self-consciously American. Painter Thomas Hart Benton, writing early in the Depression of the search for an American expression in the arts, explicated this view perfectly when he boldly proclaimed that "no

American art can come to those who do not live an American life, who do not have an American psychology, and who cannot find in America justification for their lives."[35] Although his comments were directed toward his associates in the visual arts, it was as though Benton were speaking directly to the era's European-trained composers. When Benton announced that America's true soul could only be found and expressed from the heartland, away from the East Coast and its urban centers, many composers heeded him, shifting their focus from city-bred jazz to folk music from the Appalachians, Midwest, and West Coast. Indeed, from the late 1920s, the idea resurfaced that music of "the folk" was a form of cultural expression different from, and ultimately more satisfying than, popular commercial music or that of the cultivated tradition.[36]

Across the forty years before the Great Depression, composers had been convinced that a national musical culture could be based on a vernacular genre—if they could only find the correct one.[37] This conviction carried over into the Depression's use of Anglo folk cultures, and caused composers to approach those sources in the same ways in which they had approached Native American music and jazz. Although composers successfully followed the path marked by painters like Benton, many did not learn from their compatriots in the visual arts and merely adapted the techniques of composers who used exotic elements in their music. They approached this aspect of American heritage, one with which many had familial connections, as a decoration, an exotic overlay to their current style rather than a new style with which they could engage conceptually.

Still, the situation was not so black and white. A few composers made strides toward a conceptual engagement by occasionally allowing folk music to dictate the framework of their composition, even though that framework was expressed through the harmonic language of modern musical techniques.[38] This trend is most apparent in symphonic works produced during the Depression, and Roy Harris's *Folksong Symphony* provides the clearest model, despite the awkward merging of the two genres in its title.[39] Originally titled *Folksong Jamboree*, the choral *Folksong Symphony* is in seven movements: "The Girl I Left Behind Me" (based on a Civil War song of the same name, as well as "Good Night Ladies"), "Western Cowboy" (based on three cowboy songs), "Interlude—Dance Tunes for Strings and Percussion" (orchestral movement based on "The Irish Washerwoman"), "Mountaineer Love Song" (based on "He's Gone Away"), "Interlude— Dance Tunes for Full Orchestra" (orchestral movement based on "The Blackbird and the Crow" and "Jump Up My Ladies"), "Negro Fantasy" (based on two spirituals), and "Welcome Party" (choral movement based on "When Johnny Comes Marching Home"). Harris found some of his folk songs while coediting the book *Singing through the Ages* (a collection culled from the Library of Congress); he used his chosen melodies not only for thematic material in each movement, but for the figuration, motives, and accompaniment material as well.[40] The symphony's large arc structure opens with the sending of a child off to war, and it closes with his welcome return. Within the arc, the even-numbered movements are regional pieces representing diverse American geography: "Western Cowboy" depicts the loneliness of the cowboy lifestyle, interspersed with its tragedy and comedy; "Mountaineer Love Song" is a straight-forward setting recalling the simplicity of Appalachian life; and "Negro Fantasy" looks at life in the American South through the lens of the minstrel show tradition.

Conceptual versus Decorative Exoticism

Even though Harris was a Parisian-trained composer who engaged Anglo-American folk sources in a more meaningful way than simply using a collected melody, his use was still a form of decorative exoticism. Before discussing the foundations of Partch's approach, briefly comparing Harry Partch's *Barstow* to the "Western Cowboy" movement of Roy Harris's *Folksong Symphony* provides a clear way to differentiate between decorative and what I term "conceptual exoticism." This term is both needed and useful to this study because, as Ralph Locke cogently pointed out, most discussions of exoticism have ignored how nonmusical elements impact a musical work, focusing instead on what exotically coded musical styles exist in the music.[41] Using this term helps train our attention on how music engages materials from another culture on a structural and aesthetic level. Instead of mining merely for a cultural flavor, conceptually exotic works use a given culture's organizational principles and philosophical basis as the foundation to attempt a true hybrid, a music that rests comfortably in neither the composer's nor the borrowed culture. This notion is at play in *Barstow* and easily seen when compared to Harris's work. Both pieces were composed around 1940 and are almost equal in length. Both use texts collected from the Western frontier. Both focus on an iconic Western figure, the hobo and the cowboy respectively. But there the similarities end.

By choosing the cowboy as his Western figure, Harris tapped into the image of Western conquest familiar from page and screen. Partch focused on a group that also symbolized Western freedom and was equally recognizable, but was regularly ignored, shunned, or used as a object of ridicule prior to the Depression. Harris culled the texts for his songs, "The Lone Prairie," "The Streets of Laredo," and "The Old Chisholm Trail," from the Library of Congress and particularly John Lomax's collection; Harry Partch collected his texts himself from a highway railing while hoboing in California. Harris does not specify a professional choir, but "Western Cowboy" is supposed to be sung by a choir with some degree of training and certainly led by a professional conductor, while the vocal lines of *Barstow* are to be performed by instrumentalists who lack a trained voice and therefore sound like the hoboes that Partch heard. Harris alters text and tune to declaim the text dramatically: after the men's voices finish the line "Oh bury me not," he adds a six beat rest before the women respond "and his voice died there."[42] Partch, by contrast, bases *Barstow*'s structure and musical material on the inflection of hoboes reciting the lines he collected; he is more interested in preserving the inherent drama than in adding any externally. Finally, Harris's depiction of the cowboy is a romantic, sentimental one similar to Roy Rogers's or Gene Autry's, a nostalgic depiction of a bygone lifestyle that never existed as presented.[43] Partch's presentation is neither sentimental nor exploitive—he presents life as hoboes lived it and allows the audience to infer what it will.

Harry Partch's American Sound

Partch's conceptual engagement with American sources in composition touches on several of the trends seen in this panorama. He briefly flirted with Native American music as a young man. In February 1933, Eleanor Hague hired him to transcribe Edison cylinder recordings of Native American ceremonial music housed at the Southwest Museum in Pasadena, California. Hague hired Partch because she felt that his experiments in microtonality made him uniquely qualified to notate the field recordings accurately. Partch was able to notate each singer's melody precisely, but as he worked he began to notice that, contrary to his expectations, the singers moved toward intervals in the lower overtone spectrum rather than discrete microtones. As a result, he used a scale in equal temperament to notate the melodies. In his introduction to the transcriptions, Partch rationalized its use, saying, "Notating the melodies for the tempered scale also is perhaps justifiable since its falsity is no doubt less than the element of human fallibility mentioned."[44]

Even though Partch worked closely with these Native American materials, he never used them as Farwell or Cadman might have by setting a

Native American melody. This omission is actually a little surprising, given that he always listed the Yaqui Indian ritual as one of his primary musical influences. The only place Partch ever used a melody he transcribed is when a Cahuilla chant appears in *The Bewitched*, though he refused to call attention to the melody's origin. He simply used it as an ephemeral motive and let it disappear into the others that accompanied it.[45]

So, Partch had a connection with Native American music, but not in the context of a search for an American-sounding music. What of the 1920s jazz craze? Although Partch was an almost exact contemporary of Aaron Copland, he did not study composition in Paris, did not live for long in New York, and did not compose jazz-inspired music during the 1920s. That particular fad seems to have moved past him. Not until the 1950s, with *Revelation in the Courthouse Park* and *Water! Water!*, did popular music influence his compositions.

Only during the Depression-era search for an American sound did Harry Partch intersect fully with dominant compositional trends and with the more conceptual early traditions in American experimental music. Charles Ives, often considered the founding father of American experimentalism, regularly mined the folk songs, hymn tunes, and patriotic marches of his youth for compositional material. However, Ives did not use his melodies as decorative overlay, but rather drew on their harmonic structure and even their texts as structural elements. Although the resulting sound was startling and new, it was virtually unknown during the search for an American sound in the early decades of the twentieth century. Ives's music, in many ways more American than his contemporaries', did not become known until other composers began, fortuitously, to mine the same sound sources as Ives. Likewise, Harry Partch, often classed with Ives as an unrepentant experimenter unconcerned with the traditional concert world, fits perfectly into the search for an American sound, as if he had heard Thomas Hart Benton's proclamation and decided that the best way to respond was to live an American life in order to compose an American music. He collected texts and music among a largely Anglo-American subculture. He wrote works based upon those collections. He considered the role a composer should play in society as he moved among the hoboes. Like so many Americans hit hard economically, physically, and personally by the Depression, Partch turned to American folk culture to survive. His experiences, and responses to those experiences, over the following decade and a half, gave him the impetus to develop a self-consciously Americanist attitude toward his music. His was a distinctive approach to sounding American.

As with Ives, here is where Partch's connection with the search for an American music separates from the mainstream. Partch's approach to using folk sources in his music differs from that of most other composers, in both intent and manner. While the music chosen to represent America had changed from generation to generation—from Native American melodies to jazz and then to Anglo-American music—the way composers used that music had not. They continued to operate in a decoratively exotic framework, choosing a melody or style of music and attempting to distill its essential characteristics: Native American music became open fourths and fifths, in a pattern of two eighth-notes followed by a quarter-note, representing ritual drumming; jazz was a series of syncopations and blue notes and a reduced ensemble, and Anglo-American folk music became singable melodies accompanied by openly-spaced harmonies. Composers combined those elements with a Western-derived structure or a harmonic progression owing more to European common practice and gave the result an "American" title. If the music had a bit of an exotic "kick," a taste of something American, it was still European in its basis and derivation.

Partch, on the other hand, began his Americanist compositions as an attempt to capture the essence of American speech and American custom. One of the reasons he initially adopted just intonation in the late 1920s, and subsequently divided his scale into forty-three discrete microtones, was his desire to recapture the power of Greek music, which he believed was based intimately on speech. This notion of everything arising from human speech, from what he called the "One Voice," became his conception of music from this period forward, one that he termed Monophony.[46] Rhythm, melody, and, to a limited extent, harmony all rested on precisely notated speech. He would simply find an appropriate subject, write down the inflection of that subject's speech in his notebook, and then turn those notations into music. As a result, when Partch considered folk music, he saw not raw, abstract musical material but folk singers. He found that those singers "personify a directness of word appeal, characteristic of this age and this land, and characterized by suggestions of actual times, actual localities, actual identities, and actual human situations."[47] Because of this focus, the music resulting from his use of folk melodies and themes was not a form of decorative exoticism. He was so invested in Monophony that the speech-rhythms of hoboes created his music's rhythms, and the inflection of their speech formed the basis of his works' melodic lines. Everything else rose from this foundation. Instead of taking a folk melody and weaving it into a theme and variation, or using it as a contrasting theme in a sonata-allegro symphonic movement, Partch extracted musical structure from the materials he used. Engagement with the material is so transformative and generative in his music that even aspects of the instruments he built to perform these Monophonic compositions arose from the sound of the folk culture he collected. Partch recognized that his use of this material created something special, even remarking on using "hillbilly, cowboy, and popular music, which, whatever its deficiencies, owes nothing to sciolist and academic Europeanisms."[48]

Partch's use of material from his own nation but outside his typical culture is conceptually exotic. For Partch, the idea was not to sound, but to *be* American: to use the patterns of hobo cultural products to create something distinct and true. As a result, his music became American—perhaps not in the way some expect, having been conditioned by decorative exoticism in music that simply features moments intended to mimic a musical style, but nonetheless indebted in ideation and execution to the land and the people who originally created that music. He created music that in facile description might seem to be decoratively exotic but in performance upsets those expectations by sounding completely different. The resulting music is a snapshot of a time, place, and people; it is documentary rather than the ethnographic fiction of decorative exoticism.

The Documentary Perspective

To use the word "documentary" to categorize Partch's exoticism may be startling for several reasons. Our documentary vision is skewed toward the visual art of film or the written art of memoir. It is seen today as an attempt to preserve contemporary memory, life, and culture. Most documentary art urges progressive action, illuminates social injustice, exposes corruption, or simply shares a slice of life. Contemporaries view it as a narrative art form and rarely consider music in that vein. But in many ways, the aims of conceptually exotic music align with those of 1930s documentary art. In fact, documentary photography and literature, as practiced during the Depression, are themselves conceptually exotic.

William Stott has argued that the search in the 1930s among practitioners in all artistic fields to define what was unique about American culture was brought about by a documentary impulse or motive. Attempting to engage the period through its documentary products is a relatively new endeavor. Not until the 1970s did Stott first persuasively argue that understanding the documentary impulse of the 1930s and 1940s was essential to understanding American life during the period.[49] His groundbreaking study, *Documentary Expression and Thirties America*, surveyed the vast amount of documentary literature and images, carefully examining almost every prominent field of artistic endeavor during the decade. Significantly, he left music unexamined. Stott found evidence of the documentary impulse, the desire to rediscover America through artifacts of its heritage, in literature, film, painting, photography, and dance—but not in music. He even spent several pages detailing Martha Graham's ballets and her search for the American soul through movement while offering only the odd statement on such collaborators as Aaron Copland.[50] From his survey, one might assume that music, unique among the arts, resisted a pull toward Americana before which all other fields were powerless. In fact, the opposite was true. The beginning of compositional use of Anglo-American folk sources coincided with the rise of the documentary impulse. But in its essence, Stott's disregard of music was correct: few composers other than Harry Partch engaged with a culture's music in the conceptual manner conducive to documentary aims.

In essence, the documentary impulse resulted from American weariness of abstract promises that things would get better. Americans believed only what they could see and feel. The documentary impulse responded to this skepticism through communication that made images, words, and sounds appear truthful and credible.[51] The search for roots that preoccupied so many artists in the face of Depression-spawned insecurity focused this impulse on "authentic" Americans as both Depression victims and victors. Books, ballets, paintings, and photographs extolled "the folk," the everyday person, as the nation's true soul. Even New Deal cultural programs focused on preserving the common people's culture through oral history projects, music collecting trips, photojournalism, and state guidebooks that collected local lore.[52]

Why did this search for America's roots manifest itself in a concerted move toward documentary expression in the arts? Why did Americans feel that they needed tangible, objective truth in their art? Why did artists feel the same? Certainly, as Stott avers, it was a need for commonality, a knowledge of shared suffering. But Stott did not address the reality that documentary is an art form produced by artists. Although many documentarians claim to be objective, they always present a dramatized version of the truth from their perspective. They travel to locations, conduct interviews, take pictures, gather notes, and discover how their subjects live, before returning home and using their impressions to craft an artistic response to their subjects. This description of 1930s documentary as artists using lived experience to create and structure art is a definition similar to that of conceptual exoticism. By using what they found in the field to formulate their art, documentary artists fashioned new genres during this period because the materials gathered, whether photographs or stories or patterns of life, determined the manner in which the documentarians presented them. The art produced was nevertheless a form of exoticism, albeit more conceptual than decorative: it still asked people outside a culture to look in and observe differences. For this reason, Stott's "documentary impulse" can be better understood as a documentary imagination. This slight change in nomenclature highlights the subjective side of Depression documentary and the methods by which artists approached their subjects. During the Depression, the public desired voyeuristically to see the harsh truth of the nation's predicament while simultaneously escaping from their troubles. Documentarians spoke to both desires by providing a romantic view of the nation's past, of its roots, and of people currently suffering. They took an outside group, an Other, used the experiences of that group both symbolically and personally, and presented them to a public as the truth about contemporary American life. It is a documentary process still in evidence today that creates a form of universal humanism in which "we" are all alike, but "they" are still separate and different.[53] As an art form, it is conceptually exotic.

Harry Partch's compositions collectively titled *The Wayward*, and his journal *Bitter Music*, are filled with the documentary imagination. Each chronicles people marginalized and hurt by the Depression. Each presents a text either collected from the people it describes or based on Partch's experiences as a member of that group. Each has the "texture of reality" in its musical presentation of the way its subjects spoke, from the joy of finding a job to the despair of being chased by police.

The compositions that form Partch's Americana works each relate a story from the lifestyle of American outcasts, the primary figures on whom the documentary imagination centered. Americans wanted to know more about hoboes during the Depression, and along with photographs, novels, and newspaper articles, Partch's compositions fed that fascination. Through the music for *U.S. Highball*, *Barstow*, and *The Letter*, Partch gave his audience a feel for what it was like to hop a train or hitch a ride and listen in on conversations in a boxcar or in the back seat. They wanted to comprehend the Depression's effect on children, and *San Francisco*, which sets the cries of two newsboys, spoke to that interest. Finally, *Bitter Music* chronicled the groups of outsiders that, even more than hoboes, captured America's documentary imagination—migrant families and transients. The music journal laid bare the devastating effects of Californian policies toward migrants and transients, in a manner similar to John Steinbeck's *Grapes of Wrath*. As a result of that book and Dorothea Lange's Farm Security Administration photographs, no group drew more documentary attention. Americans looked to migrants' stories to understand, cope with, and conquer the devastation wrought by the Depression. Because Partch lived as a member of that group, his recollections rang true to publishers interested in producing *Bitter Music*.

The Documentary Imagination and Exoticism

In order to see the connections between exoticism and the documentary imagination more clearly, it is useful to compare a documentary work featuring music with Partch's output. In 1935, the Resettlement Administration of the New Deal hired a young film critic named Pare Lorentz to craft a documentary film that would examine the ecological devastation caused by the mismanagement of land in the Midwest and sway public opinion toward assistance for the dust storm ravaged Plains. The resulting film, *The Plow that Broke the Plains*, remains one of the most influential documentary films ever made, the first film placed in the Congressional Archives and subsequently named to the National Film Registry in 1999. Although it was his first film, Lorentz knew he wanted an established concert composer, and after interviewing Aaron Copland and Roy Harris among others, he settled on Virgil Thomson. Shortly after hiring Thomson, Lorentz brought him a rough cut of the film.[54] Thomson was impressed by the film's detailed and heartbreaking images of dust storms reaching to the heavens and farmers desperately trying to coax food from the dry land. Having grown up in Kansas City, Thomson knew the area and, following a period of research into cowboy songs at the New York Public library, suggested that he use songs from the Midwest to depict the landscape. Lorentz agreed.

This close collaboration between director and composer was unique to documentary film. In narrative films from Hollywood during this period, composers scored pictures after they were locked, with no input in the final cut. Their music was to be "inaudible," secondary to image and dialogue, and similar in sound to all other films from the studio. In documentary film, and particularly in this pairing of director and composer, there was much more give-and-take.[55] Thomson composed his score, inspired by the rough cut. He then played his material for Lorentz while the director was cutting the film, later noting that "When he gets the final recorded music track, then he goes back to the cutting room, finds inspiration for expressive visual narration through the musical detail, and wholly recuts his film."[56] This process allowed for the source material to shape the documentary's form in a more conceptual way.

Thomson's musical material came from a variety of sources. He evoked the Plains through the use of Protestant hymns such as the "Old Hundredth"; he used typical Hollywood musical codes for Native Americans, echoing those used by Indianist composers in the early part of the century (such as a pentatonic melody in perfect fourths over a timpani ostinato); and he drew on cowboy songs, such as "I Ride an Old Paint" and "Git Along Little Dogies."[57] Through his sensitive use of these quotations, Thomson managed to conjure the sweep of time and place that the filmmaker required to communicate his message.

Together, Lorentz's images and Thomson's music tapped into the same documentary imagination. In fact, in its intent and function Thomson's music for these two films comes the closest to conceptual exoticism of any of his compatriots. Its powerful impact worked with the film to help convince Americans of the Dust Bowl's devastating effect on the land and its people.[58] But even Thomson's music does not feature the same level of connection with the people depicted as does Partch's. Thomson certainly knew the Protestant hymns he quoted: as an organist in both a Southern Baptist and an Episcopal church growing up in Kansas City, he could have played the "Old Hundredth" every week. But the cowboy songs he used came from Margaret Larkin's 1931 *Singing Cowboy*, and he represented Native Americans through Hollywood stereotypes.[59] Partch's exposure to hobo songs and their structure came from firsthand experience. Like Lange, Steinbeck, James Agee, and Walker Evans, along with other documentarians of the 1930s, Partch traveled among the cultures he was documenting. Both Partch and Thomson composed documentary that brought the life and travails of an outcast people to light; what varied was their remove from the situation they were chronicling.

Uncovering the Past

Like most composers during the Depression and immediately following, Harry Partch was drawn to indigenous American music for multiple reasons. However, he engaged it through methods more common to documentarians than to other composers. His compositions provided the texture of reality for a group often marginalized and overlooked but who, for many, symbolized the freedom and expanse of the United States. The compositions' documentary nature helps explain why Partch's music was successful and why, even today, his Americana works remain his most popular.

With the exception of *Barstow*, these works also remain among Partch's least studied.[60] Perhaps common statements about the composer's early years, such as "little will ever be known of the first forty years of Partch's life,"[61] have led many to see the works as surrounded by an impenetrable haze. It is true that Partch's itinerant existence during this period generated a paucity of reliable evidence, but other sources shed light on the works. By following the documentary impulse to the people Partch chronicled, elements of the works' composition, structure, and meaning become clear. And only by digging into the context of the works, the people they portray, and the ways in which those groups were understood by those who performed, heard, and judged the works can we begin to understand this conceptually exotic music.[62]

The ideas of conceptual exoticism and the documentary imagination are the lenses through which this study explores Harry Partch as a hobo composer. Each chapter follows Partch's life chronologically, from his earliest memories through his final compositions, teasing out the hobo-like figure that lives in each era. Chapter 1 outlines Partch's life until and through the early 1930s, including his early experiences hoboing, as a way of uncovering his philosophical, aesthetic, and practical reasons for creating his singular musical system. The next two chapters explore his time as a Depression-era transient in the mid-1930s, an existence Partch recounted in *Bitter Music*. Transients were men who left their homes and families during the Depression to find work, but unlike hoboes were not directed in their wandering and took advantage of governmental assistance. While the transient life was closely connected to the documentary imagination of Dorothea Lange, John Steinbeck, and Woody Guthrie, three figures who feature prominently in "The Transient Journey," these authors in fact chronicled the migrants, families who moved to California with the express intent of putting down roots and establishing a new life in the state. The shift from transients to migrants, from wandering men to immigrating families, had enormous repercussions on how Partch (and American society) ultimately viewed his work. Chapters 4, 5, and 6 delve into Partch's life in the late 1930s and early 1940s and the hoboing he ultimately transformed into the works of *The Wayward*. Partch consciously chose the hobo during this time as a figure who moved for his work, never put down roots, and in general cultivated a lifestyle unencumbered by traditional mores. Chapter 7 explores Partch's attempts from 1943 to 1945 to ensconce himself in a New York City musical culture then fascinated by the folk and the hobo, before chapter 8 traces his rejection of and then slow reconciliation with the hobo image over the following twenty years. Interspersed with these chapters are two Interludes that explore the contemporary views of the transient, the migrant, and the hobo, seeking clues to Partch's achievements in the texture of their lives. Like the chapters, these Interludes follow the chronology of Partch's life, so the first Interlude looks at the transients and migrants among whom Partch moved in the early 1930s, while the second Interlude focuses on the hobo he later became. As the documentary imagination is based on then-current conceptions of these figures, observing the role of each group during the Depression reveals the importance of the works rising from their voices—they are in truth the significant voices of musical Americana.

Film critic Roger Ebert was fond of saying that a great movie is not what it's about, but how it's about what it's about. The same can be said of any great work of art. Literature, film, painting, and music can all be reduced to a simple story—a plot, the use of color, harmonic progressions—but while art may be made of those elements, it also rises above them. What follows can be seen in some respects as an attempt to explore Harry Partch's art using Ebert's dictum. It looks at the composer's life and music to uncover not only what it's about, but how it's about what it's about. This study reveals that even beyond their roles as musical milestones or documentaries, Partch's hobo-inspired compositions are substantial works of art. They emerge as the meaningful work of a "hobo composer."

CHAPTER ONE

THE HOBO IN PARTCH'S EARLY LIFE AND AESTHETIC

In the second part of Jack Kerouac's novel *On the Road* (first published in 1957), narrator Sal Paradise and his friend Dean Moriarty pile into a car with Dean's wife Marylou and Ed Dunkel, and take off from the East Coast headed for California. Watching the miles slip away beneath them, Sal exults, "We were all delighted, we all realized we were leaving confusion and nonsense behind and performing our one and noble function of the time, *move*. . . . [Dean] and I suddenly saw the whole country like an oyster for us to open; and the pearl was there, the pearl was there."[1] To post–World War II Americans the idea of the frontier seemed lost in the distant past, but many young men and women still wanted to go West, to seek their fortunes beyond the horizon, to move. The road, stretching from every front door to every point imaginable, became a dominant artistic metaphor for self-discovery, and a particular character arose to inhabit it. Through Sal and Dean's exploits, Kerouac solidified the "road hero," a character who found redemption and release on the open road.

The road hero is an enduring cultural mythic figure in American music, film, literature, and life that speaks to a strand of American reality. However it did not spring fully formed from the years after World War II, emerging rather from an exceptional figure in American cultural and societal history: the hobo. Since he first appeared on the scene over a hundred and fifty years ago, the hobo has been a compelling symbol for generation after generation of young Americans eager to leave the daily grind and responsibility and strike off on their own. For them, although he has symbolized the degradation associated with homelessness, he has also symbolized absolute freedom. Harry Partch was one such young man caught up with the hobo. He was entranced by the notion of living where and when he wished, carried about by his imagination instead of someone else's whims. He believed that "into eternity the hobo mind seeks something different, something better, something beyond."[2] And he wanted to go beyond.

Beyond Childhood Musical Experiences

Harry Partch's entire life can be seen as a hobo's attempt to escape traditional rules and go beyond traditional limitations. When asked late in life what his musical influences were, Partch ignored composers and compositions from the Western classical tradition and instead listed "Christian hymns, Chinese lullabyes [sic], Yaqui Indian ritual, Congo puberty ritual, Cantonese music hall, and Okies in California vineyards."[3] This diverse grouping, which might seem improbable, stems directly from his biography. The first four derive from his upbringing in America's desert Southwest, the fifth from his young adulthood in Los Angeles and San Francisco, and the sixth from his years spent wandering during the Depression. Together, they forge an accurate portrait of how Partch's life experiences shaped his music and musical philosophy.

Since Partch clearly delineated all three eras as crucial to his aesthetic development, it is prudent to approach them chronologically.[4] Although he often claimed China as the site of his conception, since his parents were Presbyterian missionaries there in the late nineteenth century, Harry Partch was actually conceived in Oakland, California, and born there on June 24, 1901.[5] When he was two-and-a-half years old, his mother's tuberculosis necessitated a move to a drier climate, so Partch's father Virgil obtained a post first in Tucson and then in Benson, Arizona, as a Chinese inspector for the US Immigration Service. Partch's earliest memories were of Benson, a small town he later remembered as dependent on the railroad, with "about three hundred population and with eleven saloons for transient railroaders along its board walks."[6] As a young boy in that desert town, he customarily used his telescope to watch dramas unfold along the railroads and would surely have seen numerous hoboes "holding down" a car or climbing underneath to "ride the rods."[7]

Partch was also surrounded by different cultures and different musics during his childhood. First and foremost among these were Christian hymns. His father's spiritual journey upon his return to the United States took the road to atheism, but his mother retained and attempted to pass on her faith to her children, including Harry's two older siblings, Paul and Irene. She gathered them around the reed pump organ in their home and taught them all manner of hymns, including "Rock of Ages." This family hymn singing was among Partch's earliest, but not his only, musical memories. His mother also retained an abiding love for China, sang Chinese lullabies to the young Harry, and taught him Chinese songs when he grew older.[8] Additionally, she insisted that her children learn a musical instrument and mail-ordered "a cello, a violin, a mandolin, a guitar, a cornet, and numerous harmonicas" for them to play.[9]

A naturally curious and lonely child, Partch sought out musical experiences beyond what his mother presented. When he was ten, he began listening to music collected on Edison cylinders. Although later in life he could not recall specific recordings, he did remember hearing and being struck by Congo rituals.[10] He also observed from afar the Yaqui tribe in the Southwestern landscape. Though the tribe was declining, they still performed their rites and ceremonies, their music drifting into the edge of Partch's small hometown. He found the Yaqui personally timid and aloof when he encountered them, but their music remained haunting and familiar throughout his life.

In 1913, the family moved to Albuquerque, New Mexico, where they remained until Partch graduated from high school in June 1919. Here the composer's love for and devotion to music and the idea of music began to flower. He began pursuing the piano seriously, playing it and the organ in the Pastime Theatre, Albuquerque's main movie house. This occupation provided an unexpected advantage in high school: local bullies left him alone, knowing that if they hurt his hands he would be unable to play in the evening.[11] The job also shaped his musical development. He later recalled that playing for silent films "strengthened my belief in dramatic or theatrical music," a belief evident in the small works he began composing for the piano.[12] The earliest of Partch's known works is *Death on the Desert* (1916), a melodrama meant to be read accompanied by piano figurations that served to heighten the tension and dramatic effect. Even at fifteen, Partch's musical taste leaned toward combining instrumental music and the human voice to exploit music's dramatic possibilities— interests nurtured by playing for silent films that found fruition in this early composition.

In Albuquerque, Partch first encountered the people who would shape his life, his music, and its reception. When he started high school, his mother began attending the University of New Mexico, in pursuit of a BA in social science. She was soon championing women's rights, visiting the local jail to campaign for better treatment of female prisoners, and occasionally bringing prostitutes home to spend a night off the streets. Partch's father likewise brought home hoboes, but instead of giving them charity, he put them to work for food and bed. Partch later mused that while his father made the hoboes work in the home, his mother never demanded the same from the prostitutes.[13] It is tempting to consider what Partch might have gleaned from those outsiders and wanderers around the supper table. Hoboes were typically marvelous storytellers, so perhaps the young composer became entranced by the freedoms of their lifestyle and the glory of their adventures as they regaled the family with tale after tale. These encounters mark the beginning of Partch's interest in hobo culture and mystique, and were important enough to him to include them in the brief autobiographical sketch in *Genesis of a Music*.[14]

Beyond Traditional Music Study

A few months before Partch graduated high school, his father grew gravely ill and died. The juxtaposition of these two events caused Partch to mark the summer of 1919 as his entry into adulthood. In the preface to *Genesis of a Music* he wrote, "In 1919, as I recall, I had virtually given up on both music schools and private teachers, and had begun to ransack public libraries, doing suggested exercises and writing music free from the infantilisms and inanities of professors as I had experienced them."[15] Although he was certainly exaggerating the timeline (he had yet to experience professors), that summer he did have his first full encounter with classical music. With nothing to keep them in New Mexico, Partch and his mother relocated to Los Angeles. Once in the city, Partch began finding his way in a new musical milieu by regularly attending classical musical events, including concerts of the Los Angeles Philharmonic's inaugural season. This contact with the concert world simultaneously attracted and repelled the young composer. Ushering at concerts so as to see them for free, he loved the color and drama of symphonic music, but hated the performances' class-based segregation, the stiff attire, the separation of audience and performer, the stolid atmosphere, and the sea of "blue-haired ladies" he observed.

Partch presumably moved to Los Angeles in order to begin formal music studies, but his growing uncertainty about the musical world, combined with an untimely tragedy, initially kept him away. In November 1920, a streetcar struck his mother while she was traveling to meet him. She died almost instantly from a skull fracture. While few letters and records remain from this decade of Partch's life, her death must have profoundly impacted the young musician, as it appears that he did not begin music studies until the following spring. He did, however, begin studying piano in 1920 with Olga Steeb, head of the University of Southern California piano department, some months before he formally enrolled in the university. Whether he enrolled because of his mother's wish that he gain a college degree or because he still hoped to make a career in Western music is uncertain, but he was diligent enough in his practice that his piano skills stayed with him: into his sixties, he could play Chopin nocturnes, Brahms intermezzos, and the John Field concerto. Partch continued attending USC on and off through the summer of 1922, then ended his formal education. By that time, he had discovered that he could learn as much from reading through a library as he could from teachers, and that by so doing he could focus on topics that most interested him.

Other issues in the 1920s caused Partch ultimately to go beyond tradition. The end of his schooling was likely also caused by a medical condition that lasted throughout the decade. He wrote to Elizabeth Sprague Coolidge in 1932, "At nineteen came the first of a succession of physical breakdowns—as the result of a heady ambition, overstudy, overpractice, and many long hours in a newspaper office—that turned a love of the piano and tradition into a devastatingly intense aversion to the piano and to music as it now exists."[16] His growing awareness and acceptance of his homosexuality also precipitated these breakdowns.[17] In 1920, Partch befriended a young actor and vaudeville singer named Ramon Samaniegos, who ushered at the Los Angeles Philharmonic with him. By the following year they had become lovers, but they had to end the relationship suddenly in 1922 when Samaniegos, under the screen name Ramon Novarro, became a movie star with the release of *The Prisoner of Zenda*. Novarro's rejection of Partch in favor of fame, combined with the sense of decorum instilled by his late mother, caused Partch to be discreet in his relationships thereafter.

Information on Partch's activities during the rest of the 1920s is sketchy at best, which is unfortunate given that between 1923 and 1928 Partch moved from being a Chopin devotee to a maverick rejecting equal temperament. From the documents that do remain, we know that he spent those five years composing music in a European vein, such as the symphonic poem he submitted to a Los Angeles Philharmonic composition competition and a piano concerto whose second movement featured the piano only playing "two notes, F-sharp and the F-sharp an octave below."[18] He also worked as a proofreader at the California State Legislature in Sacramento, taught piano in La Jolla, and continued his study of violin and viola. He then moved to San Francisco, became reacquainted with Chinese music by attending Cantonese operas at the Mandarin Theater in San Francisco's Chinatown, and began returning his music to a basis of acoustically pure intervals.

Beyond Equal Temperament to Monophony

This last event, the most pivotal for this story, entailed a search that proceeded in fits and starts during this period. It began in 1923, the year of which Partch always said that he decisively broke with the Western musical tradition and struck out on his own. That year, while working as a proofreader, he discovered Alexander J. Ellis's 1885 translation of Hermann Helmholtz's *On the Sensations of Tone* in the Sacramento Public Library. Partch devoured the book, utterly convinced by its theories on the physics behind auditory perception. Helmholtz's theory of consonance and dissonance was based on the acoustic properties of the harmonic series, or as he termed it, the series of *oberpartialtöne* (upper partial tones). Above any musical tone there are frequency components that vibrate at set relationships to that fundamental tone. These upper partials, or overtones, as they are commonly called, relate to the fundamental through whole-number ratios in the proportions of a vibrating string. For instance, the first partial vibrates twice as fast as the fundamental, resulting in a sound an octave higher and a ratio of 2/1. According to Helmholtz, this natural property of sound means that the closer a tone is to the fundamental—or put another way, the simpler the whole number ratio—the more consonant it is.

Helmholtz's explanation of the harmonic series was nothing revolutionary: Pythagoras discovered the relationship between musical intervals and the proportions of a vibrating string. What was radical was Helmholtz's endeavor to break down "the boundaries of *physical and physiological acoustics* on the one side, and of *musical science and esthetics* on the other."[19] Those connections were what excited Harry Partch in 1923, and ultimately provided the foundation for all of his future work. Over the following five years, Partch began to process the full implications of Helmholtz's theories, and with each new bit of research he became more and more convinced that he was finally on the right track. At its core, this path was a retreat into history. Helmholtz led Partch to seek a reestablishment of the connection between science and art that he believed had existed in ancient Greece. He began scouring the library, reading the history of tuning, and finally pinpointing composers' search for and adoption of tuning methods divorced from acoustics as the moment Western music had lost its moorings. For centuries, musicians had used various schemes to divide the octave into twelve discrete steps. From Pythagorean tuning (which is based on a series of six fifths at the ratio of 3/2) to meantone temperament (which flattens the fifths to temper the syntonic comma to a unison) to Werckmeister III temperament (which uses mostly pure fifths but flattens four of them), various schemes had tried to preserve acoustically pure intervals, while allowing for modulation. Partch was persuaded that musicians had finally fumbled when they embraced equal temperament, which divides the octave into twelve steps by distributing the octave across equally spaced intervals with identical frequency ratios. It necessarily fudges some of the intervals, making them slightly smaller or larger than their acoustical models. It is a compromise to which musicians have adapted over the past century and a half, but it is not the only solution to tempering.

After reading Helmholtz, Partch gravitated toward a return to just intonation, the tuning system used in Greek modes and favored by Renaissance music theorists, in which each pitch in a scale is determined by simple whole-number mathematical ratios without tempering. Most pitches in the diatonic scale are found in the lower levels of the harmonic series—after the octave (2/1), follows the perfect fifth (3/2), perfect fourth (4/3), just major third (5/4), and just minor third (6/5). However, just intonation precludes simple modulation to another key, as the intervals are tuned to a single note: if one tunes justly from C and then plays a scale starting from D, the interval size makes the scale sound strange: the second scale degree (E) is not a second above D, but rather a third above C. Tempering those whole number ratios makes modulation possible so that the E is the same whether one starts on C or D, but it also limits the number of pitches available in an octave.

Partch began investigating these justly-tuned intervals. As he explained in 1933 to the Guggenheim Foundation:

> The years from 1925 to 1928 were spent in experiment with theories and the composition of music to demonstrate them. In 1926, with the intention of experimenting with instruments of unfixed tones I took up the study of the violin, and later the viola.... These theories and compositions, all since destroyed, came to a climax in May 1928, when the first draft of *Exposition of Monophony* was completed. That might be called the first of my accomplishments.[20]

In that first draft of what later became *Genesis of a Music*, Partch declared his wholesale implementation of just intonation up to the eleventh partial of the harmonic series. Practically, this meant that he used the musical intervals created by the pitch relationships between any two of the first eleven pitches found in the harmonic series, and their inversions. Taking those intervallic relationships, removing any duplications, and folding them all down to their simplest whole number ratio so they fit into one octave, produces a scale of twenty-nine different pitches, or "the 29 tones within 11" as Partch termed it—the twenty-nine pitches within the 11-limit.[21]

Over the years from 1928 to 1935, Partch continued to test his scale's makeup. With the twenty-nine intervals of the 1928 scale he still had several large crevices between pitches, so he began adding what he termed "secondary ratios" to smooth out the scale. The total number shifted from twenty-nine to fifty-five and several numbers in between before finally settling, in 1935, at forty-three tones to the octave.[22] This kaleidoscope of pitches is important to the hobo period in Partch's compositions, for it shows that he saw the intervals in his scale as a compositional resource, what he termed a "fabric." As he heard and notated hobo speech, and attempted to realize the infinite gradations of pitch present in spoken inflections, he naturally fine-tuned his scale. Partch's use of just intonation was an intricately woven system that allowed him to find in it the patterns and colors he needed for any given composition.

Beyond a fascination with the physics of music, Partch's research led him to believe that any kind of tempering destroyed music's power; that when music does not correspond to naturally occurring pitches and intervals, people do not respond to it in an instinctive way. Reading through music history, Partch discovered ancient Greek reports of the impact of music on a person's ethos, or ethical character. Pythagoras's followers theorized that since the human soul was ordered by numerical relationships and music was numerical relationship made audible, music had the power to alter the soul's state directly: Greek stories recounted instances of music sending its listeners into frenzies, from the heights of exultation to the depths of anguish. Plato's writings sanctioned only two modes, Dorian and Phrygian, because they cultivated courage and self-control. Inspired by what he found, Partch vowed to recapture that power of ancient Greek music through the use of just intonation.

Partch also believed that there was one other key to reclaiming music's influence over a listener's ethos: close coordination between music and text. Greek music distinguished between *melos*, a performing art that simply featured individual instrumentalists or multiple performers playing a single melodic line, and perfect *melos*, an art that combined melody and text and stylized movement into a unified conception. Reaching for perfect *melos*, most Greek drama and lyric poetry was not only spoken, but sung and danced to instrumental accompaniment. For Partch, the lesson of ancient Greek music and drama was that composers had gone astray by throwing away the acoustic basis of music, and by ceasing to build music on the expressive ability of human speech. While composers from Monteverdi to Mozart to Janáček and Schoenberg had sought a connection between music and spoken language, Partch's approach differed in its insistence on the acoustical properties of speech. Partch's term for his revitalization of "the intrinsic music of spoken words" and the corollary to just intonation in his music was "Monophony": it grew out of the "One Voice": "Of all the tonal ingredients a creative man can put into his music his voice is at once the most dramatically potent and the most intimate. *His* voice does not necessarily mean his own voice and it certainly does not mean the specialized idiosyncrasy known as "serious" singing. It means his conception as expressed by the human voice and it means *one* voice."[23]

Just as all intervals grew out of a single pitch in just intonation, so all melodies grew out of a single voice intoning a text. For Partch, all music literally developed out of one sound. Composing music in this fashion felt natural to him. As he later remembered, "I came to the realization that the spoken word was the distinctive expression my constitutional makeup was best fitted for, and that I needed other scales and other instruments."[24] Going even further, in December 1930, in a short article titled "The Art of Song," Partch discussed his attempts at writing songs in the previous two years as building from his "determination to allow the spoken words of lyrics to govern the melody and rhythm of the music." This explanation is the core of the Monophonic concept. Going into more detail in his late 1920s draft of *Exposition of Monophony*, Partch described the "principles upon which the songs are created. First, the line of the spoken inflection determines the melody for the words; second, the rhythm of the words is the intrinsic rhythm of the music. The words are meant to flow in about the spoken tempo, without inordinate sustaining of a single syllable."[25]

Practically, then, Partch's compositional process during this period seems to have begun with his transcription of speech patterns as he heard them, whether his own or others'. He then attempted to match the pitch nuances he heard in the spoken sounds with pitches in his microtonal scale, notating the speech-music even more precisely. In many ways, his Monophonic process was a form of documentary that attempted to preserve the way people sounded at the time. Nevertheless, his music was not simply a recreation of speech: it existed somewhere between speech and song, a transformation that places it firmly within the documentary imagination. In the best Homeric tradition, Partch ended his compositional process with a close reading of a given text and its notation, observing the repeated notes, cadential patterns, implied harmonic movements, and pitch relationships, and crafting a song based on them.

Partch may have viewed the rejection of speech as a basis of composition and later adoption of equal temperament as the greatest mistakes of musical history, but since every school of music taught these errors as musical truth, he was bucking the musical establishment by rejecting them. Nevertheless, after 1928 he was committed to this path. He wanted to return Western music to its condition before equal temperament, to restore the primacy of the acoustically pure intervals found in Greek music and the power that went along with them. He began denying his training altogether, situating himself as far from institutionalized music-making as he could by removing his schooling at the University of Southern California from his biography and defiantly stating that he was "without institutional musical training."[26] He began immersing himself in musical cultures, like the Chinese, that used intonational systems outside equal temperament, seeking alternatives to Western practices.[27] He struck out on his own, both musically and creatively. He became a homeless musician.

Beyond Traditional Lifestyles

Not coincidentally, precisely at the time he was completing his first draft of *Exposition of Monophony* Partch had his first hoboing experience (see table 1.1). Partch had that draft notarized on May 20, 1928, in San Francisco. The following month, he was living in Santa Rosa, California, as a tenant in one of the rental units of Martha Zoller and her three children. It was a comfortable situation: his rent was free because he provided music lessons for the children, and he had become a part of their family, taking his meals with them and even admonishing the children to develop good manners.[28] But he felt restless. His position was a bit too comfortable. His music was not progressing. He began to need a change to reignite his creative passions, and so, as he later recalled, "I rebelled in another direction. I'd lived outdoors so much of my early life, and I resented this adventureless existence punching time clocks, even soft beds and regular meals. So in 1928, I quit the job I was on in Sacramento and started out on the fruit harvest. This was my first real hoboing, and it came at a time when jobs were fairly easy to find. I followed the harvest most of the rest of that season, then shipped out on an oil tanker."[29]

Table 1.1. Harry Partch's movements and life as a hobo, from his first hoboing experience in 1928 to the end of what he termed his "personal Great Depression" in 1943.

Month and Year	Partch's activities and place of residence, if known
Fall 1928	Partch's first hobo experience, following the California fruit harvest.
February 1930	Arrival in New Orleans, where he burned his compositions to that point in what he termed "a kind of adolescent auto-da-fé" (*Genesis of a Music*, x).
August 1931	Returns to California and stays with the Zollers in Santa Rosa.
September 1931	Moves to San Francisco to promote his music and gives concerts around the region.
Spring/Summer 1932	Hoboes along the Southern California coast and especially in Los Angeles, where he performs lawn work (pulling weeds, mowing grass, shoveling gravel) while forming contacts in the area.
Fall 1932–Spring 1933	In Los Angeles, promoting his music through concerts and taking small jobs.
Summer 1933–Summer 1934	In New York and New England, writing and promoting his music and applying for grant support.
September 1934–April 1935	Studies in Europe under a Carnegie Corporation grant.
April 1935–May 1935	Returns to the United States and travels to California, where he stays with the Zollers in Santa Rosa.
June 1935–January 1936	Takes to the road again, living in New Deal work camps. Chronicles this period in *Bitter Music*.
January 1936	Stays with friends in the Los Angeles area, where he begins notating *Bitter Music*.
February 1936	Finds a job proofreading in San Bernardino, his first steady job since 1931.
August 1936	Travels to Tucson, Arizona, where his older brother Paul has invited him to visit.
September 1936–July 1937	In Phoenix, rewriting sections of the Works Progress Administration's *Arizona: A State Guide*, under the auspices of the Federal Writer's Project.

(continued)

Table 1.1.—*(concluded)*

Month and Year	Partch's activities and place of residence, if known
July 1937	Leaves Arizona to spend two years wandering; his movements are partly traceable through "care of" addresses found on the few letters to Partch that remain from this period.
September 1937	In Boise, Idaho.
October 1937	In California; letters sent "care of" an address in Glendale.
Spring–Summer 1938	Working on the Devore-Camp Cajon link in the Cajon Pass Highway (US 395), San Bernardino County.
Autumn 1938	Follows the fruit harvest up the Western Coast all the way to Spokane, Washington.
Spring 1939	Returns to Los Angeles and befriends composer Noel Heath Taylor, who writes two articles about him that summer.
Summer 1939	Works on *California: A State Guide* for the Federal Writer's Project.
January–February 1940	Embarks on a photojournalism trip through the desert Southwest; finds the inscriptions that form *Barstow*'s text.
Autumn 1940–September 1941	Moves to Anderson Creek, on the Southern California coast, and works as a proofreader, writes articles about music, and composes *Barstow*.
September 1941	Hoboes to Chicago, later enshrines the trip as *U.S. Highball*.
October 1941–July 1942	Promotes his music around Chicago, creates the first Chromelodeon, and records a few of his pieces.
Summer 1942	Follows the fruit and grain harvests up through Michigan, ultimately working in a lumber-camp dining room.
Fall 1942–Winter 1943	Travels throughout New England and to New York City, promoting his music and applying for grant support.
April 1943	Awarded his first Guggenheim Fellowship.

Although Partch was not in Sacramento when he gained his first taste of hoboing, the year is correct; it was one when the United States was still prosperous, and railroad cars had not begun to swell with the ranks of the Depression's unemployed. Judging from other contemporaneous hobo accounts, Partch's first experience could not have been as easy as he described. Still, living by his wits, sleeping underneath the starry skies and, more importantly, adopting the image associated with hoboes at the time seemed to suit him. Over the next fifteen years, whenever Harry Partch could not find money or support, he would drop out of society for a while and follow the closest harvest.

Hoboing was by no means an easy life, despite its appealing image in early twentieth-century art and culture. Hoboes frequently died young, and the life left its mark. Partch later remarked that while he wanted that life, "it finally became very onerous."[30] But even more than wanting to live as a hobo, Partch craved the image. He was no down-on-his-luck musician forced to beg and wheedle hearings for his music. He was a hobo, a rugged individualist actively working against modern industrial society and clinging to an older, better way. This antimodernist view fit perfectly with the musical aesthetic Partch created during the 1920s. In fact, his beginnings as a hobo must have reinforced his developing views and provided a sense of validation for his new path.

Like any hobo, Partch left behind the familiar and comfortable tentatively at first, still grasping at tendrils of the musical culture he was renouncing. By the fall of 1928, he was back in San Francisco with a new job as proofreader for the *San Francisco News*, a job he enjoyed because "Proofreading took nothing out of me. I could be almost as fresh after eight hours as I was at the beginning."[31] The occupation left him free to pursue his experiments and to engage in an unexpected activity—playing viola in the University of California Symphony Orchestra.[32] Although it is not clear why Partch participated in a ritual he later decried as "bring[ing] to music a mandarin artificiality that attracts too many of the wrong kind of poets,"[33] Bob Gilmore plausibly suggests that as Partch had only begun learning stringed instruments a few years earlier, playing in the orchestra gave him a chance to test out his new skills and allowed him to see firsthand how ensembles successfully functioned—information that proved invaluable in his later career.[34] On evenings he was not rehearsing or performing, Partch continued his experimentations in just intonation in almost complete isolation, certain that he was finding an older, better way. He later quoted Adlai Stevenson's reflection that "much of life is a conspiracy against freedom" and firmly wanted to be free, even if the cost was loneliness and derision.[35] During his time in San Francisco, Partch slowly realized that he was ready to leave behind what he viewed as the decadent aspects of Western musical society and to become a voice in the wilderness, mapping out a new musical frontier.

In the fall of 1929, after a decade of searching, Partch finally embarked on his idiosyncratic path. As he had done the summer before, he began following the fruit harvest across the United States, this time finding his way to Philadelphia by December. On the last day of that year, Partch did something that was an outlier even in an admittedly unsettled life: he registered for the Merchant Marines. Perhaps under his navy brother Paul's influence, Partch shipped out on the MS Sunoil, a diesel oil tanker that plied intercoastal waters transporting crude oil from the fields to the refinery for Sun Oil Company, or "Sunoco," as an ordinary seaman. His enlistment lasted all of three weeks: on January 22, 1930, he was discharged with "very good" marks in character, ability, and seamanship. Whatever the reason for this short excursion, Partch seems to have worked diligently to leave little trace of his time in the Merchant Marines. He registered under the pseudonym "Paul Pirate," his songwriting *nom de plume* from the previous few years, and gave his age as twenty-four when he was in fact twenty-eight.[36]

Leaving Philadelphia in January, Partch used the next month to hitchhike and ride the rails down to New Orleans. Arriving in the dead of winter, he lived on green bananas scavenged from the docks and ten-cent soup until he secured a job proofreading for the *Times-Picayune*.[37] Although Partch always pointed to 1923 as the fulcrum on which his apostasy pivoted, not until he arrived in New Orleans did he complete the break with Western music that he had begun when he discovered *On the Sensations of Tone*. There he took a stack of music, fourteen years worth of compositions, including a symphonic poem, an unfinished piano concerto, several solo piano pieces, and a string quartet in a nascent form of just intonation, and burned it all in a pot-bellied iron stove in what he later called "a kind of adolescent auto-da-fé." The act was "a confession, to myself, that in pursuing the respectable, the widely accepted, I had not been faithful."[38] With that single act, Partch rejected wholesale his European-based musical training and devoted himself wholeheartedly to the ideas that he had developed over almost a decade. Starting over with only the fingerboard of a cello upon which he had begun marking ratios, he set out to craft a music based on a justly-tuned scale and wedded to the voice and movement of the human body.

His first practical step in crafting his new music marked the rest of his life. Later that year, with the help of New Orleans violin-maker Edwin Bentin, Partch created his first instrument—the Monophone, christened after his Monophonic idea of basing a music on a single vibrating string (see glossary). The Monophone was a hybrid instrument, consisting of a viola body, a cello fingerboard, tuning pegs, and strings (except the first string, which was a double-length violin E string); and brads hammered into the fingerboard to the left of each string to serve as guides to the fingers, not frets, marking the desired ratios. Its sound resembled a viola's tone, but with a greatly expanded range: the lowest string was tuned two octaves below g′, or, as Partch would have termed it in ratios, two 2/1s below his fundamental 1/1-392.[39] He played the instrument like a viol – placed between the legs and bowed, but with an overhand instead of underhand position on the bow.

The Monophone proved the perfect vehicle for Partch's new vision of music, and he composed exclusively for it over the next several years, completing his first characteristic compositions: the *Seventeen Lyrics by Li Po*; the "Potion Scene" from Shakespeare's *Romeo and Juliet*; and his *Two Psalms*, "By the Rivers of Babylon" and "The Lord is My Shepherd." Each followed the same pattern in their compositional process. Partch began composing by finding someone to recite the texts: he recited many of the Li Po lyrics, he asked a trained actor to perform Shakespeare's verse, and he recorded a Jewish rabbi canting the Davidic Psalms. He then used a shorthand notation to capture the speaker's inflection and articulation for later use. In translating his shorthand to song notation, he followed a dictum of W. B. Yeats he regularly quoted: that "no word shall have an intonation or accentuation it could not have in passionate speech."[40] Even though he referred to actual voices to compose the works' melodic lines, he granted himself compositional freedom to alter them if needed: in Gilmore's words, "His intention in these settings was not to reduce melody to the less distinctive contours of speech, but rather to maximize understanding of the words by showing that speech contained within it the *condition* of music."[41] Perhaps surprisingly, in many cases Partch did not notate rhythm for the singer, only pitches. He expected the singer to intone the words at the given pitch following natural spoken delivery patterns. The final part of the process was to add suitable accompaniment to the vocal line in the Monophone, and he used the instrument's full resources, asking the player to bow, pluck the strings, and perform a variety of tremolos and portamentos. In his manual on the musical and attitudinal techniques for playing his instruments, Partch called this playing technique "one-finger," in which the musician does not "perform like a pipe organ," hitting notes in "precise, discrete steps," but instead glides between notes, sometimes moving so slowly, "that one is not sure as to the point where rest has been achieved."[42]

By 1933 Partch began pushing against the Monophone's limits. Wanting additional and different sounds, he set about forming an entire instrumentarium of his own creation. He signaled his intention by changing the Monophone's name to the Adapted Viola, and then evolved a guitar into the Adapted Guitar and a melodeon into the Chromelodeon—and even reconstructed a Greek Kithara. From that Kithara to the Diamond Marimba, from the Adapted Guitar to the Harmonic Canons, and from the Chromelodeon to the Quadrangularis Reversum, Partch spent his life making instruments that would play in just intonation and allow musicians to learn new ways of approaching performance. As he noted in his manual on playing techniques:

> At no time are the players of my instruments to be unaware that they are on stage, in the act. There can be no humdrum playing of notes, in the bored belief that because they are "good" musicians their performance is ipso facto "masterly." When a player fails to take full advantage of his role in a visual or acting sense, he is muffing his part—in my terms—as thoroughly as if he bungled every note in the score.[43]

When Partch began composing in just intonation, his personal situation was precarious at best; it would remain so for the next decade. His taste for hoboing, cultivated in the late 1920s, became a way of life as the United States entered the Great Depression. Having rejected modern musical society, he found modern American society rejecting him, and he struggled to find employment, let alone acceptance, throughout the 1930s. He had arrived in New Orleans to burn his compositions and symbolically purify himself by hitchhiking and, staying there only one year, used the same method to drift back to the West Coast in the spring of 1931. After a summer spent hitchhiking and harvesting, he arrived in California that August and immediately sought lodging with his old friends the Zollers (see fig. 1.1). He accepted their hospitality for only a month, moving on to San Francisco in September.

In San Francisco, Partch approached Henry Cowell, then don of the California new music scene through his New Music Society. Sensing a kinship with Cowell, he shared his theories and music: if the latter left Cowell cold, the former intrigued the older composer. The two talked extensively about Cowell's pioneering book *New Musical Resources*, which proposed "to point out the influence the harmonic series has exerted on music throughout its history, . . . and how, by applying its principles in many different manners, a large palette of musical materials can be assembled."[44]

Figure 1.1. An early photograph of Harry Partch after he began following the harvests, probably taken by "Buddy" Zoller in Santa Rosa, California, in August 1931. Courtesy of the Harry Partch Estate Archive, San Diego.

Partch was extremely sympathetic to Cowell's notions of basing all pitch material on the mathematical relationships found in the harmonic series, and was particularly drawn to Cowell's insistence that the undertone series actually existed and was not idle speculation. The undertone, or subharmonic series, extends the principle of the harmonic series downward from the foundational pitch. Relative intervals mirror those in the harmonic series, and though the original sounding body does not create them, they exist in the sympathetic resonances of objects around that body. After his encounters with Cowell's ideas, Partch began theorizing what he called Utonalities, hexadic chords built by progressing downward from the fundamental. Utonalities became an important facet of his creation of the tonality diamond and his subsequent microtonal theory.[45] As these chords appeared in Partch's music, the clearest analogy he was able to make was that Otonalities were his "major" chords and Utonalities were the "minor."

Throughout this period in San Francisco, Partch was destitute. Through Cowell, he met Rudolphine Radil, a local singer committed to performing the ultra-modern music of Cowell and his contemporaries, and presented concerts of his new compositions for a bit of income. He also marketed himself to women's clubs and societies to demonstrate his theories and philosophies for ten dollars. But these intermittent income streams could not feed and house him. Throughout the fall of 1931, he frequented the breadlines near Howard Street, where men lined up four abreast across several blocks for a small bite to eat.[46]

Although Partch and Radil continued to concertize in the early months of 1932, reviews were tepid at best and the composer recognized that his prospects for steady employment were dim. By late spring, he was ready to head south in the hopes of finding income and an audience and so set out once more to follow the harvest. He stopped for several days in Santa Barbara to meet Mildred Couper (1887–1974), a microtonal composer whose music for a local production of Eugene O'Neill's play *Marco Millions* Cowell featured that year in a New Music Society concert. That work, which Couper called *Xanadu* (1930), was the culmination of her experiments in quarter-tones: it was written for two pianos tuned a quarter-tone apart. Although Partch roundly rejected quarter-tones as another false system perpetuating equal temperament's dominance, he was drawn to Couper because he saw potential in crafting a microtonal keyboard instrument. His discussions with her resonated deeply, and that fall he began constructing the keyboard for such an instrument, a device that resembled a manual typewriter keyboard.

Partch's activities over the remainder of the spring and summer are murky. He seems to have spent the seasons roaming, attempting to find sustenance and work but often obtaining neither. Of all his periods of homeless wandering, these four months seemed to have marked him most deeply. In the diary *Bitter Music*, he made an oblique reference to this time, noting in the August 5, 1935, entry that "it has been three years since I did this sort of thing [begging], and I never did it more than three times before. Starting again, the pain of humiliation is just as intense as it was the very first time."[47] He never romanticized the time, as he frequently did his first hobo experience of 1928. The only record from the period comes at its end, September 20, 1932, when Partch was arrested for vagrancy under California's increasingly strict laws and spent the night in the San Luis Obispo jail.[48]

Following that incarceration, Partch's mindset changed. He decided to become proactive about reentering respectable society, as he called it. He moved to Pasadena, where he supported himself through odd jobs like cutting grass for the Campfire Girls' Clubhouse for four dollars a week and transcribing Edison cylinder recordings of American Indian songs at the Southwest Museum in Los Angeles. Through the agency of wealthy Californian and music reviewer Bertha Knisely, he met Calista Rogers, one of Pasadena's best-known singers and host of an influential musical salon at her home, who agreed to perform his songs in the coming season. He also began preparing his first Guggenheim Foundation grant application, to support further study in microtonality and monophonic composition.

Beyond Hoboing

Working in the evenings from his house at 701 Bradford Street, Partch filled out only the first and last pages of the four-page application form, neatly typing in perfunctory information—name, birth date, occupation, and next of kin—as well as names and occupations of his eight references.[49] His answers to the form's opening questions betrayed the main thrust of his creative work during this period. On the line for the project's field of learning, Partch listed "theoretical music," and summarized his goals as: "Continuation of work in a multiple-tone music system based on the one natural source of tone relationships, the overtone series, the writing of a review of the historical uses of those relationships, and the adaptation of a keyboard to the theories."[50] At this point, Partch was less interested in composing for a justly-tuned scale than in finishing his book, then called *Exposition of Monophony*, and in developing a keyboard instrument capable of playing a microtonal scale.[51]

Rather than complete the application's inner pages, Partch submitted a six-page typed exegesis of his previous musical experience, his musical theory's evolution, his accomplishments, and his proposed project, categorically stating, "I am without institutional musical training."[52] He continued by succinctly extracting himself from any standard musical tradition, describing how he had rejected training at the University of Southern California and taught himself acoustics and the viola from books. Constructing this history of self-study and assuring that he had the drive to synthesize material on his own was central to Partch's proposal, as shown in his three-part project description above. The proposal's second element was the most interesting and unusual. It described how Partch would research historical tuning methods over a period of six months "at the Tokyo Academy of Music and at one or all of the following three Chinese institutions: Yenching and Peking Universities, Peiping; Shanghai University, Shanghai."[53] He would complete additional research at the Bibliothèque Nationale, the Library of the Paris Conservatoire, and the British Museum. Here, only four years after he adopted just intonation and only two after he had burned all his previous compositions, Partch was embracing his love of Chinese music, inculcated by his mother's Chinese lullabies, and opening himself and his tuning practices to the world's musics.

Partch knew that it would be difficult for Foundation directors to accept someone without institutional pedigree to work outside the bounds of the Western musical tradition. So he engaged as referees men and women who had dedicated their lives to Western music and its institutions, but were sympathetic to his ideas. His referees were as varied as his background, including musicologist Charles Seeger; Ernest Schuyten, Director of the New Orleans Conservatory of Music; Richard Buhlig, pianist and teacher of both Henry Cowell and, later, John Cage; and the established composer Roy Harris.[54] All of Partch's endorsers commented on his utmost sincerity, his ability to succeed at his chosen task, his perseverance in enduring life's hardships, and their own inability to comprehend his accomplishments fully. Only Richard Buhlig and Mildred Couper could associate Partch's theoretical work with that of others; Couper even went so far as to connect Partch's idea of speech music with Debussy's *Pelléas et Mélisande* and to argue that it represented the first step in a new musical development. Most agreed that Partch's work was interesting, important, and that "the world gives precious little attention or assistance to those few who are doing it."[55]

Unfortunately, recommendations were not enough to sway the Guggenheim Foundation, which rejected Partch's 1933 application. Undaunted, Partch and Rogers continued regularly performing what he called "tone declamations" around Los Angeles and building a base of support. But it was a fragile foundation on which to live, as Partch lamented two years later: "It was this blindness [to men's physical needs] that maddened me in Pasadena. They recognized and guaranteed my body for a time, but having done so, dropped it into a pit. Its purpose in being was not within their ken."[56] By May 1933, he had thrown himself on Bertha Knisely's graces as she concocted a plan to create a subscription series for the composer to support his move to New York City and pursue another Guggenheim application, following the failure of his first. Using the funds,

Partch bought a train ticket and traveled inside a train car to the East Coast in July, before hoboing from Gloucester, Massachusetts, to Middlebury, Vermont, and finally to New York City, where he found lodging with Clara Shanafelt, a friend of Knisely.

Once established, Partch actively pursued contacts to support another Guggenheim Fellowship attempt. On Knisely's advice, he began corresponding with Otto Luening and met composers as diverse as Aaron Copland, Walter Piston, Marion Bauer, Henry Cowell, George Antheil, and Adolph Weiss, convincing them all to write on his behalf to the Guggenheim Foundation. At Weiss's suggestion, Partch met with Henry Allen Moe, executive secretary of the Guggenheim Foundation, shortly before applications were due for the 1934 awards. The young composer's ideas impressed Moe, who nonetheless remained unsure how the Foundation would judge such an unusual proposal. Unfazed, Partch submitted his proposal and then continued to promote himself and his ideas to anyone who would listen.[57]

The 1934 Guggenheim application reveals a composer much more savvy in musical community politics than he had been the previous year. Instead of proposing a broad and wide-ranging project difficult to categorize, Partch focused on musical composition and proposed: "The setting of W. B. Yeats' translation of Sophocles' 'King Oedipus' to music through Monophony, a system of just intonation with 37 tones to the octave, and on the principle of intrinsic melody and rhythm in spoken words."[58] Partch's idea of setting the Oedipus story received a further boost when a letter from Yeats arrived, expressing interest in the idea and giving "permission with pleasure subject, in case of performance or publication, to the usual business arrangements."[59]

Partch was also more politic in presenting himself. Gilmore has argued that Partch, keenly aware that his lack of academic pedigree could hinder his advancement in New York musical circles, decided to make his self-education a positive facet of his identity.[60] Although Partch unfolded his musical experience and evolutionary period almost identically to his previous application's presentation, gone was the decisive "I am without institutional musical training." What remained was a deliberate listing of where he had taught, what he had studied, and who had recognized his accomplishments. He also added a complete list of compositions to date (his newly-finished *Li Po* settings, the *Romeo and Juliet* "Potion Scene," his *Two Psalms*), and an explanation of work completed on the project he had proposed in 1933.

Partch succeeded admirably in securing a wide range of recommendations from prominent East Coast authorities, but he made a critical mistake.

Instead of ensuring that those authorities could speak well and fluently about his Monophonic system, he assumed that he needed only their names. The recommendations are full of vague statements which range from *New York Times* critic Olin Downes's, "In regard to Mr. Partsch's [sic] work, he has done some rather astonishing things acoustically which I found very interesting to discuss with him.... I have not known him for very long" to "I can say very little about Partch" from George Antheil. One referee even refused to recommend him for a Fellowship. Henry Cowell, who had missed Partch's performance for his New Music Society in California the year before, wrote an openly disdainful letter, mentioning that Partch was "somewhat egocentric" and had not invented Monophony. Some referees worried about Partch's ability to compose the proposed works. George Antheil's recommendation observed that he would endorse Partch if he had constructed fifteen instruments, but "the orchestration outlined in his request (the instruments are not yet ready) is inadequate to support a cast and chorus for any length greater than 10 minutes."[61]

Still, Partch received mostly positive recommendations from a variety of sources. Dr. Milton Metfessel, a psychologist studying human speech and birdsong at the University of Southern California, enthused about the possibilities of Partch's speech-music system, as did the director and a professor from the School of Speech at the same university, Ray K. Immel and Cloyde Dalzell. Composers Adolph Weiss, Marion Bauer, and Otto Luening were especially enthusiastic about Partch's music and made comments akin to Mildred Couper's about it being one of music's future directions.[62]

Yet Partch's active self-promoting and the positive recommendations of established composers and scientists could not overcome the influence of Thomas Whitney Surette, the Guggenheim Foundation's sole music adviser at the time. Surette believed that his job was to help established composers like Copland, Harris, and Quincy Porter through the Depression. He saw Partch's music as too far from the mainstream to have any chance of success, and therefore deemed it unworthy of support.[63] His influence on the Foundation's board was wide-reaching and strong, and even Moe's backing and encouragement could not save Partch's proposal. The Foundation denied Partch a second time.

After a winter spent making connections with artists and composers and supporters of the arts, tired of the city and worn out from the exertion of promoting himself, Partch retreated to East Chatham, New York, in June 1934, where he lived with the Flanders, friends of Clara Shanafelt who were sympathetic to his music. That month, he received word that ended his unsupported homelessness for the following year: though he did not receive a Guggenheim, Henry Allen Moe arranged for a $1,500 Carnegie Corporation grant to fund his proposed study of microtonality in Europe. Overjoyed, Partch immediately began preparing for the coming year, including buying a guitar to take with him and adapt to his ever-increasing microtonal scale. He set sail for England on September 22 aboard the *S.S. Gourko* to study at the British Museum and find further evidence for his theories, thinking that perhaps his long years of hoboing, his "personal Great Depression," were finally at an end.[64] He could not have known that eight more years of restless wandering awaited him upon his return, nor that his response to his hoboing would define and contain him for the remaining years of his life.

INTERLUDE ONE

TRANSIENTS AND MIGRANTS

When Harry Partch began picking fruit, riding the rails, sleeping under the stars, and discovering the bounty and arduousness of hobo life in 1928, that very existence was vanishing from the American scene. Having filled the West, railroad mileage peaked during the Great War and then slowly began decreasing, restricting the hobo's movement. Tractors, combines, chain saws, and steam shovels all came into widespread use in the years after the war as machines replaced human labor.[1] As settled towns sprang up throughout the West, timber, mining, and farming companies began to rely on a local labor force instead of a wandering one. As Partch discovered firsthand in the early 1930s, hoboes were forced to roam farther and farther afield, with fewer options for movement, to find enough work to survive.

Although faster harvesting techniques and more and newer equipment stymied the need for hoboes throughout the West, no invention threatened the hobo way of life more than the automobile. Suddenly, hoboes were not the only Americans who regularly took to the road. The freedom to go where they wanted when they wanted, a defining characteristic of hobo subculture, belonged to anyone who could afford a car. And Henry Ford determined that anyone would mean everyone. Instead of gleaming tracks moving masses of people in single directions, slivers of highway threaded the nation, moving individuals in multiple directions. The nation became one on the move culturally, socially, and economically.

The new form of transportation disadvantaged hoboes. Families took to the road and took over hobo jobs. Traveling only a few miles away from home by car, these wageworker families earned extra money by working in the fields, pushing out the hobo workforce. Farm owners and manufacturers much preferred this "casual labor"; some even posted notices that single male "floaters" should not bother applying for work.[2] The neighborhoods in the cities that housed the railroads' main hubs—the so-called main stems where hoboes once gathered to find work in Chicago, St. Louis, San Francisco, and other large cities—began to shrivel, and even noted authorities like Nels Anderson lamented that the hobo seemed to be vanishing.[3]

The Rise of the Transient

Although the hoboes Partch met around the dinner table of his childhood still existed in the 1930s, a new generation of train riders emerged as Partch took to the rails for the first time. As a result, his first artistic products about homeless populations in the United States did not focus on hoboes, but instead on this new population. They still traveled by train and used governmental services; by 1932, riding freights illegally was more commonplace than at any other time in American history and overflowing municipal shelters were turning away applicants.[4] But the men who used those services had new faces—they felt they had no other choice, in leaving home for the unlimited horizon. With the widespread loss of jobs caused by the crash in the fall of 1929, young, unmarried men, unable to find work in their own communities and not wishing to burden friends and families, ventured out to find work in the various harvests.[5]

During this decade, newly-unemployed men under the age of twenty-five comprised 70 percent of the migratory worker population.[6] This new army of migrants learned its craft from the old-time hoboes who still wandered and worked and, following their lead, swelled the jungles and main stems of Chicago, St. Louis, and San Francisco. The new migratory workers did not follow the old-timers' advice about when and where to work, however. Unlike their forebears who worked from early spring to late fall, these new hoboes needed, sought, and found work intermittently all year. This pattern strained the labor market and the already shaky relationships between workers and owners and manufacturers throughout the West. As the decade progressed, year-round work became scarcer, leading to a second drastic drop in hobo numbers even while the number of unemployed remained steady.[7] As the automobile became more and more commonplace and good roads stretched across the countryside, families that in earlier years had only traveled a few miles to work now made cross-country moves. This new generation of unemployed workers in the 1930s created a stark division between "old time" hoboes and those they called "newcomers," between the wanderers themselves and the general public.[8] Instead of "hoboes," who were virtually extinguished by the diminishing importance of the train after World War II, these men were known as "transients": the demographics of America's peripatetic population changed so drastically that the word "hobo" all but disappeared from print.[9] This shift in nomenclature ignited connotations of sordidness in the public mind. Unlike the hobo, the transient does not make his own luck, rising above whatever governmental or business systems throw at him. Instead, he is the system's victim, dejected and impoverished by a society that cannot or will not support him.

This popular understanding of the term transient perhaps first appears in the closing pages of John Dos Passos's 1936 novel *The Big Money*, the final chapter in his *U.S.A.* trilogy. Whereas the first chapter of the first book in the trilogy, *The 42nd Parallel*, features Mac, an independent individualist roaming the closing Western frontier and using his passion for his life on the road for political change, this final chapter closes with an unnamed wanderer referred to as "Vag." Over the course of three pages, Dos Passos paints a portrait of a man destroyed by vagrancy:

> Head swims, hunger has twisted the belly tight, he has skinned a heel through the torn sock, feet ache in the broken shoes, under the threadbare suit carefully brushed off with the hand, the torn drawers have a crummy feel, the feel of having slept in your clothes; in the nostrils lingers the staleness of discouraged carcasses crowded into a transient camp, the carbolic stench of the jail, on the taut cheeks the shamed flush from the boring eyes of cops and deputies, railroad bulls.[10]

Although Dos Passos opened the trilogy with an optimistic hobo, he closed it with a man who has lost hope, who is bitter and disillusioned, and who is no longer in control of his destiny. He is a transient.

A New Deal for Transients

In its initial attempts to assuage the growing unemployed population during the Depression, the federal government focused on these unemployed male transients. Those men who rode the rods and found handouts and work where they could, were, in Walter Stein's words, "more spectacular and more visible than the families crossing the nation in search of new homes."[11] Transients therefore received the most federal attention among homeless populations through the New Deal, first by way of the Federal Emergency Relief Administration (FERA), then the Works Progress Administration (WPA), and finally the Relief Administration.

All over the country, the growing number of unemployed homeless who crowded the cities were a cause for concern. Homeless men congregated in seas of makeshift dwellings formed from cardboard, canvas, wooden planks, and industrial waste. These tent cities, or "Hoovervilles," as they were nicknamed, appeared on the edges of most major cities, unnerving many residents. The most famous sprouted in Washington D.C. in the year before Roosevelt took office and FERA was created. A group of World War I veterans, calling themselves the "Bonus Expeditionary Force," marched on the city and demanded restoration of their discontinued pensions. This "Bonus Army" of over twenty thousand men camped in the city, vowing not to leave until their demands were met (see fig. I.1). President Hoover grossly overreacted, sending troops to disperse the demonstration. In attempting to short-circuit any ensuing furor over their plight, Hoover provided the nation's newspapers with front-page pictures of the army attacking its veterans. The plight of transients, now recast as United States veterans, was thrust into the national eye.[12] Demands for reform blossomed over the next year and a half.

On May 12, 1933, Congress first moved toward economic relief when it established the Federal Emergency Relief Administration and appropriated $500 million to supplement state money. FERA faced the daunting task of providing direct relief to millions of unemployed during the Depression's darkest year. To head this unprecedented new program, President Roosevelt turned to Harry Hopkins, a man who shared Roosevelt's attitude that direct relief, money simply handed out to needy people, was an ineffective, short-term solution to a long-range problem. They favored work relief instead. Hopkins believed that while direct relief would only produce shame, work relief could provide that measure of self-respect that would keep people from depending on relief their entire lives.

By most estimations, FERA was one of the New Deal's most resourceful and innovative agencies. It responded to its Congressional mandate with a series of programs aimed at specific segments of the population, a trial-and-error approach to discovering what kinds of work relief the public would accept.[13] The program's short history is littered with initiatives. Some succeeded, but many more failed either in public relations or from lack of state participation. Fortunately for its directors, despite the Congressional mandate for state involvement, the Emergency Relief Appropriation Act of 1933 authorized FERA to give block grants to states "to aid needy persons

Figure I.1. A small contingent of Brooklyn veterans in the Bonus Expeditionary Force camped in Washington, DC, 1932. Library of Congress, Prints and Photographs Division, Theodor Horydczak Collection, LC-DIG-ppmsca-05576.

who have no legal settlement in any one state or community" rather than only residents of that state.[14] Hopkins and his top staffers decided early on to give direct-fund grants first to Colorado, Illinois, Iowa, Michigan, Mississippi, Ohio, and Texas. Awarded on May 31, 1933, FERA's first day of operation, these grants were to purchase commodities that were needed for direct relief to "resident, transient, and homeless unemployed."[15]

With those grants made, Hopkins began creating a nationwide system of work and direct relief programs for unemployed, homeless men. He established the Federal Transient Bureau, or Transient program, on July 11 with the single directive to help State Emergency Relief Agencies (SERAs) set up work programs for transients and administer direct relief. In the contentious issue of transient care, the program's dual nature of assisting SERAs while providing relief on its own was a blessing and a curse. By forming its own camps and shelters, the Transient program ensured that aid went directly to transients rather than to fund state projects. But the approach forced the already understaffed and overworked FERA to duplicate state operations. Despite the headaches it caused (many throughout the decade called the migrant problem the "migraine problem"[16]) it was the first area in which FERA showed definitive results from its relief efforts. In fact, this small subdivision of FERA, managed by only six full-time staffers, cared for over 500,000 people at its peak.[17]

On July 26, 1933, the Federal Transient Bureau began its mission in earnest, releasing a memorandum to state governors and relief organization administrators enumerating areas needing immediate attention:

> (1) central registration and case-work facilities; (2) shelter, food, and clothing, adapted to individual needs; (3) medical and health service; (4) transportation either to place of legal residence or other destination when found desirable and necessary on a case-work basis, for families and unattached persons; (5) work, adapted to the physical handicaps of the clients, if any; the possibility of work opportunity should be sought through local work projects, public works, and employment bureaus; (6) preventive programs.[18]

It then proceeded to divide the men it served into categories to facilitate their aid. The program defined any person who had resided in a state for less than twelve months as a federal transient, all others as state transients. Beginning in 1933, Federal Transient Bureau statistics show that over 57 percent of federal transients had been homeless for less than six months; these were the men Roosevelt would later call "employables."[19] They were on the road for various Depression-related reasons, but primarily (as Nels Anderson reported) "economic transitions, marital and sexual problems, alcoholism, physical injuries or illness, cultural conflict, and detachment."[20] However, the same statistics reveal that less than 10 percent of the total transient population moved constantly. Most settled for a time, then moved again.[21] Hoping to ease these people's suffering, the Transient program worked through each SERA to organize a series of shelters and work camps around the country. Agents directed transients to area shelters where they were registered and then given medical examinations, a new set of clothes, two meals, and a bed for two nights. Then they had the choice of returning home or accepting work in a camp. Local and state homeless went to state camps, which provided treatment similar to that in federal ones. At the camps, segregated by gender and age, transients worked on public work projects, mainly in national or state forests. From their inception, the camps were successful, housing over 67,000 people in their first summer of operation.[22] They were so successful that, even though the Transient program began shifting control of its various services completely to the SERAs by the end of 1933, it continued to operate its own federal camps for a few more years.[23]

Even with these accomplishments, many were not pleased with the Transient program. Cooperating states questioned FERA policies of slowly reducing transient dependency on the dole while improving aid standards: this produced huge federal intervention in state policies, as state services had to match those in Transient program camps.[24] Transients, however, questioned the type of aid provided. Despite Transient program regulations, or perhaps because of them, many states based eligibility and type of transient care on their old poor laws or work tests, and continued operating unsupervised flophouses and breadlines. As a result, many work camps provided room and board of poor quality, insufficient and even below that found in hobo jungles. Work was repetitious and often consisted of make-work such as digging and then filling ditches, with no purpose other than making transients earn their handout. For people used to moving when and where they wanted, camps restricted small freedoms, with defined physical boundaries and set times for meals and sleep.[25]

Even with these failings, FERA exceeded governmental expectations— and every other New Deal agency—in supplying relief. Depression-era records show that the high point of relief came in February 1934, at the height of FERA and the Civil Works Administration, when New Deal programs supplied aid to twenty-eight million people, roughly 22 percent of the total population.[26] Later that same year, FERA responded to criticisms with a policy change to make the work it provided of "economic and societal benefit to the general public." But by then FERA was running out of steam, as the country's mood and official pronouncements conspired to change the conception of who should be helped.[27]

In a move that resonated throughout the decade and ultimately affected the perception of Partch's transient-based works like *Bitter Music*, the Transient program transgressed its own rules and began providing assistance to transients in family groups.[28] Migrant families were supposed to be excluded from the program's auspices in order not to compete with such low-wage economic sectors as farm work. But within two years of the program's inception, national concern had moved beyond the Bonus Army's veterans to rest with women and families as well as single men.[29] The division between transients and migrants put in place by government administrators to convince legislators of the program's parameters was breaking down. The public saw FERA administer relief to migrant families, transients, and bums; although train-hopping hoboes retained their status as a separate class, the other three became indistinguishable in most people's minds.

This situation had unfortunate consequences for migrant families who were leaving the dust-ravaged plains even as early as 1933. Congress and the public grew tired of supporting transients, and the Emergency Relief Appropriation Act of 1935 officially closed FERA on April 8 and replaced it with the Works Progress Administration (WPA).[30] After FERA's cessation, the Federal Transient Bureau announced on September 6, 1935, that "after midnight September 20 no more persons shall be accepted for service and relief from special transient funds."[31] Although it continued dispensing relief to transients through local relief offices using general funds, by year's end Bureau funds had been transferred to the WPA.

The Transient program was ultimately disbanded for several reasons. Its beneficiaries were always marginal, and many in government openly despised transient relief as an unnecessary drain on federal resources. Operating in almost every state, the program was an administrative and logistical nightmare, exacerbated by the speed of its conception and implementation. The most compelling reason, however, was the establishment of the WPA, which changed Federal policies on relief and relinquished the reins completely to the states, not even attempting the kind of direct relief the Transient program had pursued. Many transients received WPA jobs, Partch included, but only if they were state residents and supported by local relief agencies.[32] This decision left many transients without work or relief after 1935 and contributed to the rise in homeless, jobless migrants. After federal and state camps in California alone peaked at a combined high of sixty-nine in February 1935, by December that year only twenty-one camps (seven federal and fourteen state) remained, and only two state camps were still operating by July 1936.[33] Few states were ready or able to assist the migrants, sick, and unemployed left on their hands when FERA closed at the end of 1935.[34]

The FERA policy of work relief altered national leanings early in the Great Depression toward opening the system to all who needed it. The Civilian Conservation Corps (CCC), which offered young men employment on public works projects in exchange for room, board, and a small stipend sent directly to workers' parents, proved to the nation that there were good alternatives to simply handing out money, food, or clothing. It seemed a fair decision to sacrifice marginal people like transients for the welfare of those deemed more deserving of federal government aid. Still, when a 1939 Institute of Public Opinion poll asked Americans what they considered the New Deal's greatest accomplishment and worst program, the Works Progress Administration was ranked highest in both categories.[35]

The Transient in California

Individual state programs even more clearly reflected attitudinal shifts from desiring to help transients to openly disdaining them, and from viewing homeless men as vagrants to calling all migrants vagrants. As *Bitter Music* is set primarily in California and Harry Partch primarily dealt with attitudes toward transients in that state, it is fortunate that the only two states in which Transient program state initiatives have been studied in depth are New York and California.[36] California must have been singled out because of the state's long history of transient and migrant problems even before the stock market collapse, when it had the nation's largest migrant labor population.[37] The state's extremely long growing season, variety of crops, and relative ease of movement had long lured men looking for work.[38] Yet this long season did end, and, come late fall, a large percentage of the Californian transient population was left in the cold. With such a large community out of work during the winter, the state was a logical choice for early programs that catered to that demographic.

Prior to the Depression, the SERA, and the Transient Bureau, California communities typically dealt with transients in three main ways. The most popular method became known as the "'passing on' principle." Cities and towns adopting this principle provided temporary care in the form of cheap housing and two meals, but encouraged transients to move on after one night. Secondly, in the absence of any official plan, local police routinely rounded up those they called vagrants, arrested them for the evening to clear the streets, and then released them at the edge of town the next morning. Thirdly, the jauntily-named "hobo express" existed as an amalgam of the "'passing on' principle" and police intervention where officials corralled transients, loaded them into a truck, then physically removed them to the county or even state line.[39]

The rise in transients caused by the Depression's onset forced cities to realize that their hobo express was a revolving door: towns in the next county simply returned transients the next day through their own express service. This constant cycling of transients did nothing toward solving the problem, so California created state labor camps in spite of local antagonism toward transients.[40] As the transient problem was at its worst during the winter months, in the winters of 1931–33, California sponsored 250 such camps that employed over 15,000 men. The men mainly performed conservation work on public lands: cutting fire breaks in state forests, grading roads, and maintaining already-functioning services. They received no weekly wage for their work, only room and board for the camp's duration and five dollars when the camp closed as incentive to complete the program and be on their best behavior.[41] Although it was not a perfect solution to the problem—it only supported men able to work and did not care for families—the camps' success inspired the FERA directors' decision to include camps as part of Transient program directives.

The Transient program first attempted to quell California's transient problem by forming its own shelters in five major cities. This idea did not sit well with most Californians, especially as 73 percent of Californians lived in urban areas (compared to 56 percent for the rest of the United States). The California SERA countered by proposing that city shelters hold transients only one night and that their main purpose be to examine and group men for transportation to camps located outside of major residential areas.[42] This move effectively communicated to Californians that the state government was defending their interests while the federal government was meddling in their lives.[43] As a result, residents were happy for camps to expand their operation throughout the year and trusted SERA policies far beyond those of the federal government.

These SERA proposals to remove the transient menace are but one symptom of the state's wide-spread enmity toward, and fear of, single, homeless men. States other than California exhibited these same feelings. Most Americans during the Depression maintained pre-twentieth-century notions of homeless men and were frightened of transients, a fear fed by popular media that featured stories of burglaries, assaults, murders, and abductions and fingered transients as the culprits. Transients provided convenient scapegoats, since although they were typically voracious newspaper readers the likelihood of their responding, positively or negatively, to the attacks was scant. As Harry Partch learned, the hobo lifestyle did not encourage social engagement outside its own community. But public fear required little evidence: although most transients had indeed served jail time, it was usually only for vagrancy. Spending a night in jail was a common method of finding free quarters on a cold night. Violent crime among transients was relatively rare.[44]

Suspicions of transients' motives were nevertheless rampant, particularly in 1934. That year, Upton Sinclair ran for California governor on the Democratic ticket. The novelist's platform became known as EPIC (End Poverty In California). A staunch Socialist, Sinclair had many conservative opponents who, when he misspoke in a rally in early October, cunningly combined his slip with Californians' fear of transients to damage his bid seriously. On October 4, the *San Francisco Chronicle* quoted Sinclair as saying, "If I am elected, about half the unemployed in the whole country will climb aboard freight trains and head for California." He later explained that he had made the comment in jest, but the damage was done.

Sinclair's opponents passed out leaflets warning of "the bum invasion" and produced newsreels about waves of migrants uprooted from their homes. The press also ran stories and political cartoons showing bums flocking to California, attracted by Sinclair's promise to end poverty and by routinely high federal and state government relief payments. Although full of obvious embellishments, the films and leaflets had the ring of truth. All a Californian needed to envision the result of a Sinclair governorship was to look out the window. Migrants from the country's Dust Bowl had been making the trek to California for at least a year. Now they often arrived with their beat-up jalopies carrying a sign reading "Sinclair here we come, where's the job?" "Sinclair for Governor," or some similar slogan.[45] Although the migrant tide from the plains had been small, the Californian reaction encouraged the inevitable equation of migrant families with the homeless transients who came to the state looking for work.

An academician helped crystallize the issue. In July 1935, Paul Taylor published his first study on the growing transient problem. Taylor, a University of California agricultural economist who would later gain fame, along with his wife Dorothea Lange, for chronicling the problem, was interested in the Depression's impact on those at the bottom of the state's agricultural industry. Surprised at what he found, Taylor quickly shifted his research focus to the new migration patterns he uncovered.[46] His subsequent article was notable for several reasons. It was the first to draw attention to the migration from the Dust Bowl and Southern United States. It aroused interest in the plight of farm laborers who had been largely overlooked during the first half of the decade. Furthermore, by attracting public attention to migrants' plight, Taylor's article initiated a new phrase for the national lexicon. Those he initially called "drought refugees" became known as "dust bowl refugees" after the publication of this first article.[47] Finally, by highlighting the growing influx of migrants during the previous year, when FERA and its Transient program were at their height, Taylor commenced a blurring that would culminate within four years. The terms "dust bowl refugee" or "dust bowl migrant" and "transient" slowly merged in Californians' minds, and the predicament of the first became synonymous with the degradation of the second.

Taylor's article appeared on the heels of a May 30 *Los Angeles Times* report that "between 25 and 40 percent of the nation's transient unemployed are already in California." The newspaper's statistics were inaccurate (only 14 percent at most of the nationwide transient population was in the state), but they closely reflected Californians' heightened concern about the increased tax burden and social ills that roaming men would produce.[48] In light of this statewide concern about transients launched by both Taylor's article and the *Times*'s report, the legislature considered, and narrowly defeated, a bill that would close the state's borders to all unemployed migrants.[49] When this bill failed, Los Angles police chief James E. Davis declared that he would save the state from all alien transients. On February 3, 1936, he dispatched 125 Los Angeles police officers to sixteen border crossings, some over eight hundred miles away.[50]

State officials initially did little to impede Davis's popular "Bum Blockade," as the press called it, beyond decrying his actions. The blockade underwent court challenges by the American Civil Liberties Union, the Attorneys General of Arizona and Oregon, and even a California resident named John Langan, who was unable to return home after a business trip to Arizona. State officials finally reacted to national press ridicule by pressuring Davis to recall his officers. He complied in mid-April, while pointing to the 6,044 transients reportedly rebuffed and maintaining that the blockade had saved the state millions of dollars and provided national publicity.[51] Although an extreme example, the Bum Blockade aptly demonstrated the severity of resident reactions to the transient situation, as many favored starving out transients and shutting state borders permanently.[52]

The Coming of the Migrant

Reactions to transients served as a prelude to the reception Californians afforded homeless families who began flooding the state in the mid-1930s, the Dust Bowl refugees. Driven from their Midwestern homes by dust storms caused by land mismanagement, and believing their situation hopeless, these migrant families took to the road and moved westward, following the migration pattern that continued to resonate in the American subconscious, even though the 1890 census had shown that the United States was settled from coast to coast and the "frontier line" no longer existed. By traveling en masse to California, they ignited a nation-wide discussion of their plight. Two opposing claims clouded an accurate understanding of why more Depression-era migrants seemed to go to California than to any other state. The first was postulated by the growers' associations that sprang up to protect established agricultural systems: their propaganda held that migrants and transients came to California for relief wages that were higher than the national average. In other words, Dust Bowl refugees had heard from friends and family that money was being given away in California, so they came to live off the fat of the land and do no work. By contrast, the second, engineered by state reformers and perpetuated by Steinbeck's *Grapes of Wrath*, averred that migrants came because greedy landowners, hoping to keep labor prices down, advertised heavily in the drought-stricken Plains in order to swell the worker population. Growers, only concerned with hoarding their wealth, engaged in dishonest and immoral practices to do so.

While both myths contained elements of truth, both were vastly overstated. Recent immigrants did write home that they found work and support in California, but most migrants and transients were proud people who wanted to work for a living, not simply collect relief checks. The impetus behind their migration was to find work, not handouts. Similarly, growers did advertise in the Plains for workers, but these advertisements were neither as widespread as portrayed in *The Grapes of Wrath* nor part of a sinister plot.[53] The truth behind migration to California was at once more complex and simpler than these myths imply. California was a victim of its own propaganda, which for years had promised the fulfillment of the American dream. Migrants, fully aware of the state's image, chose California not just for work in orchards and fields, but also for the lifestyle they believed they would have amongst towering natural wonders in a state where excitement waited around every corner.[54]

The state's tourism board was not the sole creator of these fantasies. California was home to Hollywood, manufacturer of dreams, and the film industry was one of the few unimpeded by the Depression. Whatever their troubles, Americans did not stop going to movies. If anything, attendance went up as people attempted to escape their problems in the darkness for a few hours.[55] Movies encouraged audiences to equate California with an earthly paradise, and so many packed up and moved to California, following a centuries-old American impulse to go West when times were rough, seeking this time a place where people lived happily ever after.[56]

What migrants found when they arrived differed vastly from the images they carried in their minds. California's agricultural system, exposed in 1939 by Carey McWilliams as nothing more than *Factories in the Field*, was built on large farms assembled by owners and on exploitation of agricultural labor.[57] The "migrant problem" merely exposed an issue inherent in the system. As Dust Bowl migrants arrived, they displaced traditional Mexican workers. Unlike Mexicans, who often returned home after the harvest, or even hoboes, who traveled on to the next job, these refugees wanted to stay, to establish homes, and eventually to buy their own farms. They congregated in the fertile valleys and eked out an existence even through winter. In other words, they were visible. By 1937, migrant shanty towns were a local embarrassment, forcing city governments to legislate against them; by 1938, their presence was a state concern as lawmakers debated how to support the residents; by 1939, with the publication of *Factories in the Field* and *The Grapes of Wrath*, they were a national scandal.[58] Attention focused on farming practices forced growers and owners to decide how they would deal with the spotlight and, more importantly, react to migrants.

After initial pity, growers, and indeed most Californians, responded to migrants in typical fashion—with fear and loathing. They had learned this response when transient camps were formed in 1934 and continued the pattern two years later as the Farm Security Administration (FSA) began establishing similar camps for migrant families. The following letter, written to President Roosevelt by Mrs. Effie Ball Magurn in 1940, aptly summarizes Californians' reactions to migrant families:

> A Federal migratory camp is being established adjacent to my property at Porterville, Tulare County, California. Knowing the character of migrants from my experience in dealing with them, I object to these hordes of degenerates being located at my very door.
>
> The fact that they are leaving their native land unfit for human habitation is not surprising. Their ignorance and maliciousness in caring for trees, crops, vines, and the land is such that California will be ruined if farming is left to them.
>
> Please do not put these vile people at my door to depreciate my property and to loot my ranch.[59]

In the battle between stereotyping and tackling the immense agricultural problems migrants exposed, gross generalizations held sway. Migrant families quickly began to replace Mexicans, Chinese, and even transients as the most despised segment of California society, in spite of their race and religion. In fact, while in the early years migrants' ethnicity prompted an open-minded response and social action, by decade's end the situation had reversed. One sociologist, spurred by the situation's national attention, reported that locals perceived migrant families as a slovenly, degraded form of white folk.

Walter Goldschmidt, studying the social consequences of California's agricultural system, discovered that many Californians ascribed to migrants the physical, mental, and emotional traits formerly attributed to transients: they described both groups as "ignorant and uneducated, dirty of habit if not of mind, slothful, unambitious, and dependent.... Not rarely is he accused of being dishonest. These characteristics are sometimes considered innate (a local physician spoke of them as a separate breed); sometimes lack of education is held responsible."[60] Viewing a migrant as, in John Steinbeck's words, "a dirty son-of-a-bitch" was not limited to those who had daily interaction with the migrants, like large farm owners, or those who lived next door to FSA camps. Many Californians unassociated with agricultural production viewed those who accepted government handouts as "poor white trash." Even workers charged with supporting and ministering to migrants saw them through this lens. Doctors, social workers, and teachers who worked with them filed reports full of assertions that migrants suffered from the severe social and cultural deprivations posited by those who actively opposed migrants.[61] Californians held that, like transients before them, migrants were uneducated, lazy, backward people, a race alien to society in manner and deed.

The terms used to designate migrants were similar in style and use to racial epithets. Stuart Jamieson reported that "'Okies,' 'Arkies,' and 'Texies' have taken the place of 'Chinks' and 'Dagos' in rural terminology."[62] The sobriquet "Okie" came to denote any migrant who came to the state seeking work, no matter his state of origin. Carey McWilliams later noted, "They were promptly stereotyped, exactly like a racial minority. They were called Okies and Arkies: they were shiftless and lazy and irresponsible and had too many children, and if we improve the labor camps and put a table in, they would chop it up and use it for kindling. Once I went into the foyer of this third-rate motion picture house in Bakersfield and I saw a sign: Negroes and Okies upstairs."[63] Although this stereotyping existed on all levels of interaction with migrants, it was limited to newcomers. People had been arriving from the Plains and the Southern United States for many years, but no one ever called residents from those areas Okies. In keeping with the social system perpetuated by agricultural monopolies, the distinction between an Oklahoman who lived and worked in California and an Okie was class.

Exceeding even James Davis's Bum Blockade, by the decade's end, Californians were attempting to keep all newcomers out of the state. Animosity toward transients and the New Deal programs that supported them in the mid-1930s was redirected and focused almost exclusively on Dust Bowl migrants. The line separating migrant from transient had been erased and, in the final three years before the United States entered World War II, the migrant completely replaced the transient in popular imagination.

This transformation reverberated through all forms of popular entertainment, but media coverage led the way. Throughout the 1930s, newspapers had afforded extensive coverage to the dust storms ravaging the country's midsection. Journalists traveled to Texas and Oklahoma, Kansas and Colorado to witness curtains of dust descending on the region, covering it in their folds.[64] In 1936, Pare Lorentz released *The Plow that Broke the Plains*, a documentary funded by the New Deal's Resettlment Adminstration to chronicle the disaster and its causes visually. When national attention shifted from this natural disaster to its human fallout, newspapers dispatched reporters to FSA camps. Where newspapers went, magazines were not far behind. In 1940, *Life* magazine featured a three-page spread on the migrant problem.[65] Its pictures purported to prove, with documentary evidence, the truth behind the novel. Even Hollywood had a boomlet in migrant movies, including *Gold Rush Marie, You're Not So Tough*, and *Doctors Don't Tell*.[66]

In erasing the mid-Depression transient by focusing on migrant families instead, these image-makers accomplished a curious feat—they transformed migrants from a destitute group of outsiders, worthy of fear and scorn and equated with transients who had roamed the West for decades, into a symbol for Depression-era failure.[67] They permanently changed impressions of homelessness by painting a subculture let down by many different people and systems on many different levels. They demonstrated how the business world had failed migrants early in the 1930s when the stock market collapsed. While few farmers had money in the market, banks that held mortgages on and loans to farms and homes did. When the market fell, banks called in loans—or at least did not extend them. When the economic downturn coincided with bad crop years and farmers could not pay their debts, many lost farms and homes. There was nowhere to go but west.

Through the Agricultural Adjustment Act, the Relief Administration, and the Farm Security Administration, the New Deal promised those who kept their farms a new chance at success, at personal and economic freedom. Yet government assurances could not stop the drought's devastation. As Americans watched, read, and listened, they came to see the possible failure of an American dream in the migrant situation. Although it was only gestational during the 1920s, by the Depression the idea of a lifestyle guaranteed to all Americans was fully formed. Migrants had no home, no security, and no way to succeed in their chosen undertaking. Children would probably inherit their parents' poverty. In the midst of a land that was supposed to provide richly for its people, here was a group that it had failed. Fascinated, Americans asked if the American Dream would fail them as well.[68] They wanted assurance that America was still America, still the land of opportunity. Dust Bowl migrants became the mirror in which Depression-era America viewed itself.

With the transformation of transients into migrants and the layering of American insecurities during the Depression onto that group of people, migrant society came to offer a folk culture for many to study and admire without active engagement, just as many artists were turning to "the folk" for inspiration. It was another wellspring from which to draw artistic inspiration for the documentary impulse, in the creation of novels, musical scores, and journalism. It was another place to turn in the retreat from modernism, in effect since the turn of the century, and from a system that had failed spectacularly on the economic front. Salvation for the world and, more importantly, modern culture could be found in the lives and cultures of "ordinary Americans." Unfortunately, this turn toward folk cultures often disguised deeply held expectations on the part of artists who made the move. They supposed that they would find simplicity and backwardness, and came armed with a feeling of superiority. They believed that they could transform the borrowed and supposedly insignificant culture into something truly significant.[69] In the case of migrant culture, these presuppositions caused artists and scholars to overlook the less "real" aspects, those they did not expect to find, in favor of more "authentic" folk expressions. It was a move that would ultimately haunt Harry Partch's reception as he began shaping his own music's focus and defining its imagination in the coming years.

CHAPTER TWO

THE TRANSIENT JOURNEY

Harry Partch's year in Europe could hardly have been more productive or promising. Upon arriving in London in the fall of 1934, he quickly ensconced himself in the British Museum, where he poured over ancient manuscripts on tuning and began sketching out an idiosyncratic history of the practice. He made his way to Dublin to meet with W. B. Yeats, explain how he used the intoning voice in setting speech to music, demonstrate his theories, and receive enthusiastic affirmation from the poet. He met with Arnold Dolmetsch to discuss new musical instruments and with Kathleen Schlesinger, who was then working on her book *The Greek Aulos*, to discuss old ones. He finished his Adapted Guitar and engaged a local builder in creating the Ptolemy, a keyboard instrument with forty-three tones to the octave (which he would abandon in a California shipyard a year later). He even met with Ezra Pound in Rapallo, Italy, during an excursion to Malta. In each of these encounters, Partch found encouragement and, if not understanding of, at least an openness to his ideas. After a frustrating few years during which he had struggled for any sort of recognition and had resorted to hoboing, it seemed as though he were finally realizing his goals and the time was ripe for his acceptance.[1] As he prepared to return to the United States in the spring of 1935, he must have envisioned riding his upward trajectory to greater and greater acclaim in his homeland.

As though a premonition of things to come, Partch's return to the United States was not auspicious. He appeared at the Institute of International Education in New York City, under whose aegis he had traveled abroad, to make his final report. Minor functionaries shuffled him from office to office until finally someone informed him that the six-month report he had sent while on vacation in Malta had been incomprehensible and, indeed, no one could grasp what exactly he had accomplished. Frustrated, Partch left the Institute, the city, and the state, and began the long trek to California.[2]

Partch's Bitter Eight-Month Journey

Partch had been a California resident for much of his life, but upon his return to the state, he faced life for the first time without support. His earlier patron, Bertha Knisely, was overseas, and he did not want to impose upon old friends or family. Without a place to live or financial support he was willing to accept, Partch followed the path of so many young men not wishing to burden their families and struck out on his own. Although he had hoboed on and off for the previous seven years, he later marked April 1935 as the beginning of eight years of homeless wandering. As he later summarized: "My return was to a jobless America, and I took my blankets out under the stars beside the American River (the river of gold!), carried my notebook, kept a journal, and make sketches."[3]

Partch did not call the seven years prior to 1935 ones of hoboing because of their less itinerant nature. He was often in one place for long periods and worked primarily as a proofreader, not as a harvester. From 1935, however, he hoboed the majority of the time, although he was often settled and still worked as a proofreader on occasion. Perhaps, then, even more than the amount of time spent wandering (because the line between settled and wandering was a fine one throughout the composer's life), the country's general mood led him to label these eight years his "hobo years."

In spite of Partch's nomenclature, following New Deal terminology developed under the Federal Emergency Relief Administration (FERA), his early experiences in 1935 should properly be called his transient year (see Interlude 1). Although Partch's most famous works today, from *Barstow* to *U.S. Highball*, deal specifically with the hobo and Partch's life as a hobo in the late 1930s and early 1940s, he did write a work that vividly detailed his short life as a transient under the federal system—*Bitter Music*. Part diary, part songbook, and part sketchbook, *Bitter Music* is unlike any other account of the Great Depression or those who suffered through it. The journal was, as Partch wrote, "an excursion into an art form as old as history," a personal communication from artist to audience that resonated with the

Greek concepts of art he so loved.[4] In it, he chronicled his life almost daily for the nine months following his return from Europe, but he also painted concrete examples of government responses to the suffering caused by the Great Depression. During those months he was supported by FERA work camps. His journal recorded the effect this had on transients, especially when the camps closed in late 1935. The way Partch moved around, from federal and state shelters in California to federal camps in Oregon and back again to work camps throughout California's valleys, makes it appear that he intended *Bitter Music* to catalogue the various avenues open to transients to receive help: he participated in almost every initiative FERA and the California State Emergency Relief Agency (SERA) established. Through *Bitter Music*, Harry Partch demonstrated the semantic shift in the public's consciousness from hobo to transient as well as his conscious choice to identify with the former.

Partch initially encountered the difficulty FERA and SERA had in distinguishing between federal transient and state homeless. For FERA purposes, a federal transient, any person who had resided in the state for less than twelve months, was eligible to receive aid at federal shelters and camps. Although a California resident and even born in Oakland, by the time he was searching out support through the camps Partch had only been back in the state for a month and a half. SERA did not consider him a resident, and he was therefore allotted only bed for one evening and one meal.

Partch's treatment by SERA reflected the extent of governmental and societal confusion over the criteria for residency. Transients and migrants were commonly at a loss in dealing with the complex FERA and SERA system: Partch even commented, "I am bewildered, not knowing whether to protest or deny California residence."[5] The system quickly thrown up by two agencies, FERA charging ahead, SERA dragging its feet, produced chaos in the shelters. The California government, obviously wishing that FERA would take all homeless so that it could publicly wash its hands of the affair, set up stringent and complex guidelines for citizenship. Many transients, caught like Partch between the two systems, shuffled back and forth several times before they were ultimately claimed, usually by federal shelters.

FERA established five major shelters in California, the largest and most important being the one at Stockton where Partch was first registered and processed. There, his fine clothes from Malta were confiscated, and he was given a "monkey suit" to wear. These tan coveralls usually had "FERA" in large letters on the back, branding those who attempted to walk into town and prompting animosity from townspeople who already despised the camp's proximity and its residents. Partch was also deloused and given a surprise early the next morning before checking out: the shelter at Stockton was one of the few that checked for venereal disease, prompting *Bitter Music*'s humorous musical speech, "I've had my pants down so many times the last two weeks there's not much use pulling 'em up."[6] In spite of FERA orders for medical care at all shelters, most ignored the directive as too costly, even though Californians greatly feared that migrants would unintentionally spread disease.[7]

As shelters allowed only one day's stay, Partch quickly moved to a federal work camp. The Stockton shelter funneled transients to the mountains or the San Joaquin valley, mainly offering farm work of all sorts, from dairy farms to cotton fields to vineyards.[8] Of the three options open to Partch, two were in the mountains and one in the valley; he elected to go to Harrington Ranch in the valley and work on the farm. (The Sierra Nevada work camp Partch turned down in favor of Harrington Ranch was Hetch Hetchy, one of the largest and most successful camps, where groups cleared brush and roads around the San Francisco municipal water project.[9]) Although most of the protagonists of *Bitter Music* appear at this early stage, upon his arrival at Harrington, Partch was dispirited and quickly felt alienated. The camps housed mostly older men, younger ones having found their way into the CCC by the end of 1935. Partch encountered few kindred souls there with whom to converse. Fortunately, he met Pablo, whom he immortalized in *The Letter*, and Jimmy, known in the journal as "Kain-tuck." Through them, Partch vicariously experienced more of life in the camps.

Through Pablo's reasons for vagrancy and his hopes and fears, Partch verified Anderson's observations, quoted on p. 51 above, that transients were forced to leave home by "economic transitions, marital and sexual problems, alcoholism, physical injuries or illness, cultural conflict, and detachment."[10] As Partch noted, "Their whole lives are a continual escape—they try to escape their boredom in trivial arguments, they try to escape their impotence in alcohol, they try to escape the necessity of continual effort in crime, in begging, in institutions such as this, and they try to escape reality itself in a crazy dreamworld."[11] Kain-tuck was on the road after his father and "sexually wanton stepmother" turned him over to the police for reform school, and he fled following his incarceration. Pablo likewise fled family problems. Each had a drinking problem: Pablo was eventually forced to leave the camp a step ahead of expulsion under FERA rules; for the same reason Partch abandoned Kain-tuck when he left the camp.[12] Their lives exhibited the detachment and need for escape that many saw as characteristic of transients, feelings that hung over Partch's head throughout the journal.

Pablo was also the instrument through which Partch examined homosexuality among transients and its repercussions. Moralists and commentators at the time regularly decried what they characterized as rampant homosexuality among transients, and used it as a wedge to argue against federal transient aid. From Partch's perspective, those writers were accurate regarding the pervasiveness of homosexuality in the camps. *Bitter Music* is replete with sexuality, from reporting the open discussions of sex carried on by men in the camps to humorously noting the affairs they consummated. But unlike the moralists, Partch characterizes most of this as nothing more than bodily urges. As he observes early in his time among the camps, "If the homosexuality in prisons, navies, and in any other circumstances which segregate men is similar to such tendencies as I have seen in this camp, it is mostly pure lust. Few of these men desire tender affection. A female sheep would often prove satisfactory."[13]

In his personal life, Partch always desired deep relationships and was at pains to show that most men in camp were actually not homosexuals because their encounters were loveless. His more nuanced portrayal of homosexuality among transients is best seen in the entry for June 16, 1935. Pablo is sitting with Partch, showing him pictures of the women he has loved, when he pulls out a picture of his buddy in the camp, who had left right before Partch arrived. He shyly confessed passionately kissing his friend and the guilt and turmoil he felt for an act that he would not have considered outside transient life. Dismissing the opportunity to include any of the lurid tales that comprise so many other period accounts, Partch simply acknowledged his friend's distress and comforted him with a quiet "any real love is a beautiful experience" and then continues on to ask the reader "Who cares who loves who? It doesn't matter, anyway, so long as the music is good music."[14]

Instead of responding to the dominant condemnation of homosexuality, Partch turned the question into one of intimacy and connection and wrapped it all up in his musical philosophy. Pablo was open about his concerns, and Partch assured Pablo that he had experienced something other than the lust that characterized the encounters of so many homeless men. This episode reveals that Partch's own sexuality may have been one reason he struck out on the road, but not in the manner usually thought. Partch was not after casual sexual encounters; instead, after years of pretense and false faces in the musical worlds of Los Angeles and San Francisco, he was eager for honesty and openness, something he found in small measure among transients.

At the end of July Partch headed north to Oregon, where he found refuge in a Portland federal shelter. Following the same trajectory as in

California, he then moved to another federal work camp, this time Camp Milan in Washington, where he replicated his Harrington Ranch experience. Frustrated with the FERA system, Partch soon returned to California and, at the SERA shelter in Redding, was finally accepted as a California resident. The Redding shelter was established to stop transients coming over the Siskiyou Mountains from Oregon before they could fully enter the state.[15] The transient stigma Partch had encountered in Stockton was small compared to Redding's outright hostility. When he first stopped in the city on his way to Oregon, he asked a passerby where the transient shelter was located. Until he asked where the bums went, he could not get the man to give him directions.[16] He fared no better upon his return a few weeks later. Walking through town in his SERA coveralls, he noticed that "the outside world has few smiles for the transient stigma."[17]

State rules matched those at federal shelters, and after a few days in Redding, Partch moved to a state work camp in Ingot. Surprisingly, considering the response of most Californians and their government to the transient problem, Partch found that SERA camp more comfortable, better run, and more tolerable than the FERA one, and he stayed there for a month. There he met Cisco, a young man through whom he learned the caste system among transients and the expectations of those who helped them. Cisco worked with the camp doctor and therefore earned a slightly higher salary than other residents. Unfortunately, his position exacted a high price. The doctor for whom he worked expected him to associate only with better-paid transients and forced Cisco to cut off his friendship with Partch.[18] Representatives of the society most transients had left behind, such as this doctor, were interested in aiding the unfortunates only if they were willing to rehabilitate themselves, fit back into, and become useful members of that old social order again.

In September, Partch learned that FERA had announced the cessation of its transient shelters and camps. He and his fellow workers were moved to a public works project in the Ohio Valley in Plumas County, California, one of a handful of measures taken by the government to move transients slowly from FERA's care to that of the Works Progress Administration (WPA). Partch worked there for four weeks before developing trenchmouth, a disease not permitted on work projects and which cost Partch his job.[19] He then struck out on his own. Since the government had closed its shelters by the time he recovered, like so many other transients he was left with nowhere to go, no one to turn to. He camped along the California coastline, stayed for three days with the "Godmother" of the first chromatic organ (presumably Mildred Couper) in Santa Barbara, and eventually made his way to San Bernardino. There he found a job that pulled him out of the transient jungle, if only for a short while.

The Documentary Imagination Shifts to Migrants

Harry Partch's *Bitter Music* experiences align more closely with those of Depression-era transients than hoboes. Like those wayward men, Partch used FERA shelters, found employment at SERA work camps, and wandered the California coastline. But both his later reactions to the events recorded in *Bitter Music* and the changing responses to homeless wanderers in the late 1930s equated his transient experiences with another class of people. By the time Partch began to leave his itinerant existence in the early 1940s, the documentary imagination at play in literature, newspapers, and photography had moved from transients to a new group of wanderers. *Bitter Music* began to resonate with commonalities with the period's great iconic migrant, the Dust Bowl migrant. This transformation in popular conception of the homeless played an enormous role in the way Partch marketed himself and, perhaps more importantly, in the way people received him and his music.

Although daunting, understanding the Great Depression through its own lens is not impossible. Because of the work of numerous artists and the period's advances in printing, few eras are as embedded in the collective imagination of the United States. The 1930s, along with its perceived antithesis in the World War II years, retains an uncanny grasp on Americans' sense of themselves and their country. The conception of hard-working, plain-folks America originates in the constant stream of Depression-era images that Americans imbibe from an early age, from Dorothea Lange's striking photographs to John Steinbeck's novel *The Grapes of Wrath*, studied in many high schools. Through these and other sources, most Americans can still conjure iconic images of Depression-era life: unshaven men standing in bread lines, hats and posture slouching; vast expanses of prairie covered by huge clouds of dust, like a wall up to the sky, with nothing but a cow skull visible for miles; college graduates returning home with no job in sight; suicide rates skyrocketing as investors jump from buildings; former businessmen selling pencils or apples on street corners or sweeping streets in suits; an extended family of grandparents, parents, and five or six children riding in a jalopy burdened with all their worldly possessions; an open boxcar with hoboes sitting in the doorway, a bundle nearby (see fig. 2.1).[20]

Figure 2.1. This iconic image of the Dust Bowl, that of the family jalopy loaded down with possessions, features a family of five from Missouri on US Highway 99 in California, 1937. Library of Congress, Prints and Photographs Division, FSA/OWI Collection, LC-USF34-T01-016456-E.

These images are so powerful, and their impact so pervasive, that any attempt to understand Partch's conceptually exotic approach, his hobo music, and the way he and his artistic creations were viewed, both during the time and after, must grapple with them. They are, in many ways, an exoticizing force. These images originated in the same desire that drove American composers like Copland and Harris to turn their gaze westward. When Americans looked for what was unique in their country during the Depression, they looked outside their own heritage to "the folk." When composers searched for a true American voice in music, they looked to "the folk." When documentary artists looked to catalogue the Depression's harshest effects, they looked to "the folk." By the Depression's end, "the folk" most in need of assistance were Dust Bowl migrants. In another semantic perceptual shift, the transients of the early 1930s became migrants, victimized by society and by nature and, most importantly, deserving of help.

The documentary imagination, this impulse to respond to insecurity and suffering through the presentation of reality, began to place the migrant image at its center, building upon decades of tramp, hobo, and transient impressions. Pictures, articles, and books chronicling the migrants' experiences flooded the market. Local, state, and national meetings were held to discuss the migrant situation. Americans discovered the Depression's soul in families who were forced from their homes and urged to travel to California, but found conditions there as harsh as those they had left. As one, the country moved to care for them. It was a remarkable expression of empathy for a group usually seen as an Other.

The Documentary Imagination in Photography (Dorothea Lange)

Traditionally, literature was the most important medium through which Americans encountered migrants. But a new form of artistic expression depicted Depression-era wanderers: photography. Literature had long grappled with pressing social issues, but at the Depression's beginning photography was only starting to do so. During that decade, photographers began to explore their medium's ability to combine aesthetic considerations with a visual record.[21] This move coincided with the Roosevelt administration's desire to document the Depression's effects for governmental studies. Those two conditions ultimately met in the Farm Security Administration (FSA), the New Deal agency charged with recording the range of the Depression's effects. FSA administrators decided that photography would accomplish their assignment and employed the best photographers they could find throughout the United States, including Walker Evans, Dorothea Lange, Russell Lee, Ben Shahn, and Marion Post Wolcott. By 1942, the FSA had amassed over 270,000 pictures, which were used in photomagazines, newspapers, and books, effectively defining the Depression visually.

Ruminating about the impact of images by FSA photographers on America's desire for knowledge of the folk, administration head C. B. Baldwin remarked, "I think our most lasting contribution was this collection of photographs. I think it more effectively dramatized the plight of poor people than anything else done in thirty years. It was accidental. We just happened to hit on the medium."[22] More than any other artistic form, that medium, documentary photography, shaped Americans' view of the Depression then and now. The documentary imagination manifested itself in photography through pictures that focused not on glossy posed portraits or majestic natural landscapes, but rather on flatly-lit, stark images of suffering and the resolve to survive. Through these new images, photographers sought to restore faith in the idea that government, through the media, might deliver the truth of a situation.[23]

Since its inception, no woman has had more influence on, and no name has become more identified with, documentary photography than Dorothea Lange. Her images define the Great Depression in many minds and reflect, in Karin Ohrn's words, a "widespread movement to integrate art, literature, journalism, and social science into documentary forms having social significance as their primary purpose."[24] Lange's first documentary photographs illustrated a 1934 report meant to convince the California government to establish camps for transients. As she and her husband, economist Paul Taylor, worked on the project, both became convinced that a photo alone could not reveal everything about a situation or person. Amidst misery, poverty, and fortitude, they found that the old axiom "a picture is worth a thousand words" did not hold up. Lange wanted verbal comments to add to her photo's power, not simply to explain the picture. She later said, "I don't like the kind of written material that tells a person what to look for or that explains the photograph. I like the kind of material that gives more background, that fortifies it without directing the person's mind."[25] As a result, while Lange took photos, Taylor would strike up conversation with the people they were documenting, gathering what information he could. When they left the site, the two would sit in their car for over an hour, furiously writing in an attempt to remember and record exactly what they had been told.[26]

Although unorthodox in its day, the method's success bespoke its utility. Lange's photographs appeared in "newspapers, magazines, government pamphlets, and books; they were exhibited at schools and libraries, department stores, museums, and professional conventions; they were presented as evidence on the floor of the Senate."[27] It is not too much to say that of all FSA photographers, Dorothea Lange was most responsible for the migrant image supplanting that of the transient in the Depression's latter half.

Lange almost missed her most famous and iconic picture, "Migrant Mother." In early March 1936, she drove through a rainy, miserable day along California's Highway 101, returning home to San Francisco after a month-long assignment photographing state migrant camps. She passed by a hand-lettered sign indicating a pea-pickers' camp and a few miles later, turned around to investigate: "I was following instinct, not reason; I drove into that wet and soggy camp and parked my car like a homing pigeon. I saw and approached the hungry and desperate mother, as if drawn by a magnet." She took out her camera and, eschewing her usual style of engaging her subjects in conversation, began taking pictures immediately.

Lange took a series of photos that day, wide shots of the camp and collections of families living under tents, but it is one of the last, a close-up of a young family, that is the most striking (see fig. 2.2).[28] In it, a mother gazes out into nothingness, her hand resting lightly on her chin and worry knitted into her brow. She cradles an infant in her arm while two older children of unknown gender lean on her shoulders, their backs toward the viewer. It is a remarkably intimate photograph, shocking in its raw emotive power. Because it is a close shot focused on the mother and her children without any relevant context, the picture presents a striking image of victimization, one that transcends the situation and translates, to any and all, the Great Depression's impact.[29] When Lange published the photograph in the *San Francisco News* on March 10, 1936, scant days after it was taken, it created an immediate stir and connected strongly with its first audience—so strongly that it brought in $200,000 in contributions for migrant relief.[30]

After its appearance, "Migrant Mother" quickly spread across the country. In October of that year, it appeared in *Midweek Pictorial* with the headline "Look In Her Eyes." Numerous publications used the photograph to illustrate American perseverance in the face of hardship. By appealing to the universal concern of mothers for children, it succeeded more than anything else in raising middle-class concern for and interest in the situation and became a national symbol of the Depression.[31]

Like Partch's conceptually exotic music, Lange's photography engaged its subject in a deeper and more personal way and, as a result, developed new genres. Its most significant genre was the photo-documentary book, a publication that matched images and literary text in a format that fit Lange and Taylor's working method perfectly. Since Americans wanted the semblance of reality, they wanted more than a book of pictures, a novel, or a piece of music; they wanted genres that combined to enrich their understanding of a people. Perhaps the most notable Depression-era photo-documentary book was James Agee and Walker Evan's *Let Us Now Praise Famous Men*. Agee and Evan's work focused on three tenant families in the rural South: the Ricketts, the Woods, and the Gudgers. Like most

Figure 2.2. Dorothea Lange's famous image "Migrant Mother," 1936. Library of Congress, Prints and Photographs Division, FSA/OWI Collection, LC-DIG-fsa-8b29516.

photo-documentary books, it grew out of a journalistic article, extensively rewritten and enhanced by biography, autobiography, recorded conversations, bits from other newspaper articles, and reflections on the state of an American society that produced this level of suffering.[32] Harry Partch's *Bitter Music*, with its maps, its sketches of characters, conditions, and the countryside, and its musicalized migrant speech, fits perfectly into this tradition. As a result, several publishers, including Story Press, considered the manuscript for a time in the late 1930s as a unique example of a new hybrid genre.

Lange and Taylor's photo-documentary book, *An American Exodus*, is a "paper movie" where, instead of linear narrative, constantly shifting perspectives confront the reader. The book's story, such as it is, recounts the effects of agricultural mechanization on farming, of economic consolidation on small farmers, and of drought on families. It is the tale of a battle between nature and machine that caused the Dust Bowl, a battle in which migrants are only victims.[33] And it is a record of human erosion in which "we have let them speak to you face to face. Here we pass on what we have seen and learned from many miles of countryside of the shocks which are unsettling them."[34] Evidence from studies, newspapers, and surveys reinforce the pictures rather than, as is usual, literary text.[35] The photographs appear in sharp focus with great depth, at times overshadowing the text and overwhelming the viewer by filling the page. Text and pictures engage in a dialogue, each informing the other and imparting different perspectives. But in spite of the couple's stated desire to provide their subjects with the "opportunity to tell what they are up against to their government and to their country men at large," the men and women profiled are left as symbols, not as fully formed, complex, contradictory humans.[36] They are left to be seen as separate, as distant, as Other. *An American Exodus* is documentary, but it is exoticization as well.

The Documentary Imagination in Literature (John Steinbeck)

An American Exodus never achieved the currency of "Migrant Mother." That one photograph, taken on a rainy March day, became an icon, representing the anxiety caused by Depression dislocation. Its iconic status also helped link Dorothea Lange and John Steinbeck, the era's foremost proponents of migrant images in literature. Those two artists did more than any other in their respective fields to draw attention to the plight of migrants and make them the focus of documentary art. Both used descriptions culled from migrant interviews to add verisimilitude to their claims. Both thought in photographic terms, as a quick perusal of Steinbeck's working diary from the period aptly demonstrates.[37] Both did more for the migrant cause than any politician of the day.[38] And both felt that their job was to educate Americans about the damage inflicted on people they considered the true American folk.

Since its publication, critics have argued over the outrage *The Grapes of Wrath* engendered, over Steinbeck's aims, and over the novel's ability to penetrate the national consciousness. In one historian's words, "the book captured the deprivation and disorientation of the migration, the hostility of the Californians, the heroism and the bigotry of the Okies. Finally, *The Grapes of Wrath* made the dual nature of California's problem crystal clear: the first half of the book told of interstate migrants, the second half of agricultural laborers."[39] Still, considering the animosity of Californians toward migrants and transients, it is instructive to explore the popular appeal of Steinbeck's novel and uncover some of the reasons behind the shifting tide of public opinion.

The Grapes of Wrath benefited from a trio of factors. First, it came after a decade of Depression, when men and women sought assurances, through tales of those less fortunate than themselves, that they were better off than some. In the novel's protagonists, the Joads, Americans found a family sufficiently like their own with whom they could sympathize and for whom they could demand justice.[40] Second, when *The Grapes of Wrath* was published, many Californians worried about the state's image and worked to ban the book on charges of obscenity, vulgarity, and false depictions of migrants.[41] Other groups around the nation joined the movement and the novel gained a reputation as a "dirty book"—a label that only fueled interest. Third, the book delivered its social problem as a gut-wrenching story, appealing to emotions as well as intellect. Readers reacted to the social shock delivered by its visceral nature.

The social power of *The Grapes of Wrath* lay in the way it made the plight of the Dust Bowl migrants into a national problem.[42] By painting a picture of a life his readers could not endure, though lived by people his readers understood, Steinbeck made Americans acknowledge the migrants' humanity.[43] Americans saw Steinbeck presenting grainy, gritty reality. As viewed in the readers' documentary imagination already crafted by images from FSA photographers, the novel was a mythic American story and Steinbeck an author who held the mirror to real American life while prophetically depicting his country's future. His characters were bleakly hopeful and optimistic that America and its people were capable of change and worthy of redemption, in spite of grievous faults and failures.[44] Although it flew in the face of the American dream, in the face of American ideals—that with hard work and perseverance one can and will succeed—*The Grapes of Wrath* held out hope that the country would emerge from the Great Depression a better and more perfect people. It was a message that Americans wanted to hear.

The Documentary Imagination in Music (Woody Guthrie)

Americans were so eager for that message that, by the time World War II was in full swing and Harry Partch was beginning to ply his music based on his experiences among the homeless in California, migrants had been mythologized and their plight almost forgotten. As Warren Susman commented: "This search for some transcendent identification with a mythic America led Americans in a few short years from deep concern for the Okies of the Dust Bowl as a profound social and human problem to the joyous "Oh! What a Beautiful Morning" with the "corn as high as an elephant's eye" of Rogers and Hammerstein's *Oklahoma!* (1943), a hugely successful if sentimental effort to recapture the innocent vitality of the historic American folk."[45] Partch would have preferred to avoid this kind of sentimentality, but if he had published or performed *Bitter Music*, it would have been seen through this lens. Partch assuredly benefited from the fanatical interest in the migrant plight and the search for an American sound, for America's soul, through the folk, but that interest proved to be a double-edged sword. Musicians had a definite idea of how Anglo-American folk sources should be used, one predicated on a decorative exoticism with which Partch did not agree. Even more limiting, when they looked at his works, they did so through the eyes given them by artists like Dorothea Lange and John Steinbeck. In some ways, Partch could not help but be seen as a migrant, but as he wanted neither pity nor nostalgic attempts to frame his music; he had to choose between hobo and migrant, between an image that seemed to be fading in American memory and one burning bright with associations that Partch did not desire. His ultimate decision charted both the course of his life and his own reaction to his works from this period.

The way in which writers and visual artists portrayed the migrant affected how Partch's *Bitter Music* and compositions like *Barstow* and *U.S. Highball* would be seen. But Partch's music has never been associated with Dust Bowl migrants, primarily because of the composer's conscious choice to set texts about, and promote his wandering years as associated with, the hobo. He was a single, white male in his thirties who rode trains and went from job to job; he perfectly fit the hobo demographic. Another man fit the same demographic, but his songs, particularly those in his *Dust Bowl Ballads*, presented the Depression's effects on individuals through a music then-understood to be straight from migrants' mouths. Woody Guthrie's music, life, and career offer illuminating insights into *Bitter Music* and Partch's choice of the hobo image over the migrant or transient. The two musicians share striking similarities, but in New York's and the musical establishment's responses to them, the impact of the multitudinous layers of historical meaning in those terms hobo, transient, and migrant, becomes ringingly clear.

The legend of Woody Guthrie's career begins with *The Grapes of Wrath*. All the furor over the novel inevitably led to a benefit function for migrants; it had sparked America's imagination and outrage, and something had to be done. On March 3, 1940, almost a full year after the book's publication, Will Geer organized a "*Grapes of Wrath* Evening," a benefit concert with proceeds going to the "John Steinbeck Committee for Agricultural Workers." It was held in New York City at the Forrest Theater and featured "American Ballad Singers and Folk Dancers: Will Geer, Alan and Bess Lomax, Aunt Molly Jackson, Leadbelly, Woodie [sic] Guthrie, the Pennsylvania Miners, and the Golden Gate Quartet."[46] Although Guthrie had never performed in New York before that evening, he had been slowly gaining credence as an authentic folk singer, a Dust Bowl migrant who sang the songs and travails of his people. When he stepped out on stage that evening, scratched his head with his guitar pick, mumbled about how happy he was to be performing on a "Rapes of Graft" concert, and began to sing, he fused his name with Steinbeck's.[47] For better or worse, Woody Guthrie came to personify the Joads in music.

During the year and a half that Guthrie spent in New York City following the concert, many saw him as a type of documentarian, chronicling the migrant's plight in musical pictures. Guthrie's success in this vein was so great that when Harry Partch arrived in the city less than a year after Guthrie's departure, comparisons necessarily colored the composer's reception. Both had lived as hoboes and written music about their adventures, both arrived from California, both based their music on the patois of the people they depicted, and both had ideas slightly outside the mainstream. The figure Partch cut onstage only strengthened this connection. In lecture-demonstrations around New York City and New England in 1942 and 1943, Partch accompanied himself on the Adapted Guitar while performing his hobo-inspired works *Barstow* and *U.S. Highball*. Although he would have been dressed in a simple black suit instead of the workingman's clothes Guthrie sported, the visual impact of Partch's picking style and the easy, joking personality he cultivated was strikingly similar to Guthrie's performance aesthetic.[48] Similarities continued behind the stage. Although unrecognized at the time, even Partch and Guthrie's writing and drawing styles were quite similar. Guthrie finished his autobiography *Bound for Glory* in 1943, and it is akin to *Bitter Music* in several ways. The two books are full of sketches, drawings of people and places encountered across the country (see fig. 2.3). They carry and preserve each character's voice through written-out dialect (Guthrie) or speech music (Partch). Finally, the settings are comparable: numerous episodes occur in migrant camps and among hoboes. *Bound For Glory* even opens bouncing along in a boxcar, before Guthrie begins singing.[49] The scene could have easily occurred in *Bitter Music*, *Barstow*, or *U.S. Highball*.

But however similar their surface interests and performance demeanor, the two men's music differed vastly in philosophical, topical, and especially audible terms. Since the 1940s, those differences have caused Woody Guthrie's music to be celebrated for presenting the Depression's effects on individuals, while Partch's musical documentation of migrants and hoboes has been sidelined. Surprisingly, however, in 1940s New York the opposite was true. Composers caught up in the furor of creating a discernibly American music ignored Guthrie's songs while they tentatively embraced Partch's ideas. This dichotomy in reception lay not only in the exoticized framework in which composers understood uses of folk music, but also in how the two men presented themselves against the sound of their music. How effectively they tapped into the image of the hobo and migrant crafted by the FSA photographers and *The Grapes of Wrath* can be seen in stark relief when their most important documents of Depression-era life are compared.

Upon his return to California in 1935, Partch had difficulty entering the state, discovering that either money or deception was required to enter, as typified by this exchange he recorded in *Bitter Music*:

"How long have you been in California?"

The old, question. My inquisitor is neither very bright nor interested. If he had been, he would have seen an expression of strained patience before him. . . .

"Just a month and a half, but I was born in Oakland and have lived in California most of my life."

Figure 2.3. Comparison of Partch's line drawings in *Bitter Music* (*left*) and Guthrie's in *Bound for Glory* (*right*) shows not only similarities in drawing style, but also in the subjects they depicted. Drawing of "Hoodlum" from Partch's *Bitter Music*, October 29, 1935. Courtesy of the Harry Partch Estate Archive, San Diego. Woody Guthrie, *Walking in the Wind*, 1942, pencil with pen-and-ink on poster board illustration for Guthrie's autobiography *Bound for Glory*. © Woody Guthrie Publications, Inc.

"Bed tonight and breakfast tomorrow is all we can give you," he says.

"That sort of induces one to lie," I say, smiling.

"Yes, it does," he says.[50]

In February of 1936, only a few months after Partch's arrival in the state, Woody Guthrie traveled to California on the suggestions of many Oklahoma residents.[51] Arriving at the California border, he encountered the remnants of and stories about Los Angeles Police Chief James Davis's Bum Blockade. Guthrie was able to enter the state with no trouble, but later, angry over the blockade's injustice, he wrote the song "Do Re Mi" about the whole affair. In the song he opined that the police were not letting people into the state unless they had money, a clever turn of phrase based on the homophone "Do" and the colloquial use of "dough" for money. Where Partch had trouble entering because, having grown up in California, he was classified as an in-state transient, people from Oklahoma like Guthrie had trouble getting into a state that viewed them as out-of-state migrants. California's SERA viewed both groups as hazardous to the economy.

Settling in the state, Guthrie initially tapped into the craze for the singing cowboy in Los Angeles, performing on the radio with his cousin Jack Guthrie and then Maxine "Lefty Lou" Crissman. But as he traveled the state at the urging of Frank Burke, the populist owner of KFVD where Guthrie did his radio show, the singer heard migrants' anger at their situation and their frustration that they had come for work and food and had found neither. As he performed a few songs in migrant camps and hobo jungles, he learned both the extent of bigotry toward migrants, especially those from his native Oklahoma, and the uniting power his songs had over those who felt oppressed by government, society, and business. Guthrie began to agitate for them by writing politically charged songs expressing the migrant situation, such as "Dust Bowl Refugee," which opens by recounting the difficulties encountered by many migrant families on the westward trek, as they made their way to a land filled with fruit and water and false promises; and "Dusty Old Dust," which pins the move migrants made to California firmly on the dust that not only filled houses but caused many to loose their homes when they could no longer earn a living from the land. Guthrie then sang these songs on the radio, in concerts, and almost anywhere he could get "a couple of dollars, or a couple of drinks, or a meal."[52] The songs that grew out of his experiences with drought and bankers in Oklahoma, and his anger over the oppression suffered by migrants in the camps and throughout California, formed the basis for *Dust Bowl Ballads*.

The differing perspectives of *Dust Bowl Ballads* and *Bitter Music* illuminate one crucial distinction between Partch's and Guthrie's philosophies concerning their music and its use of Anglo-American folk culture. Guthrie's songs spring from stories he heard from men and women in migrant camps. When he observed their living conditions and the verbal abuse they endured, Guthrie wanted to use his commercial radio pulpit to rile his audience to take action on behalf of migrants. He wanted to speak for people who had no say. Partch, on the other hand, was not interested in being an advocate. Instead, he wanted to demonstrate his Monophonic system's ability to capture the tenor and inflection of the human voice. He found in hoboes, transients, and migrants people who, to his ears, spoke with a musical richness found only in the United States. He wanted to capture this "fountainhead of pure musical Americana," as he later called it, and let it speak through his music.[53] While Guthrie wanted to speak for the people, Partch wanted to let the people speak.

Their music's reception related directly to these philosophies. Guthrie's ultimate fame came not in California among Dust Bowl migrants, to whom he was nothing more than another hillbilly performer trying to scrape by, nor among composers and musicians, who saw him as recycling folk songs, but among New York intellectuals, who considered him the quintessential "Okie troubadour," the voice of an oppressed proletariat.[54] *The Grapes of Wrath* had helped imprint leftist ideals on the migrant, who came to be seen as having socialist leanings, an image immediately applied to Guthrie by his New York supporters and only slowly taken up by the singer. His success rested on that image. He never challenged the tacit assumption that he spoke for Okies exclusively, but by the time he had reached New York, he desired a wider reach and approach showing "that the experience of displacement, movement, homelessness, and transit was not simply a condition but a fundamental fact of American life."[55] Guthrie quickly realized that the circles in which he moved in the city wanted to pigeonhole him; so in January 1941, less than a year after arriving in New York, he left.[56]

Partch's reception was almost the opposite. His initial acceptance in New York came from his ability to use the hobo voice within a setting deemed art music. Most of the composers attempting to create an American music based on folk sources were ethnically not part of the communities from which they drew their music, nor did they want to be. Likewise, they did not want to abandon European musical structures in favor of ones based on folk music. The Othering that occurred when they used those sources as a decorative overlay was a welcome barrier. It allowed composers to see "the folk" as unblemished Americana and therefore worthy of use. Guthrie was too authentic. By speaking for the people, he was seen as one of them. By singing their songs, he obviously lacked professional training. He could be a source for tunes, but not a composer of cultivated music. Partch, on the other hand, was seen as a composer first and foremost, who had happened to live as a hobo out of necessity, but fundamentally was not one. Reading his pamphlets and promotional materials, composers in New York must have felt that Partch had similar aims in his use of "the folk." To them, Partch simply used folk sources in a novel manner, one that was personal but still aspired to be art. Furthermore, the sources he was using had captured the American imagination through Steinbeck's work. Composers wanting to achieve a synthesis between European art music and American folk music were eager to hear the results and, for a time, the idea of Partch's immersive use of the aesthetics and styles of hobo and migrant music entranced them.

But what of their music? Does public perception fit private reality? In some ways, yes, but in most ways the perception was as skewed as the works' reception. *Dust Bowl Ballads* did not begin life as a unified collection. Woody Guthrie had worked on the songs that comprise the album since first traveling among the migrant camps in 1938, but the idea to assemble and record them was Alan Lomax's. Following the "Grapes of Wrath Evening," Lomax had actively promoted Guthrie, even recording him for the Library of Congress archives over three days in March. In May 1940, Lomax went a step farther and convinced RCA Victor Records to record and release a commercial album of Guthrie's songs. Victor was interested in the burgeoning folk music market and agreed on one condition: they wanted Guthrie to write and add a song about *The Grapes of Wrath* to cash in on the popularity of both book and movie.[57] Over the course of an evening with the book, Pete Seeger, and a half-gallon jug of wine for inspiration, Guthrie wrote a seventeen-verse song titled "Tom Joad" that summarized every major plot point and even included Tom's last words to his mother. Victor was so happy with the results that they recorded all seventeen verses, even though it took up both sides of a record.[58]

Recorded in a two-day session, *Dust Bowl Ballads* was a two-album set of thirteen songs. Viewed collectively, the songs are firmly in the rhythmic and melodic pattern of Southwestern United States folk ballads—in fact, many use preexisting tunes. What makes these particular ballads work as a unified whole is the thematic and metaphoric consistency of Guthrie's lyrics. He presents Dust Bowl migrants as refugees of an almost Biblical trial straight out of Exodus. There are numerous allusions to the plagues sent down on Egypt during the Exodus, and on the whole earth during the apocalypse of the New Testament book of Revelation. Migrants are presented as noble victims, willing to work hard in order to make their way in life, but denied opportunities by nature, business, and government.[59] *Dust Bowl Ballads* recounts migrants' stories, tales that were used to understand and frame their problems rather than to present the historical facts of their plight. It is a work of documentary art that, through its authenticity, purports to tell the harsh truth—but acts instead, much like Steinbeck's work, to draw attention to a national scandal and inspire action.[60]

Much of the authenticity of *Dust Bowl Ballads* rested on Guthrie's professional image at the time. In his liner notes for the original release, titled "The Dustiest of Dust Bowlers," Guthrie was conscious and deliberate about how he presented himself. He understood that intellectuals were interested in him because of the image of America that he presented and represented—and he was careful to preserve it.[61] Yet he was also careful to begin framing his songs as having wider implications. As he wrote,

> This bunch of songs ain't about me, and I ain't a-going to write about me, 'cause every time I start to do that, I find that I run out of material.
>
> They are "Oakie" [sic] songs, "Dust Bowl" songs, "Migratious" [sic] songs, about my folks and my relatives, about a jillion of 'em, that got hit by the drouth [sic], the dust, the wind, the banker, and the landlord, and the police, all at the same time ... and it was these things all added up that caused us to pack our wife and kids into our little rattletrap jallopies [sic], and light out down the Highway—in every direction, mostly west to California.[62]

By contrast, Partch's work was personal; *Bitter Music* recounts his time in federal and state work camps, and *U.S. Highball* dramatizes a transcontinental hobo trip he took in 1941. In the works, characters complain about their treatment at the hands of society. They share small triumphs, such as getting a ride on the highway as opposed to jumping another train. They use stories to frame their subjects' troubles. Whether relating an anecdote about getting a new suit dirty or the tragedy of a life prematurely aged by the rails, these works reveal the homeless character through vignettes of grace and perseverance. They are works of documentary art as surely as *Dust Bowl Ballads*, but instead of calling for social justice they merely present a dying way of life.

Comparing Harry Partch and Woody Guthrie initially seems odd, even though the two men narrowly missed crossing paths, but that does not mean that Partch was unaware of Guthrie's work. Outside any connection that Partch's audiences may have drawn between his work and Guthrie's are the connections Partch made himself. The notion that Partch knew of Woody Guthrie's music and was thinking about it when he wrote works like *Barstow* and *U.S. Highball* is not illusory at all. In a letter to the Rockefeller Foundation on July 21, 1973, a year before he died, Partch revealed that Woody Guthrie and Leadbelly were sources of his Americana works. He even went so far as to note that singers wondering about vocal production when performing *Barstow* or *U.S. Highball* should listen to those two singers for accurate models.[63]

Beyond those quirks of fate that led the two men along parallel lines and the revealing suggestion that Partch's hobo works should be performed in Guthrie's style, the crucial difference between Partch's theoretical use of Anglo folk culture and Guthrie's utilitarian one highlights areas of divergence between the two categories of exoticism. Harry Partch's engagement with this "folk" was fundamentally different from Guthrie's, although many composers in New York and its environs in the early 1940s thought that it emerged from the same impulse. Partch's conceptually exotic approach used its sources as foundational to each work's basic structure rather than applying those sources as an overlay. Partch did not adopt the common exotic practice of infusing a European-modeled work with strange sounds from a different culture. His approach involved serious study and immersion in a musical culture to the point that its patterns, aesthetics, and styles merged with his own.[64]

The Documentary Imagination and Partch

Partch's engagement with homeless culture was even unique among documentarians. Interest in migrants was so intense and widespread that it prompted *America's Town Meeting of the Air*, a popular radio program, to ask in 1940, "What Should America do for the Joads?" From early in the Depression various New Deal agencies worked to relieve the migrant situation, but that situation received little attention until artists, acting under a documentary impulse toward the rawness of the American experience, focused America's gaze on the problem. The impact of these documentary products was so pervasive and powerful that they became iconic in American culture. As evidenced by its use in *America's Town Meeting of the Air*, the name "Joad" stood for any migrant in trouble. Similarly, through its reprinting in newspapers, books, and even Congressional reports, Lange's "Migrant Mother" symbolized Americans' concern for the downtrodden among them. Americans' fascination might not have been piqued had it not been for this series of publications in the late 1930s and early 1940s, which formed an image of the migrants in the public eye that retains its power and remains pervasive to this day.

Pictures from the Farm Security Administration's photographic unit, especially "Migrant Mother"; the stories concerned with the downtrodden, such as that of the Joad family; and period music, like Guthrie's *Dust Bowl Ballads*, combined to portray the migrant as the quintessential American. Migrants were understood as ideologically part of the "plainfolks Americanism" that was championed by intellectuals of the time and took root in the use of Anglo-American folk tunes in Depression-era art music. As Charles Alexander persuasively argued, "'The people,' denounced as yahoos, yokels and Ku Kluxers in the previous decade, took on heroic qualities in their poverty. And America, which had seemed so dull, commercialized and hopeless when prosperous, looked vital and exciting, just awakening to its national promise in the depths of depression."[65]

But this is a frankly Romantic view of migrants, one at odds with the common assumption of documentary as an objective art overcome by a predilection toward harsh truth. For this reason, Depression-era documentary art is most in line with Partch's approach to his hobo and migrant subjects. During the Depression, Americans reacted viscerally to the migrant images presented to them, clamoring for a solution to the harsh migrant situation and sending in money to support migrant families. Through Lange's photographs and Steinbeck's words, Americans identified with migrants, cried over their situation, but, strangely, remained distant from the situation's reality. They paradoxically and sentimentally viewed migrants as "the folk," the foundational basis of American culture, yet perversely cast them as an intriguing Other. This exoticized duality persists into the present through the images that remain. When dealing with modern economic calamities in the United States, it is no longer simply the stories of the Dust Bowl and the Great Depression that are used metaphorically to link past tragedy to modern predicaments, but the images given to us by Steinbeck and Lange. These images' power is enhanced by application of the period's music—music that drew differently from the same ideological well. Partch's music fits the aims of this documentary impulse better than Roy Harris's symphonies, Aaron Copland's ballets, or Douglas Moore's operas, certainly utilizing a sense of the Other, but foundationally embracing it.

Although their documentary nature cloaked migrant images in objective truth, the words and images produced were little more than fertile ground for artists to plunder in search of social commentary. Documentarians knew what message they wanted to convey and used migrants, transients, and hoboes to deliver it. Therefore, when artists presented migrant images back to the public, their form, shape, and even meaning were already determined. The ideal of objectivity was a readily accepted, elaborate fakery best seen in the case of Woody Guthrie. Championed as the voice of Dust Bowl migrants because of his dress, speech, and birthplace, Guthrie was understood to be an honest-to-goodness migrant, a poor farmer who had emigrated to California to find work in the fields. He was presented as someone who wrote and sang songs that migrants performed, and that cultivated presentation impacted Guthrie's performances and compositions. Yet Guthrie grew up middle class and moved to

California to find fame in the entertainment business: when various collectors travelled among California's migrant camps, collecting songs and stories, they did not find or record a single lyric that Guthrie had penned. Like Lange and Steinbeck, Guthrie was shocked and appalled at migrant conditions, especially since migrants were his friends and neighbors, and wanted to dramatize their plight to stir social action. But he was also interested in subjectively using his migratory experiences to further his own ambition. Because of his appearance, the seeming authenticity with which he spoke, and the desire among many in New York for an Okie troubadour, he was cast in a mold. It was a mold that allowed him to achieve his first celebrity, but it was also one that he quickly abandoned when he left New York.

This same desire for documentary exoticization that simultaneously buoyed and trapped Woody Guthrie was at work in Harry Partch's reception. When Partch began promoting the works based on this period, musicians and intellectuals were still caught up in the attempt to redefine European music as American music through the decorative use of an exotic Other. He was fresh from a protracted period among hoboes and Dust Bowl migrants and his music, like Guthrie's, dealt with that folk. Yet, in many ways, Partch was able to bridge a gap for musicians through the persona he adopted. The texts Partch used in his compositions were collected sayings and inscriptions, not his own words. Also, although he occasionally used folk or hymn tunes and always based the vocal line on human inflections, his music was firmly rooted in the origins of Western musical heritage. In fact, by basing his tuning system on ancient Greek musical ideals, he was exoticizing the culture commonly understood as the foundation of democracy, as well as tapping into the craze for migrant images. He brought "the folk" to a segment of society interested in them in an abstract way, in a manner and form they could understand and appreciate.

CHAPTER THREE

BITTER MUSIC

Dorothea Lange's reputation as the most astute photographic chronicler of the Great Depression provides ample reason to examine two of her photographs of hoboes and transients, both as prelude and accompaniment to Harry Partch's musical journal *Bitter Music*. In many ways, these three works of art achieve a certain synergy. Partch's words reveal the minds of the men Lange's camera captured, sharing their passions, their failures, their sense of humor, their sense of themselves and of the world around them, and all the quixotic depths of their characters. His music floats their words through time to conjure them afresh for us. Lange's photographs bring concrete reality to Partch's words. Here, in black and white, are the men of whom Partch wrote. The slope of their shoulders, the tilt of their heads, the condition of their clothes—all say something about their lives. And, beyond anything Lange's work unveils about *Bitter Music*, by delving into her choice of images for the FSA, the Depression-era perception of homeless wanderers becomes abundantly clear.

The first photograph, Lange's "Toward Los Angeles, California. 1937" (fig. 3.1), has two prominent features. The first to catch the viewer's eye is the human component: two men walking a dusty, deserted road. Their backs face the viewer and their heads are bowed. One carries a bindle on his back and the other a small, hard-shelled suitcase at his side. Both men wear hats, hands dangle wearily at their sides, and shoulders ride forward, toward their chest and away from the viewer, making them appear smaller than they actually are. Their entire posture exudes exhaustion and they seem to be so tired that they cannot even keep up with their shadows, which stretch in front of them across the landscape on

Figure 3.1. Dorothea Lange, "Toward Los Angeles, California. 1937." Library of Congress, Prints and Photographs Division, FSA/OWI Collection, LC-DIG-fsa-8b31801 DLC.

their left. These two dark figures contrast with a large white billboard, an advertisement for Southern Pacific Railroads. Painted in tall capital letters is the slogan "NEXT TIME TRY THE TRAIN," followed by one word, in italics: "*RELAX.*" As if to underscore the message, a large picture of a Norman Rockwell-esque gentlemen kicking back in a reclining train seat fills the billboard. He epitomizes contentment and rest, an ironic juxtaposition to the two men who slowly trudge past.

At first glance, the none-too-subtle commentary elicits a slight grin, but reflection coaxes underlying meanings to the surface. Although the photograph does not label them as such, in dress and stance we might think that these men are hoboes. They carry their worldly possessions, are practically dressed, and meander without speed. But these men are not the hoboes who fearlessly conquered the machines that made the West. As the billboard suggests, they can no longer ride the railroad: hoboes have been evicted from that domain. No, these men are transients, wandering from town to town instead of moving where they wanted when they wanted. They are down-on-their-luck homeless, who have been forgotten by a society that speeds past them in relative comfort.

The second photograph (fig. 3.2) has a lengthy descriptive title: "Hobo wakes up early in the morning from his bed alongside a corral. Imperial Valley, California." It portrays a man who has slept on the ground, next to a wooden plank fence and a sizable bale of hay. The title "hobo" seems completely at odds with this man's appearance. His rumpled and disheveled hair and clothes imply he has recently awoken, but the shadows are not long enough for the picture truly to be early in the morning. Instead, this "hobo" seems to be pulling himself off the ground mid-morning, having missed the daily wageworkers' early morning opportunity for a full day's work. This man epitomizes the transient who arrives in California but then cannot or does not work. This is the kind of man whom Californians feared. This is a man to pity for his station in life, not one to celebrate for his freedom, his bravery in flouting the law, and his cunning. This is a new kind of homeless man altogether.

During the Great Depression, migrants and their stories fascinated Americans. Images such as these two by Dorothea Lange were imbibed with morning coffee and provided fodder for a day's discussion. They also aroused curiosity about the men and women living those lives. Words and images were not enough: Americans also wanted to hear migrant voices. The overwhelming success of *The Grapes of Wrath* both as book and, a year after its publication, as film, along with the New Deal emphasis on the common man's plight, heightened interest among Americans in folk music and its collection.[1]

Spurred in part by *The Grapes of Wrath* and certainly informed by the increasing interest in migrants across the nation, in 1940 the Library of Congress commissioned folklorists Charles Todd and Robert Sonkin to visit California's FSA camps and collect songs.[2] Sonkin and Todd recorded over two hundred songs, and, soon after their first trip, reported their findings in the *New York Times*. They reported discovering only three song types: traditional English ballads, songs of the American Southwest (cowboy songs), and newly-composed songs in ballad style about the migration.

Figure 3.2. Dorothea Lange, photograph "Hobo wakes up early in the morning from his bed alongside a corral. Imperial Valley, California, 1939." Library of Congress, Prints and Photographs Division, FSA/OWI Collection, LC-USF34-019233-C DLC.

Because Todd and Sonkin rarely mentioned the popular tunes the migrants sang, the ideal of a glorified past living in the present resonated throughout their article. Although many of the songs they recorded were common or popular tunes with new lyrics about the current situation, Todd and Sonkin only discussed English ballads. They even went so far as to write, "Strolling in the evening through one of the big Farm Security Administration's camps, past long rows of tents and metal 'units' one hears fragments of tunes that a more prosperous America has forgotten in the process of growing up and getting rich."[3] This blatantly romantic and exoticized statement strangely was not informed by the documentary imagination. Although folklorists, Todd and Sonkin were caught in the trap of only attributing ballads to the American folk. They were so ensconced in this view that they went into the camps with an ear for the celebrated and much-used folk culture of the Appalachian Mountains and could not reconcile what they discovered with their expectations.[4]

Bitter Music: **Structure**

Unfortunately, Todd and Sonkin never published a collection of the songs they found, so most composers, even if they knew of the material, found it difficult to access. But theirs was not the only collection of transient and migrant voices from Depression-era California. Harry Partch recorded the men he heard singing and speaking around him as he toured California's work camps in 1935. The result of Partch's record-keeping was the remarkable journal *Bitter Music*. It combined the documentary expressions of Dorothea Lange and Paul Taylor's *An American Exodus* through its images and words yet gave them life in a manner similar to Todd and Sonkin's collection of songs. And because of its time and the people it chronicles, it cannot help but rest within the framework of the charged conceptions of transients and migrants.

At first glance, it appears as though the journal is ordered much like any diary, with regular entries marking the date, beginning on June 11 and ending the following February 1, when Partch received his first job after his return from Europe. However Partch transcended conventional diary construction in even the simplest of ways: the arrangement of entries. On June 24, his thirty-fourth birthday, he began shuffling simple chronology by inserting an extended flashback detailing his efforts and experiences from the previous year. On October 22, he compressed time by constructing a collage of the thirty-five days that had just passed, ordering events and juxtaposing them to provide the most trenchant commentary possible on his experiences. The collective impact of these flashbacks lends his work a certain timelessness: even though the days pass, events do not seem rooted only in the journal's timeframe.

Partch did not stop at simple chronology in breaking the boundaries of the documentary book. In *Bitter Music*, he attempted not only to let his audience read about his trials and the people he encountered, but also to see and hear them as well. He framed each daily entry with an elaborate drawing incorporating the first letter of the month's name into a picture of an event or person that figures in that day (see fig. 3.3). Partch drew at least one portrait of most characters mentioned by name in the journal. He also sketched the landscapes that surrounded the camps in which he worked, rendering pictures of towering trees, desolate mountain passes, and waves crashing against high cliff faces. Nature and humanity enthralled Partch; *Bitter Music* proved a gateway to experience the essence of those creations and capture them in an illustrative form to which he would rarely return.

Figure 3.3. Partch's opening drawing ("Trees") for his August 28, 1935, entry in his journal *Bitter Music*; the confluence of two trees becomes the "A" in August. Courtesy of the Harry Partch Estate Archive, San Diego.

In *Bitter Music* Partch depicted transients in the camps musically as well as visually. "I heard music in the voices all about me," he later wrote, "and tried to notate it, and I tried to enhance the mood and drama of such little things as a quarrel in a potato patch."[5] *Bitter Music* is a work meant to be read at a piano.[6] Throughout the entries are bits of speech that have been placed over musical notes to provide a guide to the inflection with which the line was originally delivered. From lines as small as "you are" (February 1, 1936) to long, full speeches on salvation through Jesus (November 15, 1935), Partch preserved the patois of the people he encountered. He set these bits of musicalized speech in various ways, using the piano's full capabilities: their melodies appear unaccompanied, doubled at the octave, with other lines moving in parallel or contrary motion, supported by pedal points, and even harmonized.

Through these notations, the journal becomes a dialogue between Partch and the reader in which the reader is to sit at a piano and play and sing these musicalized bits of speech as they appear. Partch wanted these voices from the past to float from page to ear. He had long been intrigued by the musical nature of human speech, and his initial forays into microtonality attempted to capture it more accurately. He set early compositions, such as the Twenty-third Psalm and the "Potion Scene" from *Romeo and Juliet*, according to the notated recitation of a cantor and actor respectively. By continuing this practice with *Bitter Music*, he was beginning to capture the nuances of transient, migrant, and hobo speech, nuances that would figure prominently in his compositions over the following ten years.[7]

In a 1940 preface to the work, Partch stated that *Bitter Music* was an honest portrayal of his time in the camps and that "only such changes have been made as would clarify, not destroy, the spontaneity of the instant."[8] His reason for insisting on his veracity lay in the transcriptions of speech. In the hobo jungles and transient camps he claimed there was "a fountainhead of pure musical Americana."[9] This Americana lay not only in the way this lowest social order spoke but also in the songs they sang, and he wanted his readers to know that they were hearing those voices as directly as possible. This reasoning explains why he included compositions separate from these instances of musical speech. From the first entry on June 11, songs Partch wrote appear along with hymns, popular songs, and folk songs. In many cases, the words to these songs were altered, by Partch or the men who sang them, to fit a given situation. These songs certainly provided added depth to the depiction of the singers' world, but they can be—and have been—too easily dismissed as mere decoration. These songs and musical speech constructed a framework as surely as the dates and recurring visual motifs, and promote an understanding of the work's themes beyond those of the written text.

Bitter Music: Themes

Within these myriad artistic endeavors, the themes that *Bitter Music* encapsulates are as various as the ways to approach the work. Whether one is reading, viewing, or listening to the journal, certain ideas vie for attention. The most obvious of these is the project's historical and documentary nature. *Bitter Music* is lived experience, a first-hand account of life in federal transient camps. The journal is a compelling, honest, and accurate depiction, from an insider's perspective, of how men in the camps viewed the work they were asked to do, their interactions, and their situation. It is a brutally open and personal work, and although others from that era detail the despair and humiliation of transient life, most notably Tom Kromer's autobiography *Waiting for Nothing*, none goes into lives lived under the New Deal's shadow like *Bitter Music*.[10]

The people among whom Partch lived in the camps were very different from those who had "tramped" America between 1870 and 1920. Returning to his study of homeless men in 1940, almost twenty years after he pioneered the field, Nels Anderson noticed a change in the men's attitudes. He found a distinct difference between old-style hoboes, who worked and traveled in the century's first twenty years, and modern transients and migrants, groups he did not consider to be hoboes. Pride in their situation, defiance in the face of opposition, and resolution in their decision to adopt the lifestyle marked old-style hoboes.

By the mid- to late 1930s, transients and migrants were by-and-large frustrated by their predicament. They were ashamed to beg, ashamed of unemployment. They adopted the lifestyle out of necessity, not choice.[11] What is most remarkable about the Californian reaction to transients is that it was completely the opposite of the view that transients had of their own station and situation. Far from believing that the government owed them anything or enjoying the homeless life of handouts and flophouses, the transients' overriding emotion was shame. They were ashamed to ask for help, ashamed that they could not support themselves or their families. Louis Banks, who felt forced to leave his family and relieve them of the burden of his care, related, "The shame I was feeling. I walked out because I didn't have a job. . . . And God help me, I couldn't get anything."[12]

Much of that same feeling of shame pervades *Bitter Music*. Partch peppers his commentary with statements such as: "It has been three years since I did this sort of thing [begging], and I never did it more than three times before. Starting again, the pain of humiliation is just as intense as it was the very first time."[13] Unlike in most first-hand accounts, such instances are countered by the joy Partch found in freedom and the excitement of hearing his theories on human speech being music played out before him daily. This mix of emotions is precisely what makes the journal so compelling and worthwhile. Many extant documents and diaries of the period read like a grocery list:

> *June, 1934.* Worked as a circus hand with Al G. Barnes Circus for 4 weeks at $4.60 a week and board, Seattle to Wallace, Idaho.
>
> *July, 1934.* Tree shaker at 25 cents an hour, averaged $2 a day for 25 days near Fresno.
>
> *August-October, 1934.* Picked oranges and lemons at 25 cents an hour, working an average of 6 hours a day, for 60 days, near Fresno.
>
> *December, 1934.* Houseman in hotel, Fresno. Received 50 cents a day and board for 1 month, and 25 cents a day and board for 2 months.[14]

Instead of providing the mindless monotony of many transient accounts, where the days are simply laid out in "I did this and then this," fashion, Partch provided impressions and psychological depth through his musicalized voices, in effect humanizing a group of people who at the time were consistently treated as sub-human. In effect, he was aligning not with documentary's touted objectivity, but instead with its ready tendency toward advocacy on behalf of the dispossessed.

Partch's insights into and explanations of the Federal Transient Bureau's inner workings mark *Bitter Music* as an important historical document. The journal, as lived experience, has the same kind of gossipy attraction that many autobiographical works exude. Certainly the sketches and music that it contains provide a unique dimension and deserve attention, but other factors also undergird the text. Partch developed and intertwined several themes within the text itself, themes that layer the historical experience and help account for some of the fascination the journal still generates.

Three pervading themes colored Partch's experiences and run throughout *Bitter Music*. The first is the physical and psychological impact of his sojourn in transient camps.[15] At the journal's beginning,

Partch has just returned from a period of recognition and acceptance in Europe, where a Carnegie grant had allowed him to study and where W. B. Yeats (amongst others) had been encouraging and understanding. These reactions were new for the composer. When he returned to the United States, he experienced rejection once again, and the journal is full of the despair and utter aloneness of transient life. On July 13, he wrote, "Nothing to hear but functions. Nothing to read but purchased words. Nothing to do but attend this painless existence gazing in vacuity."[16] Behind the monotony of his existence, and in many ways making that monotony even less bearable, lay the knowledge that he had no real connections. No one worried about his condition: "It is always move, move, move—where? Nobody knows nor cares."[17]

The curious aloofness with which Partch carried himself exacerbated his solitude. Although he made connections with a few, whom he mostly mentioned by name, Partch wrote about transients as though isolated from them, detached from their situation. "I am sure that in time I would develop an affection for them, something like Pablo's," he wrote on June 26. "They do not understand me, and I seem to ignore them, but I am not ostracized for it."[18] Most of *Bitter Music* has this detached tone of an observer not participating in the events, although Partch endured the same repudiation and filth as the men of whom he wrote. Ironically, he noted the lack of intellectual and emotional intimacy among the men, even while distancing himself from them. Partch believed that they could not connect intellectually because of the widespread ignorance he found among them. As a result, he categorized most of the men as hopeless and irredeemable.[19] Yet for all his aloofness, Partch genuinely cared about the way society treated these men, as well as himself. Beginning with his encounter with Kain-tuck and continuing through his later dealings with a convict known as "The Hoodlum," he was eager to show that just as American society had caused the transient's situation, so musical society had created his. Partch knew from experience what FERA tried to advocate—that the transient's plight was less a result of genetic predisposition than of the nation's hard times.

Partch's indictment of the musical establishment formed *Bitter Music*'s second theme. He recognized a pervading lack of respect for and appreciation of American music, especially music of the common people. In many instances in the journal, Partch recounted his discussions with educated people, from London workers to the director of the Carnegie Corporation. Time and time again he heard that America was not a musical nation: "Germany and Italy are the musical countries," Partch was told, "whereas England and America are not musical." Understanding the bias, he contradicted that assumption with the argument "I think you are only familiar with the least interesting stratum of American life. I know the music of American hoboes."[20]

Partch believed that any physical exploitation of California through mining or overfarming was nothing compared to the destruction brought upon music by wealthy Californians patronizing it without bothering to learn anything about it. Furthermore, the music with which they were familiar was not even relevant, according to Partch. They might know Beethoven, but he knew the speech music of Americans. "Hallelujah, I'm a Bum," Partch proclaimed, quoting the old hobo hymn from the Industrial Workers of the World (IWW) Little Red Songbook, as he had found a life-giving strain of music among wandering Americans. He knew that migrants, transients, and hoboes sang constantly, even if educated Americans did not. Following the documentary impulse that pervaded artistic expression, he intended to record the songs they crafted and the popular songs and hymns they sang. In a sense, all his Americana works, from *Bitter Music* to *U.S. Highball*, were attempts to refute the myth of America's lack of musicality and "give myself, and others, a good basis for a new and great music of the people."[21]

This theme reveals one of the primary motivations behind Partch's writing of *Bitter Music*. He had been working on his theoretical treatise for years, but each time he showed it to someone, the response was akin to that of the Carnegie Corporation after he submitted a six-month report of his time in Europe under its auspices: no one understood it. In this narrative musical journal, he was able to offer a nontechnical explanation and demonstrate theories of music arising from speech in a way that more people could grasp. Furthermore, he could spark more attention to his work by showing that his musical ideas flowed from the speech of the people, from "the folk." By tapping into the fad of intellectuals turning to the folk for inspiration, Partch generated an acceptable basis for his ideas. In this light, the purpose of the extended flashback to his work in Europe that dominates his June 24 birthday entry becomes clear. Partch not only provided an American basis for his work, but also used W. B. Yeats's endorsement to offer evidence of intellectual and artistic precedent. Combining an intellectual foundation with this narrative of despair, Partch showed that his art had been born out of suffering, and was worthy of further investigation. While some have been tempted to view *Bitter Music* as a departure for Partch, it was actually firmly in line with his ideals. Even in this work, so different from his other projects, he refused to compromise his principles.

The final textual theme plays directly into the music in a way that even Partch's constant refutation of the musical establishment does not. Laced throughout *Bitter Music*, from the first page to the last entry, are religious songs and Christian imagery. This theme is a striking innovation for Partch, considering his religious background. Although Partch followed his father in religious apostasy, he retained vestiges of his mother's continued faith. Her convictions accompanied him on his descent into the transient world, and throughout the journal, he strove to understand, as did many other transients, whether some sins of his had caused his situation. Indeed, until 1940 he called the journal *Cause All Our Sins Are Taken Away*.[22]

Christian images primarily appear in connection with the old hymn "Hand Me Down My Walking Cane." The hymn's strophic, sixteen-bar melody became the journal's *idée fixe*. Although it often appears with altered words, mode, or accompaniment, according to its place in the narrative, the "Hand Me Down" lynchpin holds the work together. It appears more often than any other musical figure, surfacing at every point where Partch changes his situation or mindset.[23] "Hand Me Down" also became the vehicle through which Partch confronted his own demons concerning his predicament. The hymn's initial appearance implied that Partch's sins were taken away by the act of leaving polite society and joining the transients. But, by July 22, he wondered if he would be out of jail and free from sin if he had only listened to what his mama had said—that he should follow Christian doctrine.[24] His sins, in effect, had caused his situation, and he was being punished for them. By early August, Partch had begun to think differently, and in September concluded that he was being punished for nothing more than trying to "broaden and beautify" the petty respectable life by introducing decidedly non-Western musical elements.[25] This realization immediately precedes one of *Bitter Music*'s most outstanding scenes. Partch was picked up alongside the road by a Filipino who, in an eight-page musical setting, laid out his salvation through Jesus. Partch juxtaposed this passage with insertions of "Rock of Ages," the hymn his mother had sung, beneath which flowed his own stream of consciousness. His soft response to the Filipino, "May God bless you," demonstrated that he was no longer lashing out against his circumstances but instead beginning to accept his lot in life. By the last extended musical setting—a grand quodlibet of popular songs, hymns, musical speech, and even a setting of Everett Ruess's poem "Wilderness Song"—Partch had come to terms with his supposed sin and reimagined the religious imagery. In the entire sixteen-page setting, only one line of text was not set to music: "Have you confessed your sins to Jesus?" On the heels of this line followed a torrent of music that included "Rock of Ages" transformed into a cascade of chromatic runs. Partch ended the outburst and the quodlibet with a pianissimo setting of "Since I may wander anywhere I will draw there what I will."[26] With this Benediction, Partch was effectively saying, "I no longer need to confess my sins as I have found what I need for my future artistic life, wandering here among the people." He was ready to leave the past completely, an action to which he had committed five years earlier, and to stay true to a new course. Freed of its original connotations, "Hand Me Down" was then available for one last use, this time in a completely secular setting. Partch connected it with "There Is a Tavern in the Town," as he said adieu to the transient life, literally offering his completed journey to God, in a suitably ironic ending.

Bitter Music: Musical Patterns

These complex psychological and religious themes join *Bitter Music*'s historical and biographical value. In preserving transient speech in music, Partch crafted a new kind of documentary form that has never been replicated. He demonstrated his assertion that the rise and fall of everyday speech is music, and that notation can accurately be used to represent it.

As an apologist for his speech music theories, *Bitter Music* is a resounding success. But the journal's most striking feature remains the music Partch used to depict his characters. Rather than produce new music, Partch relied on the musical quotations that litter the manuscript. Since he was attempting to depict the transients Monophonically, through the inflection of their own words, it is strange that he also relied on preexisting melodies: these arcane fragments of songs, many identified by Partch in his 1940 preface, are surely nothing more than musical allusions, a trick to add depth to his characters. It would seem that he used these songs because he actually heard them while living in the transient camps. But while Partch may have included songs he heard on the road, he was obviously selective in his choices. Upon close examination, it is clear that these songs are more musically connected than they seem at first glance. Since *Bitter Music* is neither a purely musical composition nor a purely textual one, Partch seems to have latched on to these songs as a way to unify this new form he was creating. In many ways the songs form a structural web as tight as the chronological-textual one of daily diary entries.

Bitter Music contains the following songs (listed in order of their appearance): "Hand Me Down My Walking Cane," "I Left My Gal in the Mountains," "Standin' in the Need of Prayer," "Miss Jenny Lee," "While My

Heart Keeps Beating Time" (Partch's original hobo song, which was published with different words; see chapter 4), "Red River Valley," "Rock of Ages," "1492" (also known as "Columbo"), "Oh! Susannah!," and "There Is a Tavern in the Town." It also contains two classical references—Chopin's F-sharp Major Nocturne, op. 15 no. 2, and the *Marcia funebre* from Beethoven's "Eroica" Symphony—and two settings of poetry that were never published outside of the journal: the aforementioned "Wilderness Song" by Everett Ruess and several verses from Song of Solomon[27] (see table 3.1).

A few of these musical selections are nothing more than ways to express a certain person's character and were probably songs Partch heard them sing. For instance, Kain-tuck sings two lines of Gene Autry's "I Left My Gal in the Mountains," Cisco belts out "Standin' in the Need of Prayer," and the Hoodlum sings the end of "May I Sleep in Your Barn Tonight, Mister," a hobo song based on "Red River Valley." But Partch prescribed no singer for the rest of the songs, leaving them attributable to either himself or the reader.

All of these songs are closely related. The musical materials connecting them are so similar that it is often difficult to gauge which song has entered when each first appears. As "Hand Me Down" is the musical *idée fixe* and the only song (other than "Rock of Ages") that is repeated, "Red River Valley," "Rock of Ages," "Standin' in the Need of Prayer," and "There Is a Tavern in the Town" can all be understood as being musically related to it. Most of these songs begin like "Hand Me Down," with an anacrusis that jumps from the dominant to tonic. This rising jump, usually syncopated whether or not it was in the original song, is one of the most characteristic musical features of *Bitter Music*. The songs are also related harmonically: most appear in the closely-related keys of C and G major. Regardless of key, their melodic lines center on the pitches C, G, and B—a very small pitch class. Finally, the phrases Partch quoted from each of these songs describe the same melodic shape. All begin with an initial ascending motion, rapidly reach their peak, and descend back almost to the starting pitch. This perfect arch shape is also found in many of the musical settings of speech.

When these features were not already present in his chosen song, Partch often altered it to fit into his musical scheme. The opening phrase of "Rock of Ages" does not match the above criteria, but when the first phrase is removed and the hymn begins on the second phrase, it fits the melodic shape almost perfectly. It becomes practically interchangeable with "Hand Me Down." "There Is a Tavern" likewise opens differently than the hymn, but its chorus is strikingly similar to the second half of "Hand Me Down." Both sit on c'' and $b\flat''$ and slowly work their way down to the

Table 3.1. Songs and musical citations in *Bitter Music*, along with page numbers indicating where they appear in Partch, *Bitter Music: Collected Journals, Essays, Introductions, and Librettos*, ed. Thomas Nelson McGeary (Urbana, IL: University of Illinois Press, 1991).

Title	Composer	Page reference
Works by other composers		
"Hand Me Down My Walking Cane"	James A. Bland	8, 43, 48, 73, 87, 130–31
"I Left My Gal in the Mountains"	C. J. Robinson	41
"Standin' in the Need of Prayer"	Harry Thacker Burleigh	69
"Miss Jenny Lee"	Anonymous	71
"Red River Valley"	Anonymous	90
Nocturne op. 15 no. 2 in F sharp major	Frédéric Chopin	96
"Rock of Ages"	Augustus M. Toplady (text) Thomas Hastings (music)	104–8, 126 (melody only)
"1492" ("Columbo")	Anonymous	121
"Oh! Susannah!"	Stephen Foster	124
Symphony No. 3 in E flat major, Op. 55 ("Eroica"), *Marcia funebre*	Ludwig van Beethoven	115
"There Is a Tavern in the Town"	Anonymous	131
Existing songs by Partch		
Song of Solomon	King James Version of the Bible	52–57
"While My Heart Keeps Beating Time"	Harry Partch	78–80
Text newly set by Partch		
"Wilderness Song"	Everett Ruess	117–18

tonic G major, allowing Partch to merge them successfully for the February 1 entry. He also supported the melodic line with a G minor ostinato, leading Richard Kassel to hypothesize that Partch was attempting musically to depict the unsteadiness of barroom singers.[28]

The sheer number of harmonic, melodic, and rhythmic similarities strongly suggests that Partch intentionally arranged these songs to provide a musical framework for *Bitter Music*. This idea is also borne out in the manner in which he notated the songs. Partch obviously lacked access to a piano in the federal camps when he was writing the journal. He must have simply noted in the journal which songs he might wish to add. The music was then almost completely notated in January 1936, when he stayed with friends in Glendale, La Crescenta, and Covina, California.[29] He was not finished with the journal at that time, but there is only one entry after December of 1935—that of February 1, when he received his job and departed from the transient life for a time. During that month he must have examined his options and chose the songs he could connect musically, placing them according to a preconceived scheme. Their use was a rational and artistic decision.

Beyond providing a musical structure to *Bitter Music*, the songs also presaged what would become a common technique in Partch's work. In his two extended dramatic scenes, the encounter with the Filipino and the concluding quodlibet, Partch superimposes and juxtaposes seemingly-unrelated thoughts. Songs abruptly shift from one to the other with little to no transitional material, exploring contrasting moods. Their arrangement appears to be random, a grand collage that is more descriptive than musical, but in fact is carefully planned. This "collage" technique, first attempted in these two passages, became Partch's preferred structural device in works as diverse as *Barstow, Revelation in the Courthouse Park, Delusion of the Fury*, and even in some passages of *U.S. Highball*.[30]

Unlike many transients, who sought their bodily salvation through the camps, Partch's salvation did not come from the food or work in the shelters, nor did it come from the people with whom he interacted. Instead, he found salvation through artistic creation. Partch's ability to keep a journal in which he could continue, and find validation for, his experiments with the music of human speech was a remarkable achievement. In what many would regard as the most dire of circumstances, he was able to fulfill his creative impulses and build a foundation for fifteen more years of work. Many artists could only continue producing through the WPA's assistance:[31] without such support, their creative life stagnated. E. Y. Harburg, like Partch an artist who found inspiration in his situation, noted that "someone who lost money found that his life was gone. When I lost my possessions, I found my creativity."[32] So did Partch, at least at first, and he produced a remarkably creative account of his eight-month sojourn. Unfortunately, the tide and tenor of the land were beginning to shift as Partch emerged from the federal camps in early 1936. Even the modicum of goodwill that the California government had shown toward transients through the California State Unemployment Commission disappeared with the arrival of the Dust Bowl refugee, a figure that ultimately brought fascination and fear and created the tense atmosphere in which Partch first began to promote himself and his journal, still titled *Cause All Our Sins Are Taken Away*. In the Southwest corner of the nation, there was fear and misunderstanding about the transients and migrants who flooded the landscape, even while throughout the rest of the country "the folk" were the intellectual trend of the day. In the midst of this cacophony of ideas and interests, and through a variety of jobs and coincidences, Partch came close to getting his journal published, riding this surging tide of interest from both views of migrants. But in the end, it would not be enough. When they viewed those displaced by the Depression both sides saw not the men Partch knew and documented, but a constructed reality. This circumstance ultimately worked against Partch. As he encountered resistance and the common views of migrants in the Southwest, Partch began to recount his experiences of 1935 and 1936 through a new lens. In a few short years, he would feel quite differently about his ordeals and they would turn bitter in his mouth—so bitter that he would want to forget them entirely.

Put to Work in the WPA

Bitter Music ends on February 1, 1936, with Partch in San Bernardino having a conversation with an unidentified man. From their conversation, the man divines that Partch truly is "a practical newspaper proofreader" and offers him a job starting within the next week. Partch sang "adieu" to his wandering existence, and its eight-month journal, to the melody of a barroom piano. With this farewell, he hoped to end his transience.[33] That proofreading job was his first steady employment in almost five years, but with the end of his journaling, all trace of his movements and activities disappears for seven months, by which time he was in Arizona.

During these months, Partch was extremely active in completing his musical journal. In January 1936, he had stayed with friends in Glendale, La Crescenta, and Covina, California, who provided him rest from the road, time to reflect upon and polish entries, and pianos on which to notate the hastily drawn sketches that had been the extent of his recorded vocal inflections, as well as to compose full accompaniments to several tunes.[34] By the time he left the camps and shelters for good the following month, Partch was ready to send the manuscript out to publishers. He mailed copies that summer to Viking Press and Covici Friede, but both politely refused the work.[35]

Partch most likely went to Arizona at this point at his brother Paul's invitation, dejected from the lack of progress in finding support after emerging from his self-imposed pilgrimage. Once there, he attempted to get another proofreading job. But as happened so often during his *Bitter Music* days, residency became an issue, and he was unable to secure employment. Fortunately, luck intervened for the first time in a long while, and he was referred to Ross Santee, Arizona director of the Federal Writers' Project (FWP).[36] The arts projects, branches of the WPA, were established in 1935 in an attempt to put artists to work through a three-pronged approach consisting of the Federal Writers' Project, the Federal Music Project, and the Federal Theatre Project. Although the WPA was as controversial as FERA from its inception, the arts programs were particular hotbeds of controversy. Congress was unsure whether or not the government should be funding art without having a say in what was created. This burgeoning censorship debate added to the one already raging within the administration as to what type of art to fund: classical versus modern, cultivated versus vernacular, and traditional versus avant-garde.

In spite of these hesitations, Harry Hopkins, who headed the WPA after FERA was dismantled, felt that the arts projects might provide the most benefit by giving hope and establishing "a new base of American life." President Roosevelt agreed, wanting artists to be "inherently rediscovering and defining American culture." The Federal Writers' Project was the most pro-active project in this pursuit. While the Theatre and Music Projects sought American playwrights, directors, actors, composers, and musicians to create new works on a multitude of themes, the Writers' Project set out to document and define America.[37] One of its first undertakings was a series of American Guidebooks, one for each of the forty-eight states. The project hired authors to visit every corner of each state and construct essays describing the noteworthy and unusual sights, paths, and even festivals that made the state unique. Ross Santee was in charge of finding and organizing authors for the Arizona guidebook. When Partch wrote to Santee in August 1936, he averred that music was the focus of his artistic aims, but he also sent *Cause All Our Sins Are Taken Away* for Santee to read, as well as offering his resumé of reading "proof in various offices—*Los Angeles Times*, Sacramento State Printing Office, *Spokane Spokesman-Reviews*, *New Orleans Times-Picayune*."[38] Impressed, Santee forwarded the manuscript to George W. Cronyn, national associate director of the FWP. After finding a way around the residency requirement, Santee hired Partch in September to edit and rewrite sections of the Arizona guidebook for eighty-five dollars a month.[39] Partch was obviously grateful for the job and felt satisfaction in what he was accomplishing. He wrote to Henry Allen Moe, executive secretary of the Guggenheim Foundation and an early supporter, in December that "to be doing work for somebody which pleases him and for which there is immediate recognition is a beautiful and a long lost experience."[40]

While he may have enjoyed working for the Writers' Project, Partch was surely still as frustrated about not finding musical support as he had been in California's transient camps. However, Harry Partch was not the only out-of-work musician in the 1930s. Due to the recent addition of sound to motion pictures, "canned music" in restaurants, and the closing of bars under Prohibition laws, together with the dismal economic climate, in 1933 the American Federation of Musicians estimated that in New York City, 12,000 of its 15,000 members were unemployed. Across the country, two-thirds of musicians lacked work. By 1934, with opera companies and orchestras folding around the nation, 70 percent were out of work and the remaining 30 percent made less than a living wage.[41] Statistics like these, which did not improve until the onset of World War II, encouraged the creation of the Federal Music Project (FMP) as a branch of the Federal Arts Projects.

For all its good intentions, after its establishment, the FMP encountered many problems. The greatest of these, and the primary reasons composers like Partch were never employed by it, were its aims and its director. Nikolai Sokoloff, the Russian-born head of the FMP, was biased against American composers, often remarking that "the American composer or artist will get no place playing stupid things."[42] The project itself was biased against vernacular musics and composers, leaning instead toward supporting performers. This is not to say that American composers were never performed. On the contrary, statistics in the FMP's final reports indicate that the New Deal era was one of the greatest for American composers. During the years in which the FMP operated, over 14,000 American composers heard their compositions performed by an FMP-sponsored organization.[43] But these statistics are misleading, for composers rarely received substantial aid and never commissions to compose. They had to complete a work, then submit it to the audition board. If the board accepted it, the composer would receive a small stipend for each performance, which in most cases was only one.[44] Composing without assurance of performance or even payment is a hard road, even in prosperous times. It is a testament to American composers' resiliency that so many pursued their artistic endeavours.

Partch continued his musical pursuits as well, albeit in a fashion typically all his own. Although he found it strange and it did disgruntle him that he was supported by the FWP instead of the FMP, he was grateful for the aid. After the end of FERA and the Transient program, he knew, "My only light came from the hope of the WPA. Now here were the poor WPA musicians. Surely they would accept me? Hell no! In those six years the only two brief jobs that took me out of the tomato and apricot fields and their 10 to 15 cents an hour on a straight hourly basis were with the WPA writers! Among writers one expects imagination and humanity. Why not among musicians?"[45]

Bitter Music after the Depression

Partch apparently found working for Ross Santee difficult, but the contacts he made for his journal's manuscript were encouraging. George Cronyn greatly admired *Cause All Our Sins Are Taken Away* and sent it on to Story Press to see if it could be published. Story was positive about the manuscript but refused it, quite possibly for the language or rough subject matter that "no run of the mill editor wants to read."[46] Partch had further contacts for publication which he could have pursued, but instead, in December 1936, he sent the manuscript to Henry Allen Moe in lieu of an agent: He had always admired Moe and continued throughout his life to ask Moe's professional and personal advice.[47] No record of Moe's response, if any, remains, but George Cronyn continued avidly to support Partch's writing. On May 27, 1937, as Partch's troubles with Santee were coming to a head, Cronyn encouraged him to stay with the project:

> There may be criticisms of details but the stuff is good.... Your essay style, combining color with detachment, is a rarity. You can write well about anything you turn your hand to. But if I were your classroom instructor (God forbid!) I would advise you to avoid the autobiographical form for a year or two. It's the *métier* of the present school but has pitfalls. There are few enough people in America with a shrewd observing eye, but that eye, turned inward, may see too many snarls. An outsider might

consider you maladjusted; that's the penalty of looking clearly at a maladjusted world. And "adjustment" is generally the sign of insensitivity or conformity.[48]

Unfortunately, Partch felt he had to leave Arizona. One week later, Cronyn wrote to him one last time, sadly reporting that a desired transfer to the California Writers' Project was not an option due to budget cuts. He also offered, as a parting bit of advice, that Partch should consider writing another manuscript like *Cause All My Sins*, but one expanded to encompass the entire United States, which would offer greater commercial potential.[49] As enticing as the idea seems today, Partch apparently never followed Cronyn's suggestion except obliquely, chronicling his cross-country hitchhike four years later in *U.S. Highball*. He did continue trying to get *Cause All My Sins* published, sending it to Caxton Printers in Caldwell, Idaho, a small publishing house that specialized in regional Americana, but even with editor John E. Ludlow's endorsement, the proprietor decided not to accept the manuscript.[50] After he left Arizona and the Federal Writers' Project, Partch disappeared for two years, resurfacing in time to work for the FWP on California's guidebook (an ironic turn of events following his *Bitter Music* era relationship with the state), jot down some hobo inscriptions in Barstow, California, and hop a train to Chicago, Illinois.

By 1940—the next time we have a record of Partch thinking about his transient diary—both Steinbeck's *Grapes of Wrath* and Taylor and Lange's *American Exodus* had been published, igniting a furor over the plight of migrants in California. Steinbeck's novel had completed the steady erosion of the divide between transients and migrants through its dual focus on Dust Bowl migration and transients finding work through state and federal camps. In the minds of most Americans after reading the book, anyone who accepted relief in California was a Joad, someone to be pitied and looked down upon. It was a position in which Partch had found himself with the musical community more times than he cared to remember, and one to which he had no wish to return. Taylor and Lange's opus told a story similar to Steinbeck's, but in a unique fusion of words and images. With a new documentary form already expertly presented, Partch's manuscript lost part of its originality, part of its appeal. It was now just another attempt, albeit a first-person one, to depict in a new way the horrors attached to the migrant condition. It is perhaps this altered landscape that urged Partch back to the manuscript and toward a new conception. In a preface written on November 22, 1940, Partch reversed the way he viewed his work. Replacing a title drawn from the first line of text with one from the last, he called it *Bitter Music*, moving from an inherently optimistic, forward-looking conception to one that is fundamentally pessimistic. This action marked a permanent shift in his recollections of the period.

No matter which conception frames one's understanding of the work, in *Bitter Music* Partch combined the best and most original artistic expression of the period in novels, musical scores, and documentary journalism in one unique format. But his achievement was not just a new style of documentary feature or a new way of thinking about speech-music. Through this unique collection of voices from the 1930s, expertly preserved in inflection and meaning, we hear history come to life. Partch did not spend time, as did most Depression-era commentators, discussing the "migrant problem." Neither did he delve into the nobility of people struggling to craft a life in a new land. Instead, he achieved a rare balance. Partch was willing to lay open his personal travails and thereby detail the degradation and solitude inherent in transient life. Yet within that harsh existence, he depicted the importance of tenderness from relief workers and other transients, the good-humored songs and tales they shared, and the freedom of being answerable to no one. He lent humanity to what the New Deal had for so long characterized merely by statistics.

CHAPTER FOUR

A KNIGHT OF THE ROAD

As the 1940s dawned, Harry Partch was looking toward a new horizon, turning away from menial labor and its associations with the migrant and moving back into contact with musical society. Part of his new attitude toward the culture he felt had rejected him came from the increasing hardships, both physical and psychological, of his nomadic existence. The freedom he initially sought was constantly undercut by Californians' attitudes toward migrant workers and the sheer number looking for work: near Marysville he noted that "there were at least a hundred peach pickers for every job, and the banks of the American River were so thick with hobos that—at night—you'd have thought it was the site of an army bivouac."[1] Beyond the physical travails was an increasing sense of desperation about the impact of his situation on his compositional progress. He had not completed a musical work in five years and had been unable to find publication for his most recent major work—*Bitter Music*. The only instruments to play his scale remained his Adapted Viola and Adapted Guitar, with a discarded keyboard for the Ptolemy the only testimony of the previous years' work. At almost forty years old, he had little to show for close to two decades of grappling with his new musical ideas, and he felt stymied by his lack of achievement.

As had become his pattern, when Partch felt stuck he responded by moving. In January 1940, he set out from California on a photography trip documenting the desert Southwest, perhaps thinking of creating a project like Walker and Agee or Lange and Taylor. On the back of the first photograph, which shows him sitting behind the wheel of a car, he noted:

"On beginning of search for my soul into desert."[2] Most of the remaining photos give no indication that Partch found a fresh direction in the desert; the images are of natural wonders like the Mecca Hills Painted Canyon or the Colorado River or the men he encountered on the road, and have little to do with his later work. But at the trip's end, as he was turning back toward California, Partch took several pictures that presaged the direction of his work to come. Stopping near Fort Yuma, Arizona, Partch photographed hoboes jumping trains at the California border in late February (see fig. 4.1). The bridge over the Colorado River was an important point for hoboes. The section on Yuma in the WPA state guide to Arizona, which Partch may have written, noted that "to freight-car bums Yuma is the jumping-off place for California. Hoboes, arriving from points east, camp in the jungles nearby, where they cook up their mulligan stews and wash their clothes in preparation for the next run."[3] These photos show Partch's attention returning to the hobo, a direction only reinforced when the composer crossed the bridge into California and encountered unexpected words that would shape his life's work and trajectory from then on.

Words on a Highway Railing

A few days later, after hitchhiking into California, Partch was resting next to a highway railing while waiting for a passerby to take pity and offer him a ride. Looking down, he happened to notice that several former occupants of his spot had written on the railing to pass the time. He had seen short sayings like those for over ten years on highway signs, railroad overpasses, walls, and railings, but had always thought them meaningless scribbles. This time was different. He reread the scrawled lettering: "It's January 26. I'm freezing. Ed Fitzgerald. Age 19. Five feet, ten inches. Black hair, brown eyes. Going home to Boston Massachusetts. It's 4:00, and I'm hungry and broke. I wish I was dead. But today I am a man." Something deep within him stirred, and, as he knelt down for a better look, he realized "this—why, it's music. It's both weak and strong, like unedited human expressions always are. It's eloquent in what it fails to express in words. And it's epic. Definitely, it is music."[4] He diligently recorded those written fragments in a notebook, but they floated around his mind for a year. When he finally sat down to compose the work, it only took him a month to complete it. He named it in honor of the town where he found the texts and soon performed it in lectures, on recordings, and, presumably, in boxcars. *Barstow* became his gateway to making the hobo experience music.

Figure 4.1. Partch noted on the back of this photograph: "Fort Yuma Freight, Feb. 1940." He took the picture at the end of a photography trip documenting the desert Southwest, capturing hoboes as they jumped trains at the bridge crossing the Colorado River outside Fort Yuma, Arizona. The river, which separated Arizona from California, was a popular stopping point for hoboes. Courtesy of the Harry Partch Estate Archive, San Diego.

When Partch decided to compose *Barstow*, he not only made a compositional decision but one about his image as well. His earliest Monophonic pieces had all been based on established works of poetry, all seen as classic within their genre. From Shakespeare to Li Po to the Bible, Partch's works captured the speech-rhythm of the best poetic utterances. Although he continued to dabble in this type of setting throughout his life, composing on texts ranging from Lewis Carroll to Ki No Tsurayuki, after *Barstow* he turned his attention almost exclusively to his own texts. In the 1940s, most of those texts were based on or gathered during his hobo years. Unable to publish his migrant journal (and nourishing his increasingly negative opinion of it by changing its title in November 1940, five months before composing *Barstow*), Partch made the conscious decision to downplay his transient/migrant time in work camps and cultivate the hobo time riding the rails and forging his own path. He still desired a new form of documentary that brought to life the voices of the people, but sensing the country's mood, knew he needed to tap into a different documentary imagination than the one surrounding the migrant. He needed to become a hobo.

The Hobo Enters Partch's Work

Although *Barstow* was the spark that ignited Partch's musical documentation of the hobo, it was not the first time he had written about the figure. Over the previous twelve years of wandering, Partch had occasionally used the hobo, but never in any systematic way. The first hobo-based works he composed were a series of songs for voice accompanied by piano or guitar. In the late 1920s, Partch wrote songs in a popular idiom to earn a little extra money. These were not "popular" songs by any stretch of the imagination and they cannot be found on the recordings of major or minor artists of the period. As Partch explained to an interviewer in 1960:

> I forgot to say that in 1928 also I started writing songs. In a period of about two weeks I wrote one a day, words and music. At least one was obscene, and I had the nerve to send it to a publisher. He didn't turn me over to federal authorities, but he did write me a blistering letter. I replied to it very calmly, and then I had a second letter from him saying that he thought I had talent, and I ought to channel it properly. Mostly they were hobo songs. One was published, but it was certainly never popular.[5]

The result of Partch's "proper" channeling of his abilities was the song "While My Heart Keeps Beating Time," published by Lloyd Campbell Publications in San Francisco:

> I've gone away,
> Away forever,
> Away from cries and tears,
> Away from loves, hates, thrills, fears.
> The stars above,
> The winds beneath me,
> In spreading sails,
> In hobo trails where I'm

> Bound away for Sacramento Jungle—
> For the joy o' living I'm
> Strumming, a-strumming on my vocal chords a-tingle
> While my heart keeps beating time.
> California, here's your hobo baby!
> Here he is without a dime—
> Strumming, a-strumming on his baby ukulele
> While his heart keeps beating time.[6]

In comparison with Partch's later libretti and his prose writing throughout his life, the song lacks incisive satire. It was the product of a single day's work, and shows evidence of a rush job from a composer known for his laborious precision. While descriptive of the hobo life, the words seem clinical, as though the singer were fully removed from the life he was extolling. Unfortunately, the music is as anodyne as the words. A simple ostinato of a dotted quarter note followed by an eighth note and two quarter notes runs through the verse. This ostinato outlines each measure's chord—the root, then the fifth, and finally the third before falling back to the fifth on the final note. Chord changes happen like clockwork every two bars and, as the song is written in the key of D major, every chord in the verse is either D major or A major with one D diminished thrown in for spice. The refrain is more interesting—as the tempo slows, the ostinato is replaced by steady quarter notes, and the key modulates to G major. But even the inclusion of a scoop from the dominant up to the tonic on the final note does little to add any sparkle to the song (see fig. 4.2).

Partch seems to have regarded "While My Heart Keeps Beating Time" as a curiosity and little else, but it held his heart in a sentimental grasp. That grasp extends to those engrossed today by the composer's development, as it is the only piece of Partch's music that remains from the first thirty years of his life. But Partch's attachment to the song, which stretched so far that it resurfaced several times in his music over the following ten years, was marred by the treatment it received at the publisher's hand. "My hobo words were deleted," he recalled, "—that appalled me, but I went along. Ted Lewis wrote new lyrics for it—they were so silly I don't even remember them."[7] The new lyrics transformed Partch's hobo song into one related to that other mythical frontiersman, the cowboy.

The connection between the cowboy and the hobo was strong, especially since many of the new country and western singers who performed hobo songs adopted a cowboy persona like Jimmie Rodgers. And since many of those same performers camouflaged some hobo references by changing the texts to more generic Western references, perhaps the publisher felt it a wise move:

Figure 4.2. The opening lines of Harry Partch's hobo song "While My Heart Keeps Beating Time." The lyrics are not Partch's, which were never published, but new ones penned by Ted Lewis, writing here as Larry Yoell. Published by Lloyd Campbell Publications, copyright September 18, 1929.

> A cowboy's tears are slow at starting;
> A cowboy's love is sad at parting.
> A pony lies beneath the moonlight;
> A cowboy's voice is heard in pray'r.
> Now you roam alone the plains of Heaven,
> While my heart keeps beating time,
> Tho' I ride another pony daily,
> Ev'ry hoofbeat makes me pine.
> In my dreams I hear your gentle neighing
> And I'm praying for the time,
> When we'll ride the golden plains together,
> While my heart keeps beating time.[8]

Partch's ode to the hobo life became a prayer to a departed horse—which may account for why Partch published it under the pseudonym Paul Pirate.[9] Ted Maxwell ultimately introduced the song, which, when published, featured an additional poem on the front cover reminding the reader that "altho' he's [a cowboy] hardened and calloused and coarse, there's one thing that makes him soft-hearted—his horse." "While My Heart Keeps Beating Time" was a typically sentimental ballad common also to hobo songs published at the time. The detachment Partch demonstrated in his original lyrics did not fit this framework, and though he retained a fondness for the song as he wrote it, by the 1960s, he had completely forgotten the modified version.[10]

"While My Heart Keeps Beating Time" was Partch's only musical hobo work prior to *Barstow*, but he did use the hobo in several prose works during the 1930s as he struggled through his feelings of working against an ingrained musical (industrial) order while attempting to free music from its pretensions and unnatural bases.[11] He wrote the first, titled "A Modern Parable I," in 1933 while he was in New York City, seeking monetary support and entertaining questions about his lack of academic pedigree. It features two events occurring within the same city block: a young newsboy conferring with his boss and a university president conferring degrees.

The newsboy was something of a hobo figure in the early twentieth century. He was usually an orphan, constantly on the move to earn his pay, and he owned little beyond the clothes hanging on his body. He figured so deeply in the same sort of mythology that grew up around the hobo that Partch later included a newsboy as part of *The Wayward*, through *San Francisco—A Setting of the Cries of Two Newsboys on a Street Corner*. Perhaps the seeds of inspiration for that work, written ten years later, were sown in this first parable.

In "A Modern Parable I," the newsboy is a self-assured fellow who, though only thirteen years old, "was better prepared to know and understand the world than many in their prized threescore and ten." Partch paints a picture that only he can see: the true value and worth of this boy, who argues for a better corner from which to hawk his papers. "Our academicians would certainly classify him as inferior mental stuff," Partch declared in a pointed remark. "Nevertheless, he was the kind of boy who, freed from the oppressions of civilization, in certain of his more puerile moments, could enjoy Beethoven; who, in sudden flashes of witlessness, could admire Michelangelo; and who, in his deepest moronic moods, could feel something of the dark broodings of Ibsen."

Against the newsboy's rough-hewn insights, Partch placed a university president, with more letters behind his name than in it, who was ushering graduates into the "fraternity of enlightened men." At the story's climax, the boss inquires of the newsboy what he would do with the corner the boy proposed vacating, at the precise moment the university president rhetorically asks his audience "What shall we do with this magnificent learning?" Partch allows the newsboy to answer both: "'I'll tell you what you can do with it,' replied the newsboy on the corner, half under his breath. 'You can ——'" Partch then tells us that the newsboy uttered five magnificent words that were, in effect, the words Partch had for musical institutions that attempted to force him into their mold—they could "stick it up their ass!"

Partch completed the second writing, conveniently titled "A Modern Parable II," five years later on April 26. In it, he follows the pattern set out by the first, of contrasting those overlooked by society with those held up as its experts. In this case, he takes a group of bums sitting around a pepper tree in California—a sight Partch would surely have seen daily, as he wrote the story in a work camp for transients in San Bernardino County—and set them against five musicologists sitting around a walnut table on the opposite coast, in New York City. Unlike the first parable, which focused on the newsboy, the second spends most of its time in the company of the musicologists who talk constantly because, Partch informs us, "musicologists never tire of musicologists." The scholars are listening to a paper concerning scientific experiments conducted on reactions to "Yankee Doodle."[12] In a game of oneupsmanship, each points out the fallacies of the previous musicologist's thesis, and demonstrates how they address those inaccuracies in their own papers. The dialogue hilariously descends into upper-crust name calling— "pettifoggers" and "pedants"—until Partch breaks into the conversation and allows the "plain, ordinary bum" to clear the air with a resounding "BULLSHIT!"

While Partch certainly wrote both stories in response to his situations, the second also resonates with his reasons for adopting the hobo image in 1940. He places the two groups on the two coasts, paralleling the respective attitudes of musicians who live and work on each. The East Coast, tied closely to Europe and her traditions, resisted change. The West Coast, still largely untamed and full of Asian and Mexican immigrants, was paradoxically more open to Partch's ideas about reclaiming European music's ancient traditions. Throughout his life, Partch found more acceptance and success on the West Coast and in the Midwest than in the East. Partch also laughs at the notion that musicologists firmly embedded in equal temperament are conducting scientific research. His own musical philosophy, which pivoted on returning to a music based on the science of acoustics, was nevertheless routinely scoffed at by musicologists overseeing their own "scientific" experiments.

Both of these parables celebrate the shunned, the overlooked, the people who most clearly see into the elaborate ruse that is acceptance of the dominant order. Originally Partch had wanted to be part of that order, as a university-trained pianist or composer. But during the 1920s, he realized that the musical establishment was stifling human and musical creativity and power. He needed to go off on his own, to forge his own idiosyncratic and individual path and break completely with Western music as it was being practiced in order to rebuild it as it had been. That break with tradition would not have been possible without his experience of being a hobo. Living as a hobo showed him that he could survive even if no one else knew or understood what he was doing. It confirmed for him that an alternative to modern society was possible. And it gave him the strength to know that he could work within the system without having to become part of it. The image of the hobo afforded him the ability to do what he wanted and be seen as having chosen it because he refused to conform. It allowed him to be celebrated as an antimodern individualist. The hobo became central to Partch's development as a theorist, as a composer, and as a man.

Personal Resonances with the Hobo

Beyond his artistic and aesthetic reasons for adopting the hobo existence and mystique, Partch's interactions with other hoboes offer glimpses into his personal reasons for the move. Only a few letters remain from his years of wandering, and most of those deal with attempts and successes in promoting his music. But a small handful of letters written to him while on the road allow us to peek into the nature of his hobo friendships and ascertain the subjects that crowded the hobo mind at the beginning of the 1930s. Of immense importance to our conception of Partch's time as a hobo, they also create ripples beyond simply understanding an American composer.

These letters contrast and confirm the fears, warnings, expectations, and allure that we have seen other writers layer upon the culture during the first three decades of the twentieth century. They bequeath a firsthand account of how the hobo viewed himself.

The chief concern among Partch and his correspondents was movement. Hoboes moved constantly; they only remained in one spot for an extended time when they earned or came into a decent amount of money. This "jungle stake," as it was known, quickly became a burden, as hoboes existed in a culture founded on surviving by one's wits and not one's frugality. Tradition dictated that hoboes with a stake spent it fairly quickly, then moved on to find new work in a new locale.[13] Most hoboes did this, either in deference to tradition or to remove the new "friends" who inevitably came with the money. Some would stand still when they came across a decent job, but even then they settled in only for a little while; most hoboes abhorred the idea of settling down permanently.

Because movement governed hoboes, the bulk of their letters to each other concerned past and future movements. All of the hobo letters Partch kept embody this feature. Jack Brooks, one of Partch's most common correspondents from the period, included a second postscript that runs a third of the letter's full length to describe his trek from Tucson to "Portland, Oregon. And from there to Marseilles, Illinois by way of Idaho, Utah, Wyoming, Nebraska, and Iowa. After spending a few weeks in Marseilles, I came here to Niagara Falls." He admits that he's been in Niagara Falls for three months on a job, but also that he plans to leave and visit "N.Y.C., the Fair, West Point, Annapolis, Wash. D.C., and parts of W. Va. and Kentucky and Indiana."[14] Although this letter is remarkable for its length, even in the short postcards Partch kept the communication of movements predominates.

The other overwhelming feature of the letters Partch kept is their affection for the missive's recipient. Partch's personal connection to the authors surely governed which letters he saved, as most of the men seem to have had a significant relationship with the composer. In the same letter in which he listed practically every state in the union, Jack Brooks also confessed: "In some strange manner you have affected me as no one has ever done. It is true that I desired ever so much to make the Colorado trip with you. And it is also true that I was afraid to do so with you. Did it not seem strange to you, that I with a passionate nature should wear such a cold armor? You say I slipped a strait jacket over you—I also slipped one over me."[15] Brooks uses this letter to confess awkwardly that he shares Partch's feelings and wants a chance to reciprocate them. Likewise, a correspondent known only as Don ends a letter in which he graphically and freely relates the effects of a painfully swollen testicle with the line "Do you miss me just a little bit? (I do)."[16]

A few of Partch's close friends gathered the impression years later that the freedom to engage in indiscriminate homosexual sex and to pursue, as Lou Harrison put it, "male bonding," was among hoboing's most attractive aspects to the composer.[17] These types of casual yet intense relationships between men certainly marked hobo culture, much to the consternation of writers around the turn of the century. Nels Anderson found homosexuality "very prevalent" among hoboes, from one-time encounters to longer lasting relationships.[18] Many accounts included candid accounts of hobo sexual experimentation and discussions of the culture's loose sexual mores, lamenting how openly all kinds of sexual practices were allowed to proliferate. While most of these accounts were exaggerated and used to condemn hobo culture, some publications went too far in the other direction and denied such practices altogether.[19] No evidence indicates whether or not Partch was particularly drawn to this aspect of hobo life, but being homosexual himself, he certainly found relationships more easily in the hobo jungle as well as the freedom to express his sexuality in a way he could not in so-called polite society. He also would have been drawn more to long-term relationships than one-night stands, a fact borne out in these letters and in his portrayal of homosexuality in *Bitter Music*. But if at first he found the opportunity to live openly as a homosexual appealing, by the time he was ready to leave the hobo world and climb back to society at large, it had had dire results: sometime toward the end of the 1930s, Partch contracted syphilis, a cloud that hung over his relationships for the rest of his life.[20]

While these two topics of movement and affection drown out all others in the letters, one other subject rates highly enough to merit mention: food. Partch opened a letter he wrote to his hobo pal Jimmy (known as Kain-tuck in *Bitter Music*) by remarking: "They give you real butter here, and, believe it or not, a big pitcher of real cream on each table. And the pie isn't filled with cornstarch. When I saw bread pudding I though: O, O—the old stand-by, but it proved to be hoky-doke, the best I ever ate."[21] His hobo friend Bill wrote him with a similar statement: "I am still toiling on the grade; the work appears a little hard, but if they keep on feeding me this fifth avenue food, I am sure it will become easy in a short while."[22] Hoboes constantly begged food, an art they perfected in order to survive, at least according to Jack London's tale "Confession," which opens *The Road* and relates one evening he successfully begged a full sit-down supper.[23] Other contemporary literary and sociological texts share similar stories, so it is unsurprising that Partch and his hobo pals also had their minds on their stomachs.

Discussions of movement, affection, and food are connected in some of these letters through the notion of freedom—freedom to go where one wants, be with whom one wants in the manner one wants to be with them, and, with luck, to eat what one wants, when one wants. Hoboes took up the life to obtain that freedom; Harry Partch was no different. The constant self-promotion and glad-handing on top of trying to find work and find time to compose and build instruments drained him physically and psychologically. Hoboing was a chance to drop out of that existence for a while. It was not an easy life and ultimately it dealt as harshly with Partch as it did any other man who took to the road. But it did allow him freedom and an opportunity to recharge before forging ahead once more.

All in all, the hobo letters that Partch saved attest to what concerned many turn-of-the-century moralists—that hoboes were primarily concerned with matters of basic existence. But the portrait of the hobo revealed in Partch's correspondence goes beyond the lust, greed, and desire for sustenance that characterize early descriptions of the tramp and hobo. It clarifies that hoboes considered friendship and meaningful human contact a matter of basic existence. Certainly they had to survive, and they worried about food and shelter and where they would travel next, but they also recognized the absurdity of parts of their existence and responded to it with humor and ribald grace.

Adopting the Hobo Image

These multitudinous reasons for adopting the hobo image certainly resonated for Harry Partch: he knew why he needed the hobo musically, aesthetically, and even psychologically. But that adoption would have been meaningless for his acceptance and reception were it not for the continuing hold hoboes have on the American imagination. In other words, *The Wayward* would not hold our interest, and Partch would not have clung to the image, were it a forgotten one only glimpsed in history books.

There are several other themes that seem to attract scholars and popular attention to the hobo. An undercurrent of seductive danger flows through accounts of hoboes over the past century. Many characterize hoboes as modern-day Robin Hoods, rebels working and living beyond the bounds of civilized society for the good of the downtrodden, which simultaneously makes them a dangerous and a romantic figure to ordinary citizens. Remembering his first experience as a hobo in the 1910s, George Witten wrote, "Then I had my first thrilling sensation of being an outlaw. When I was pulled through the door of the box-car I was pulled into another world, a world of adventure and hardship.... I had stepped outside the law, into the realm where men lived by their wits."[24] In the first half of the century, people avoided jungles and missions, and even looked the other way whenever they met a hobo. Writers wondered openly why hoboes did not work and whether their morals reflected their base lifestyle.[25] At the same time, many envied the hobo existence. The frontier was closing, and few places remained where a man could live as he wanted without interference. Furthermore, Americans have long been a mobile people, constantly moving residentially, professionally, and socially. Hoboes represented and contributed to this feeling, showing that it was still possible to live free, following one's own rules.[26]

This dichotomy between revulsion and attraction is demonstrated by the term "Knights of the Road," a common euphemism in the early twentieth century for hoboes and tramps. In many ways, this term highlights the culture's true popular conception, conjuring images of noble, upstanding people who roam the land seeking wrongs to correct; a brotherhood following a common code. They are friends of common folks, accepting food where offered and taking jobs for little or no pay. These modern knights are free adventurers, chasing the next escapade in their eventful lives and justly flouting the rules of a society that mistrusts and misunderstands them.[27]

The historical record of Harry Partch's life as a hobo both fits into the "Knights of the Road" image and undermines it. He was not a full-time hobo; his existence on the road was not a continuous one. Although he hoboed from 1928 to 1943, stretches of employment and relative stability interrupted those periods of wandering (see table 1.1). Partch's life during this time was unsettled, but he was not a habitual hobo by any stretch of the imagination—even though he later allowed that impression to persist among interviewers and associates. Instead, he hoboed by choice, when he wanted to do so and on his own terms. In his beautiful and detailed biography, Bob Gilmore surveys this intriguing situation and asks a provocative question: in attempting to reconstruct Partch's movements in the final years of the 1930s, Gilmore ponders "why he [Partch] chose to resume, and to maintain, that lifestyle when, as his experience in Phoenix demonstrated, he could find a job if he was willing to stay in one place for long enough."[28] Having surveyed when and why Partch headed to the hobo jungle the clearest answer seems to be that once he decided upon his path, he wanted no job that took him away from it. Proofreading came easily to him and did not require the type of dedication or concentration that other jobs did. Unlike Charles Ives, who could simultaneously compose while holding a full-time nonmusical job and allow his creative personality to surface in both, Partch seems to have needed to focus on his artistic work to the exclusion of all else, resulting in a lifetime of creative surges and dry spells related to his employment. When a job or a person or people began to impinge on the direction in which Partch strongly believed he needed to go, he would leave to find a new vista. This pattern existed not only during his hobo years, but in later decades as well.

The months following his photojournalism trip through the Southwest continued this pattern, even while Partch contemplated what to do with the Barstow inscriptions. In the fall of 1940, he hitchhiked to Big Sur, found a job proofreading a novel for Lillian Bos Ross (perhaps *The Stranger in Big Sur*), and moved into the superintendent's office at the recently abandoned convict camp at Anderson Creek. There he charted his course for the next decade. He finished a seventh draft of his theoretical treatise on intonation. He resumed work on his instruments, collecting remnants of redwood to finish his first Kithara (based on Greek designs and discussions in London with Kathleen Schlesinger) and to construct a model of a new Ptolemy. He wrote four newspaper articles for the *Carmel Pine Cone* that respectively decried equal temperament's influence on Western music ("Bach and Temperament"), celebrated speech music ("W. B. Yeats"), and detailed his recent activity ("Barstow" and "The Kithara"). And, perhaps most importantly, he broke five years of compositional silence with a hobo concerto.

Barstow as Hobo Composition

The hobo experiences detailed in *Barstow* are remote. These are not Harry Partch's trials and hopes, nor his insights and expletives. They are the raw emotions left on the roadside by a mingled community of men and women wasting time while searching for salvation. That salvation might have appeared in the form of a ride, as Jesus Christ, or as matrimonial bliss, but however it manifested, the stranded hoboes outside Barstow, California were all straining for a glimpse of it. The inscriptions they left were short, mostly unrelated to each other, and antinarrative in their staccato sentences and far-ranging foci. Many must have looked at them, read them, and even leaned against them without seeing or hearing their group potential. Partch heard their voices that February day in 1940 and collected them all, unsure of how they connected, but certain that they did.

In April 1941, Partch began ordering the eight inscriptions that had been running in his head for a year, creating a sense of cohesion among them by ordering them into a dramatic structure. *Barstow* begins with the words of nineteen-year-old Ed Fitzgerald, quoted on p. 111 above. Hungry, broke, and freezing, Fitzgerald is heading home cross-country to Boston. His inscription is the second longest and introduces us to the work's themes: the marking of time, the struggles of the homeless life, and the various forms of salvation sought. These are themes reminiscent of *Bitter Music*, but instead of the hopelessness that ultimately characterizes that journal, *Barstow* is full of the irony and sly humor popularly associated with hoboes. The six short inscriptions that follow list the forms of rescue available: an easy handout (Inscription 2), a stable and perhaps rich mate (Inscriptions 3, 4, and 7), religion (Inscription 6), and physical movement (Inscription 5). They each contain moments of great humor and intimate pathos, and all overflow with humanity. The final Inscription, the eighth, is the longest and serves as a culmination of the utterances that came before. Johnnie Reinwald from Los Angeles narrates his hobo trip in an open boxcar from Chicago and expresses his hopes upon his return home, ending "the best of luck to you." Following Johnnie's inscription, another hand had evidently scrawled "Why in hell did you come, anyway?" as a sarcastic response to the long narrative.[29] Partch picked up on these words as a refrain and ultimately ended his work with them: not only does he ask the eight correspondents why they elected this life, he also rhetorically demands of his audience what they hoped to gain from the piece and, in line with the responses pouring out from Lange and Steinbeck's work, what they intended to do about the situation.

In addition to the textual structure, Partch added a musical one.[30] Each Inscription proceeds through the same four sections: an instrumental introduction, a spoken declamation of the Inscription's number, a setting of the text in speech-music, and a setting of a portion of the text in a sung chant. The only Inscription to break this pattern is Inscription Eight, where Partch skillfully interweaves the speech-music and sung sections to create a running commentary and a musical climax that matches his textual one. Although in the first version Partch performed all the vocal parts while accompanying himself on Adapted Guitar, by the second version of the work, completed in December of 1941, he had split the vocal line into two parts, the "Intoning Voice," which performs the speech-music sections, and the "Chanting Voice," which takes the sung sections. This division serves to highlight his recurring musical structure, one that is made more obvious through his treatment of the work's melodic lines. The Intoning Voice ranges over all forty-three pitches of Partch's scale, while the Chanting Voice confines itself primarily to the justly-tuned diatonic intervals.[31] The expressive result is that of someone reading the Inscription and then ruminating upon its meaning before proceeding to the next writing. The vocal sound Partch sought is similar to any piece of American musical folklore in its lack of pretense and unforced vocal production.

The instrumental introductions are the same for all Inscriptions, a short descending motive of chords built on the foundational pitch 1/1, moving from "G minor" through what Partch termed a "C-sharp auxiliary" and several versions of "C major" before landing on "E-flat augmented." Rhythmically, Partch presents each chord with an arpeggiated figure that spans one quarter note: a thirty-second note alternation followed by two falling sixteenth notes. The collective impact of these introductions is similar to that of the "Promenade" sections of Modest Musorgsky's *Pictures at an Exhibition*. Partch had long admired the Russian composer, particularly for his explorations of the musical possibilities of human speech in the operas *Boris Godunov* and *Khovanshchina*, and perhaps was thinking of how the "Promenades" gently introduce and guide the listener through each of Musorgsky's evocations of Viktor Hartmann's paintings.[32] However, Partch's introductory sections are shorter and more connected to each Inscription, and in their structural use are best related to ritornello form, one that harks back to the the Baroque concerto. It was this connection that probably led Partch to nickname the work his "hobo concerto," especially after a friend sent him a clipping from the *New Yorker* in 1942, detailing a concert in Cleveland that included "a Brandenburg Concerto and an orchestral suite by Bach, a Concerto Grosso of Vivaldi, and the Concerto for Hoboes, Tramps, Hitch-Hikers, oboes and strings by Handel." Whoever sent the clipping to Partch helpfully noted "So you let Handel get ahead of you, eh?"[33]

As *Barstow* was Partch's first extended composition using the hobo, it is instructive to see him grapple with how to write a work that was based on a figure in American folklore, without falling into the easy pattern of decorative exoticism. Many composers at the time were readily picking melodies related to the figures they were musically portraying, and then weaving those melodies as a spice into their composition. Partch wanted a music whose melodic, rhythmic, and harmonic material would derive organically from the voices he recorded; he did not want to rely on external musical associations. The model that he heard and knew, however, was the traditional one of decorative exoticism. As a result, *Barstow* shows the composer picking out his new path, trying different approaches with different Inscriptions and discovering a more conceptual approach. It also shows him trying out how subtly to evoke connections to ideas and music outside of the composition, without relying on blatant musical quotation. Some of those connections he links directly to the hobo in stylistic terms, and some exist simply to add to the piece's humor, but each is generated by the work's textual references. The most obvious example of this kind of borrowing is in Inscription Six, which features *Barstow*'s shortest inscription text: "Jesus was God in the flesh." After the Intoning Voice finishes the first reading, the Chanting Voice begins singing a mixture of "Hey Hey Hey" and the original text. Partch fluctuates between monophonic chanting with a regular and propulsive beat (reminiscent of the Native American music he transcribed in 1933) and slow, homophonic sections that have the strong flavor of the Methodist hymnody of his childhood. Each of the hymn references is marked "suddenly slow" in the score, omits the "Hey Hey Hey" text, and moves through a cadence that is a close cousin of the traditional plagal Amen. This musical signpost is subtle—just long enough to draw a knowledgeable listener's mind to stories of hoboes taking advantage of missions that provided room and board in exchange for sitting through a sermon, for example—but not long enough to draw a listener out of the composition, as it barrels on to the next Inscription.

Partch's other requisitioning of a musical style results in a striking connection. In the final Inscription, as Johnnie Reinwald is narrating his trip back to California from Chicago, Partch has the Intoning Voice deliver the "Why in hell did you come, anyway?" refrain before letting the Chanting Voice take up the inscription. The arrangement is reversed in the lines "I'm on my way. One half of desert to the east," which he gives to the Intoning Voice. Underneath those lines, Partch reached back to his teenage years playing piano for silent films in Albuquerque, and his first composition, a melodrama for reader and piano titled *Death on the Desert*, to compose stock "traveling" music.[34] In a 4/3 otonality (a hexad created by going up the harmonic series from 4/3, or "C" in Partch's tonality), the Adapted Guitar drops into a figuration that sounds similar to the horse clopping along in "While My Heart Keeps Beating Time" or any number of compositions from the 1930s, including, Richard Kassel speculates, the third movement of Ferde Grofé's *Grand Canyon Suite* from 1931.[35] The resulting sound is a nod to tradition, a tongue-in-cheek salute to how film composers would have treated any mention of the desert, even if just for ten measures.

These few stylistic borrowings are unique to *Barstow*. The only time in *The Wayward* Partch clearly uses this type of musical decoration comes when he signals the uneasy relationship between well-meaning Christian missions and the hoboes they served in *U.S. Highball*. In that passage, he writes in homophony but without the signifying plagal cadence. Lacking the "Amen" featured in *Barstow*, the connection is likely to pass by all but the most careful listeners, and beyond that connection there are no other such musical appropriations. After trying out this kind of borrowing in

Barstow, Partch stopped using the music associated with hoboes or life in the western United States and instead used hobo musical styles as foundational material, in a more conceptual fashion. No more did he write "concertos" or use ritornello form; rather, he constructed hobo conversations and events in music. His works began relying on formal structures generated by the men he depicted instead of Western European theorists and musicians. With *Barstow*, he pivoted from the more decorative exoticism of *Bitter Music* toward the conceptual exoticism of *U.S. Highball*.

Still, the features that make up *Barstow* combine to craft a work both witty and profane, wonderfully rich and vibrant but strangely distant, as though you were watching hoboes come and go, sit on the railings, and scratch out their messages, but were never able to interact with them. In this way it is, like all of Partch's works from this period, a piece of documentary. From its outset Partch seems to have recognized this aspect of the work as he framed *Barstow* as presenting a slice of life ignored by modern society: he inscribed on the first version, "[The inscriptions] are generally written in pencil, or carved in the wood with a pocket knife. Every so often highway workers come along, and these little stories, epics of American hitch-hikers, come to oblivion in a few strokes of white paint."[36] He presents the work as saving a bit of Americana, bringing to light a segment of Depression-era life usually covered over, in a similar manner to *The Grapes of Wrath* or Lange's photographs. He even increased the composition's veracity by letting his audience learn the hobo's real names—Ed Fitzgerald, Marie Blackwell, Johnnie Reinwald. Rather than allowing listeners to become intimately acquainted with them, however, Partch uses these hoboes as cyphers to address larger issues, focusing on our reaction to these men and women on the edges of society.

"Why in Hell did you come, anyway?" In Partch's hands, this is a question that demands a response from the audience, one we can imagine Lange's Migrant Mother asking: "What did you expect to find, and what are you going to do about the situation now that you know?" As with most documentary of the period, Partch never allows listeners to penetrate beyond the hoboes' facade any more than he does himself as a composer. He keeps these men and women at a distance, documenting them for the world to hear but hesitant about admitting in any of his writings that accompanied *Barstow* at the time that he not only gathered these inscriptions, but was a hobo himself. Consider, for example, a performance Partch gave of *Barstow* a year and a half after composing it. On November 3, 1942, he walked into Kilbourn Hall on the campus of the Eastman School of Music and demonstrated his musical theories, ending the lecture with a solo performance of his first hobo piece. His performance, which was recorded, began with the characteristic guitar refrain that frames the incriptions; he then launched directly into "Inscription One." But Partch's recitation of Ed Fitzgerald's writing is almost a monotone, each sentence ending with the same slight falling off in pitch. Only on the line "I wish I was dead," does he show any emotion by slowing the tempo and dropping into the bottom of his vocal range. The inscription then moves into the sung section and Partch remains uncommitted, punching the words "man" and "dead," but softening almost to *sotto voce* by the end. Although he wants his audience to hear these inscriptions and imagine their authors, Partch seems tentative in equating himself with those authors.[37]

In spite of the vocal attitude of parts of this performance, the remove at which Partch kept his hobo experiences was beginning to shrink only a year after he penned *Barstow*. In introducing the work to the Eastman students, Partch related that one inscription showed how hoboes often had to sit on the railings for days before getting a ride. He followed this statement with a moment of candor, musing "I don't know what he did eventually . . . but speaking from my own rich experience, I would say that he eventually took a freight train." Partch was beginning to realize that in that age of various searches for an American sound, during which composers plundered other cultures to find musical treasures, creating that sound out of something personal would speak more directly and powerfully to his audience. Accordingly, that November performance was one of the last where *Barstow* was prominently featured.

Not until he lived as a hobo and created music and instruments that were simultaneously part of that culture, part of Western musical culture, and something completely their own, did Partch find his own voice. Those hobo works and his experiences living that life helped forge him into the rugged American individualist recognized today, a composer fighting against modern musical culture to regain the grandeur cast aside in the crush of progress. This distinction makes Partch's works from this period conceptually exotic—part and parcel of who he was and needed to be, yet effectively between and of two cultures. We have seen the impact of the migrant and the transient on American culture and Partch's creative process; now it is time to explore not only the hobo as a cultural figure, but how by living as a hobo and pulling from those experiences, Partch managed to make one of the twentieth century's most personal, original, and compelling collections of artistic works—*The Wayward*.

INTERLUDE TWO

HOBOES

In order to understand fully why Partch adopted the hobo persona, we must first explore the hobo as construed by artists, writers, filmmakers, and the news media. Decades of use by various crusaders, intellectuals, and politicians created a multilayered image of the hobo by the 1930s and 1940s, which Partch accessed as a way to define himself. Most Americans of the time fell roughly into two camps in their attitudes toward the hobo. One side viewed the hobo as a rugged American individualist, flouting the law to live as he liked and reveling in the absolute freedom to control his destiny. This hobo lured many artist-intellectuals with the promise of experiencing America, including writers from Carl Sandburg to W. H. Davies, Vachel Lindsay, Harvey Kemp, Jack Kerouac, Robert Service, and Jim Tully.[1] The other side viewed the hobo as a pitiful figure, victim of the rising industrial order. As manual labor on and around the railroad subsided, crusaders held up the unemployed hobo as the dismal future of American society. Homeless legions would overrun cities, these reformers argued, unless society took action. Although they were historically contradictory, these two representations persisted through the early twentieth-century's silent screen, with images such as Charlie Chaplin as the Little Tramp being bested by life, only to gain victory through humor, perseverance, and the freedom to be himself. From our vantage point it is difficult to grasp the full impact of the composer's adoption of this image, to see why his audiences found the persona compelling in a composer and why Partch latched onto it throughout his life. However, exploring how these disparate views came to coexist, and mining the space between them, offers the first glimmer of what the hobo image meant to Partch, why he would choose to celebrate that particular folk figure, and what impact his choice had on his musical career.

Who was the historical hobo, and how did he become saddled with so much cultural baggage? Broadly speaking, hoboes were young, unmarried, English-speaking migratory workers who roamed the United States from the 1860s through the 1940s.[2] Within this definition are myriad ways of survival and a variety of public responses. Consider the many names with which Americans burdened a member of this group of hired workers throughout history: in the Gilded Age, he was a "tramp," so-called because he walked or "tramped" most places he traveled; in the Progressive Era, he was a "hobo," a member of "hobohemia,"[3] who wandered and worked throughout the western United States; and after World War II, he firmly became a "bum," living on skid row.[4] Each term represents a different conception of the same group of people, and even though one was dominant at any given period of time, they also existed simultaneously. Recognizing this reality, Dr. Ben L. Reitman, who studied hoboes in the 1920s for the Chicago Health Department, crafted a precise definition in an attempt to distinguish linguistically among the various types of men who rode the rails and inhabited cities during that decade: "The hobo works and wanders, the tramp dreams and wanders, and the bum drinks and wanders."[5] Central to all these formulations, and perhaps the key concept for understanding hobo history, is that of freedom, freedom to move where you desire and do what you dream.

Tramping in the Nineteenth Century

Historically, hobo culture arose on the Western frontier in the nineteenth century's closing decades. Its growth was a reaction to two concurrent forces: industrialization and the railroad. As industrialization expanded in the United States, trains drove it westward. At the Civil War's end, only 30,000 miles of rail had been laid; by the 1910s, there were over 254,000 miles. Sustaining the rapid industrialization that had opened the Western frontier demanded laborers and machines. At first, men followed the trains, grabbing up land for timbering, ranching, and mining. But those industries, as quickly as they were established, needed a second wave of men to sustain them. Large ranches employed nomadic workers, popularly called cowboys, and timbering, mining, and farming enterprises needed workers as well. Hoboes initially grew from the same impulse as cowboys, riding trains rather than horses, sometimes carrying their bed rolls instead of guns, and working the harvests, the mines, and the key instrument of their culture, the railroad. The railroad's growth, therefore, mirrors that of hobo culture. As long as there was a frontier with a rail line running to it, hoboes would travel there to work. In fact, for almost fifty years, the hoboes' sweat equity ensured their continued existence and mobility.[6] But more settlers, arriving in larger and larger numbers through the 1890s and 1900s and building towns and permanent labor pools, forced the hobo out. Rapid industrialization brought work for the hobo at first, but it also created a curious new feature—unemployment. In a situation strikingly similar to factory workers in the East, the hobo did not own the property he used to make a living. He was dependent on wages.[7] As increased mechanization decreased the need for human labor, the hobo ranged farther and farther for work that would barely sustain him. Eventually he faced unemployment, and so began to find other ways to continue to live a mobile existence.

These unemployed, or at least minimally employed, "tramps," as hoboes were popularly called in the late nineteenth century, soon became a vexing problem for middle- and upper-class America. The petite bourgeoisie believed them a dangerous breed, criminals who threatened both themselves and society's fabric because they did not work. This notion of the hobo as a threat to society can clearly be seen in Allan Pinkerton's popular 1878 book *Strikers, Communists, Tramps, and Detectives*. In it, Pinkerton equates hoboes with labor unions and "communists" and especially Native Americans, unapologetically writing that they are "human beings so devoid of all conscience, pity, or consideration, that it is hard to look upon them as possessing the least of human attributes."[8] From these fears, myths began to spring up about tramps' origins and why they refused to settle down, find a home, and find a sustainable job. One of the earliest myths cast tramps as Civil War veterans, so alienated from everyday life by their wartime experiences that they could not return to their previous lives. This army "tramped" or walked from job to job, enjoying the same camaraderie they had previously found in army camps with the other men in hobo "jungles."[9] This myth was tightly interwoven with the popular idea that tramps had lost touch with all feminine influences that might impel them to remain home. According to this theory, men would naturally roam and wander and shun society's graces and benefits were it not for the saving impact of women in their lives—first mothers, then sisters and wives. These feminine influences kept men devoted to home and kept them working to provide for others. In short, women held civilization together. But lack of those influences spelled disaster for men. Women who did not properly nurture their children, and wives who did not properly care for their husbands, were pushing those men into tramping. This notion explains perhaps the most pernicious myth about tramping origins—that tramps were men who, through insufficient social conditioning, lacked the self-government and moral rectitude to compel themselves to work.[10]

While polite society debated the origins and effects of tramping, by the 1890s the men themselves had managed to find a solution to this problem. They had developed their own subculture, with its own language, societal codes, and even neighborhoods called "main stems" where they looked for work, slept in a bed or hammock for a few days, and decided where to travel next. Meeting with other tramps there and in jungles along the rails, they traded stories of good places to bum a meal and tips on how to find clothing and shelter. They told and retold stories of other tramps' adventures. They strummed and sang popular songs with new lyrics of their own invention and then rechristened the songs to suit tramp taste. Despite the lack of "feminine influences" feared by moralists and writers, tramps formed a society.

Still, mainstream American society greeted this new subculture with suspicion and fear until the turn of the century. That fear was probably bolstered by statistics published at the end of the nineteenth century, showing that tramp society was growing. Starting with the Long Depression of 1873–79, recession after recession rocked the United States, forcing more men out of their jobs. They then faced a choice between taking a dead-end job in the new factory production system for a salary that barely kept them and their families above starvation, or taking to the road.[11] Unsurprisingly, many elected the road. They became tramps, learning the pattern of begging and moving from one job to the next from other tramps they met and swelling the country's main stems.

At first, commentators roundly proclaimed that tramps were victims not of economics, but of drink. Scathing articles declared the tramp a poor worker, despite Western industries that relied on his labor for survival.[12] But as the calendar's numbers edged toward rolling completely over, impressions of the tramps became more complex. *Atlantic* editor William Dean Howells began to write novels such as *A Hazard of New Fortunes* (1890), in which he used tramps to criticize the inequalities of industrial capitalism and encouraged middle-class readers to consider aiding tramps. Other writers followed suit to such an extent that, by the 1910s, social worker and Superintendent of the New York Municipal Lodging House Stuart Rice admonished Americans to try and "imagine yourself a beggar."[13] Instead of seeing the tramp as Other, Americans began to sympathize with what was perceived as their plight, and moved en masse to aid them through organizations such as the Salvation Army.

Hoboing in the Twentieth Century

This new view of tramp as victim deserving of assistance grew concurrently with another view of the culture, one best expressed by the new term that writers, social workers, and the men themselves began to apply broadly—hobo. No one is certain of the word's etymology. Writers variously describe it as a derivation of the Latin *homo bonus*, which roughly translates as "good man"; as being a shortened form of the greeting "Hello, boy!"; as coming from the slang "hoe boy" for an agricultural laborer; and as being an Anglicized version of the French *Haute Beau*.[14] Regardless of its origin, Josiah Flynt's writings first granted the term "hobo" currency. Flynt was a journalist who spent time as a tramp during the 1890s.[15] His 1899 *Tramping with Tramps*, a collection of essays about his tramping experiences, has been celebrated since its publication as the first ethnographic study of hobo life. But it is a study in contradiction.[16] The hobo lifestyle, and those who tramped with him, fascinated Flynt, but his middle class upbringing nurtured the notion that he had morally failed in some fashion by undertaking the life. As a result, much of his work vacillates between extolling and denigrating the hobo. *Tramping with Tramps* is a grim portrait of life on the road, in both its physical and psychological hardships. But the book was also the first to discuss the opposite side of the coin, the attraction life on the road held. He wrote sympathetically about the hoboes he encountered and dispelled rumors about their propensity for murder and depravity, while moralizing about the reasons behind their plight. He dispelled much of the nation's paranoia about tramps and gave them a new name, but he also solidified many commonly held stereotypes. Overall, Flynt succeeded most in molding the hobo's image into a proactive one, rather than one that reacted to economic and societal pressures. Through his activities as author and expert on the hobo culture, Flynt began the transformation of the homeless wanderer from tramp to hobo.

The popular image of hobo as frontiersman, working hard while free from worry and responsibility and following his own path as the true American individualist, first appeared in *Tramping with Tramps* but did not come to full flower until Jack London's *The Road*, a collection of vignettes first given life in serial form inside the pages of *Cosmopolitan* and then published in 1907 in book form. That London owed a great debt to Flynt is clear from *The Road*'s dedication to the journalist as "the real thing, blowed in the glass." But though *Tramping with Tramps*'s success certainly aided *The Road*'s publication, London's experience as and depiction of a hobo radically differed from that of his predecessor.[17]

In 1894, when London was eighteen years old, a severe economic depression gripped the United States. Jacob S. Coxey, a young man forced into tramping by the downturn, concocted a scheme to organize tramps to march on Washington and there request federal funding of construction projects. Like New Deal programs forty years later, these projects would furnish labor for the masses of unemployed and help alleviate the depression. Coxey's Army, as the group came to be called, gathered in Massillon, Ohio to begin their march, and though they never made it to Washington, the images of a sea of politically motivated tramps moving in concert briefly inflamed American fears.

Coxey's call lured the young Jack London to leave his home in Oakland, California and ride freight trains to join the army. Over the next year, he traveled across the United States and, in a move echoed by Harry Partch thirty years later, kept a diary of his adventures riding trains: being arrested at Niagara Falls and locked up for thirty days, talking his way out of trouble and into supper, and living an unencumbered life. Although he only hoboed for one year, the experience imprinted itself upon him and urged London toward his later socialist leanings.[18] The year also found literary voice in the series of stories that make up *The Road*. In these tales, London demonstrates none of the guilt that plagued Flynt's writings of ten years previous. Instead, London celebrates life lived on the road outside the bounds of normal society. He imbues his hoboes with a mythic aura of complete freedom and self-reliance. In the story that opens the collection, "Confession," he paints the picture of a hobo who, through lying so artful that he begins to believe it himself, can gain almost anything he needs and give the upper crust their comeuppance when necessary. In "Road-Kids and Gay-Cats," he gives the reason for hoboing as wanderlust in the blood, not the necessity of work. And in the book's most stunning episode, "Holding Her Down," he gives a tense recital of a night when he eluded two brakemen, a conductor, a fireman, and an engineer to stay on a train. He recounts how he jumped blinds, rode atop and beneath the train, made a desperate lunge for the caboose, and mastered the railroad, the symbol of American industry. As he boasts:

> As I wait in the darkness I am conscious of a big thrill of pride. The overland has stopped twice for me—for me, a poor hobo on the bum. I alone have twice stopped the overland with its many passengers and coaches, its government mail, and its two thousand steam horses straining in the engine. And I weigh only one hundred and sixty pounds, and I haven't a five-cent piece in my pocket![19]

London detailed an epic figure: an individual who refused to conform to society; a man with rugged strength; a member of the brave West and not the "effete East";[20] a youthful, healthy, quick-witted vagabond who eschewed the trappings of urban society to live on its fringes and embrace the frontier's fading glimmers.

The Hobo as Frontiersman

The hobo's connection with the frontier was no accident, and explains much of the culture's potent allure through the Second World War. By the time London's essays first appeared in the pages of *Cosmopolitan* the frontier was closed but, thanks to Frederick Jackson Turner, the myth of the frontier was stronger than ever. In a lecture delivered at the 1893 American Historical Association's meeting held in conjunction with the Chicago Exposition and World's Fair, Turner postulated his "frontier thesis": that the frontier was key to America's cultural identity and had bred democracy, the independence of owning property, and individualism. But the 1890 census showed that the unbroken line of uncivilized territory that stretched from Canada to Mexico and marked "the frontier" had disappeared, so, as he later wrote, "four centuries from the discovery of America, at the end of a hundred years of life under the Constitution, the frontier has gone, and with its going has closed the first period of American history."[21] According to Turner, Americans needed the safety valve the West offered to provide for men who lacked property. This longing for the idealized frontier appears in the period's clamor for Frederic Remington paintings and Owen Wister writings, the popular appeal of Theodore Roosevelt's public image, and the intrigue that surrounded the hobo.[22] London's *The Road* appealed to an America afraid that the frontier's passing and the escalation of creature comforts had made the nation soft.

Tramping with Tramps and *The Road* combined with other pieces of popular journalism to encourage men to explore the frontier as a hobo. Following Flynt's and London's lead, writers in the 1910s and 1920s produced a rash of books, both narrative and poetic, about the glories and trials of hobo life: W. H. Davies's *The Autobiography of a Super Tramp* (1908); Vachel Lindsay's *Rhymes to be Traded for Bread* (1912), *The Tramp's Excuse and Other Poems* (1912), and *A Handy Guide for Beggars: Especially Those of the Poetic Fraternity* (1916); and Harvey Kemp's *The Cry of Youth* (1914) and *Tramping on Life* (1922). These writings, among others, helped solidify one facet of the modern view of the hobo: that of the freedom-loving frontiersman. But the other part of the hobo image that was most prominent in the 1920s, and that equally drew Harry Partch—that of the hobo as a critique of modernization and industrial society—traces its roots elsewhere.

William Dean Howells's *A Hazard of New Fortunes* (1890) used tramps to underscore his problems with the growing gap between the captains of industry and their galley slaves, but not until the Industrial Workers of the World (IWW), or the Wobblies as they were popularly known, appeared on the scene were hoboes regularly used by those wishing to critique modern industrial society.[23] Although the IWW began in 1905 as a coalition of disparate labor organizers who hoped to create a new union to replace the American Federation of Labor, it quickly schismed and disintegrated into a strictly Western labor union. Eager to find recruits, the IWW focused on the hobo as its core and began actively courting members of that culture. In the hobo, the IWW saw a potential force for political action, a force that had been ineffectively harnessed in 1894 during the failed Coxey's Army march. As Melvyn Dubofsky wrote in his history of the IWW *We Shall Be All*: "Few workers in America were better adapted to the doctrines and tactics of the IWW than the migrants who followed the harvest on the West Coast, from the fruit and hops fields of Washington and Oregon to the ranches of California's San Joaquin, Central, and Imperial Valleys. No workers were more mistreated by their employers, and none so lacked the elementary amenities of a decent life: a home, a family, and an adequate diet."[24] The IWW was only fully active, striking and working for migratory laborers, between 1909 and 1914; for most of its existence it functioned primarily as a hobo social club. But although the IWW left little impact on American unions (it failed to create the "One Big Union" it desired) or American industry (by World War I, its strikes were quickly shut down as un-American), it had a disproportionately large impact on American culture. The Wobblies were able to cast a large shadow, fooling both their membership and the American public into overestimating their power.[25] Their propaganda, in the form of literature, cartoons, and especially songs, created a myth of the hobo that still resonates a hundred years later.

In the view of the IWW, the hobo was a product of Social Darwinism's natural selection and Turner's frontier thesis. He was a revolutionary figure who went West, removed the confines of the East Coast's bourgeois society, broke free of domestic bondage, and became a true man and a true American, forging the nation anew in spite of the industrialization for which he worked but did not serve. The Wobblies helped formulate the myth that hoboes had single-handedly built and sustained the West, and that the West, once established, had subsequently turned its back on that labor. For the IWW, the hobo became the true proletarian. For the rest of America, he became a symbol of the masculine romance of the road and, divested of the radical aspects of Wobbly folklore as the IWW faded away, a figure safe for popular consumption.[26]

The Hobo as Individualist

By the 1920s, Americans firmly embraced the view of the hobo as the last frontiersman, at a time when the frontier was closing, and as a man who, notwithstanding his conquest of the frontier, had been cast off by an urban-industrial world. Gone were images of beady-eyed criminals wandering the countryside living by avarice and malice. In their place was a man surviving in spite of a system that shunned him. As the United States entered a period of prosperity for many in that decade, and shifted even further from an agrarian to an industrial society, hoboes came to be admired as among the last American individualists. Nels Anderson's defining study *The Hobo: The Sociology of the Homeless Man* clearly delineates this new view. One of the first works to come out of the Chicago School of Sociology, Anderson's book grew out of firsthand information. He lived as a hobo, following the various harvests until he gained acceptance into the University of Chicago's graduate school. Then, at his adviser's urging, he turned to his personal experience as the cornerstone of his graduate work. While his thesis and the resulting book focused on Chicago's "main stem," which he nicknamed "hobohemia," it also took on the mass of workers roaming the countryside. Anderson laid blame for the hobo's situation firmly at the feet of society, attempting to eradicate once and for all the notion that men hoboed from a defect in personality or human nature. But he also emphasized the rebellious nature of many hoboes, as they rejected the monotony of industrial work, the strictures of small-town life, and the prevailing definitions of what constituted the good life. In Anderson's view, hobo life was hard but at least men lived it on their own terms.

Anderson's conception of the hobo as a rugged individualist held great appeal for 1920s Americans, and his study received a great amount of academic and public attention when it was published.[27] *The Hobo* was a popular success for reasons beyond the diminishing echoes of Turner's frontier thesis. Part of its success, and the subsequent transformation of the hobo's image in that decade, rests on a strain of antimodernism that began sweeping the public at large, and artists in particular. Upper and middle class Americans began to feel that modern culture watered down life and had replaced uniqueness with mass conformity and consumption. They began to believe that material and spiritual progress were less tightly sewn together than previously thought. In this view, modernism's march of progress excluded authenticity, or at least layered it with enough consumer trappings to render it unrecognizable and sap its power. In response, many began to seek "authentic" alternatives to modernism, as they called standard cultural authorities into question. Antimodernists turned from the assembly line to medieval craftsmanship, they ignored religious ritual in favor of religious ecstasy, they rejected urban life for rustic existence, and they replaced institutionalized systems with pure experience.[28] In this view, it is easy to see how antimodern sentiments drew men and women to the perception of the hobo's earthy spontaneity.

The Hobo as Bohemian

Among artists, antimodernism led first to an examination of American culture for those artists, writers, and intellectuals who personified authentic American life and ultimately to a revival of Walt Whitman.[29] They quickly focused on Whitman's "Song of the Open Road"—in which the poet issued a challenge to middle class values by extolling the open road as "the idealized model of American democratic culture"—as the key to regaining features of American life that were fast slipping away. That poem in particular, along with many others of Whitman's, came to be seen as the progenitor of the American vagabond in life and letters because he so clearly called for a transformation of—indeed, an assault on—the materialism, class-consciousness, and artistic conservatism that held sway.[30]

One major 1920s literary figure to take up Whitman's mantle was John Dos Passos, and to Dos Passos, the hobo above all others represented Whitman's America.[31] Although he treated the hobo figure in his books *Streets of Night* and *Manhattan Transfer*, it was in the *U.S.A.* trilogy of *The 42nd Parallel*, *Nineteen Nineteen*, and *The Big Money* that the hobo spoke the clearest, and his voice was "the speech of the people."[32] The *U.S.A.* trilogy was Dos Passos's attempt to trace the nation's political fortunes over the course of the first three decades of the twentieth century, fortunes he saw decaying because of industrial interests. Hoboes made the perfect foil for industry because they deliberately existed outside factory life and could therefore speak the truth.

The first character in *The 42nd Parallel* is Fenian O'Hara McCreary, better known by the hobo name he takes on, "Mac." Through Mac, Dos

Passos demonstrates how hoboes can gain individual freedom outside society's bounds.[33] Mac first begins hoboing because his family collapses: his mother and father die and his uncle descends into drink. Mac supports himself as a politically active hobo until getting married, but that social institution robs him of his freedom and individuality, and when the marriage ends, he feels relief. He returns to the road and to political activism, eventually settling down as a bookstore owner. Significantly, Mac then disappears from the narrative, the only major character in *The 42nd Parallel* who does not appear elsewhere in the trilogy.

The world changed radically in the late 1910s and early 1920s and, as Dos Passos's epic moved into those years, he did not see a place for the hobo any longer. He had used Mac to show how life could be, and perhaps should be, lived—as a free, politically active, unique character. But he knew that the world did not treat that kind of person kindly and so conceded that his Romantic figure of rugged individualism could be, and often was, crushed by modernity's encroaching wave.

Dos Passos made the hobo not only a figure of hardship, but also one of American adventure.[34] However, at the same time, the hobo's connection with the IWW and his burgeoning role in the period's arts helped form him into a bohemian, a symbol of uprooted intellectual freedom and leftist thinking. Nels Anderson solidified the connection between the hobo and socialist (and later communist) radicalism and artistic experimentation, with his designation of hobo culture as "hobohemia." Anderson's appropriation and alteration of bohemia snapped together the two formerly disparate ideas of the hobo and artistic experimentation with a bond that intensified as the decade wore on. This impression, directly tied to the Whitman tradition of true American democracy, helps explain why the hobo attracted authors such as Dos Passos. They could portray themselves as inheritors of the hobo's bohemian rebellion and draw strength and inspiration from that notion.[35] While a small point during the 1920s, in subsequent decades, becoming a hobo and using those experiences in creative work gave one a clear artistic veneer of starting art from scratch and rebelling against contemporary standards. It was a veneer that Harry Partch ultimately used to his advantage, as did later writers like Jack Kerouac.

The Hobo as Nostalgic Icon

So the hobo became a rugged individual, the last frontiersman in a land without a frontier, and a Whitmanesque symbol of American democracy living a leftist artistic bohemian life. But there is one more layer that accrued to the hobo persona in the 1920s. Although by that time the sheen of criminality had been wiped from the hobo, the old undercurrents denominating him a lazy dreamer still remained. On the cover of the *Saturday Evening Post*'s October 18, 1924, edition, Norman Rockwell painted a third component of hobo perception in the 1920s, one not as powerful in the early 1940s when Partch took on the hobo, but that perhaps resonates the strongest in the public mind today. An older man sits roasting two sausages over a small fire in a tin can, while from between his legs a dog strains toward the meat. The hobo's clothes are too big, threadbare, and obviously cobbled together, and his bindle and pocket knife rest next to his feet. His eyebrows are lifted and his forehead wrinkled, as though lost in great thought, while his posture signals a man with no cares, no worries, nowhere to go. He is lazy and a dreamer, but not threatening; no trace of malice or danger keeps him from being a man completely comfortable with himself and everyone else. The painting represents the character most Americans see now when they conjure the hobo. Rockwell's depictions of American life resonate so deeply with the strain of nostalgia that runs through the collective American psyche that much of the bohemian and socialist traces have been all but squeezed out. The hobo is, in some minds, harmless.

Although admittedly powerful, Rockwell's painting alone did not freeze the bindle-carrying, bowler-hat-wearing hobo in the American consciousness; stage and screen ably aided this. But what is most fascinating about cinematic representations of the hobo is how they play to all competing hobo images at once. Perhaps nowhere is the dichotomy between the hobo as victim of society and self-assured frontiersman stronger, the transformation of tramp into hobo, from dangerous drifter to individual striving against industrialization and modernization, clearer than in Charlie Chaplin's "Little Tramp" character. Chaplin offered many explanations for the Little Tramp's origins, but apparently he created the outfit spontaneously for *Mabel's Strange Predicament* and based the character's mannerisms on real people. The walk, for example, came from an elderly coachman named "Rummy" Binks, who tended horses at The Queen's Head pub.[36] Chaplin also maintained that elements of the Little Tramp persona emerged from a conversation with a homeless man in San Francisco. Entranced by the man's story (hoboes have always been noted for natural storytelling ability, honed through years attempting to beguile people out of food) and realizing the complexity such a character could bring to the screen, Chaplin crafted elements of his alter-ego around this encounter. Whether or not Chaplin's (or the hobo's) tale was true, he created one of film's first lasting characters.

When he first appeared on the screen in 1914, the Little Tramp was not the everyman character found in *The Kid*, *Modern Times*, or *City Lights*, who was pushed about by the caprices of fate. He primarily popped up in short films as a frankly vulgar and bawdy slapstick character. He was a clown figure, playing to the audience (which even at this point was mixed in class and ethnicity) and its basest sensibilities, making them laugh by any means necessary.[37] This comedic tramp had roots plunged deep into history before Chaplin transferred him to celluloid. By the end of the nineteenth century, the tramp was one of the most popular figures on the Vaudeville circuit, especially as played by Nat Wills (the "Happy Tramp") and Billy McDermot (the "Last of Coxey's Army"). These figures were essentially cartoons come to life, men who had no wish to alter their station in life and so were portrayed with a happy-go-lucky attitude, no matter what ill befell them. They dressed in oversized clothes full of patches and often smoked large cigars. They played jokes on other characters on the stage. They danced, they cycled, they performed pantomime and slapstick, and they even juggled. Their songs showed them to be doing the best they could in bad situations, such as in "Happy Hooligan" where the titular character is described as a man "who means to do good, but is misunderstood. / He must have been born on a Friday! / Though chuck full of pluck he plays on hard luck; / His face and his clothes are untidy."[38] This was the character upon whom Rockwell based his painting and Chaplin his Tramp. But although an outlandish character, the comic tramp played an important role off stage as well as on. When he first appeared in the late 1800s, the American public still equated the tramp with criminality and sedition. Seeing a tramp played for laughs and depicted as victim certainly discomfited early audiences. Here was a man whom they believed to be anything but benign, and yet by laughing at him they felt sympathy for him. The comic tramp was a necessary step in helping audiences move past seeing the tramp as a criminal toward viewing him as a welcome figure and ultimately as an iconoclastic rebel. It aided the shift from tramp to hobo.[39]

Chaplin's early films played off this character beautifully, but as the nation's economy turned down, harsher elements crept in. He was a bit of a thief, and the films abound in stylized violence. Early reviews of the shorts praised the laughs they generated but castigated their baser aspects as "disgusting."[40] The tenor of the nation, and of the character, had changed by 1921, when the Little Tramp made his feature film debut in *The Kid*. Vestiges of the comic tramp remained in the Little Tramp's outfit and

Chaplin's impeccable comedic and physical timing, but in settings and activities he was transforming into the 1920s hobo. By *The Gold Rush* (1925), the Little Tramp had become a frontiersman, bravely pioneering in the Klondike for personal gain, and by *Modern Times* (1936) he was a leftist agitator, symbol of all that was wrong with modern industrial society. With that film, Chaplin could have renamed his character the "Little Hobo," as he ably used his creation to criticize the loss of individuality and devaluing of personality that comes with increasing mechanization and monotonous factory work, as well as the dead-end social position of the poor. *Modern Times* even ends with the Tramp and the Orphan Girl, played by Paulette Goddard, walking down the street toward nothing but the rising sun, the open road calling them to a more secure and hopeful future.

Singing the Hobo Life

Chaplin's efforts in film, Norman Rockwell's in painting, and London's and Dos Passos's in writing were not the only popularly consumed products that shifted public perception of the hobo. The final artistic piece to the puzzle of the hobo image can be found in music, as songs lifted from the jungles found their way into parlors and Vaudeville circuits. Songs like "Big Rock Candy Mountain," "*The Wabash Cannonball*," and "Hallelujah, I'm a Bum" moved into popular culture and caused Americans to rethink the criminality commonly ascribed to hoboes.[41] These songs assumed a curious position in American culture. Many were altered or at least cleaned up, as in the removal of verses pertaining to pedophilia in "Big Rock Candy Mountain" or to hoboing altogether in "*The Wabash Cannonball*," where the phrase "she's the 'boes' accommodation" became "she's a regular combination."[42] Often the mythology surrounding the song was cast off as well: *The Wabash Cannonball*, originally a perfect, ghostly train that would take a hobo anywhere, became little more than a powerful and fast locomotive. Once these songs had shed their uniquely hobo elements and reemerged with a new skin, the culture quickly acclaimed and adopted them. In fact, "Hallelujah, I'm a Bum" became so popular that many churches reported being unable to use the hymn "Revive Us Again"—whose melody was co-opted into the basis of the hobo song—in services.

No singer was more important or influential in both the development of country and western music and the acceptance of hobo songs into that genre than Jimmie Rodgers. Rodgers actively cultivated the image of a railroader throughout his career (even adopting the nickname "Singing

Brakeman" early on), and although he recorded for only six years before dying in 1933, his legacy cast a long shadow on the genre he helped popularize.[43] Rodgers's recordings of hobo songs were distinctive because he did not whitewash their origins. Two of his more popular hobo songs, "Hobo's Meditation" and "Hobo Bill's Last Ride," proudly wear their ancestry in their titles and use unadorned sentimentality to draw listeners into sympathy with and for the hobo. "Hobo Bill's Last Ride," while featuring Rodgers's distinctive yodel, ends with the lines "It was early in the morning when they raised the hobo's head, / The smile still lingered on his face, but Hobo Bill was dead; / There was no mother's longing to soothe his weary soul, / For he was just a railroad bum who died out in the cold."[44] By naming the character "Hobo Bill" and then ending the song by calling him a "bum," Rodgers placed the blame for his cold, lonely death on the conscience of a nation that still occasionally labeled hoboes good-for-nothing vagrants and looked the other way when they cried for aid. Songs like Rodgers's and others that wove their way into the American popular cultural fabric helped create a folkloric hero out of the hobo.

All of these images, from Jack London's adventurous frontiersman to Nels Anderson's bohemian and from Chaplin's comedically triumphant Tramp to Rodgers's creator of American musical culture, swirled around Harry Partch's decision in the early 1940s to portray himself as a hobo and to use his experiences to craft hobo compositions. From today's perspective, it may seem strange that Partch would adopt a figure we equate with Norman Rockwell's painting. Why would any composer attempting to secure support and acceptance in musical society clothe himself in a garment that said frankly "I don't belong here?" But, thanks to the tenor of a country emerging from the Great Depression; a people in thrall to the documentary imagination of Lange and Steinbeck; and an impression of the hobo as a rugged, American, bohemian, Whitmanesque individual, that question would never have occurred to Partch's first audiences. Partch adopted the hobo image because American culture of the time allowed him to do so. It offered a shorthand description of the type of musician he was becoming, and gave his music an allure it might otherwise have lacked.

CHAPTER FIVE

U . S . H I G H B A L L

Becoming a Musical Hobo

*B*arstow clearly placed Partch on a new compositional path, but two final years of homeless wandering passed before he began to travel it. When he did return to the hobo in his music, he crafted a composition that became the cornerstone of his passage from the hobo jungles to the periphery of the American musical culture that he so scorned. That piece, based like *Barstow* on scribbled passages from a pocket notebook that reveled in hobo voices, was substantively different from the hitchhiker-inscribed work. These scribbled passages were words spoken by and to the composer, and the hobo voices were his own as often as those of others. *U.S. Highball* recounted Partch's own hobo journey and as such was a distinctly personal work, casting his triumphs and tragedies out for the world to share. Ultimately *U.S. Highball* became the work through which he demonstrated his version of a conceptually exotic American musical sound, and first argued for a renaissance of ancient musical practices in a modern language. It is such a pivotal work in Partch's output that it also acts as this study's cornerstone, the work through which Partch's full engagement with the hobo is most clearly defined.

U.S. Highball's reception throughout its lifespan clearly reflects Partch's success in communicating his adventure. Most who heard the composer sing the work to the accompaniment of his Adapted Guitar in the early 1940s eagerly embraced it, and it remained a staple of Partch's ensemble performances in the 1950s and 1960s. Even forty years after its creation *U.S. Highball* retained its power, reducing men who hoboed during the Depression to tears: after a staged performance in the late 1970s, a man who claimed to have been a hobo in the 1930s approached conductor Danlee Mitchell and calmly explained, with tears in his eyes, that the piece made him reexperience the sights, sounds, and even smells of that almost-forgotten lifestyle.[1]

The enthralling power of *U.S. Highball* comes from a unique intersection of Harry Partch's life and art.[2] The work seems to spring directly from Partch's daily existence as a hobo; certainly, throughout the rest of his life, Partch never used personal experiences so explicitly as the basis of composition. Understanding the work requires us to begin with the transcontinental train trip Partch made late in 1941. We have to discover how he lived as a hobo and if his movements, his tricks for riding both the rails and the road, and his recorded sights and sounds align with the experiences of other hoboes. Yet only fragments of the journey remain to reconstruct this period: hopping freight trains and hitchhiking do not lend themselves to a trail of documentary evidence. Instead, Partch left behind his own accounts, in the form of two articles written in 1943 and 1957, and jottings in the notebook he carried on his journey.

Catching a Highball to Chicago

In the summer of 1941, soon after completing *Barstow* and while still living in Carmel, California, Partch met a young divinity student visiting the Pacific Coast. They struck up a conversation, and he began to explain his ideas of Monophony, that all music and musical materials are an expansion from one pitch. The student expressed interest, so Partch took him back to his cabin to show him the recently finished instruments. Although the acquaintance lasted only a day, the student was evidently impressed by Partch's ideas and designs—so impressed that he mentioned the encounter to a friend in Chicago. Two weeks later, the Chicago friend, who Partch was sure must have been both a musician and a religious man, wrote inviting him to come to Chicago, ply his musical ideas, and live there until he could become established, ending his letter "May God's richest blessings be upon you." Partch later wrote that "if one wonders why God's richest blessings should direct one to Chicago, the answer is that after several years of pioneering in California and the West came to no good end—in fact no end at all—the mere suggestion of some good end in the East, or anywhere else, represented God's richest blessings indeed, even though the idea of coming from California to pioneer in Chicago is certainly a reversal of usual form."[3] Weary of life

Figure 5.1. Harry Partch on top of a boxcar, riding as a hobo. The date and the photographer are unknown, but even though he is wearing a cap similar to one in which he was pictured in 1919, he appears to be in his thirties, placing this photograph in the 1930s. Courtesy of the Harry Partch Estate Archive, San Diego.

in California, he took the ferry to San Francisco and jumped a train on September 17, 1941, with $3.29 in his pocket (see fig. 5.1).[4]

On the second day of his trip, Partch began writing on a pad that he always carried for notes, dates, and addresses, transcribing "fragments of conversations, remarks, writings on the sides of boxcars, signs in havens for derelicts, hitchhikers' inscriptions, names of stations, thoughts."[5] Although he later said that this act of committing to paper small bits of conversation was not a conscious effort on his part to create a text for a composition, it became the first act of composition for *U.S. Highball*. After his experience with *Barstow*, Partch surely knew the possibility for composition that rested in his journaling and that his notebook could easily become a font of ideas. Indeed, by recording only "those remarks, signs, and inscriptions which made him laugh, think, or merely startled him," Partch was already composing, using only the sounds that exhibited promise for later use.[6]

Starting out on the trip, Partch attempted to hitchhike. He had ridden the rails many times over his previous twelve years of hoboing and knew that jumping trains and riding in an open gondola coated one with soot and grit. The police knew this as well and counted on the tell-tale grime to aid in their train-yard roundups of derelicts. For this reason, most hoboes avoided the yards and were extremely conscientious about cleanliness, regarding dirt as an enemy. One hobo recalled, "I hitchhiked down there in order to stay as clean as I could, and you sure can't stay clean when you are riding trains."[7] Unfortunately, Partch had little luck on the highway and was forced to travel by train. A few days into the trip, in Green River, Wyoming, the oil tank car he was riding left without him, and he was stranded, dirty and broke. Dispirited, he wandered to the nearby town of Little America. There he was able to get a job as a dishwasher and spent a week saving money, resting, and cleaning away the dirt of travel.[8] Clean and fed, he was able to convince people to give him rides, and he traveled on through Wyoming, Nebraska, Iowa, and Illinois primarily by car. He arrived in Chicago early in the morning of October 1, 1941.

Although Partch's transcontinental trip may appear extraordinary from an outsider's perspective, in fact this sort of journey was not uncommon in the hobo community. Hobo writer Charles Fox habitually followed the same path from California to Chicago during the Depression,[9] and Graydon Horath, a hobo who corresponded frequently about life in hobo jungles, recollected a similar trip made just four years prior to Partch's.[10] Horath was a twenty-year-old Illinois native working in Oregon and California in 1937. In November of that year, with the harvests finished and winter approaching, he decided to travel home. He left Portland on a Saturday morning, catching a ride with a traveling salesman and arriving in Maryville, California, the next day. To travel east from California to Illinois, Horath was forced to jump a train: that evening he climbed in a gondola and headed over the Sierra Nevadas, listening to a fellow hobo regale travelers with a rendition of "Red Sails in the Sunset." Following a freezing night, he rolled into Salt Lake City, a major Rocky Mountain division point.

Here Horath's path crossed the one Partch would take a few years later. Horath had to switch trains and probably climbed aboard the Denver & Rio Grande Western, the same D&RG Partch mentioned in *U.S. Highball* and ostensibly took. Unlike Partch, Horath did not get left behind and stuck in Green River or Little America, Wyoming; rather, he sailed right through the Rockies, sharing the feeling of relief experienced by the hoboes in *U.S. Highball* in crossing the mountain range. He commented that "I felt I was now at the big hurdle, the Rockies; if I could jump them, I should be able to coast in home."[11] Horath remained on the D&RG through Colorado, disembarking at the Kansas border to continue due east to southern Illinois. Although he attempted to hitchhike several times across the Great Plains, he was covered in coal dust and grime and unable to secure a ride. Partch's interlude in Little America may have been frustrating, but it allowed time to make himself presentable enough to hitchhike into Chicago, a luxury Horath did not enjoy. Horath arrived home a week and a day after departing the west coast, besting Partch's two weeks only because he did not stop along the way.

Graydon Horath's memoir confirms many aspects of Partch's account. Riding through the mountains in an open car, Horath saw the fires of hobo camps and during stops would dash to one to get warm before the train started out again. Partch recounted the same memory from the other side in *U.S. Highball*: "We'll build a fire so when the next drag stops all the 'bos'll come runnin' over to get warm. Then we'll know where there's a [sic] empty." Hoboes would often jump off at divisions as the trains stopped long enough to restock with fuel and water, run around to get their blood circulating, and then climb back on as the train left. Trying to avoid frostbite (or even freezing) crossing the Rockies was a common and ever-present concern. In *U.S. Highball*, the protagonist Mac is asked "Is that blanket big enough for two?" Horath recalls dropping into an empty refrigerator car with another hobo and huddling together under two jackets, one for their upper body and the other around their feet. Yet even with these hardships, both accounts resonate with the joy and freedom of travel and overcoming the odds. There are tough times behind and ahead, but during the journey, life is an adventure.

Like *U.S. Highball*, not all accounts extolled the fun and excitement of making a transcontinental hobo trip. In 1936 Erling Kildahl, a nineteen-year-old living in Idaho, needed to travel to Jamestown College in North Dakota. Riding the rails on the Northern Pacific with his brother Harold and later recording the trip, Kildahl's account mainly concerns the harshness of life on the road.[12] He writes about the pain of squeezing his body into awkwardly-shaped compartments and the mind-numbing monotony of watching the countryside slip by through a crack in a boxcar door. The police apprehended him and his brother, and he almost lost his leg to the train wheels with a poorly-timed lunge. He spent the journey's final 150 miles grasping a rung on top of a boxcar, hurtling through a night that bombarded him with rain mixed with soot and smoke. Every moment was torture, and they ended the trip bruised, stiff, and covered with grime. Kildahl swore never to undertake such a journey again.

On the Road to Composition

Whatever his physical and emotional condition after the two-week trip, and whatever his immediate feelings concerning the ordeal, Partch likewise never attempted another transcontinental trek. Instead, he channeled the trip's discomfort and exaltation into his work, later writing to Henry Allen Moe that "a new period of creative or compositional work is opening up for me, of which *Barstow* is the beginning."[13] On February 14, 1943, he sat down and began composing *U.S. Highball*, completing version A for voice and Adapted Guitar, both notated in ratios, in only five weeks. He began revising the work a few weeks later, on May 1, expanding the instrumentation to include his new Chromelodeon (an adapted foot-pump reed organ, retuned to Partch's microtonal scale; see glossary) and Kithara. He wrote this second version (version B) in a combination of his own system of notation and pitch ratios, and completed it on October 1. The revision ended one of Partch's most productive compositional periods, one that saw the completion of most of the works of *The Wayward* as well as revisions of several other compositions.

Although he continued to tinker with orchestration, voicing, and structure over the following year, after a May 1944 concert at Columbia University Partch did little work on *U.S. Highball*. In April 1945, he added a second singing voice to the intoning voice already present, and a part for the Double Canon, later known as the Surrogate Kithara.[14] Eleven months later he completed a recording of the work, but after hearing it decided that he needed percussion instruments for his musical language to evolve further.[15] Almost ten years later, in 1955, after having expanded his arsenal of instruments, Partch returned one last time to *U.S. Highball*. This revision, version C, remains the most commonly performed and recorded of the work's three incarnations. He removed the Adapted Guitar, rescoring its part for the Kithara and Surrogate Kithara, and added the Diamond Marimba, Bass Marimba, Cloud-Chamber Bowls, Spoils of War, and newly-designed Boo (Bamboo Marimba).[16] All percussion instruments (described in the glossary), they broadened its timbral palette rather than adding rhythmic vitality to the work (an element that was already present and necessary to its success), creating what Partch felt was his final musical statement.

Although 1955 marked his last musical revisions, Partch continued to reenvision the work's origins and meanings and to promote it in ways incongruent with the actual circumstances of composition. More misconceptions surround this work than any other of his hobo-inspired compositions, and most of these originate with Partch himself. The two articles that outline the inspiration, form, and intent of *U.S. Highball* contain the kernels of misdirection; chronologically at least, they neatly bookend the three revisions. The first article was attached to a copy of the libretto sent to Otto Luening in July of 1943 at Luening's request, while Partch was completing version B. Partch wrote the second article in July 1957, as the preface to the script for a filmed version of the work he planned with filmmaker Madeline Tourtelot. As these two articles are the only statements Partch issued during his lifetime about the work, they have been the starting point of all subsequent research about *U.S. Highball*. (While the expanded second edition of *Genesis of a Music*, published in 1974, does contain a short description of the work in chapter 14, the text appears to have been drawn exclusively from the 1957 film script.)

Throughout the articles, Partch deliberately fostered conceptions about the work that eventually coalesced into legend. The most romantic—and therefore most pervasive—of these conceptions concerns the purity of its text. Partch firmly asserted that he collected every word found in the libretto, and consequently in the score, from a hobo's lips, or at least during the journey from California to Chicago: "In effect, the text of *U.S. Highball* consists of *some* of the words that assailed Slim's consciousness on this trip, in exactly the order they assailed, and not a single word is introduced which did not actually assail."[17] In the 1957 film script he reiterated the text's purity, adding, "I really didn't do any editing, as such."[18] This level of purity is possible, but also highly improbable. In *Barstow*, the inscriptions closely resemble the way Partch originally took them off the railing, but he did edit them slightly and said as much.[19] If he was willing to admit to altering hitchhiker inscriptions in *Barstow*, why the hesitation with *U.S. Highball*? Most likely, he recognized that the work needed a sheen of veracity if he was claiming it as a true account of a personal experience.

Along with asserting the text's authenticity, Partch felt it necessary to explain why he recorded conversations and other fragments of lore in the first place. Even though he faithfully and completely recorded the hobo voices along the road and then used only those fragments from the notebook in composing the work, Partch claimed that while on the trip, and even during the following year in Chicago, he never fully understood why he had been compelled to take notes: "I did not know when I wrote them down that this is what they would become. But during the next year and a half, I would run across the little notebook and wonder exactly why I had gone to all this trouble."[20] As though a man possessed, he precisely recorded his environment while not cognizant of the rationale behind the act.

Again, this statement could be true, but it is more likely an exaggeration: as noted above, Partch had used statements scrawled in his notebook to compose *Barstow* after letting the inscriptions sit for over a year, so he surely knew the possibility for composition dormant in his jottings. Partch fostered this misconception to ensure that audiences heard *U.S. Highball* as a work of directly personal inspiration. In order for the work to be both personal and inspired, Partch could not admit to textual additions in later revisions, especially if those additions were out of the order preserved in the notebook or from another source. So Partch began covering over that problem in his preface to version C, the work's third and final version. He noted that the revision "omits the Adapted Guitar, and cuts the total length considerably. Otherwise there are few changes."[21] Those few changes were alterations to the text as well as the music, but by phrasing it with "otherwise" after the mention of new instruments, Partch insinuated, and led others to believe, that no textual additions were made and that the last revision did not substantively alter the composition, even though it was significantly shorter than earlier versions.

Most scholars have taken Partch at his word. There has been little question of whether or not the phrases attributed to hoboes were part of the culture's vernacular; no one has questioned Partch's claim of not knowing why he bothered to write down hobo speech, even after the publication and dissemination of *Barstow* and his comments on its genesis. But comparing his statements with historical data on hoboes, extant notes, and scores produces an altered notion of *U.S. Highball*, one that questions the candor of his claims, redefines Partch's compositional practices, and re-dates the creative process of the work's composition.

Memoirs of hoboing throughout the twentieth century's first forty years hold several recurring elements and episodes in common with *U.S. Highball*'s libretto.[22] Most accounts are episodic, a series of short stories and images strung together without a supporting coherent narrative. All include, in some fashion, a tale of decking a fast train, of holding down a hard train, of riding through a rough spot, and of an unusual and wise person who taught the author something about riding the rails. They tell of death or injury after someone rode freight the wrong way, of nature's beauties only visible from atop a boxcar, of run-ins with the law in the form of railroad "bulls," and of skills at begging food. These are all features found in Flynt's *Tramping with Tramps*, London's *The Road*, and the multitudinous hobo tales published in the late 1910s and 1920s, and they all appear in some form in *U.S. Highball*.

Likewise, many of the small, specific details found in *U.S. Highball*'s libretto ring true with other hobo accounts. Each version of the libretto includes the inscription "That Cheyenne, huh. That used to be a bad town, but not any more, so much. They used to have a school there for railroad bulls. But the school's moved to Denver." Cheyenne, Wyoming, was notorious among hoboes in the early twentieth century and myths grew up around the chief bull there, Jeff Carr. Carr was a physically imposing man who sported a long black mustache that twirled around his mouth and wore pistols strapped to his waist. According to legend, Carr rode a large white horse alongside the train, grinning and cackling as he tried to knock hoboes off with a two-foot-long hickory club. Dislodged hoboes would fall and the train's moving wheels would slice them in half. If Carr could not reach a hobo with his club, he was also known to shoot them off the top of boxcars. Although he died in 1925, killed by a gang of vagrants, his memory lived on, striking fear in the hearts of most hoboes. Carr's specter, combined with the bull school that supplied over twenty railroad bulls for duty at all times in the Cheyenne railyards, kept hoboes out of the city for most of the Depression.[23]

The admonition Partch received that "if you wanta stay in one piece sleep on the back end of the oil tank, buddy," would have been a common remark from a seasoned 'bo to a prushin, a young, inexperienced hobo. Getting on a moving train was a learned skill, but an extremely dangerous one to acquire. In order to maintain balance so as to not fall between the moving cars, a hobo would always embark a train on the car's front end.

If he lost his balance, the train's momentum would slam him back into the car he was boarding instead of dislodging him between cars.[24] Then, in order to avoid being crushed by the cargo in oil tankers, refrigerator cars, and gondolas when traversing a steep decline, adept hoboes would move to ride toward the back. This is the exact manner in which London recounted jumping on and off the train in "Holding Her Down," as he narrowly avoided falling off on several occasions.[25]

Throughout the libretto, numerous inscriptions complain of jerks on the trains. These complaints are heard on three separate occasions, more references than to any subject except Chicago, and range from "There she jerks again! That engineer don't know how to drive this train," to "There she jerks again! I can stand everything but them jerks. They make me nervous." The jerks were constantly in a hobo's thoughts and dreams, as mention of them appears in every hobo recollection. Jerks were sudden movements when the train changed speed. The farther from the engine a hobo rode, the more powerful the jerks. More often than not, jerks were nothing more than a nuisance, but they could become deadly. Hoboes sometimes chose to ride in precarious positions, either on top of a car or in the baggage blind. A false move could send them flying off the train and occasionally under the wheels. A strong jerk could snap the neck of a hobo sleeping peacefully in a boxcar, or signal to him that the train was slowing to a halt and that bulls would soon be coming.[26] The unexpected nature of jerks kept hoboes on edge and rightfully nervous.

Even Partch's use of the name "Mac" for his protagonist squares with the historical record. Hoboes commonly took on and gave each other nicknames, or monikers, in hobo parlance. From the text of the first draft libretto, we learn that Partch's moniker was "Slim." He changed the protagonist's name to Mac for the later versions, an appropriately generic and common name. It appears in numerous sources, including a slice-of-life article written by a hobo for the *New Republic*, in which the author refers to his traveling companion as Mac.[27] Perhaps most prominently, especially at the time, Mac was the hobo name of Fenian O'Hara McCreary, John Dos Passos's protagonist for the first novel of his *U.S.A.* trilogy, *The 42nd Parallel*. Although the name's alteration was logical and culturally accurate, it was a departure from Partch's stated conception of the text's purity. It appeared as he began to move audience expectations of the work from the particular to the general, from "my journey" to "the journey," from narrative to myth.

U.S. Highball's Textual Evolution

The historical context surrounding *U.S. Highball* has immediate bearing on the music itself, especially in light of the misconceptions Partch propagated. Their truthfulness—or lack thereof—necessarily informs understanding of the work and its reception. By returning to the beginning and tracing the various incarnations of *U.S. Highball*, from notebook to version C, and highlighting those facets that relate directly to the misconceptions, we will see not only how closely Partch's statements resemble documentary sources, but also how deeply the work's musical genesis reflects his unwavering emphasis on the power and expressiveness of a single human voice, and how much it depends on hobo culture, both as experienced and constructed, for its meaning and power.

Opening Partch's palm-sized brown notebook, you cannot help but be immediately struck by the amount of scribbling and scratching on every page.[28] Place names, station calls, and phrases were systematically recorded and then crossed out. If the scratched-out jottings are compared with later draft librettos, the impetus behind the seemingly maniacal crossing out becomes clear: as Partch used phrases and town names, he marked through them in order to ensure that he did not reuse them.

While the notebook's first twenty pages contain inscriptions from the two-week journey, the majority of the inscriptions used were presumably recorded before Little America, where Partch was stranded for a week "pot-wallopin'" (hobo slang for washing dishes). The main evidence for this assumption appears on page 9 of the notebook, which shows the inscription "U.S. Highball: Musical Account of a Hitchhiker—Freight Train—Bus trip from Sacramento to Chicago" (see fig. 5.2). This title occurs amidst other inscriptions that appear in the "Little America, Wyoming" section of the libretto. On the reverse side of this page is a listing of every major city through which Partch had already traveled, beginning with Monterey and Sacramento, California, and ending with Green River, Rock Springs, and Little America. Inscriptions and slang on the remaining ten pages begin with food references that correspond to and are drawn from his job "pot-wallopin'," and then move to hitchhiker references that correspond with the last part of his journey: on page 17, "Julian Biggs, the highway bum" appears, and three pages later we find "St. Louis. 2 days trying to catch a ride here." Each reference located after Little America in the notebook occurs after that city in all three versions of the score.

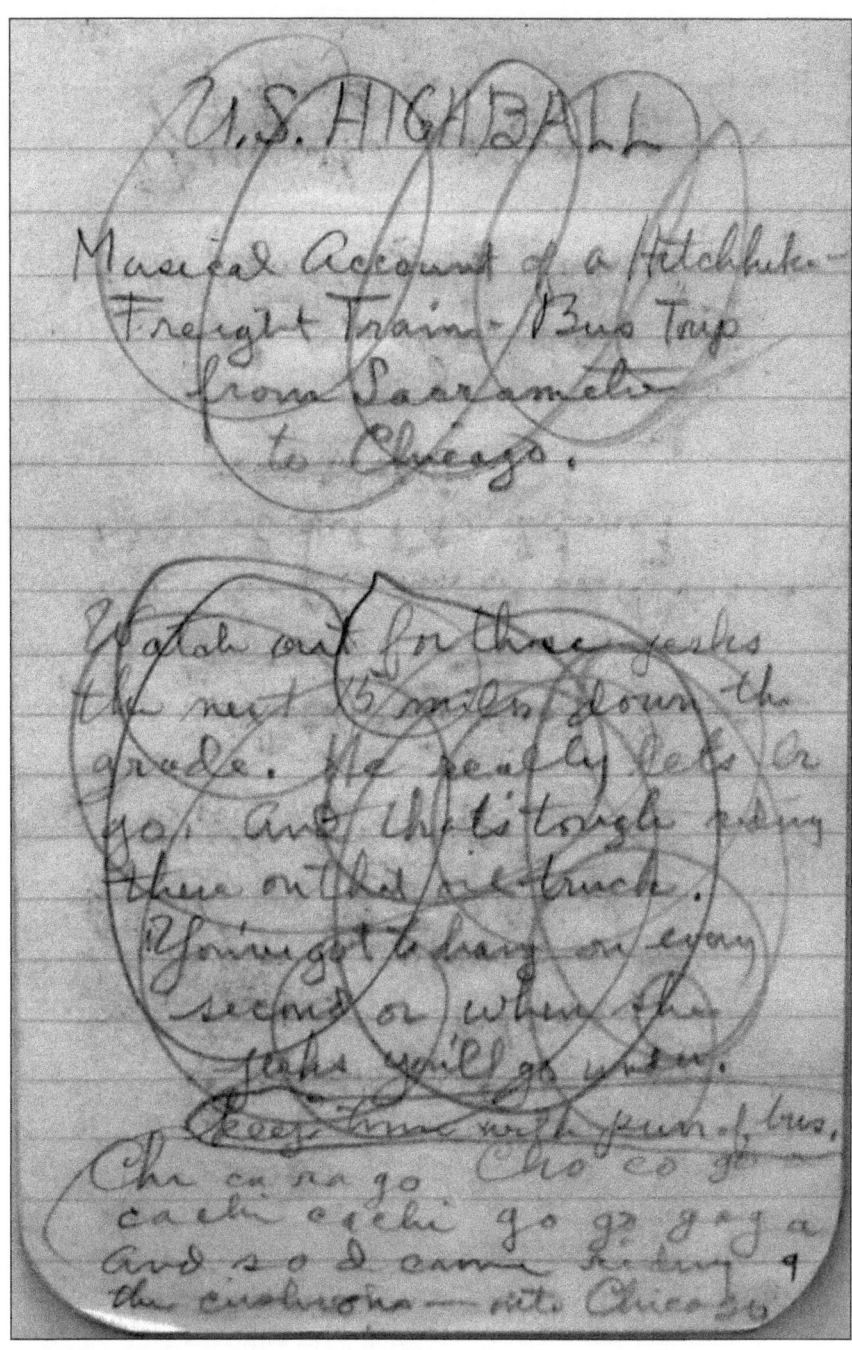

Figure 5.2. Pages 9–10 of the notebook Partch carried as he hoboed from California to Chicago in 1941. On page 9 he noted a possible name for the composition; on the next page he listed the cities through which he had traveled at the journey's halfway point. Harry Partch Estate Archive, Sousa Archives and Center for American Music, University of Illinois at Urbana-Champaign.

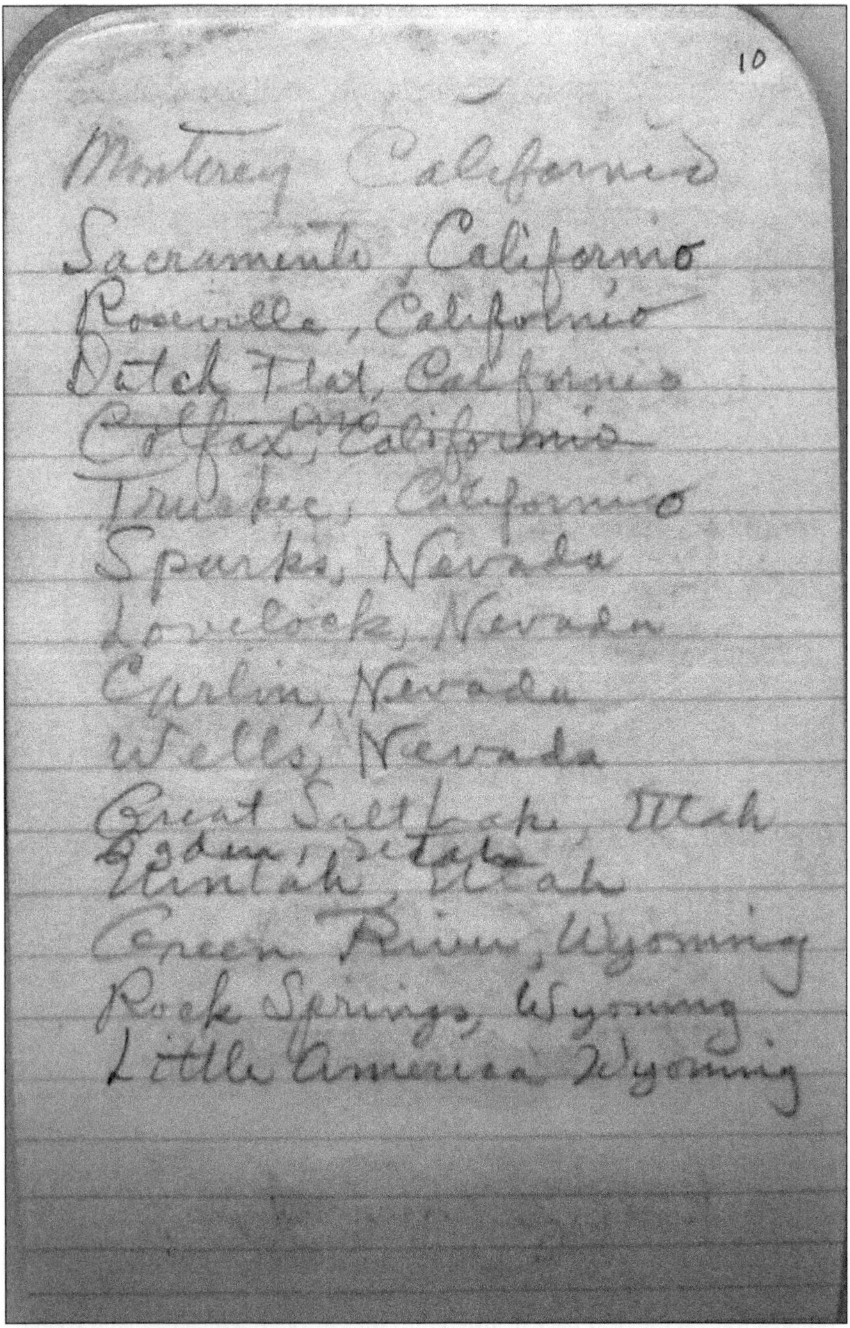

Monterey, California
Sacramento, California
Roseville, California
Dutch Flat, California
Colfax, California
Truckee, California
Sparks, Nevada
Lovelock, Nevada
Carlin, Nevada
Wells, Nevada
Great Salt Lake, Utah
Ogden, Utah
Uintah, Utah
Green River, Wyoming
Rock Springs, Wyoming
Little America, Wyoming

Figure 5.2.—*(concluded)*

This layout supports an assumption of chronological entries. It appears that while working out his week in Little America, Partch formulated the idea of composing a piece based on the trip. Although at that point he was unsure what form of transportation he would use to finish the journey, he hoped to hitchhike or take a bus for at least part of the remaining distance, for cleanliness if nothing else. Whether he was unable to save the bus fare or decided to conserve his money is unclear, but Partch did not ride a bus on the trip; he dropped the portion of the title that referenced it and never used it in any version of the libretto or score.

As Partch conceived the idea that his composition's structure would follow the journey's progress, he began recalling the various places through which he had traveled and listed them in order on the page immediately following the first appearance of the work's title. He then went back and inserted the names of cities in and above inscriptions recorded before he arrived in Little America. Irregularities in both the thickness of the pencil lines and the size of his handwriting differentiate these additions from original inscriptions. He even inserted some city names into the middle of a phrase, where they would not naturally occur had the names and phrases been recorded simultaneously. Partch later highlighted these additions when he gave those phrases to separate vocal performers and paired them with the newly-added station names.

While he was stranded in Little America, Partch not only developed the idea of *U.S. Highball* and experimented with its structure, he also began work on its composition. On page 9, where the title first appears, he sketched the work's flow and proportion. Circled three-quarters of the way down the page is the note "keep time with purr of bus." Immediately beneath are playful manipulations of the word "Chicago," ending with "and so I came riding the cushions—into Chicago." The bus trip never materialized, so he kept time in the final work's last portion with the car's purr instead, ending the piece riding an automobile into Chicago.

As his musical theories rested on a connection between speech and music, on page 11 of the notebook, directly beneath the listing of cities through which he had traveled, Partch began experimenting with the intonation of various words by marking crescendos and decrescendos under them. On the next page he began preserving definitions of the hobo slang he was considering using in the text. He did not use and mark out all of this slang, but its presence is notable in that it demonstrates his intent of creating as authentic a remembrance of his hobo encounters as possible. In creating the myth he spun around *U.S. Highball*, Partch also later claimed that the rhyming of state names with city names, so characteristic of the sound of the work in performance, was a way for hoboes to while away long hours on the trains.[29] From all accounts it appears as though hoboes often did create rhymes in this manner, yet in the notebook, none of the cities and states rhyme with each other. That facet of the text was added in later drafts.

Following notes taken during the trip, pages 22–23 of the notebook include the first listing of the "Monophonic Cycle" proposed in Partch's Guggenheim application in September of 1942, a set that was to include *U.S. Highball*. Differences between the cycle as listed in the notebook and on the application point to the former as the earlier incarnation. *Dark Brother*, proposed on the application, was listed in the notebook as "Stern Brother"; instead of setting excerpts from *Finnegans Wake*, Partch was planning on using Lewis Carroll's poem "Jabberwocky"; *U.S. Highball* was listed as "now in course of composition" and *God, She* as "not yet started" whereas in the Guggenheim application both were listed as existing in rough drafts, with no music yet written.[30]

The notebook's jottings encompass many unexpected features. Seeing how Partch took down what he heard hoboes say, and how he then transformed those statements into music, proves that the notebook is the beginning of Partch's creative process for *U.S. Highball*: he began working on the piece a year and a half earlier than previously thought. The process of formalizing the ideas expressed in the notebook and codifying them into a libretto, however, lacks the clear dating of his notebook sketching. Partch usually conscientiously marked colophons on all of his scores and librettos, so it is surprising to find the earliest typed libretto for *U.S. Highball* undated.[31] As all changes marked in pencil on this undated copy were made in the other extant libretto, dated February 25, 1943, it is clearly an earlier version, though its exact date is unknown. The title of this draft is "U.S. Highball: Musical Account of a Transcontinental Hitchhike—Freight Train Hegira" (see table 5.1).

It appears that Partch transferred notebook inscriptions to this draft before scribbling through them. Every word and phrase in the first draft libretto matches the notebook, except for a few place names, which he left blank (he drew a line where the name should have been, then later filled it in with pencil; see fig. 5.3), and, more tellingly, an extended monologue in Little America. In the latter passage, a man emerges from a piano, where he has been living for some time, and lectures a group of young hoboes about the homeless life, ending his soliloquy with the impassioned words, "I was a bum once myself."[32] Every notebook inscription is a short jotting; the only wording even resembling the monologue is the final plea. Despite

Table 5.1. Versions of *U.S. Highball*

First draft libretto	Title: *U.S. Highball: Musical Account of a Transcontinental Hitchhike -Freight Train Hegira*
Second draft libretto	Title: *U.S. Highball: Musical Account of an American Transcontinental Freight Train - Hitchhike Trip*
Original score	Title: *U.S. Highball: Musical Account of an American Transcontinental Freight Train - Hitchhike Trip* Scored for: Adapted Guitar and Voice Written: February 14, 1943 to March 24, 1943
First revision	Title: *U.S. Highball: A Musical Account of Slim's Transcontinental Hobo Trip* Scored for: Adapted Guitar, Kithara, Chromelodeon, and Voices Written: May 1, 1943 to October 1, 1943
Second revision	Title: *U.S. Highball: A Musical Account of a Transcontinental Hobo Trip* Scored for: Subjective Voice, Objective Voice, Kithara, Chromelodeon, Diamond Marimba, Bass Marimba, Surrogate Kithara, Castor and Pollux, Spoils of War, and Boo Written: completed June 30, 1955

his claims simply to report faithfully the words of others, as a dispassionate observer, Partch inserted personal experience, memory, and commentary into the libretto. This act shattered the work's purported chronological and textual accuracy. But it also points to the personal nature of *U.S. Highball* in comparison with *Barstow*: Partch wrote himself into the text as participant. It is significant that in recordings of the work Partch always delivered these lines himself, his a voice of experience to the young hoboes just starting out.

The first typed draft libretto preserved the notebook order of phrases, but Partch further altered the work's timeline in penciled markings for later revisions. Circles and arrows show the movement of texts, usually to a few lines away. Additionally, the characteristic rhyming of cities and states that was absent from the notebook makes its first appearance in this draft. Although typed correctly, Partch added rhyming alternatives in pencil over the endings of more than half the state names. Contrary to his later declarations, Partch was altering the thoughts and phrases he recorded on the trip as early as the first draft libretto.

> 2.
>
> Leaving ~~Ocala~~ Nevada—
>
> "Hey, Slim, don't sleep with your head against the end of the car—you'll get your neck broke when she jerks. ~~How are the bulls down where you come from, Slim?~~"
>
> Leaving Lovelock, Nevada—
>
> "She's gonna hole in to let a couple of passengers by."
>
> ~~"Let 'er highball when that next passenger gets by."~~
>
> "There, she jerks again, that engineer don't know how to drive this train."
>
> ~~"How are the bulls down where you come from, Slim?"~~
> ~~Leaving Winnemucca, Nevada—~~
>
> ~~"I hope he really throws that old throttle out this time."~~
>
> Leaving Imlay, Nevada—
>
> "Freeze another night, tonight, going over the hump. That Cheyenne, Hm, that used to be a bad town, but not any more, so much. They used to have a school there for railroad bulls. They taught the rookies the best [sadist] way to beat up on defenseless [poor] bums. But the school's moved to Denver now. It moves back and forth, from Cheyenne to Denver. Stay out of Denver, Slim."
>
> "If you want to eat today, boys, better get it here. The next division is just a little hole in the desert—not even a store."
>
> ~~Leaving Winnemucca~~, Nevada (see next page)
> Leaving Carlin, Nevada—
>
> "They've gone and sealed up our empty. And all the rest are sealed refrigerators. Shuck, not even a gon-<u>do</u> - la."
>
> Leaving Valmy, Nevada—
>
> "No water here in these corrals. They only turn it on once a year—round up ~~town~~ [time]. No water for us today."
>
> ~~Leaving Elko, Nevada—~~
> Moleen, Nevada—
>
> "Wait for the next drag—there'll be lots of empties on it—

Figure 5.3. Partch first draft libretto of *U.S. Highball*. Note the large-scale movement of text as well as the later addition of specific place names such as Ocala, Nevada. Harry Partch Estate Archive, Sousa Archives and Center for American Music, University of Illinois at Urbana-Champaign.

The second and final extant draft libretto bears the name "U.S. Highball: Musical Account of an American Transcontinental Freight Train—Hitchhike Trip." Several features suggest that this draft was the text from which Partch composed. On the second page, Partch wrote the colophon, "1st draft finished Feb. 25." Partch's testimony and surviving documents all place the composition of the first score version between February 14 and March 24, 1943; the second draft libretto falls within that timeframe. There are fewer markings denoting moved sections of text than in the first draft libretto. Instead, instrumental and vocal themes are penciled in the margins and between sentences of text along with annotations indicating when and what the Adapted Guitar, Kithara, or Chromelodeon are to play. The date on this libretto, combined with the instrumental notations, give the appearance that Partch used the text as an outline within which to organize his ideas before commencing the music's actual composition. Although Partch wrote version A of the score for Adapted Guitar and voice, these annotations, in the same hand and pencil thickness, point to Partch wanting to score it for other instruments from the beginning, instruments to which he lacked access in Ithaca (they were stored in Chappaqua, New York).

The most telling markings on the second draft libretto concern Partch's plans for vocal and instrumental interplay. In several sections, he noted that the vocal inflections, specifically of the station calls of cities and towns passed on the trip, were to be reinterpreted as themes in the instrumental parts. In other words, every main instrumental theme in the work had its origin in the inflections of the human voice. Delivering the text through the medium of human intoning that accurately conveyed the meaning of the words was of primary importance to him at this time. To that end, he carefully connected instrumental and vocal themes in a tight web, each instrumental theme organically referencing the human voice from which its lines arose. *U.S. Highball* is a prime example of Monophony, a Monophony that references ancient European musical traditions but flowers in American soil through hobo voices.

Following the completion of the second draft libretto, Partch barely altered the placement of phrases and station names in the text. Differences between this final draft text and the text used in version A are small but illuminate the composer's intent. All the nonsense syllables of "na," "la," and "lo" that are sung and intoned in every score version were added to the text in version A, as well as the phrases "buddy—she's tough goin' down the other side o' the Sierras," and "since the drags don't stop at Rock Springs." Neither the syllables nor the two phrases occur in the notebook. They were most likely inserted as connecting phrases to add flow to the libretto or to allow further musical development where Partch discovered it was needed after he began to compose. Recognizing the demands that the music was making on the text, he altered the latter in such a way as to not disrupt meaning while facilitating its transmission by increasing the connection between music and words.

The text for version B is almost identical to that of version A. The only changes include the completion of rhymed endings, so that every state rhymes with its city, as well as a few small cuts of musical interludes and the addition of one inscription: "Jack Parkin, 111 West William St., Champaign, Illinois. Telephone 8426 if hungry when there." Strangely, although this inscription, like all the others, was taken directly from the notebook, it is the only one Partch used but did not mark through. Its inclusion in the text appears to have been an afterthought; it is the longest continuous inscription in the notebook and the last one recorded. Parkin is the only named person in the work other than Partch himself, but the Champaign county archives reveal nothing of his story. Champaign, Illinois, was a good-sized town, the home of the University of Illinois, and on a major rail line to Chicago while close enough to drive to the city in two or three hours. Parkin's stepfather's house was within walking distance of the train tracks and the station, and he was evidently willing to part with food for a man down on his luck. But as to who Jack Parkin was, whether a bum, tramp, hobo, home-guard or, more fancifully, the generous soul who gave Partch his final ride into Chicago that grey October day in 1941, is not revealed, nor are the reaons why Partch added the name and inscription.

Partch made the most substantial cuts in version C, shortening the work from over forty minutes to roughly twenty-five. These deletions of the musical material, however, entailed only a single textual change: as noted above, the protagonist's name was altered from Slim to Mac. Beyond the familiarity of "Mac" as a hobo name, this alteration resonates deeply with Partch's changing conception of *U.S. Highball*. In the 1943 introduction to version B, the composer painstakingly demonstrated the personal nature of his trip. Concurrent with the search for an American sound and his promotion of himself as a hobo composer, Partch wanted his audience to understand the difficulties and exhilarations of not just any hobo life, but his own. Instead of romanticizing the lifestyle by using an iconic hobo, as so many literary figures since Jack London had done, he wanted listeners to identify with the protagonist. So, after a lengthy discourse on the protagonist's thoughts and feelings through the trip, Partch tipped his hand, concluding with the words, "Finally, I am Slim. It would almost have to be so, and I may as well confess it."[33] "Slim" had been Partch's hobo moniker for eight years, and with those final sentences, he compressed the universal into the personal.

Fourteen years later, in an introduction written to his 1955 version C, Partch began to reverse the process and universalize his experience and the work that resulted. In place of the conspiratorial confession "I am Slim," he claimed that "although I am hardly a typical American of my generation, my nonheroic and nonepic experiences were very typical of those times (the overcrowded transient shelters were eloquent evidence), and this fact endows the concept with a tie to other men."[34] Partch seems to have decided that for his music to survive beyond himself, and to translate successfully into film (his intention at the time), it required vast, humanistic application. In contrast to the situation in which he found himself in the 1940s, he saw that the hobo's image had shifted again and that he needed to make his hobo iconic: a simple two-week trip from California to Chicago could also be the journey of a human soul, the progression of a life from birth to death, or any number of nonliteral interpretations of a hero's archetypal journey.

U.S. Highball's Musical Evolution

Throughout his life, Partch sought to give his work increased resonance by aligning text and music closely, each depending upon the other for its power and expression. In *U.S. Highball*, he attempted a unique synthesis of the two, even writing of *Highball* that "I intend the words to grow with the music, a highly experimental procedure.... It will be incumbent on the music to carry much of the significance and emotional import of the setting."[35] Knowing that station calls and snippets of conversation could provide linear narrative but were not enough to create the personal emotional connection he desired, Partch placed more weight on the work's musical craftsmanship than he had in its earlier incarnations. Despite this written observation, his theoretical work has kept writers focused on his use of intonation to the detriment of a pursuit of *U.S. Highball*'s musical structure and language. Most have followed the earliest reviewers by focusing on the prose libretto's intrinsic worth as Depression-era literature. But *U.S. Highball* is not *Bitter Music*. The integration of text and music force a consideration of *Highball*'s music more than its chronological companion.

The close connection of text and music marks *U.S. Highball* as fundamentally different from other musical "Americana" works of Depression and World War II–era culture. Those other works often used American voices, but set to European-derived music with melodies and rhythms that did not naturally fit American inflections. Likewise, they often used American folk songs in their compositions, but with settings harmonically advanced beyond the simple chords of their origins, pulling in progressions gleaned from centuries of European development. Whether through words or melodies, much of this music simply added American flavors to a European stew. By collecting hobo voices and then basing his music on those voices' inflections and rhythms, Partch was making a new art, related to that of other composers similarly inclined to speech rhythms such as Leoš Janáček or Modest Musorgsky, but unique in its documentary nature. His hobo-inspired form of Monophony was conceptually exotic in its use of hobo material as a theoretical as well as structural basis. By the time he was writing *U.S. Highball* he may have decided it was time to leave the hobo jungle, but parts of it remained with him throughout his life, especially in this work.

To integrate text and music completely, Partch required a broader musical palate than that readily available in Western music. His use of forty-three pitches to the octave was not a musical gimmick; he was not seeking a hook with which to snag the attention of potential patrons. His stated aim of having the words grow with the music was basic to his Monophonic concept, and his microtonal scale was basic to the application of Monophony. The bards of legend and those of the hobo jungles sang monophonically. They accompanied themselves on simple string instruments while intoning the words of their songs. These ballads were not sung or spoken with twelve pitches to the octave; their power to enthrall came from subtle vocal pitch gradations. Partch wanted to capture musically, as though in an aural snapshot, the hoboes' precise inflections. The use of microtones as a compositional and notational device was therefore intrinsic to the development and impact of *U.S. Highball* and to its existence as a conceptually exotic art. If he had attempted to shoehorn his and other hobo voices into the standard equally tempered twelve-tone scale, he would have sacrificed those voices, merely imitating rather than embodying them.

Partch's use of microtones, however musically fruitful, has long been a roadblock to scholarship. In his study of *Seventeen Lyrics by Li Po*, the first works Partch wrote in his microtonal idiom, Bob Gilmore rightly stated that "the daunting prospect of having to confront Partch's complex work in the field of intonation theory in order to analyze the pitch usages in his music, and even in order simply to read his notation, has been the most significant deterrent to the detailed study of his music."[36] For the Li Po settings, this problem originates with Partch's use of what he termed "the language of ratios"[37] rather than conventional notation to write the score. The major triad G-B-D, in standard notation, would be similar to a 1/1–5/4–3/2, one on top of the other, in ratio notation, but pitches and ratios are not exactly the same (just as intervals on the equally tempered piano are not acoustically pure). Partch therefore discouraged people hoping to understand his system from always converting ratios back into letters. Once a performer is conversant in this acoustical/mathematical language and familiar with the playing techniques of Partch's early instruments, rather than seeing a graphic representation of a pitch (as in standard notation) one actually reads the pitch acoustically. It is similar to English speakers recognizing the layers of meaning in a Japanese *kanji* instead of relying on an English translation. However, for most trained musicians, the attempt to memorize forty-three ratios and not make the almost inevitable conversion back into musical letters creates a large stumbling block to analysis. Although they recognize the the ratios intellectually, much is lost in translation to performance.

Version A of *U.S. Highball* was the last composition Partch wrote completely in his language of ratios.[38] By the time he wrote version C, Partch had developed a complicated notational arsenal, with a different system for each instrument. These graphic systems were based on the five-line, four-space staff of conventional musical notation, but produced sounds vastly different from those expected. He no longer used ratios in the score (although playing his instruments requires at least surface knowledge of ratios, as they are printed on the instruments' bodies in place of musical letters). At first glance the score seems standard, as easy to read for Western-trained musicians as an orchestral one. When reading along with a recording, however, it is easy to become lost without the sounds usually associated with the visual cues. The notational system's esoteric nature, tied Corporeally to the instruments themselves, has hindered musical analysis as much as the language of ratios.

With obvious direct avenues into *U.S. Highball* obstructed, it becomes pertinent to search out and use a back door. With a basic route in, and a sense of the work's overarching conception, it becomes less problematic to enter through Partch's notational path. Studies of his sketches are among the most useful starting points and have shown his technique to be rather typical of Western composers.[39] He customarily began composing by writing the libretto or selecting the text, going through several revisions in that process. The libretto finished, he next defined the melodic line. For both *Seventeen Lyrics by Li Po* and *Barstow*, the two large-scale compositions completed before *U.S. Highball*, he transcribed the text completely above the staves and then composed the vocal line by filling in pitches underneath the words.[40] "Song flowering from speech" was Partch's stated aim, and so his first compositional act was to record the inflections and intonations of people reading the text, occasionally including himself. He would then transfer the recorded inflections to the score's first version. For *U.S. Highball*, the beginnings of this compositional creative process appear in the notebook. Using crescendos and decrescendos, Partch marked the rise and fall of inflection for "back to the freights for you, boy," a line that would become key to the work's structure. But the markings he employed are strange. Partch always notated pitch extremely precisely, but here the dynamic markings are quite offhand, as though he were thinking quickly and did not want to be bothered by exactitude.

The fact that this single notebook page contains the only known sketches of pitch material, and that most inscriptions are unornamented, poses an interesting dilemma. After he arrived in Chicago in 1941 we have no record of Partch ever riding the rails again, although he did continue to hitchhike. For his setting of the Psalms, he recorded a Jewish rabbi chanting; for his Shakespearian settings, he recorded an actor reciting the scenes. But if he did not record a "knight of the road" for his hobo settings, whose inflections form the basis of *U.S. Highball*? The work seems to signal a turning point in his compositional process, as nothing survives indicating that he was ever again as diligent about finding the right voice to intone the text before composing. If Partch's voice is the sole source of all inflection and intonation, there are important ramifications for performance practice as well as scholarship. Perhaps all performances should be based on Partch's various recordings, on his voice intoning the words.

Unfortunately, while many sketches for the *Li Po* settings and *Barstow* remain, besides the one page in the notebook and instructions to himself left in the margins of the second draft libretto, the only sketches of *U.S. Highball* that have been found are a series of rhythmic variations on the word Chicago.[41] As early as the ninth page of his notebook, while stuck in Little America, Partch began experimenting with the rhythmic implications of the word. This obsession with "Big Chi," as hoboes called the city, came to dominate the last half of his journey. In Bruns's words, Chicago was at that time "the hub of the nation's rails, the migrant mecca, Hobohemia. For the 'boes, all roads, it seemed, led to Chicago."[42] In hobo lore, a mythopoeic aura surrounded the city. One went there to stay warm in the winter, find companionship, maybe even a job to provide relief from the hobo lifestyle. It was the basin into which northern rails spilling over the continental divide emptied. Once over the Rockies, every hobo and tramp kept his eyes on the eastern horizon with expectation, so it is fitting that in the last section of *U.S. Highball* some variation of "Chicago" is always being chanted, whether it is "Chicago," "Chicago-cago," Chicogo," or "Chicaga-ogo-aga."

This typical hobo obsession lends a propulsion to *U.S. Highball*'s final section not found in earlier ones, while aptly coloring the mixture of emotions Partch surely felt as he approached the city. The destination is second in importance only to the work's desire for movement. For a piece that opens with the line "and that's why I'm going to Chicago," it seems fitting that what seems to have been the first section composed are variations on the name. The surviving draft for this section shows twenty-four variations on four pages, each separately numbered and numerically ordered (see fig. 5.4). Following his usual pattern, Partch appears to have written the words first. The city name and nonsensical syllables rub up against each other companionably, not conforming to their arrangement in the final score. They are written fluidly, with natural lifts of the pencil and spaces deliberately marked with a dash. The notes, which simply indicated rhythm and not pitch, were then applied atop the words. Partch did not use manuscript paper, as he had in earlier attempts at recording inflections. Instead, he used plain notebook paper turned so the lines ran vertically instead of horizontally, eliminating any inclination to read the noteheads on a staff. Uncharacteristically for the work, Partch did not notate any singing or intoning inflection for the Chicago variations to be sung or intoned; in these surviving sketches he made no attempt to match the words to pitch movement.

The progression of variations from numbers one through twenty-four is logical. The first three focus on the unembellished name in eighth notes. The difference among these three is found in the rests placed between iterations of the name, whether one, three, or no rests. The next ten variations, through the bottom of the second page, likewise concentrate on the unadorned name, but change rhythmic values for the various syllables. In at least half of them, "Chi" is treated as an eighth-note anacrusis while "ca" and "go" are extended through quarters, eighths, and triplets. These two pages represent a systematic exploration of ways to set "Chicago." With page 3, the variations become much more complex and inter-textual comments begin to appear. Syllables are broken down, repeated, and combined in new ways. Words based on, or beginning with, single syllables are added, to humorous effect: "Chicagogoing, Chicagogoing, Chicagogone." The comments added below these variations prove to be the most interesting and raise the most questions.

Figure 5.4. The first page of Partch's sketches for the variations on the word "Chicago" (*U.S. Highball*). Harry Partch Estate Archive, Sousa Archives and Center for American Music, University of Illinois at Urbana-Champaign.

Under each syllable in variations eleven, sixteen, seventeen, twenty-one, and twenty-two, Partch added lower case letters. The letters are confined to the first seven in the alphabet, the same set used in equal temperament to denote the seven white-key pitches. Further, in variations eleven, twenty-one, and twenty-two, the E has a flat sign written above and to the left of it. While not conclusive, it appears that Partch scribbled in vocal pitches, especially since the first appearance of these hastily notated pitches revolves around G, his fundamental. The letters also match the natural inflections of someone reading the text dramatically. The "Chicagogoing" example from variation seventeen, cited above, vacillates back and forth, G to A, until "Chicagogone," at which point the instinctive exclamation of "gone" is annotated with a C underneath it, a fourth above the G.

Version A substantiates the hypothesis that the marks in the notebook mentioned above are indeed preliminary vocal pitch notations. The "Chicagogoing" line appears on page 38, where the movement of pitches matches that of the sketch; but instead of the fundamental serving as the basis, the 3/2 (fifth) acts in that role, with a final jump on "gone" up a 4/3 (fourth) to the 2/1 (octave). This pattern holds true with variations sixteen, twenty-one, and twenty-two as well, each having been moved up a 3/2. Variation eleven is the only one whose score version does not match the sketch. It is also anomalous in that it is used in conjunction with another variation; it is the only sketch of the five to survive the cuts between versions B and C.

Other comments Partch added after sketching out the variations are diverse. At the bottom of the third page, he made a note to himself regarding the use of the Chromelodeon in this section: as noted above, even at this early stage, Partch was intending to orchestrate the work for his four instruments, as he would do with *Barstow* that same year. The note concerns the development of Theme 3 (which I have designated as the "highway theme") through the Chicago variations. Partch was concerned that the variations not begin until after the theme's first announcement, and that they start slowly and then gain speed, pushing toward the work's end. This conception remained intact into versions B and C. Other comments are significantly shorter. They primarily deal with which syllable should be accented in a given variation, and whether any are to be used in conjunction with another variation. He also writes below the final variation that by the end, the word "Chicago" will have completely broken down into babble, with only "gahgo," "cogo," and plain "go" remaining. The logical progression from simple exploration of the name in eighth notes to complex, prismatic, syllabic destruction evidenced through the four pages is the result of careful structural planning.

At the beginning of each variation is a large circled number. Comparing these with the various score versions reveals a correspondence with the number of iterations of that formula in the score. Also, as in the early libretto drafts, Partch covers the sketches with arrows and circled passages. The arrows denote accents or tempo, but the circles resemble the circled crossings-out that litter the pocket notebook. Partch circled the variations he used, ultimately employing all but about five. Although he did not use every variation, their logical progression in these sketches aptly demonstrates the organic growth of words and music that he sought.

Partch composed version A for voice and Adapted Guitar so he could use it (like the early *Barstow* drafts) in lecture demonstrations and solo concerts.[43] Although it was quickly supplanted by version B, it was version A that he first performed in and around New York, before premiering the second version at his League of Composers concert in April 1944. He composed version A in ratio notation, writing each pitch in the forty-three-note octave as its corresponding ratio, and stacking three ratios upon one another for a chord. He wrote rhythms as stems without noteheads, and flagged and barred them according to their relative length, an endeavor which does not help in deciphering them since he marked no meter in the score.

Partch must have had trouble himself in reading the metrical notation on occasion. On a few particularly overmarked pages, he wrote in beats for certain measures by adding circled sequential numbers in the middle of the staff. Performance aids like this also extend to the synchronization of text and music. Although the text was written above the voice and Adapted Guitar parts, it is often difficult to ascertain which ratios belong with which words, since they do not line up precisely. In a few cases, Partch drew a quick line to show which word went with which ratio. Like the first draft libretto, the score was heavily marked with circles and arrows, and alterations and addenda were written sideways, slanted, in the margins, and even on the backs of pages. These corrections exponentially increase the confusion when searching out the development of the work. Partch may have used version A as a performing copy, but in many ways it remains a sketch. Throughout its pages are measures that have been forced into place, the resulting text compressed and arching.

Though Partch scored the piece for Adapted Guitar, the Kithara and Chromelodeon were never far from his mind or the written page. As early as page 10, the Kithara made its first entrance, situated in place of the Adapted Guitar and boldly underlined twice. Oddly, no music, no ratios, are written next to it. In fact, with the exception of perhaps ten chords in the entire draft, whenever the Kithara appears, the music stops and the vocal line continues unaccompanied. In later drafts, Partch would evocatively set these passages to solo Kithara, with the Chromelodeon holding a pedal point. Never explicitly added like the Kithara, the Chromelodeon haunts this version in cryptic remarks and on the backs of pages. Indeed, its first appearance is likewise on page 10, but on the verso: Partch noted that he wanted the Chromelodeon to move in "widely separated parallel motion" on one of the Chicago themes. The two instruments are paired on page 16 when Partch questions, in another verso annotation, whether or not the Chromelodeon should join the Kithara on station calls or anticipate them.

These and other additions show that Partch had a full conception of *U.S. Highball* from the outset, from orchestration to structural necessities. Composed completely in ratios, and covered, in many cases front and back, with experimental lines in ratio notation, version A also puts to rest any questions that may have been raised by the use of letters for pitch notation in the Chicago sketches. By 1943, Partch had fully adopted and was fully conversant in the language of ratios, so much so that whatever shorthand he might have employed for sketching pitches, his ever-active mind was thinking in ratios.

Partch wrote version B in what seems at first glance to be more standard notation.[44] Each instrument appears on its own staff, in a manner similar to scores from the modern orchestral repertoire. Partch used pitch notation to demonstrate the general movement of the voice and the relationship between intervals. While notes spread over both the treble and bass clefs of standard staves, the implication was not that the voice sings more than one octave (see fig. 5.5); rather, it was a guideline for the singer to comprehend visually the desired inflections. In terms of pitch, the Adapted Guitar part remained essentially unaltered from the earlier version; the amendments are a few upper and lower neighboring tones added for embellishment. The rhythm underwent more substantial modifications: in version A, the Adapted Guitar played primarily eighth notes in simple rhythmic patterns that Partch could play while singing. As version B would require an ensemble, which entailed rehearsal time, Partch felt free to increase the Adapted Guitar's level of difficulty by adding sixteenth notes along with some syncopation. Harmonies also shifted throughout, often to add a bit more bite, and apply more color, to the work. For example, the second time "May God's richest blessings be upon you" is sung, Partch amended justly tuned major triads (3/2-1/1-5/4) to slightly wider spaced chords: a 4/3-16/9-10/9 for the word "on," and a 16/15-4/3-8/5 on the final "you." Opening up the sound, these harmonies depicted aurally the implied possibilities of God's richest blessings in Chicago.

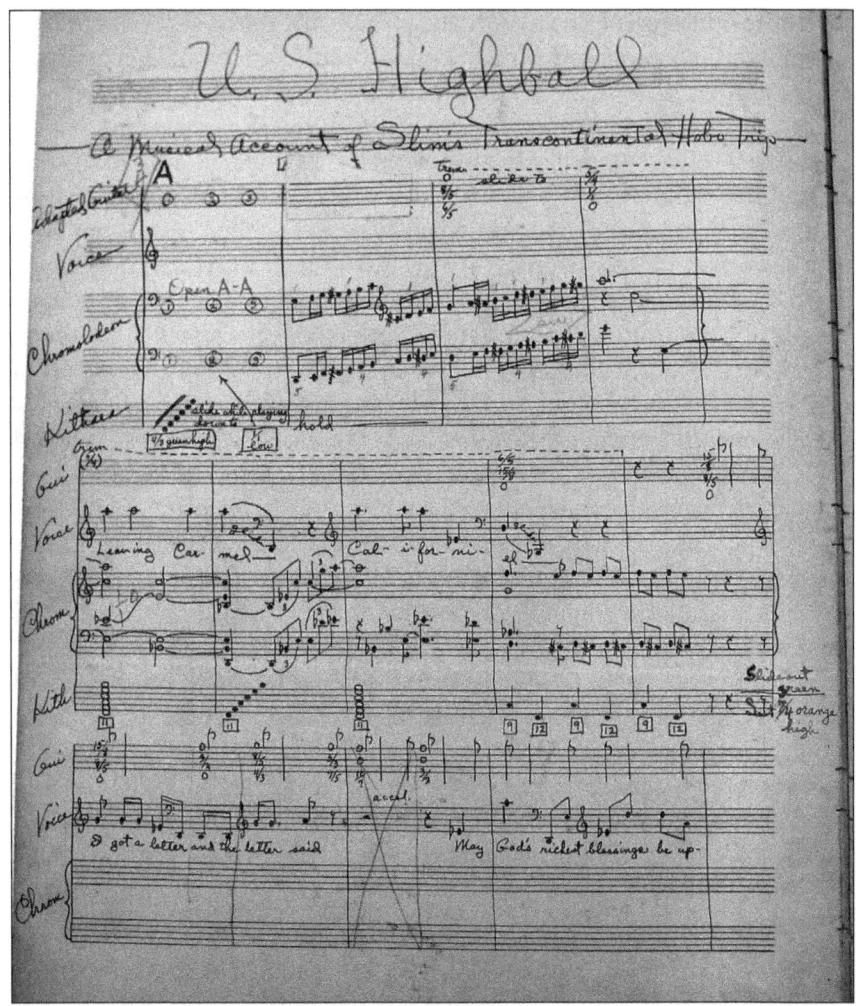

Figure 5.5. First page of version B of *U.S. Highball*, scored for voice, Adapted Guitar, Kithara, and Chromelodeon. Although the score appears to be in standard notation, the Adapted Guitar line is still written in the language of ratios and the other lines are written in Partch's tablature for each instrument and voice. Harry Partch Estate Archive, Sousa Archives and Center for American Music, University of Illinois at Urbana-Champaign.

Besides these few modifications to the Adapted Guitar part and harmonic progression, the variations on the word "Chicago" in the last section received the most extensive reworking. Both sixteenth notes and triplets joined the rhythmic devices deployed, and in several instances Partch raised the fundamental pitch a perfect fifth. Interludes between the voice parts widened in both this section and the work's opening but, strangely, no new material appeared. Instead, Partch simply repeated the rhythms and pitches already present, emphasizing the monotony of long distance travel. All in all, these adjustments of adding two new instruments and rhythmic interest and altering a few harmonies, are minor; the two versions are textually and melodically identical.

Throughout the pages of the first two versions, Partch wrote notes to himself and the performers. The majority addressed the relationship between instrumental parts and the intoning voice: on page 13 of version B, he noted that there was "no planned rhythmic incidence between words and guitar in this section, except the starting point of each spoken phrase, about the 2nd beat of each measure."[45] In other words, the instruments emphasized the phrasing of the text to communicate its meaning more effectively. Only after the voice had completely intoned a line did the instrumental parts pick up their pitches and rhythms. This imitation format is especially prevalent after station calls. Partch assigned each state a characteristic rhythm and intervallic structure, components mimicked in the instrumental lines more often than the shapes of the hobo sayings. Examining the differences between the first two versions and the final one makes it evident that the rhythms and pitches used to intone station calls remained fairly consistent: changes merely doubled or halved the note values, leaving their fundamental pitch characteristics the same.

Partch seems to have built *U.S. Highball*'s entire structure not on the order in which he heard the hobo inscriptions, as he intimated, but instead on repetition and the linear movement through towns and states as well as through the composition. This structure explains why the order and rhythms of station calls changed the least from the earliest libretto through two versions to the final product of 1955. He could change where he placed an inscription in the work, but he could not alter the geography of the stations to match.

Twelve years separated version C from the previous revision. While the composer's and the general public's impression of hoboes had changed by this time, revisions to the work in the intervening years had been limited to minor additions of new instruments as they were developed. Following the March 1952 production of *King Oedipus*, Partch's notion of music and its role in human society had turned away from a single voice delivering a text full of power and meaning, and toward elaborate theater works focusing on the percussive aspect of purely instrumental music that mined what he termed "the ancient rhythmic magic."[46] Considering this philosophical shift, it is not astonishing that Partch revisited *U.S. Highball*, the work in which he had most completely explored Monophonic principles, and which he had proclaimed his most creative. Similarly unsurprising are the changes he made, especially in light of his evolving musical aesthetic and view of his past hobo life. The text, as detailed earlier, remained relatively intact, but he enhanced the number of instruments and the complexity of their respective parts.

The addition of marked meters is the most striking feature of version C. The meter changes almost every bar, but always in a form of four—2/4, 3/4, 4/4, 5/4, or 6/4—or a form of eight—3/8, 4/8, 5/8, 6/8, or 7/8. Yet even with continually shifting meters, the rhythmic pulse is basically unchanged from previous versions: as Stravinsky did with *Le Sacre du printemps*, Partch sought to uncover the easiest way to notate difficult rhythmic passages. Whether in a meter of four or eight, the underlying pulse over the course of a phrase is always in two or four. Partch lengthened rhythms by doubling, which maintained the rhythmic relationship between pitches, and altered some bar lines separating measures to fit the new meter changes, but he never compromised the basic beat. While local rhythmic complexity increased, the work's tempo decreased. Versions A and B contained no percussion sounds other than knocking on the Adapted Guitar's body. As a reed organ, the Chromelodeon even lacks the usual percussive hit of a keyboard instrument. In order to compensate for this lack of percussion and maintain a feeling of propulsion, Partch had designated a brisk tempo, especially in the vocal lines. For version C, he dramatically relaxed the tempo, but the instrumental complexity and the quick pace of instrumental changes retained the sensation of movement he sought.

Partch also tightened rhythmic control of the pitches in the two vocal lines, essentially highlighting his new, more objective view of the work. In versions A and B, he notated only pitch in many sections, leaving performers free in their rhythmic intonation of text. In version C, Partch removed that freedom and rewrote the sections in strict rhythm, leaving few instances of intoning without set rhythms. He also introduced the distinction between the Objective Voice and the Subjective Voice: the former intones the hobo texts and is sung by instrument players; the latter is essentially the original vocal part that sings the station names. While in every section the vocal phrase shapes are similar, in this version he condensed the role of the

Objective Voice while keeping the range of the Subjective Voice roughly the same. This division between vocal parts was present in practice if not in the score in version B. In a recording made in 1946 in Madison, Wisconsin, one voice sang the station names while the other players, Partch included, intoned the hobo texts.[47] In these instances, changes to version C simply codified what was already occurring in performance.

U.S. Highball's Structural Evolution

The musicians and audiences who first heard *U.S. Highball* and Partch's other hobo compositions had not seen the sketches that reveal his organic intertwining of voice and melody, harmony and rhythm. Instead, while intrigued by his theoretical ideas and instruments and enthralled by the documentary exoticism of his hobo persona, many critics derided Partch's compositions as amateurish and amorphous. In his 1949 review of *Genesis of a Music*, Henry Cowell wrote, "However, the music to prove that a scale of forty-three tones to the octave is as valuable as twelve has yet to be written. As [Partch's] attention has been directed almost exclusively to problems of pitch, rhythmic interest is at a minimum in his compositions and consequently give an oddly formless and wandering impression."[48] Although by the final version of *U.S. Highball* Partch had added significant rhythmic interest through the interwoven patterns in his percussion instruments (an act that was perhaps a direct response to Cowell's criticism), to the charge of amateurish the composer has long been considered guilty until proven innocent. Virgil Thomson, like Cowell a colleague and erstwhile supporter of Partch during his New York City years, was characteristically more pointed in his critique: "A specialist in true intervals and their commas, he has built his own instruments for sounding these. His aim of producing music with true tunings is admirable. One regrets that his work sometimes lacks intellectual sophistication, though it can also be very beautiful."[49]

This assumption—that Partch's music is naive and perhaps a little artless though not without beauty—has entered the public and academic consciousness. The argument goes that Partch's music is amateurish with interesting sounds and promising direction; it has inspired others along similar paths but will never stand the test of time. While he was a skilled craftsman of wood and string, his musical workmanship lacks the same structural and artistic integrity. Partch believed that these criticisms arose primarily because of his lack of institutional pedigree, from either Europe or the United States, and that his detractors felt that without an academic stamp of approval there was a deficiency in his composing that he was unable to overcome. While some of the composer's critics certainly looked down upon him for this reason, it is unlikely that the majority did so. Partch was always sensitive about his lack of formal education. He was an extremely educated and well-read man, but was easily provoked into a defensive stance concerning his education and often cut off discussion of his background by castigating formal musical education as at best a hindrance to true creativity. Some of his opinions on why critics did not appreciate his music, especially in the 1930s and 1940s, seem to have been projections of his own insecurities.

Instead, it seems that part of the critical reaction came from audience members and critics projecting onto Partch their impressions of the hobo. Certainly the hobo was romanticized as a rugged individualist, a natural philosopher, and even a bit of a buffoon, but never as an intellectual or a sophisticate. He was a physical creature, living outside the society that created well-crafted, effective, and lasting pieces of art. Hoboes in popular culture, from movie characters like Chaplin's Little Tramp to literary ones like Dos Passos's Mac, changed their world in spite of their actions, never through concerted effort. They lacked a key element for full participation in American society: a strong work ethic. The perception of Partch would have been that having been part of hobohemia, he could not have had the perseverance or the discipline necessary to produce anything other than slipshod work. When Partch promoted his music as coming from his own hobo experience, that intriguing persona came with the baggage of popular assumptions. How, his audience must have asked, could anyone believe that he aspired to refined artistic expression?

The response Partch encountered points to a problem with conceptually exotic music more generally. Decorative exoticism is of the established artistic culture and simply brings in elements from outside itself as objects to study. It never fully leaves the confines of expectations. Conceptual exoticism, on the other hand, straddles the line between two cultures and so is more easily seen as part of the culture it represents. In other words, by making a personal hobo work like *U.S. Highball*, Partch became identified as a hobo beyond the reality of his situation. He had been a hobo, but he was a composer first and foremost, one who, like Henry Cowell himself, was largely an autodidact. He knew a great deal about composition and had been composing for many years, but his hobo persona partially obscured that history.

Other composers in the early decades of the century were also producing conceptually exotic music and were largely self-taught and -trained. These composers, men like Charles Ives, Henry Cowell, and John Cage, were slowly being accepted and celebrated for their compositions. Why not Harry Partch? Part of the answer lies in the circles in which he chose to move. Partch wanted to resurrect older conceptions of music instead of discarding or altering them for something new. But more importantly, Partch's writings doomed him. Most composers of the time, including Cowell and Cage, brought to New York theoretical treatises on their music. These treatises detailed and validated the structure as well as the new materials in their music. Partch's only theoretical writing at the time was concerned exclusively with new pitch resources through acoustic means, was unpublished when he arrived in New York City, and was so radical in its tuning practices that it was seen as opposed to the Western musical tradition.

This combination of factors adversely affected Partch's acceptance and reputation. Composers trained in Western conservatories routinely learn music with no discussion of the science, particularly the math, behind it.[50] Partch's theories were so far beyond the scope of most musicians that while they accepted that he had new, important ideas in the area of pitch, they could not fully understand them without reading his treatise. Those who were fortunate enough to read the sole copy of this treatise found nothing relating to new musical structures. Indeed, they discovered quite the opposite: Partch derided the very idea of formal structure. In his 1943 preface to *U.S. Highball* he wrote, "To this point all three instruments have been used liberally, but with no regular structure of composition, since the music is sensitive to every word uttered, every idea, every act."[51] As a result, many assumed that since an obvious unifying device such as sonata form could not be heard, and since the composer himself claimed that there was no regular structure, no structure existed.

Lack of audible structure is not synonymous with lack of structure altogether. The conspicuous absence of a complex Western structure, as well as Western temperament, caused Partch to look back fondly upon *U.S. Highball* in 1957 and call it "the most creative piece of music I ever wrote."[52] Yet solid construction and organization underlay the piece. Examining *U.S. Highball* abolishes the charge of amateur formlessness. The arrows, circles, and notes that litter Partch's sketches, drafts, and completed versions tighten the narrative and aid dramatic musical flow. In the same year that he heaped praise upon it, Partch began to reveal the piece's inner workings. Whereas in the 1943 introduction he carefully sidestepped the question of structure, in the final paragraph of the 1957 one he wrote: "The work falls naturally into three parts: first, a long and jerky passage by drags to Little America, Wyoming; second, a slow dishwashing movement at Little America; third, a rhythmic allegro by highway to Chicago. The one word—*Chicago*—is the end of the text."[53]

The opening (A) section consists of station calls, hobo inscriptions, and flexible rhythms with tempi that abruptly speed up and stop. The central (B) section begins with the protagonist becoming stuck in Green River and his subsequent employment in Little America. This section is textually offset from the outer ones by the length of inscriptions and its clear personal voice. The final section (A') is similar enough to the first section to be considered a variant with important distinctions. The station calls and flexible rhythm from the opening section are present, but as the protagonist travels by car, hobo inscriptions are significantly less of a factor, having been replaced by the "Chicago" variations. Also, first section themes are either transformed or replaced, aurally alerting listeners that Mac's situation has changed.

Partch clearly received artistic sustenance and inspiration from his years of hobo wandering. Many experiences that seem fantastic to the uninitiated were in fact quite common in "hobohemia." It was as if he lived in another country, which in a sense he did—one with its own language, customs, and music. It stands to reason that some vestige of hobo song styles might have helped mold aspects of *U.S. Highball*, in the same way that the language and customs did. Finding those vestiges is the last element in understanding how Partch shaped his conceptually exotic work; but this is also among the hardest of analytical tasks. Many, even among folklorists, are unaware of the range or impact of hobo song. The assumption has been that the nature of the community, single young men constantly on the move, prevented any kind of musical folk culture from developing among hoboes. Indeed, few collections of American folk music contain hobo song: the Lomaxes's collection includes just one example, and Carl Sandburg's *American Songbag* four. But these ideas too need reassessment. In one of the few studies of hobo songs, Richard Phelps writes, "it would seem that in spite of the hoboes' transient behavior and down-to-earth life style, a folk society and culture was fostered and represented, in part, by song."[54] The shared hardships of the jungles and railroads, hiding from bulls and the general public, caused hoboes to form a unique culture. They used song to express their misery in being dirty, broke, and jerked around by life and trains, and to convey their expectations and joys in constantly moving from place to place. Their songs reveal a belief that life is hard and death certain, so why not have some fun.[55] In the words of one hobo, "In a way the tramp is a modern troubadour."[56]

Fortunately, George Milburn, a friend of Sandburg's, began collecting songs among the country's migrant workers, traveling in boxcars and living in the jungles. In one year he was able to collect enough songs for an entire book, publishing the results of his fieldwork in 1930 as *The Hobo's Hornbook: A Repertory for a Gutter Jongleur*.[57] Milburn was also able to discern patterns in the songs and linguistic games the hoboes played. Extemporaneous rhyming was one of the best skills a hobo could cultivate. Watching the world pass by the open door of an "empty" or waiting for Mulligan stew to cook in the jungle was much more pleasant when two hoboes engaged in a battle of rhyming, using monikers or nonsense words to get over rough spots where no one could find an appropriate rhyme.[58] Being able to sing while rhyming, create jingles on the spot, craft new words to old songs (as Woody Guthrie did), or create puns on proper names, was enough to win a reputation and encourage other hoboes to overlook your bad habits.

Milburn's lengthy exposure to hobo songs allowed him to categorize them and enumerate each category's characteristics. Hobo ballads and songs never dealt with such mainstays of country songs as love, loss, grief, or the subtle relationship dance with the fairer sex. Instead they always narrated the "feats and adventures common to the vagrant life."[59] Hoboes loved to sing of "railroads, of solitude and pain, of working and doing time, of the grandeur of the country, of the power of the railroads, of the virtues and freedom of the open road."[60] The songs were replete with tales of hoboes besting railroad bulls and finding the pot of gold. In one of the most famous, "The Million Dollar Mulligan," a group of hoboes finds a boxcar full of squawking birds. The 'boes lift the lot of them and prepare a feast that evening in the jungle, singing and dancing to their good fortune. Only later, when reading the newspaper, another favorite pastime, do the 'boes discover that the flock they had stolen and eaten was part of a long-term scientific experiment and was being transferred to California for further testing. The song's payoff is in the birds' price tag: upward of a million dollars.

One of the most popular types of song among hoboes Milburn categorized as a "monika song." The recitation of ballads and monikers in jungles was a common way to while away the hours, but in order to keep the litany from becoming stagnant, hoboes would begin to rhyme monikers and place names. In true Monophonic fashion, these recitations soon gave way to accounts sung by hobo bards, often unaccompanied. Monika songs were largely improvisatory and combined a hobo's love of rhyming with a recitation of where he had been or whom he had known. Hoboes crafted them according to a set framework, whose formula lived in oral tradition. The improvisatory nature of monika songs, combined with the lack of a written source, caused them to be excluded from most collections.

As trains ceased running and the jungles dried up, monika songs disappeared; today fewer than five are known, all variations on two tropes. The framework is fairly simple. An object, event, or trip is used as the basis, as in monikers found under a bridge, an annual hobo convention, or the geographical progression of an extended train ride. The balladeer uses the recitation of names as a skeleton upon which to hang a basic story. Proper names are rhymed in usual hobo fashion using altered endings and nonsense words where needed.[61] The following monika, from *The Hobo's Hornbook*, is a good example of a song based on an object, in this case a water tower:

"Monikas Seen on the Water Tank"

Oh, we left the Coast a month ago,
    Eastbound for Chicago.
The head shack ditched us in a burg
    The other side of Fargo.

Says he, "And if you are a tramp,
    And not a bum or chronika,
Mooch on down to the water tank
    And there chalk up your monika."

I went down to the water tank,
    It was all marked up with chalk.
There was stiffs from every state
    From 'Frisco to New Yawk.

Your attention for a while
    One and all I'll thank.
And I'll mention some monikas
    Seen on that water tank.
. . . .
There was K.C. Jack and Mobile Mac
    Spokane Slim and Biff 'n' Bim.
Wingey Ed and young Chi Red
    and also Porkey Tim.[62]

This monika song clearly exhibits the influence of this genre—which Partch undoubtedly knew well—on not only the form of *U.S. Highball*, but on the conception of several pieces from *The Wayward*. The core idea of a monika was to use a personal collection of names, places, even inscriptions found on a water tank, as the basic text. While he traveled, Partch assembled just such a collection in his little brown notebook, from highway overpasses, underpasses, and railings, the sides of boxcars, and the endless prattle of his traveling companions. He then reshaped his harvest into the texts of both *U.S. Highball* and *Barstow*, as though he were crafting a monika.

For *U.S. Highball* Partch went a step farther than with *Barstow* by actually borrowing the framework, in addition to the ideas. In his 1943 preface, Partch pointed out the regular repetition of place names throughout the work as its unifying device: "The action and words have no integration but geography and the implied fortunes of the protagonist, the composition as a whole no integration but music."[63] Yet the hobo monika provided an integration and a precedent for this unique construction. Notice how lines four and twelve of "Monikas Seen on the Water Tank" securely situate the song's action in Fargo and mention hoboes from San Francisco to New York. A community with no clear roots required this kind of geographical specificity and would only break the pattern of naming places visited for a moniker recitation that replaced geography with individual names. Partch's pattern of naming locations in *U.S. Highball* remained unbroken because his monika concerned a trip and the recitation therefore centered on proper place names.

Neither were hoboes above nonsensically rhyming place names. In line twelve, the creator altered New York to New Yawk in order to facilitate a rhyme with chalk. In practice, this rhyme was similar to Partch's "Council Bluffs, I-o-wuffs," or "Winnemucca, Neva-ducca." He may not have recorded this rhyming in his notebook, but its addition in later drafts clearly originated in hobo culture.

Although Partch never specifically identified monika songs as a source of influence, they were certainly widespread through the hobo community. In one year of travel, George Milburn heard enough to designate them as a separate category of hobo song; Partch traveled on and off for fourteen years and must have heard many more. Reefer Charlie, a hobo who began riding the rods in the 1930s, recalled that "there was always lots of music in the jungles.... A lot of times we met under bridges—bridges and railroad trestles.... Anyway, we'd just get together and play. You'd hear the name of a song, and most of them guys were good enough musicians that if they didn't know it, they'd listen to a few bars, pick up the tune, and join in."[64]

Partch stayed in jungles during his two-week journey to Chicago; the long soliloquy that comprises *U.S. Highball*'s central section takes place around a fire in the Little America jungle, where one of the men references the Roseville jungle, one of the larger of its kind. Partch certainly picked up songs among the hoboes and might even have regaled his fellow wanderers with tunes on his Adapted Guitar.

Music was all around, rhyming was all around, and Partch concocted the idea for using a monika song framework when he first decided to compose the work, in the Little America jungle. *U.S. Highball* is therefore one of the few remaining monika songs, and could be called the genre's pinnacle. *U.S. Highball* also is revolutionary in the way it incorporates this particular kind of folk music. Through his intimate connection to the culture and its music, Partch took the monika song's essence and used it to create something larger and weightier. This distillation has more in common with Charles Ives's compositional methods, but operates within the genre's framework as well as the musical substance of the tune. In other words, Partch's use of the monika song is the clearest example of his conceptually exotic approach to the use of folk sources. He immersed himself in the hobo tradition and, instead of creating music that merely mimicked the sound of hobo music, he actually created hobo music using his own Monophonic technique. Partch achieved an integration of folk music and the Western cultivated tradition to create something truly "less influenced by the forms and attitudes" with which he had been raised. He also sculpted a lasting portrait of hoboes in a song style uniquely their own. In the clearer focus of this knowledge, *U.S. Highball* becomes an even more accurate and poignant representation of a dying culture.

While the monika song supplied the work's structure, Partch expanded and refined that framework in several ways. Indeed, he reinforced *U.S. Highball*'s ternary and monika song structure through three methods in particular: the overture's arrangement, textual repetition, and musical cues.

It is easy to dismiss the first, and most obvious, way in which Partch defined the work's structure as merely an unnecessary addition. The first two pages of version C's score comprise what Partch called an "Overture to *U.S. Highball*—Introduction of Instruments." In this overture, which does not appear in the other versions, each instrument enters in turn and plays a passage of music from the work to follow. In sound, it is roughly equivalent to a planned orchestral warm-up before a concert and, at first listen, appears to have little to do with what follows. When the Bloboy (see glossary) sounds out over the ensemble, mimicking the sound of a Southern Pacific train whistle, there is an abrupt shift to the first line of text and music.

The overture was an afterthought, added to allow audiences unfamiliar with Partch's instruments a chance to hear them individually before hearing them in concert. This awkward shift is painfully noticeable on Partch's 1958 Gate 5 recording where an obvious and maladroit splice connects the overture to the work's main body.[65]

While the overture may have been added to introduce an audience to Partch's instruments, closer examination reveals that it also functions like a thematic opera overture, preparing the audience for hearing the work and taking the trip along with "Mac." It opens with the Kithara playing one of two newly composed parts. As one of Partch's oldest instruments conceptually, it is fitting that the Kithara announces the work.[66] Following the Kithara's five measures, the Surrogate Kithara enters. The Surrogate Kithara was built three years before the completion of version C of *U.S. Highball*, as a substitute and help for virtuosic Kithara parts that would be almost impossible to play on that upright instrument. For his 1957 revision, Partch developed and exploited a new technique idiosyncratic to the instrument, which is displayed in the overture. This is the only piece in which, while the right hand is plucking a string, the left hand presses down on that string, rhythmically releasing it an eighth note later. On most monochord-based string instruments, this action would produce a dampened "thub" when plucked and a softer resonance on the string's pitch when released, but on the Surrogate Kithara a Pyrex rod separates the hands on the string. The resulting sound is a rhythmic pitch bend without a rearticulation of the note, much like the characteristic sound of the Japanese koto. Partch used this device to mimic the sound of the pulsations of train wheels on a steel rail while moving. This sound, tied to the movement of trains, first appears in the work proper immediately following the cry of "Let 'er highball, engineer!" Throughout the "A" section, and befitting the definition of the slang "Highball," it occurs only when the text refers to a train moving at high velocities. Once Mac is picked up on the highway, the rhythm and technique never return. Their use in the overture foreshadows Mac's move to the freights.

The Chromelodeon's overture music is the opposite of the Surrogate Kithara's. It evokes the sound of the highway, a theme not found in the piece's first two sections. After the overture, the instrument is heard only following Mac's final plea, "Going east, mister?," when he finally gets a ride on the highway and the "Chicago" variations begin. Following the Chromelodeon in the overture, the Harmonic Canon II (also known as Castor and Pollux; see glossary) enters. Its musical lines act as referential parentheses, confirming its placement at the overture's center. Pollux plays first and sounds a section of music taken from the first pages of the score proper. Castor overlaps the end of Pollux's music with a section lifted from the final two pages. The instrument, which Partch jokingly called the Gemini of his Harmonic Canons, serves to bind the beginning and the end infinitely together. By creating that unending circle, the Harmonic Canon lets us know that while the physical trip might end, Partch's psychological one was just beginning.

The remaining instruments complete the chronological trek to Chicago foreshadowed by the overture's first half. Following Castor and Pollux, the Bass Marimba's music complements the Chromelodeon's passage. In the score, this material accompanies the Chromelodeon highway theme and is the point of fastest and most complex Bass Marimba playing. It is followed by the Bamboo Marimba, playing material that occurs right after Mac gets a car ride and is leaving Laramie, Wyoming, while the Diamond Marimba continues this forward progression through the piece's journey by performing music from Cheyenne, the middle of the Chicago variations.

By adding the overture, Partch was tipping his hand, mapping out the coming journey by train and then by car. As in any standard overture, the main themes of rail and road, train and car, are introduced to help prepare the audience for this transcontinental hobo trip. By the time the final instruments of the overture are heard, the Spoils of War and Bloboy simultaneously, Partch was ready to move the audience back to the rail yards to board a train. The Bloboy's whistle combines with the ringing of two shell-casing pitches on the Spoils of War to signify an engineer calling "All aboard!"[67]

In addition to including the overture for version C, which delineates structure by providing a musical roadmap, Partch also used a second major method—a textual one. We have already seen how he differentiated the sections A, B, and A′ by using only inscriptions that were found on, or refer to, the method of transportation in each part of his journey. He also organized the station calls geographically, moving from Carmel, California, to Chicago. But he employed other subtle textual markers as well that were not based on the work's documentary nature. At the opening of both the A and A′ sections, protagonist Mac reminds the audience why he undertook this journey, reciting his letter that invoked "God's richest blessings." This passage operates as a call to movement and, when intoned, marks a new section. Mac's line "Going east, mister? Going east, mister? Going east, mister?" acts in a similar manner. Partch, a hobo who, through his keen observations, seems to have held himself apart from the community even while participating in it, wanted to hitchhike as much as possible to

Chicago. Thus the beginning of each section finds Mac beside the road attempting to bum a ride. Each time, the answer to his plea accords with the action and mode of transportation of that particular section. In section A, Mac remarks to himself that, "It's the freights for you, boy," and traipses off to the rail yards. In section B, his situation having become desperate, he supplies the disheartening response, "There are lots of rides, but they don't stop much, do they, *pal*?" Dejected, he lumbers to the jungle, lamenting to himself, "Back to the freights for you, boy." His luck turns, as does the text, at the beginning of section A'. After saving enough money in Little America, Mac finally catches a ride on the highway. His joy is almost palpable, and Partch originally had his protagonist, named Slim in earlier drafts, cry out "Whoopiday! I've got one!" The decision to drop this line for the final version was part of the textual and philosophical change from Slim, who was Partch, to Mac, who represents Everyman. As Partch realized that his audience had been through the rejection along with Slim and understood his excitement, he began to move *U.S. Highball* from the particular, which forced him to explain motivations, to the general, which relied more on listener identification and interpretation. Mac no longer needs to respond.

Partch's third structuring method reinforces these textual cues with musical ones. Instrumentation and rhythm mark key moments in the overall framework and match the protagonist's emotional state. Mac's repeated line "Going east, mister?" is echoed each time by the Diamond Marimba and the woodblock from the Spoils of War. In rhythm and inflection, the Diamond Marimba perfectly mimics the voice while the woodblock accentuates syllabic stress. Partch even wrote in the score above the Diamond Marimba, "Not too fast—as though the marimba were saying these words."

The dynamics in the measures immediately following his line also articulate Mac's responses clearly. Dynamic markings are important indicators in Partch's music. Unlike most early twentieth-century composers, he rarely inscribed dynamics; as far as traditional expressive markings are concerned, he under-marked his scores. When Partch penciled in "soft" or "loud," he obviously intended a drastic dynamic change for effect.[68] In the first two iterations of "Going east, mister?" the dynamics grow from *pianissimo* to *piano*. This small swell adds a touch of hopefulness to the line's instrumental echo, mirroring Mac's state of mind. The woodblock, however, undercuts that hope in section B. It is used on the second iteration of the word "going," adding a harshness to the question and indicating that the hero will not be able to get a ride; it is over even as he asks. The third and final time the reverse happens. The question is asked only twice, the second echo *pianissimo* to the first's *piano* with the woodblock striking on the word "mister," creating a high rising terminal on the final syllable, popularly known as "uptalk," by emphasizing the weak beat. It is as though Mac is so completely dispirited that he cannot even utter the inquiry a third time.

In the measures following, Partch sets up his structure more explicitly. On page 5, the Kithara setting of "It's the freights for you, boy," the response to Mac's plea, is identical to the Diamond Marimba one preceding it. The Kithara copies the voice's inflection and rough rhythmic outline, but accompanies the voice, rather than answering it. It is a straightforward, dispassionate setting. On page 24, a similar response appears. With the Diamond Marimba replacing the Kithara, Mac's self-effacing line is granted more force, more despair, but a crescendo signals remaining hope. After the third setting on page 29, Mac's doubt of receiving a ride is depicted instrumentally. As the Bass Marimba enters, it quickly descends from a 10/7 starting pitch to a 10/9. The sub-bass 7/6 on the Chromelodeon is also heard, a rumbling, reedy sound that is only used two other times—once to underscore an ironic hymn and, at the end of work, as Mac apprehensively approaches Chicago. Here it adds a similarly ominous portent to the proceedings, as though saying, "You have to get a ride this time; you will not survive if you try and ride the rails any longer." Yet this instrumentation lasts only a measure and a half, and the audience quickly learns that Mac's prospects are improving. With the Boo, Bass Marimba, Diamond Marimba, and Surrogate Kithara all playing sixteenth notes, Partch asks for a combined accelerando and crescendo leading into the Chromelodeon's entrance with its highway theme. Hearing and examining these three settings of similar texts back-to-back affords a clear view of Partch's use of textual and musical clues to define overall structure.

U.S. Highball's Instrumental Evolution

This structural view also provides interesting insight into Partch's compositional practice. Unlike the unskilled composer critics often painted him as, Partch carefully constructed, placed, and varied the themes that depicted his librettos in music: he is as successful a word-painter as any Renaissance madrigalist. While he owed his ability in this musical aspect to his desire to place text and music in a fertile relationship, it also came from the instruments he designed and built and the unique and characteristic sounds they produced. Partch turned what could have been a liability of his Monophonic system, that almost no instruments could play his tones, into a great asset. Through his creations, Partch could hear the sounds he wanted and needed to realize his works Monophonically. He refused to compromise with the approximations available through standard instrumentation and instead built the instruments that remain his most characteristic accomplishment. Hobo lore, lingo, and life play no part in this aspect of the work, but in order to understand the work fully, it is necessary to examine his instruments individually, the ways he wrote for and used them, and their specific use in *U.S. Highball*. As important as the work was to the creation of his hobo persona, it was equally important in how he would eventually orchestrate all his subsequent pieces.

It seems that Partch added percussion parts to *U.S. Highball* in response to Henry Cowell's criticism that the work needed more rhythmic interest. It seems strange that even though he added five percussion instruments in version C to balance the five plectrum and reed instruments, he gave them secondary roles. The percussion instruments appear late in the overture, rarely come to the fore, and they do not play consistently throughout the work; rather, they add color and motion when needed. By contrast, the plectrum and reed instruments open the work, have much richer and more prominent parts, and play almost continuously. The most important single instrument is the Chromeloden: it is the only instrument to appear in both versions B and C, its part remaining basically unaltered. When he originally composed the work it was Partch's newest instrument, and it carries the majority of the themes and the weight.

In adapting his Chromelodeon, Partch retained many of the manufactured features of the original reed organ but cleverly adapted them to new purposes: for example, he renamed and reconnected the organ stops to expand the instrument's capabilities. The Chromelodeon has five workable stops that are used in *U.S. Highball*: reading from left to right, the Z, AL, AR, X, and 6/5. The Z and AL stops control the physical keys from the E below middle C (a 5/4) to the bottom of the keyboard, while the AR, X, and 6/5 control the keyboard's upper two-thirds.[69]

The stops' individual functions, while familiar to users of pump organs, have a different flavor. The AL and AR stops are for regular playing, similar to a complete chorus of flute principals in traditional registral practice for organs. The X, Z, and 6/5 are all couplers of some fashion: the X and Z couple a 2/1 (a pitch octave) higher and lower respectively, and the 6/5, Partch's most inventive stop, couples a physical octave higher on the keyboard. On the Chromelodeon, tuned so that a 2/1 spans roughly three and a half physical octaves, an octave coupler adds a 6/5 above the note played, roughly a minor third.

At three points in the score Partch uses the qualities granted by the Chromelodeon's organ stops to greatest effect, each time in an attempt to emulate a train's whistle. He writes for all stops to be open except the Z. Then, with this mass of sound, he asks the performer to smear up over a keyboard octave with both hands at the same time, hold a chord at the top, and then smear back to the starting point. The resulting sound is remarkably similar to a train whistle, especially when combined with the Bloboy. In each instance, he then takes the replication a step farther. Closing the AR and playing above the E that marks the domain of the AL, the performer replays the exact same smear. With the fundamental missing, only high, reedy sounds emerge, like the Doppler echo of a passing train receding in the distance. It is a stunning effect.

Partch's pianistic skills and training from his younger years came to the fore on the Chromelodeon part. It is a virtuosic part for fingers and even feet, which must continuously pump air into the bellows to maintain a steady sound and control the dynamics. The part fits well under the fingers, and Partch took pains in particularly tricky passages to mark in fingerings to aid the performer. These markings are especially useful on the microchromatic runs that evoke freedom of movement, usually accompanying station calls. These runs span close to a 2/1 in many instances and include jumps in the middle of the runs to facilitate chord resolution.

Contrary to popular assumption, Partch peppered moments of common-practice consonance throughout *U.S. Highball*, all easily heard on the Chromelodeon. In fact, Partch often referred to the work in private as his homage to the triad.[70] A justly-tuned major seventh chord, which Partch seems to associate with moments of reflection and rest, occurs most frequently. One appears on page 8, ending a fast-moving section and leading into a welcome piece of advice to sleep on the back end of the oil tank in order to stay in one piece. In this occurrence, the Chromelodeon pitches fan out from a held 5/4 (third) and a 3/2 (fifth), ultimately including a 1/1 (fundamental) and 15/8 (seventh) with them. In a similar passage on page 17, two hoboes discuss building a fire to keep warm until an empty comes along to the accompaniment of open hexachords on the kithara and, ultimately, a major seventh on the Chromelodeon.

Far more common, however, are parodies of common-practice chord progressions. Near the piece's end, an ironic hymn combines Partch's rants against Western music as taught in conservatories with a disdain for modern Christianity inherited from his father's apostasy. The latter element was common among hoboes from their experiences in missions throughout the United States, and stories to match the biting sarcasm directed toward religion found in *U.S. Highball* and in *Barstow* can be discovered in every hobo memoir. Tom Kromer, for example, filled several chapters of his autobiography with acrimony toward so-called people of God. He wrote that for many homeless, missions were one of the few places to eat and get a flop for the night, but droning preaching and praying in a humid, stifling church house always preceded the chance to eat. After the homeless had spent at least three hours packed into pews, a woman would finally call on the men to repent, urging them to come forward and kneel at the altar. Until her quota was full, with at least five young men prostrate before her, she would not release them for supper. Many times, Kromer wrote, he would repent for the thirteenth or fourteenth time just to end the service and stay in the converts' room, which had slightly better beds.[71]

Although not all accounts related this amount of enmity, all decry the hypocrisy of Christian social workers. Hoboes were generally well-read as a population and most had read the Bible. They knew that the Scriptures held out a higher and tougher standard, emphasizing grace in salvation and toward humankind. Many believed in and followed a strict moral code, only stealing when necessary. They were understandably ashamed of the missions and the inconsistency of middle-class Christians who refused to help the poor. Most hoboes shared Reefer Charlie's attitude when he said that "I have seen thousands of them [old-time hoboes and tramps] that you could trust much farther around your wife and family than you could many people who went to church and professed to be Christians."[72]

Partch's indictment is just as devastating. Arriving in North Platte, Nebraska, Mac finds two notices from the Salvation Army, or the Sally, as the hoboes called it.[73] The first informs transients that they are allowed two meals and a bed for one night and cannot leave after 6:00 p.m. The second is a hymn, supposedly sung before the two meals and bed. The anthem, whose text is "Praise the Lord" repeated numerous times, is presented as a parody of hymnody with common-practice chord changes slightly altered by the two accompanying instruments. Its effect is similar to the "Jesus was God in the flesh" inscription from *Barstow*, but with a slight harmonic deviation that is just enough of a twist to lend a circus-like sound while retaining vestiges of the model. The accompaniment opens with a 5/4 (approximately a major third) in the Chromelodeon and a 5/3 (a major sixth) in the Surrogate Kithara. These intervals contract to a 10/9 (a major second) in the Chromelodeon and a 6/5 (a minor third) in the Surrogate Kithara. These echoes of chord progressions are underscored by a 16/11 in the subbass (a slightly flat perfect fifth or sharp tritone to the G fundamental).

Presentation in this manner, broken down into intervals that constitute a measure-by-measure, instrument-by-instrument description, makes an argument for equal temperament chords accompanying the religious text as in any chorale or hymn. The second measure of page 38 even contains a double 4-3 suspension in the Chromelodeon part. But when the actual ratios of each instrument are stacked one on top of the other, they are differentiated by a fraction of a semitone. The Chromelodeon moves from a 16/11-20/11 to an 18/11 while the Surrogate Kithara moves from a 16/9-16/15 to a 12/7-10/7. Individually the instruments form intervals that would work in equal temperament, but collectively they create an effective parody showing a skewed vision of how true hymnody, and by implication true Christianity, should look. It is a subtle form of humor, but right in line with Partch's satiric writings from the time such as his "Modern Parables."

Partch uses other small devices as Chromelodeon text painting throughout the piece, musical depictions he might have learned on the job as a teenager playing piano and organ accompaniment at a local moviehouse.[74] Each time the train stops, he notates a large *ritard*, and the Chromelodeon lines rise slowly into its register's upper limits, ultimately stopping high in the treble clef on the interval of a 33/22, an interval smaller than an equally tempered half-step. Just as a smear with all stops open aurally depicts the train's whistle upon departing, these rising lines depict steam being released from the engine as the train grinds to a halt. At the keyboard's other end, Partch creates a funereal atmosphere as the work slows to a stop in Little America at the opening of the B section. With the Z, AL, AR, and X stops open, the Chromelodeon plays slowly revolving chords in its lowest register, an effect as powerful in the popular consciousness today, thanks to countless movies, as the use of trombones to symbolize the underworld three hundred years earlier.

The Chromelodeon is not the only instrument to participate in this text-painting game, but as most of the other instruments' parts are adaptations of those originally for Adapted Guitar and Kithara, their painting is primarily connected to sounds that might emanate from those instruments. Castor and Pollux, the Harmonic Canon II, aptly demonstrate this fact. Castor is used primarily for the musical passage it plays in the Overture—a full sweep in both hands, the left playing the canon's upper half from strings 44 to 23 and the right playing its lower half from strings 22 to 1 simultaneously. As with the Kithara, occasional sweeps accompany station calls, but there are only two instances of unique passagework. In the first, which happens during a discussion of Cheyenne after leaving Imlay, the middle string, string 22, is plucked with constant sixteenth notes, a motion doubled by the Boo. The second is lifted from a passage originally for Adapted Guitar in the opening of section B. Strings 28 through 38 are caressed by the pads of the fingers, resulting in a soft, guitar-like sound that underscores this ballad-like section, which rhapsodizes on being unable to get a ride.

In contrast, Pollux is much more active, but the conceptions and playing techniques of the Kithara and its Surrogate overshadow its passages. At least half of the sweeps on Pollux are the same runs up and down over eight strings, emulating the Kithara's hexachords. On page 36, during the notice to transients from the Sally, the Surrogate Kithara pitch-bending technique, one Partch used only in this work, is transferred to Pollux. The left hand produces pitch bends, koto-like, to provide a hint of railroad travel through an association set up in the overture; but as the sound originates from Pollux after Mac has given up the rails, it serves as a memory triggered by the posted notice. This Kithara-like technique reappears one other time, accompanying the Jack Parkin inscription, as though reading it aroused a fleeting desire to return to hopping freight trains.

Partch's percussion instruments are incapable of holding a pitch for an extended period. Once the instrument is struck, the resulting sharp, dry pitch decays quickly, leaving more of an impression of the attack than a sense of pitch. This attribute caused Partch to develop a variety of methods to create different colors, almost all of which involve repeated attacks that create emphasis and movement.

Partch calls for the use of two types of sticks on the Bass Marimba. The first is a pair of large, felt-covered dowels. Holding one in each hand, the Bass Marimba player strikes the edges of the gigantic wooden blocks. These felt sticks are used in passages where the percussion parts serve mainly to push the piece along, because hitting only the ends enables the player to move up and down the marimba faster and accomplish repeated notes more quickly. They are also used to imitate and support the vocal line: each time we hear "I got a letter and the letter says," for example, the Bass Marimba doubles the voice, adding weight, importance, to the statement. However, when the line continues to "May God's richest blessings be upon you" the first time, the Bass Marimba drops out completely. On its second occurrence, by contrast, the text is repeated several times, and on the final repetition the Bass Marimba reenters with the second pair of sticks, these having large, heavy mallets on the end. Finding a ride on the highway is a rich blessing indeed, or at least so the Bass Marimba tells the audience.

Partch uses this second pair of sticks sparingly. Their mass, hitting the middle of the wooden blocks, elicits a deep, resonant pitch, one that lasts longer than that of any other of Partch's percussion instruments. He wanted a specific effect, and so placed them deliberately. The mallets are most often used for the train whistles, completing the mirage beneath the Chromelodeon and Bloboy. For the first train whistle, the Bass Marimba rolls a 5/3 as the foundation; for the second, it holds a repeated 9/8, a 2/1-and-a-half above the previous 5/3. In fact, the writing for the second and third whistles is higher in general for all instruments and is scored in an open position. Knowing that he switched trains to cross the continental divide, Partch was careful to orchestrate his various train whistles differently, giving them each unique personalities that were nevertheless sonically knit together. The mallets are also used from Kimball, Nebraska, through the notice to transients mentioned above, which has its own unusual scoring.

The Diamond Marimba does not play during the train whistles. In fact, whereas the instruments examined above are almost constant throughout, the remaining percussion often consists of nothing more than sixteenth notes on one pitch or an ostinato here and there for motion. They take their pitches from the strings and Chromelodeon and participate in the harmonies by supporting those already present in the other instruments. For the Diamond Marimba and other percussion instruments, challenging and complex passages are found primarily at the work's end, during the Chicago variations, which explains why their overture music comes exclusively from that section as well. Where the work's first and second parts are focused on tonal structures and pitch relationships supporting elaborate texts, the third and final section, with its libretto of nonsense syllables and rhymes on the word "Chicago," is focused on rhythm and the forward drive to the end.

With the exception of where it imitates or supports vocal inflections, the Diamond Marimba part is constructed principally of patterns of Utonalities and Otonalities.[75] The Marimba's blocks are arranged according to Partch's tonality diamond, and he exploits this arrangement by writing passagework that moves up the diamond for Utonalities (which he related to major chords) or down for Otonalities (which he likened to minor chords), such as a four-note pattern between Utonality hexads 4 and 3 with one note of hexad 2 thrown in.[76] He also had several tricks, repeated devices that, although initially hard to learn, could be quickly executed, providing much of the instrument's forward momentum. For instance, in these patterns among close hexads, one hand and mallet will frequently stay on one note, alternating with the other hand, which is moving rapidly.

Alternatively, one U- or Otonality will be highlighted through rapid arpeggios, sweeping through each note in a hexad. These motives are then transposed to new areas on the Diamond Marimba. Like shifting patterns on a keyboard, the hands instinctively remember the pattern and can continue easily, but with a striking new sound. Partch's notation is based on the U- and Otonalities, and it is difficult to change notation reading while reading a line. This kind of notational change constitutes the most challenging aspect of the Diamond Marimba, and while the player rarely has to switch between U- and Otonalities in the middle of a run, the alternation is found most frequently in the Chicago variations of section A′.

Partch notates and employs the Bamboo Marimba in much the same manner as the Diamond Marimba. The Boo does not play as part of the train whistles, as it cannot add to the pitch build-up Partch needed in order to form a tight tone-cluster that emulates the train's sound; rather, it would give motion to an otherwise static event. The Boo's sound lasts the shortest amount of time of all the percussion instruments. Rather than a ringing tone, like that of the Diamond Marimba, the Boo produces a curt sound that, in performance, comes across like a whip crack at a given pitch. Partch's writing for the Boo shows that pitches, while necessary and carefully chosen, are not as important as the sharp, snare-like attack and the aural experience of rhythm rising within a tessitura. For this reason, the Boo is also left out of lyrical passages. Throughout the piece, its passagework therefore consists of runs and glissandi rather than the chords and discrete pitches that mark the part for Diamond and Bass Marimba.

The final percussion instrument, other than the Cloud-Chamber Bowls, which only play in the overture, is the Spoils of War, a collection of tuned brass shell casings and a Chinese woodblock, together with other assorted percussive instruments not used in *U.S. Highball*. Besides its enunciation during the "Going east, Mister?" lines, the Spoils of War is used mainly to finish off Diamond Marimba phrases by adding a slow decay to its sound, and to create a high, ringing quality during the train whistles. In the score, it shares the same stave with the Diamond Marimba; the only other time it plays is at the very end—a four bar chime, ominously droning the protagonist's arrival in Chicago. These chimes, harsh and penetrating, play as all other parts dim and slow to the barely audible whisper of "Chicago."

Since the percussion instruments shine during the final headlong rush to Chicago, it is fitting that they end the piece. Following the whisper of "Chicago," they all roll the 1/1 fundamental, a perfect cadence. However,

Partch wanted to further nuance the anxiety of arrival in the fabled city and so, after two beats of rest, they reenter with a final, rare dissonance.

U.S. Highball, Hobo Composition

From the battered notebook to the final version submitted to the Library of Congress, Harry Partch had a clear goal in mind—a clear manner in which he wanted to depict his hobo life. But what of the legend that Partch allowed to grow around the piece, the misconceptions he fostered in his writings about it? Was he consciously manipulating his image, and for what reason? Obviously Partch's claim that every word of the text was drawn from hobo sayings encountered on the trip is an exaggeration. The composer freely added connecting phrases, ideas, and remembrances besides those explicitly recorded. He did not set the fragments of speech in the order in which he encountered and recorded them in the notebook, but instead moved them around for purely compositional reasons. Even while on the trip, he went back to previously-recorded snippets and added place names. He deliberately inserted the names of towns in the first draft libretto that were not listed in the notebook. While the majority of the libretto was indeed based on hobo phrases, lore, and slang, Partch clearly added his own interpretations of those fragments of conversation in order to facilitate the text's message. After he admitted that his compositional method called for an organic growth of the words and music, nothing less could be expected. Why, then, was Partch deliberately misleading on this point? The organic growth he sought in the composition of *U.S. Highball* would not have been possible if he had been unwilling to alter the text. For words and music to grow together in a symbiotic relationship, one cannot remain static while the other moves ahead.

Likewise, from at least the midpoint of his journey to Chicago, Partch knew why he was keeping the notebook. He had, over the previous ten years, completed works like *Barstow* based on hobo lore and experiences. *U.S. Highball* might not have been fully formed when he began the trip, but, based on previous experience, he surely knew the probability of a composition growing out of the notebook. If he were unsure of the reason for the notebook in Sacramento, California, then by Little America, only a few days later, he had formed enough of an idea to commit it to paper and to begin composing and editing fragments.

Examining his life at the time of the work's composition suggests only one reason for this discrepancy between his later writings and the notebook evidence. *U.S. Highball* was the centerpiece of his Guggenheim application in 1943. In order to obtain the fellowship, Partch must have felt that he needed to present a substantial work composed exclusively under their support. *U.S. Highball*, a forty-minute hobo epic, fit the bill perfectly. He wrote to Otto Luening insinuating that the work was written, from inception to completion, that very year. He then presented the composition to the John Simon Guggenheim Memorial Foundation and dedicated version B, the first one in full score notation, to the Foundation and Henry Allen Moe, its secretary. Just as he knew that a more personal hobo work would ring truer for an audience, he understood that fostering these misconceptions would earn the support he needed to leave the hobo jungles.

While the first two conceptions about *U.S. Highball* Partch fostered in his writing were exaggerations for a clear purpose, the final one concerning the similar nature of all three versions stands as accurate. Partch made changes between the first and second versions, but in version C, overall structure, pitch framework, and rhythms remained fundamentally unaltered. He seems to have removed dialogue passages primarily to shorten the work, possibly in response to disparaging remarks by reviewers and other composers at its premiere, or as a result of the difficulty in pressing a recording of such a large piece, or simply because of his evolving musical philosophy. Whatever the reason, the outcome evidently pleased Partch: after revising the work three times in thirteen years, in the remaining twenty years of his life he never touched it again.

Whatever the circumstances surrounding its creation, *U.S. Highball* is a uniquely American work. Although in practically every essay he composed about the work Partch maintained that it was not intended as a statement on American life, or even to have overtones of Americana, it inevitably does. Partch's experiences as a hobo, one of a group of people granted a distinctively iconic status only in America, inspired and formed the work. The combination of frontier, railroad expansion, and labor shortage existed only in the western United States, where it caused an unprecedented number of hoboes. While hoboes did exist in other parts of the world, their number caused them to be a noticeable social problem only in the United States. It was the commitment to individualism as an ideal found in American popular media and culture that elevated hoboes to the mythic status they still enjoy. *U.S. Highball* owes its considerable power simultaneously to enthrall and amuse to the mythic life of the hobo, to its sense of freedom in movement, to the awkward poetry of its vernacular, to the transience of its characters and their voices, and to its love of vast, open spaces. The ideas and sounds contained within its structure are embedded in American culture and history. Whether by intention or happenstance, Partch's use of a subject matter with deep personal import, and a process culled from hobo culture and Greek thought that could only have developed in America, enabled him to accomplish a unique synthesis of music and Americana.

In the 1930s and 1940s, composers, musicologists, sociologists, and folklorists were attempting to ferret out the characteristics that made a music American. They looked in Appalachia, among African-Americans in the South, even in prison yards. They tried to boil ballads and folk tunes down to their essence to uncover any rhythm, harmony, or turn of melody found nowhere else. Yet in all their research, they virtually ignored the hobo. Despite the attention hoboes and migrants received in photography and literature, musicians and folk collectors failed to examine their culture. A former hobo, documenting his experiences in 1925, crudely wrote that "the hoboes sang true American songs, not the odious noises composed by swart, thick-voiced aliens, but the simple, plaintive airs of long sentimental and heroic ballads which are as native to America as the prairie corn."[77] Here was an untapped resource, a wellspring of song and story.

Harry Partch documented hobo life in a way never accomplished before or since. By the time he was composing *U.S. Highball*, hobo culture was dying. The automobile was destroying the hobo and his jungle in the same way that it destroyed American dependence on rail. The itinerant family, living out of, and moving freely by, its car became the new source of migrant workers. As trucks carried more and more freight, railroads carried less, resulting in fewer trains. Hoboes moved to highways for transportation, but there, hitchhiking across open country, they found no natural stopping point like the railroad divisions. Gasoline was available in every town and along all major roads, and automobiles could stop at their drivers' will. The lack of uniform congregating points obviated hobo jungles. Without the collegiality of a rail car or jungle fire, hoboes stopped singing together, stopped passing on songs and stories. As the culture passed away, it carried with it a wealth of monika songs and hobo slang.[78] But Harry Partch's compositions immortalized those songs and stories, that slice of American life. *U.S. Highball*, his most creative work, owes its framework to a hobo creation, the monika song. It owes its flavor to the hobo argot that peppers it. And it owes its text to the lore surrounding an outlaw riding the rails. It is truly a different form of exoticism than that practiced by his chronological compatriots.

Where the piece maintained hobo culture, its composer maintained the hobo image, adopting its persona. Partch toured the New York area with his Adapted Guitar slung on his back and a repertoire of songs drawn from the words of tramps, a Woody Guthrie figure for the high-art crowd. He was an iconoclast, defying traditional methods of composition and clinging to a rugged American individualism. Even Partch's philosophy of life and attitudes toward the world align closely with those attributed to the hobo. Dan O'Brien, a hobo philosopher and celebrity in the 1920s and 1930s, wrote of the hobo, "He is an avowed optimist, laughs a great deal at the gyrations of men, looks upon politicians as tyrants, the clergy as supreme dodgers of things religious, hopes the human race, like whiskey, will improve with age."[79] It would be hard to write a more accurate description of Partch's stance on the government, religion, mankind, and even strong drink. Dismayed by the economic situation in which he found himself, Partch nevertheless embraced what he saw as a truer, more down-to-earth life. Through this identification with and respect for his composition's subjects, he was able to create a fusion of folk sources and cultivated craft, a new kind of documentary that grew organically from its sources to a new flowering of art.

CHAPTER SIX

A NEWSBOY LETTER

During the time that Harry Partch rode the rails and then transformed those trips into musical form, American perception of the hobo was shifting once more. Through the late 1930s and early 1940s nostalgia grew for pre-Depression hoboes in response to the situation brewing with migrants and transients on the West Coast. This transition can best be seen in the 1940 *New York Times Magazine* article "That Vanishing American, the Hobo."[1] The article opens with the stark observation that the hobo population had fallen from a high of a million and a half in the late 1920s to 25,000. Author Lawrence Stessin then wistfully worries over these numbers while foreseeing a future in which the hobo joins the American Indian as a vanishing people. Although Stessin views the new reliance on well-paid regular labor as a positive advance in American society, his article—printed in a prominent East Coast publication— reveals a striking change to the attitudes of even ten years earlier. Hoboes were no longer just freedom-seeking wanderers at odds with industrial society; now they were iconic figures of the Old West, new archetypes in the American psyche. No wonder Harry Partch began to highlight his time on the road as hobo: as the Dust Bowl migrant came to take the hobo's place as the most feared and despised Western figure, he naturally wished to control his persona and history and show them in the most acceptable and profitable light.

While *U.S. Highball* is certainly Partch's magnum hobo opus and *Barstow* his hobo concerto, they are not the only compositions based on his eight-year wanderings. *U.S. Highball* and *Barstow* are the anchors of *The Wayward*, a collection that includes two lesser-known works, *San Francisco—A Setting of the Cries of Two Newsboys on a Street Corner* and

The Letter. Partch later described the grouping as "based on the spoken and written words of hoboes and other characters . . . the result of my wanderings in the Western part of the United States from 1935 to 1941."[2] Each work deals with a marginalized people, the "wayward" in American life, and presents them as not only worthy of contemplation, but recognition as a genus of true Americana. The works encompass his years living as a wayward person, and a full understanding of how Partch crafted his hobo persona relies on considering the complete collection: Partch musically chronicled not just the hobo but two other iconic emblems of the homeless experience in the 1930s and early 1940s, the newsboy and the migratory transient worker.

When considered alongside each other, these two figures, and the manner in which Partch chose to present them, offer a miniature version of the larger issues that frame this study. The newsboy's image traverses the same convoluted path as the hobo's, moving from an object of scorn to one of pity to one of nostalgia over the course of a few decades. The transient worker, on the other hand, begins in scorn mixed with pity and never progresses to nostalgia, largely because his image becomes intertwined with that of the Dust Bowl refugee—much as Partch's own image did. Understanding *San Francisco* and *The Letter* reveals the shifting terrain on which Partch began promoting his Americana collection.

Images of the Newsboy

The figure of the newsboy first appears in Partch's writing in the spring of 1934, when he dashed off "A Modern Parable I." As observed in chapter 4, in this piece of writing, Partch compared the barkings of a newsboy to a university president delivering a valedictory address. At that point in his life, when he had followed the harvests on a few occasions but had not yet descended into the hobo jungles on a more permanent basis, Partch was eager to demonstrate his artistic and philosophical remove from what he saw as the more academic style of classical music taught in conservatories and universities. Since he lacked the relevant experiences to adopt the hobo as a figure with which to challenge the establishment, he recalled the newsboys who dotted the landscape of his early adulthood in Los Angeles and San Francisco, latching on to their image as a way to represent those farthest removed from the halls of academe and the native intelligence that could be found in even the most unlikely of places. Because Partch fastened on to the newsboy so early in his writings as an alternative stance from which to view the world, the arc of public perception of the newsboy from his origins through the Great Depression reveals as much about the composer's aesthetic thinking in the 1930s and 1940s as it does of *San Francisco*.

Even a cursory glance at the newsboy's cultural position reveals intriguing analogies with that of the hobo.[3] When he appeared on the scene in the first half of the nineteenth century, the newsboy was the well-nurtured yet industrious worker. He sold his papers to make a living for himself, profiting from an expanding infrastructure that allowed for mass circulation of newspapers to a citizenry that demanded up-to-date information on important matters. In the latter half of the century, views of newsboys were not so lofty. The image degenerated into a dangerous class of outlaws, feared and pitied, just as likely to pick a pocket as to sell a paper. By the turn of the century, thanks to works of popular fiction (especially the domestic sentimental novel) and sentimental art, the newsboy had become an exemplar of laissez faire capitalism, ably demonstrating why that particular economic system was so important to the health of the US economy. As reformers became concerned about child workers in the twentieth century's early decades, they portrayed the newsboy as a casualty of an industrial society desperately in need of aid. Finally, by the Depression's onset, he had become a proletarian hero ultimately displaced from home and sustenance by economics beyond his control.

This quick, depersonalized sweep reveals why Partch included the newsboy in his portrait of those who, though on the wayward side of American life in the 1930s, represented a "true fountainhead of Americana." Perceptions of the newsboy have vacillated as widely and changed as radically as those of the hobo, but they have remained curiously in line with images of the men who rode the rails. Both classes of men (and women, to a lesser extent) mirrored American opinions about those living outside societal norms and the proper response to them, and both were subject to wildly contradictory views as individualistic entrepreneurs and vagrants.

The easiest way to see the dichotomy of views is to examine two representative paintings of the newsboy from the nineteenth century: Henry Inman's *News Boy* from 1841 and James Henry Cafferty's *Newsboy Selling New-York Herald* from 1857. Inman's work (fig. 6.1) is a frankly romantic depiction of the newsboy: a nattily dressed youth with his hat cocked to one side, his eyebrows raised in a delighted look, and his cheeks rosy. He stands next to a half-eaten apple he had been munching; his mouth is open, ready to make his pitch, and he leans next to an ebony sphinx before the Astor House Hotel on Broadway.[4] The only signs of low station are the tear at the elbow of his overcoat and a small patch at his knee. Painted only sixteen years later, Cafferty's work comes after a series of depressions had changed America's view of itself (see fig. 6.2). His newsboy also sports the healthy-looking rosy cheeks of Inman's, but the face they adorn is more haggard, painted with downward lines as opposed to Inman's optimistic upward ones. Exhaustion keeps the newsboy's mouth barely open and darkness rims his hollow eyes. His clothes are more haphazard and ill-fitting, and he stands in front of a half-completed wall papered with posters. Inman's newsboy is on the move; Cafferty's is stuck. The newsboy of 1857 pleads rather than pitches; he is a beggar and a vagrant.

Most newsboys were not street urchins or orphans, as sometimes portrayed in popular literature. Certainly some were homeless, but most left stable homes to sell papers to make extra money for the family.[5] They went to school in the morning, lined up outside newspaper offices in the early afternoon, then sold papers until dusk or after. In fact, they sold so many papers that between 1900 and 1920 newspaper publishers relied on newsboys for more than half of the distribution of their evening editions.[6] Skilled newsboys working the late edition circuit could easily sell 250 to 300 papers a night.[7]

Newsboys were consummate salesmen. Every afternoon, they attempted to judge accurately the weather, the day of the week, the season, how well local sports teams and businesses were doing, and, most importantly, the size and impact of the headline in order to divine how many papers they should buy from the press. Subscriptions drove morning papers, but men bought afternoon papers on the spur of the moment or out of habit. So newsboys looked for banner headlines and attempted to communicate them to anyone who walked past through any means available. Any papers left at the day's end represented lost money, as newspapers would not buy them back. If newsboys did not sell all their papers, they would stay out all night and try to sell to dwindling numbers of pedestrians.

Late in the evenings, in cold winter months, many newsboys with leftover papers performed for passersby, playing to the popular impression of newsboys by acting the part of the poor, hungry, homeless child to coax a tip out of a customer. Most common was what the newsboys called the "last paper ploy." Pretending to be cold, hungry, and exhausted after a long afternoon of selling papers, the newsboy would beg anyone who walked by to purchase his last paper so he could scurry home to a warm house and meal. Once the customer's back was turned, the newsboy would slide over to his secret stash, remove another "last paper," and begin again. Skilled newsboys could play this ruse for hours.[8]

Figure 6.1. Henry Inman (1801–46), *News Boy*, 1841, oil on canvas. Reproduced with permission from the Addison Gallery of American Art, Phillips Academy, Andover, Massachusetts.

Figure 6.2. James Henry Cafferty, *Newsboy Selling New-York Herald*, 1857. Image courtesy of http://www.the-athenaeum.org.

After World War I, however, the era of the newsboy began to fade. Distribution companies began appearing, delivering newspapers and supplanting newsboys, so fewer Americans bought their papers off the street.[9] By the onset of the Great Depression, the newsboy had already become another vanishing American.

Also a factor in the newsboy's decline was widespread questioning, during the Depression, of the social utility of giving jobs to boys that could go to adults, especially as around four hundred daily papers folded or were absorbed during the decade.[10] Depression-era implementation of federal standards for the employment of youth sealed the coffin: the 1938 Fair Labor Standards Act (FLSA) stated that children age fourteen to fifteen could only perform work that did not interfere with school, and that no one under eighteen could work in dangerous occupations. The law did not affect children who sold newspapers directly, but societal pressure to limit childhood occupations was so strong that the 1940 Census showed a 41 percent drop in children age fourteen to fifteen who worked. Much of that decline came from the newsboy industry.[11] By the 1940s, the few remaining newsboys were licensed and the homeless ones largely off the street, prompting a small wave of nostalgia for the days when there was a newsboy on every corner, ubiquitous as lampposts. The newsboy may have held a mass of contradictions, but as Vincent DiGirolamo noted, "more than any other child worker in the United States, the newsboy has become a cultural icon, a symbol of the American character, the American work ethic, the American dream.... The newsboy figure embodies the belief that individual character, not social class, shapes the structure of opportunity in America."[12]

The Newsboy in Musical Culture

This brief newsboy history strikes resonances with the hobo story, especially in images of the newsboy as someone finding his own way and succeeding by his own ingenuity. Understanding this popular perception clarifies why Partch used the newsboy to speak back to academia in "Modern Parable I." Understanding the musical culture that often related the newsboy to hoboes likewise makes clear why Partch thought a short setting of a newsboy's cries a perfect counterpoint to the more monumental *U.S. Highball* and *Barstow*.

Songs about newsboys appeared in American popular music as long as children sold papers on the street. Most of them in the late nineteenth and early twentieth centuries partook of the sentimental parlor song tradition, songs for voice and piano accompaniment that would be sung in the home or in the newsboy foundations by members of visiting charitable organizations, especially well-meaning women. Appealing to the genteel attitudes of the late nineteenth-century middle-class woman, many of the songs written about newsboys featured dying ones. With lyrics concerning the cold nights through which they worked, the squalid conditions in which they slept, and the loneliness of their death, these songs worked to create a sense of *noblesse oblige* among their audience. For instance, "Found Dead in the Street," written in 1882 by the Louisville House of Refuge music instructor, ends with these lines:

> Once more hear him cry, "My papers, who'll buy?
> Oh! Is there not some one that cares though I die?"
> A shivering chill, and then all is still,
> While softly the snow flakes come down from the sky.[13]

Not all songs sketched the dire conditions under which newsboys labored, nor did they use a newsboy's perspective to demonstrate their situation. The famous hobo song "Big Rock Candy Mountain" originally spoke to fears of impressionable young boys being taken in by the dark characters encountered on the street or in back alleys. Homeless vagrants and hoboes alike were understood to prey on young boys, especially newsboys. In the song, a young boy falls under the thrall of an older hobo who spins tales of a land where the sun always shines, the hens lay soft boiled eggs, lemonade bubbles up from the ground, and no one has to work. But the song has a darker underside, in a stanza almost always left out of recordings:

> The punk rolled up his big blue eyes
> And said to the jocker, "Sandy,
> I've hiked and hiked and wandered, too,
> But I ain't seen any candy.
> I've hiked and hiked till my feet are sore,
> I'll be God-damned if I hike any more
> To be buggered sore like a hobo's whore
> In the Big Rock Candy Mountains.[14]

Harry "Mac" McClintock, who always asserted that he wrote the song but had dubious claims to it, related to Alan Lomax that the song was based on his own experience:

> But my new trade of singing for my supper brought new dangers on the road and in the jungles. As a 'producer' I was a shining mark; a kid, who could not only beg handouts but who could bring in money for alcohol, was a valuable piece of property for the jocker that could snare him. The decent hoboes were protective as long as they were around, but there were times when I fought like a wildcat or ran like a deer to preserve my independence and my virginity, and on one occasion I jumped into the darkness from a box-car door—from a train that must have been doing better than thirty miles an hour.[15]

Although the song speaks to homeless boys (commonly known as "punks" in the hobo community) being taken in by older hoboes pursuing money and sex (known as "jockers"), the practice extended to newsboys as well. "Big Rock Candy Mountain" was unique in its treatment of the phenomenon because of its explicit character, a rawness in the lyrics that was cleaned up by the time McClintock recorded the song in 1928, thirty years after he claimed to have written it.[16] By that time, the hobo was becoming a figure of entertainment and the lyrics would have kept the song from becoming a hit, but at the turn of the century, most saw any young boy out on his own as potential prey for older homeless men.

Setting Two Newsboy's Cries

In many ways, Partch's *San Francisco* walks the line between these two extremes—the helpless child working in the cold who is the victim of predators in the song and the individualist pulling himself up by his bootstraps of Horatio Alger fame. As a composition, *San Francisco* first appears in Partch's 1942 proposal for a Guggenheim Foundation Fellowship. In that application Partch detailed a "Monophonic Cycle" on which he was then at work, including seven compositions. In describing number three, "San Francisco," he noted that it "is a straight musical picture or impression, without significant words, story, or especial musical direction. I have already completed a rough draft of the setting."[17] That draft has been lost, but its music seems to have been markedly different from the version completed in the summer of 1943. In what he termed a "Resume of the Music Philosophy and Work of Harry Partch, Composer—Instrument Builder and Player—Theorist," but was little more than a promotional pamphlet he printed to advertise his services as a performer and lecturer at colleges and universities, Partch noted that *San Francisco* was written for "Two Voices, Chromolodian [*sic*], and Kithara." The first full version features only one voice part.

The text, on the other hand, evidently remained unchanged. Partch was right to call *San Francisco*'s lyrics a musical impression without narrative, as he simply remembered the cries of two newsboys working for two different papers and wrote them down in dialect:

> Chronicull, Chronicull, Chronicull, Chronicull.
> Eggzaminay papay, Eggzaminay papay, Eggzaminay papay, Get your papay.
> Eggzaminay papay, Eggzaminay papay, Eggzaminay papay, Here's your papay.
> Eggzaminay papay, Eggzaminay papay, Eggzaminay papay, Get your papay.[18]

Bob Gilmore remarked that perhaps Partch's choice of the two papers had less to do with his memory than with wanting a poke at the *Chronicle* and the *Examiner*, two papers that, though they reviewed his San Francisco concerts in the early 1930s, did not always do so favorably.[19]

San Francisco presents Partch's Monophonic concept in perfect miniature. Everything arises from the One Voice, in this case the newsboy attempting to sell the *Chronicle* late in the evening. The work opens with the Kithara playing a steady rhythmic pattern while the Adapted Viola foreshadows the voice's entrance about a minute into the piece by playing the vocal melody. Partch's notation matches the natural inflection and rhythm of the spoken word: the line features a slide up to a pitch for the first syllable and a sudden dip down for the second, which is quickly left for a return up for the third syllable on a pitch slightly lower than the first. The instrument repeats this line three times, each slightly higher than the time before. The Adapted Viola begins on a 7/4 for the first syllable before dropping to an 8/5 for the third. The second line slides up from that 8/5 to a 9/5 before settling on a 5/3, and the final slide begins on 5/3 up to 11/6 before resting again on the 5/3. The intervallic space from the lowest pitch, 8/5, to the highest, 11/6, is a little more than an equally tempered major second, so the distance the Adapted Viola travels is slight. However, there is enough difference that the effect is one of mounting desperation as the line creeps higher and higher.

The voice, when it enters with the melodic line, mirrors this feeling of desperation. It repeats the line four times, moving up, then down, then up, then down, accurately gauging the newsboy's fortunes as passersby look interested (movement up), then continue on without buying a paper (movement down). Adding to the melancholy atmosphere, the Chromelodeon plays repeating pitches in the background and the Adapted Viola plays double stops behind the voice, mimicking a foghorn much as the instrument recreates the train whistle in *U.S. Highball*. The mournful quality Partch gives to both the Adapted Viola and voice, through tessitura and pitch choice, merges with the Chromelodeon to create the image of a newsboy enveloped in fog by the San Francisco Bay at the end of a long night trying to sell his last papers. He is clearly not trying the "last paper ploy," but genuinely wishing to finish up and head home.

The second newsboy contrasts the first, hawking for the *Examiner* with as much gusto as he can manage. His vocal pitch remains static but moves quickly, sixteenth and eighth notes to the *Chronicle* boy's tired quarters. He even gets into the theatrical aspects of selling papers on the street by holding out the last vowel in "Eggzaminay" the final time and embellishing it by rapidly moving above and below that held pitch to create a call, a vocal flourish to attract customers. This newsboy has the greatest pitch movement at the end of his line, when he chants "Get your papay," starting high in the range before falling a justly tuned perfect fourth, from a 5/3 to a 5/4. Compared to the *Chronicle* boy's major second range, the *Examiner* boy is quite animated. However, underlying the "Eggzaminay papay" lines the Chromelodeon continues playing the "Chronicull" motive, picking it up from the voice as the voice did from the Adapted Viola. And as in the Adapted Viola, each iteration of the line in the Chromelodeon moves higher and higher, from a 3/2 up to an 11/6. The effect is to undercut the *Examiner* boy's exuberance by adding a subtext that, before long, he will be as tired and worn out as the first newsboy and is flailing madly in an attempt to stave off exhaustion and sell his final papers. Fittingly, the piece ends as it begins, with the Chromelodeon holding one of its lowest pitches, the Kithara strumming chords, and the Adapted Viola holding long double stops, giving the feeling of great ships passing in the night.

Partch's aural realization of his memory of two newsboys crying the news has texture, ambiance, and weight through his recreation of the full range of sounds on a San Francisco night in the 1920s. Its impression is so strong because it evokes accurately what the newsboy experienced—staying out late into the evening attempting to sell that last paper no matter what, voice cracking and energy giving out as he tries to squeeze every customer who passes by his corner. This aura of a disappearing subculture that many city residents nostalgically remembered, of the sounds of a simpler time, gives *San Francisco* potency even today. More than anything else, the work's atmosphere and verisimilitude caused Lou Harrison to call out this piece in particular for praise in his review of Partch's April 22, 1944, concert, remarking that "*San Francisco (setting of the cries of two newsboys)* was the best and shortest piece. Around these cries Mr. Partch has woven a spell of about the foggiest and dampest music I have ever heard. I got homesick."[20]

Partch was evidently so taken with Harrison's remarks that when he rescored the work in 1955 for voice, cello, Kithara II, and Chromelodeon, he changed the work's title from *San Francisco—A Setting of the Cries of Two Newsboys on a Street Corner* to *San Francisco—A Setting of the Cries of Two Newsboys on a Foggy Night in the Twenties*. In fact, he was so satisfied with the work that except for the substitution of the cello for the Adapted Viola and the Kithara II for the Kithara, the rebarring of several measures, and the addition of expressive directions such as "connect! with two hands liquid!" the piece's more atmospheric subtitle is the largest change. The two versions are so closely related that he simply wrote the new parts and all alterations on top of the original score and noted on the title page that this was the "original, with re-writing July 12, 1955."

Partch Receives a Hobo Letter

Partch's satisfaction with *San Francisco* evidently did not extend to the fourth work of *The Wayward*, *The Letter*. Of the four works, *The Letter* was the only one not performed in the New York concert Lou Harrison reviewed and the only one not recorded between 1945 and 1946 when Partch was in residence at the University of Wisconsin, Madison and had a regular ensemble he had trained.[21] Its exclusion seems odd considering that Partch composed the works within days of one another—he completed *San Francisco* on July 1, 1943, and began work on *The Letter* the next day, completing it on July 4. But *The Letter* seems to have been an afterthought. It was the last new work he finished in 1943 before turning his attention to revisions and instrument maintenance. It is not listed among the seven works Partch submitted as his "Monophonic Cycle" in his Guggenheim application. And he rarely mentioned it in letters or lectures, never rehearsed it in the 1940s, and first thought to record it only at the end of 1949.[22]

Yet fully understanding Partch's hobo music requires examination of this "afterthought." Of the four works of *The Wayward*, *The Letter* is perhaps the most personal. *Barstow* and *San Francisco* both use the words of others to shed light on aspects of the transient experience in the 1920s and 1930s. The vocal inflections may or may not be based on Partch's own voice, but in either case they offer no insight into his perspective. *U.S. Highball* is the story of a train/hitchhiking trip Partch took, and he appears in the narrative as Slim or Mac. But most of the work features an objective look at the hobo life as much as it provides a subjective feeling of presence; it is still possible, as Partch himself tried, to present it as the record of another's adventure. Partch could not so obscure the origins of *The Letter*. He even originally titled it *Letter from Hobo Pablo*, as he based it on an actual message he received from that eponymous friend in early October, 1935.

Partch first met Pablo on June 14 of that year at the Federal Shelter in Stockton, California, before both were shipped to Harrington Ranch. Partch was new to the federal camp system; Pablo was an old hand. They struck up a friendship, and Pablo indoctrinated the composer into transient life circa 1935. The two men shared many intimate discussions before Pablo left the camp on July 5 in advance of being kicked out for drunkenness. The October correspondence from Pablo is the only one Partch saved from this brief but passionate friendship, and while the news it recounts is fairly mundane, the feelings undulating beneath the words are not. It is significant that we have the original letter because Partch's feelings toward Pablo are evident: he carefully recorded the details of their friendship in *Bitter Music*, where Pablo is one of just two men mentioned by name. As a result, *The Letter* serves as a musical portrait of a dear friend and the only piece of music Partch composed that sprang directly from the period chronicled in the journal.

Letter or *Hobo* Letter?

Although Partch later shortened the title, his description of Pablo as a hobo is important not only for the rhyme it makes, but also for the overtones it would have carried throughout the 1940s. In 1935, Pablo would have been recognized throughout California as a transient or migratory worker more than as a hobo. Originally from Kentucky, he evidently had sired a child out of wedlock in Ohio and then fled his responsibilities by traveling to California to work in the harvests. He followed those harvests up and down the West Coast, most likely finding work as often as not, and took advantage of the newly-created agencies to aid migrant workers in the 1930s—a fact borne out by his recommendation of Harrington Ranch to Partch based on past experience there.[23] The men who used those camps regularly fit the mold of the transient better than that of the hobo. Most did not wander throughout the United States, working the railroad and any temporary job they could find, be it industrial or agricultural. Instead, they wandered California, specializing in occasional fruit and grain harvest work. The State of California even officially classified them as transients, a label applied to Partch as well during his time in the camps in 1935 and 1936. Why, then, did Partch insist that Pablo was a hobo?

Most likely Partch's was a pragmatic decision. In the years surrounding his time among migratory transient workers, labels attached to that class of people were in flux. As seen earlier, the men and women called hoboes were of a different class and character than those routinely saddled with the label before and during the 1920s. The mutability of labels during the 1930s is evident in terms applied by journalists, sociologists, social workers, and later historians to people who traveled and worked. *Mendicant*; *casual, floating, migratory, seasonal*, and *unskilled workers* or *laborers*; *down-and-outers*; *go-abouts*; *rounders*; and *the underclass* joined *hobo, tramp, bum*, and *transient*, used and defined up to this point, in the 1930s.[24] Part of the reason for this geyser of nomenclature was the simple fact that a class of worker previously invisible to the public suddenly and shockingly became visible during the Depression and journalists needed new words as they wrote about them.[25]

The impressions the public formed about those workers were not as sentimental and wistful as those surrounding old-time hoboes and newsboys, and nowhere were they stronger and more divisive than in California. In his history of migratory workers in California, Don Mitchell perceptively delineates two sides to the Californian dream: great weather, beautiful crops, and a land of plenty on the one hand and workers who make that dream possible on the other. "The pattern and color of the California landscape are mortgaged on the backs of an endless stream of workers," he concludes.[26] That endless stream included enormous numbers of workers: as many as 200,000 followed the harvest in the early years of the twentieth century.[27] Until the 1930s, however, those workers moved and toiled largely unseen.

Two factors made Californians notice the transients who supplied food for their table. The first was the sheer number of workers in the state during the decade. Although reasons for the march to California varied, statistics on the number of people who arrived during the 1930s were sobering. Between 1935 and 1940, around 309,000 Oklahomans left their home state for fairer climes; almost one third of those men, women, and children landed in California.[28] An additional 95,000 from other states such as Arkansas, Missouri, and Kansas arrived between 1934 and 1937. Add those numbers to the workers already present in the state and it becomes clear why native Californians could no longer ignore transient workers.

Even if Californians had insisted on continuing to look away from their economy's foundation, the men and women who formed that foundation would not have allowed them to do so. The second factor in removing the blinders toward migratory labor were the series of strikes those workers staged. Strikes in California fields usually trace back to a tinderbox incident in 1913. That summer, Wobblies led hops-pickers at the Durst Brothers Hops Ranch to strike over living conditions. The Dursts called in police, who arrived to find a peaceful strike where they had expected a riot. Hoping to disperse the gathering, a deputy fired once into the air. In the resulting confusion, the deputy who fired, the local district attorney, and two anonymous hops-pickers were killed, scores were injured, and workers and growers were mobilized against each other.[29]

Although smaller incidents followed this Wheatland Riot, not until 1933 were its repercussions fully felt. That year, following a decade of groundwork, over 48,000 workers staged thirty-one strikes. To put that number in perspective, that year, across the rest of the United States, thirty strikes were held, involving just 8,000 workers.[30] There were so many strikes that one scarcely ended before another began: in March, lettuce pickers in the Salinas Valley; in April, pea pickers in Santa Clara counties; in June, cherry pickers in Santa Clara and berry pickers in El Monte; in August, pear pickers in Santa Clara, sugar beet workers in Oxnard, and peach pickers in the Central Valley; in September, grape harvesters in Lodi; and in October, cotton pickers in the San Joaquin Valley. Even into 1934, a strike of lettuce pickers in the Imperial Valley and apricot pickers in Brentwood in January was followed by one of pea pickers in February. These strikes concerned the general citizenry as well as growers, highlighting the amount of migratory labor in the state, but no one could do anything to change the situation. Throughout the early twentieth century, state officials had explored ways to clear out laborers once their services were no longer needed but had found no effective system. As a result, migratory transient workers became linked in the public mind with all the unemployment problems facing the nation during the Great Depression.[31]

Although residents were now forced to see the workers they had overlooked for so long, many disliked the new view. Transient labor became a lightning rod for an undercurrent of long-standing tensions in California society over class and citizenship.[32] Hoboes were largely white males who worked and then left. Many migratory transient workers were white, but even more were Mexican, Filipino, Chinese, Japanese, and Indian. Fears of immigrants taking jobs from American citizens were so pronounced across the country in the early part of the twentieth century that Congress responded with a series of acts culminating in the 1924 Immigration Act that put a quota system on immigration.[33] These national fears blossomed particularly in California through the presence of so many immigrant workers. Officials generated complex systems of thought to describe why

Mexican and Chinese immigrants were a social hazard and a burden to local communities but compliant enough to be the perfect agricultural worker.[34] Many Californians were unnerved to see a class of people, oxymoronically classified as more docile and more dangerous than white workers, suddenly rise up in 1933–34 with complaints of injustice.

Partch lived and worked in California while these attitudes were taking shape: his first experience of following the California fruit harvests was in the summer of 1928, during the last stage of the formative years of worker discontent.[35] Although he left for New York and ultimately Europe in July 1933, as the surge of strikes was still building, when he returned to California two years later the deluge of migrants from the Midwest was underway and attitudes toward migratory transients were decidedly changed. This distinction between the folk hero hobo and the disreputable transient makes clear one reason Partch chose to label Pablo a hobo: he was staving off prejudice directed toward his music. The other reason was his emotional attachment to Pablo, a nostalgic view more in line with his hobo time than those months living as a government-labeled transient. But even though Partch framed *The Letter* as a hobo work and even set Pablo's missive humorously and in line with hobo aesthetics found in *U.S. Highball*, the circumstances it depicts clearly point to the perceptional division growing in the Depression between hoboes, men who revel in the freedom of the West, and transients, men who travel desperately in search of scant employment.

The Musical Letter

If *U.S. Highball* is Partch's most comprehensive exploration of his Monophonic principles and *Barstow* the most accessible, then *The Letter* is perhaps the clearest and most distilled example of the concept among *The Wayward*.[36] One final aspect of Monophony deserves consideration in a discussion of *The Letter*'s philosophical basis and an analysis of its musical aspects. In addition to its basis in the One Voice—of music rising up from the natural speech patterns of ordinary people and from one pitch through the use of just intonation—Monophony has an aspect Partch rarely discussed: Tonality.[37]

Partch's "Tonality" is not the same as standard Western tonality. While both systems use a central chord or pitch to create harmonic relationships, Partch's system does not feature diatonic scales. Instead, he based his music on a hexadic grouping of pitches numerically related either by the numerator or denominator in their ratio notation. Partch took his just intonational system to the 11-limit, which is the highest odd-number factor in his overtone-generated ratios (for comparison, throughout most of musical history pitch resources have stopped at the 5-limit, leaving Partch to explore the 7- and 9-limit in addition to the 11-limit). Therefore, Otonalities that follow the harmonic series are grouped by having the same limit in their denominator (all ratios in a hexad would have an 11 as their bottom number, for instance, or a 5); Utonalities that follow the undertone series are grouped by having multiples of the same number as their numerator.

The relationships among these hexads stand out clearly in Partch's tonality diamond, which he devised while in Europe between 1933 and 1935 (see fig. 6.3).[38] The expanded tonality diamond features six pitches on each side of the diamond that, when read up and toward the right, spell out otonal hexads and, when read down and toward the right, spell out Utonal hexads. Each of the six pitches within a hexad are then given what Partch called an "Identity," a number based on the first six odd numbers (1, 3, 5, 7, 9, and 11) that provide not only exact naming for a pitch, but its position in a hexad. So an otonality based on the 1-limit would have a 1-Identity (its first pitch), a 3-Identity (its second pitch), a 5-Identity (its third pitch), and so on. This system gives the composer enormous flexibility effectively to modulate. As in common-practice harmony, each pitch has several senses, or can act in multiple ways. In the Monophonic system, pitches can be interpreted two ways, as an Identity in a U- or Otonality, and can pivot harmony from one hexad to another.[39]

The Kithara part, which provides *The Letter*'s harmonic structure, most readily demonstrates Partch's tonality system.[40] Throughout the piece, the Kithara plays almost nothing but a steady stream of eighth notes in 6/8 time outlining a descending hexad. Partch's choice of the Kithara for this role is critical because the instrument comprises twelve cascading rows of six strings each; a sweep of the hand across any grouping will give you a hexadic chord. But Partch provides the descending hexad with a sense of harmonic movement by having the musician play the first three notes of that hexad on the three strings farthest from himself on the sixth row and the last three notes on the three closest strings of the first row.[41] The effect is that while the musician is constantly strumming strings toward himself, the pitches go down. Partch grouped those pitches further into distinct triads, the second of which begins less than a minor second higher than the first. The resulting sound is one of movement and of stasis. The pitches are far enough apart to create an effect not that different from the standard I–V–I,

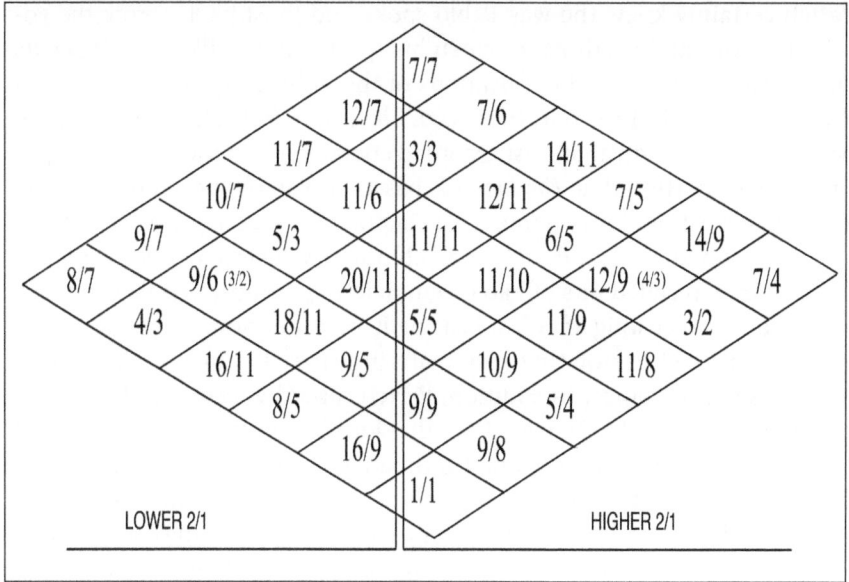

Figure 6.3. Harry Partch's tonality diamond.

"boom-chick-boom" accompaniment of many popular songs, but close enough not to create a comparable sense of tension and release. Instead, this harmonic underlay quickly recedes into the background, framing the text and voice. It is Monophonic in Tonality and purpose.

The only time this harmonic and rhythmic pattern is broken during *The Letter* is at moments of textual cadence. The first occurs after the salutation "Hello, Pal." The time signature shifts to 4/4 and the Kithara plays a dotted-eighth and sixteenth note followed by three quarter notes without accompaniment from any other instrument or voice. In the 1943 version, in the next five measures the Adapted Guitar plays a series of notes accented by tremolo while the Kithara strums full hexads on one row of strings. All movement stops, the focus switches to harmony more than rhythm for six measures, and the voice and audience take a breath, take stock of what was said, and then continue. These short interludes occur whenever there is a logical break in thought and paragraph in the letter; they follow either this six-measure pattern or leave out the Kithara's rhythmic measure, instead presenting only three to five measures of Kithara hexads accompanied by tremolo notes in the Adapted Guitar.

The music's regularity allows it to fade away while the vocal text occupies most of the listener's attention. As with many of Partch's Monophonic compositions, *The Letter* is based on the spoken inflection of a real person:

Partch certainly knew the way Pablo spoke and most likely wrote the vocal inflections and rhythms to match his speech. But unlike *U.S. Highball*, where Partch recorded the inflections of the hoboes around him and set them to music within a short time, with *The Letter*, fully eight years elapsed between Partch and Pablo's last recorded encounter and the work's composition. The assertion that *The Letter* is based on Pablo's speech might seem a stretch were it not for two mitigating factors. Although he set the letter at a remove of many years, Partch and Pablo shared a close relationship, and Partch surely recalled bits of Pablo's enunciation. If most people can recall a loved one's voice long after last hearing it, consider how much more fully Partch, practiced in notating and analyzing speech patterns, was able to revive his friend's voice. In addition, Partch carefully recorded Pablo's elocution in *Bitter Music*. On page 18 of that journal, under the entry for June 16, 1935, Partch recorded his first intimate conversation with Pablo during which the twenty-four-year-old transient related his conflicted feelings about a buddy he had not seen in over a month. At the climax of his story, Pablo breaks into song, or at least Partch began recording his inflections. Partch notated Pablo's range fairly high in the male register, sitting around a B-flat below middle C. It rises and falls from that note, but has long passages of almost monotone and characteristically falls off almost an octave at the end of sentences.

Comparing Partch's setting of the letter Pablo sent three months later (which is recorded in *Bitter Music* with no musical accompaniment) to *The Letter* provides striking similarities. The vocal part of *The Letter* is largely a monotone on B that often steps up to middle C. Although this pitch differs from the B-flat featured in *Bitter Music* since the journal was written on a piano staff and the vocal part in *The Letter* is pitched to 7/5 in Partch's scale, the visual similarity is striking, and the pitches are quite close. Likewise, each time the text cadences before the instrumental interludes of Kithara chords and Adapted Guitar tremolo, the vocal line descends, just as Pablo's speech does in *Bitter Music*.

Although certainly not conclusive, the similarities between the two vocal settings and Partch's practice of seeking out men and women to intone for him during his Monophonic period certainly point to *The Letter* being a fairly accurate representation of Pablo's speech. The speed at which Partch composed the work (he completed it in three days of steady work) also points in that direction. Partch was typically not a fast composer, and the rapidity of composition suggests that he had a firm conception of the piece from the outset. Finally, late in his life, Partch remarked that "the piece is stylized, partly to underline the perverse humor and the obviously warm regard, but mostly to convey—through sound and rhythm—the delight of reading a very unexpected letter from an old companion for the first time."[42] He was attempting to convey musically how we hear the voices of friends upon reading their letters—a sound as musically true to the music in Partch's head as anything else he ever wrote.

As personal as *The Letter* obviously was to Partch, it remains an oddity in his Americana output. He was unsure what to do with this composition and with *Bitter Music*. Because of the dominant prejudices toward the people that both represent, Partch seems to have wanted to avoid publicizing his transient works. In many ways, *The Letter* is as invisible in Partch's history as the migratory transient is in California's. Unperformed and unrecorded in the years following its composition, unlike the other pieces that would figure in *The Wayward*, *The Letter* remained underground until he brought it to the surface and reworked it in 1950, at which time he considered making it part of the series eventually titled *Eleven Intrusions*. After 1950, it disappeared again until 1955, when Partch rescored it along with *San Francisco*, *Barstow*, and *U.S. Highball*, finally collecting the four works together as *The Wayward*. Following this reworking of the composition, he retained an affection for it until the end of his life. In May 1972, two years before his death, Partch rewrote *The Letter* so he could perform it on camera in the film *The Dreamer That Remains: A Portrait of Harry Partch*. Although the recording was ultimately not part of the film, it is one of the last recordings of Partch performing any of his works.[43]

In many ways, Harry Partch's complex relationship with *The Letter* is the perfect capstone for our examination of his hobo music. With the newsboys of *San Francisco*, Partch mined a figure whose trajectory through public opinion strikingly mirrored that of the hobo. In an America looking for ways to define itself, the hobo and the newsboy became iconic figures of up-by-the-bootstraps individualism. Partch attempted to extend his nostalgic view of the hobo and the newsboy, as seen in *U.S. Highball*, *Barstow*, and *San Francisco*, to *The Letter*. Although Pablo would have been considered a transient or migratory worker in the period's nomenclature, Partch framed his friend as a hobo in the work's original title and grouped the composition with the others in *The Wayward*. All the males depicted in those works were indeed wayward, marginalized by and from the dominant society, but even though all were outcasts, society did not view them as the same. Hoboes and newsboys were strong, Western American figures like the cowboy; transients were down-and-outers. Hoboes and newsboys were making their way through the world by ingenuity; transients allowed life to happen to them. It is small wonder that Partch preferred the hobo and newsboy image to that of the transient. *San Francisco* and *The Letter* offer a glimpse into the reasons why he later called his hobo-inspired *U.S. Highball* his most creative work and ultimately abandoned his transient-inspired *Bitter Music*. In the previous chapters, we have considered the hobo in depth and the way in which that marginalized figure came to define Harry Partch's career in the 1930s and 1940s. But the story of how Partch used that figure to find a brief moment of acceptance in World War II–era New York City and the reception afforded to his music remains untold. With the next chapter, we turn our attention to how Partch interacted with the hobo image during that time, and the ways in which he eventually rejected the space it made for him in the world.

CHAPTER SEVEN

TRADING ON A HOBO IMAGE

Harry Partch was a hobo composer. At least, that was the impression held by most musicians living and working in New York City during World War II. It was an image that made him moderately successful at the time and inspired most of his music from the period, but it is also one that has clouded Partch's biography. Seeking to view this pivotal time anew, this chapter picks up the threads of Partch's life from completing *Barstow* and making his "transcontinental hobo trip" in September 1941 to his League of Composers' concert in the spring of 1944 and subsequent move to Wisconsin. This period is crucial in Partch's reception: during this time he formulated his hobo persona, first articulated his particular brand of conceptual musical exoticism, and cultivated close personal and professional friendships with composers from Otto Luening to Douglas Moore that helped him realize he would likely always work outside the musical community, no matter his preferences or his efforts to gain access to its circle.

Partch's nomadic lifestyle makes reconstructing his experiences in the early 1940s no easy task. Although he did save letters, drawings, and writings if they held special significance to him, in many cases the record is patchy at best. Furthermore, he was not given to focusing on the past. Danlee Mitchell has observed that Partch was always moving toward the next project, toward the next goal. What came before was history and of no use or interest to him. Indeed, even thinking about his previous experiences could be difficult.[1] When asked to complete a biographical questionnaire late in the mid-1960s, Partch remarked, "Autobiographies always throw me. The past comes screaming back at me, and I just want to go away and hide."[2] This feeling was particularly true of his years of hobo wandering. Partch spoke about those years so infrequently, and saved so few documents, that when Ben Johnston and Thomas McGeary began collecting materials and oral history interviews for the Partch Archive at the University of Illinois, they directed their efforts at these years, believing that saving what information remained was their first priority.[3] This chapter's reconstruction of the period is based on the documents that remain: letters Partch wrote to other composers and supporters, notices in local newspapers, and the recollections of friends and colleagues thirty years after the fact. Collectively, these documents present a nuanced portrait of a composer struggling to define himself.

Chicago: Fall 1941–Spring 1942

Early on a gray Chicago morning on October 1, 1941, Harry Partch ended the two-week hitchhiking trip that inspired *U.S. Highball*. His reason for making the trip was simple enough—he had an invitation. But the reason for the move went deeper than mere fancy. Discouraged after years of indifference shown to him by the California musical establishment, Partch decided to take his chances on a new place and eagerly made the journey to the Windy City, hoping that his Depression ordeal of homelessness and transience had finally ended. When he arrived in Chicago, Partch quickly sought out the young man who had invited him to the city, a friend of the divinity student whom he had met in Carmel, California some months earlier. Partch moved in with the friend for a short time and tried to find his place in the new city's musical milieu.[4]

Although he still had to take odd jobs such as "pot-wallopin'" in labor camps and poorhouses over the following year, Partch's move to Chicago presaged a shift in his fortunes.[5] One of his first actions was to follow up on connections he had made through the Federal Writers' Project. Meeting with Jack Scher and Stuart Engstrand of the Chicago Writers' Project, Partch presented himself as a composer chronicling the Depression experience in music, rather than as an author. In return, Partch received a recommendation to contact Alan Lomax, who was Assistant in Charge of the Archive of Folk Song at the Library of Congress and was busy collecting field recordings documenting American folk music. On October 16, just two weeks after arriving in Chicago, Partch wrote Lomax, sending his two recent articles for the *Carmel Pine Cone* ("Barstow" and "The Kithara") and a description of his work.[6] Although Lomax answered on October 30, no record of his response remains, though he did forward Partch's original letter on to Charles Seeger. Still, Partch's letter makes clear that he was beginning to see his music as representing music of the United States in a unique fashion.[7] Then, on November 18, a month and a half after his arrival, Partch performed at a multimedia concert held at Chicago's School of Design. His inclusion seems to indicate that, in a mere six weeks, he had managed to connect with and be accepted by Chicago's modern music community. The concert opened with an exhibition of work by students and faculty of the institution, followed by a history of motion pictures compiled by New York City's Museum of Modern Art. After these performances came two by John Cage, a rising young composer ten years Partch's junior. Like Partch, Cage was attempting to make a name for himself in Chicago before continuing on to New York City with compositions for new instruments. Unlike Partch, Cage wrote for both standard instruments and ensembles slightly altered, such as the percussion ensemble and his invention, the prepared piano. Cage was then teaching at the School of Design and for the concert had his students (who were conducting experiments in sound production) hold an improvisation, followed closely by the airing of recordings of percussion works by himself, Lou Harrison, and William Russell. "Tone declamations by Harry Partch using the 43 tone scale" followed these two Cage sections. The program listed two declamations: "Chinese Poem" and "Hitch-hikers Ballad," presumably a selection from his *Li Po* settings and *Barstow*, as he had just completed the second work and both could be performed by a single vocalist with either Adapted Viola or Adapted Guitar.[8]

Although Cage and Partch had radically differing views of music's expressive power and nature, the older man's ideas and his intense and unwavering devotion to them evidently intrigued Cage. To Partch, such interest meant that Cage should take an active role in promoting his work, but Cage's interest did not become action until Partch completed a working model of his Monophonic keyboard instrument the following spring. Although Partch found presenting concerts and making his name enjoyable and important, more pressing was the realization of the goal he had doggedly pursued for almost a decade—a working system of just intonation complete with a microtonally tuned keyboard instrument. To that end, after the November concert, he devoted his energies to adapting an old five-octave harmonium. Partch had attempted to create his keyboard instrument twice before. While in London in 1934 under a Carnegie grant, he had hired an organ builder to craft an instrument based on a model he had designed. In his sketches, the keyboard consisted of two manuals, the first containing push buttons, as on a typewriter, and the second having diamond-shaped keys mirroring the shape of Partch's harmonic series-based tonality diamond. The organ, built and christened "Ptolemy," was shipped to California. Elated with his progress, Partch retrieved it upon returning to the States, but soon realized that the instrument had a faulty mechanism. He salvaged Ptolemy's reeds but abandoned the rest. In 1940, he started again by constructing a new keyboard, but by the time he reached Chicago he had evidently decided that he could not wait until he had enough money to commission someone to construct a fully-functional Chromatic Pipe Organ.

Partch abandoned his most recent console in favor of adapting existing keyboard instruments, much as he had done with the viola and guitar. He first played around with a melodeon loaned him by Chicago friends Philip Manuel and Gavin Williamson,[9] then obtained a used harmonium. In January 1942, using the reeds saved from Ptolemy, he retuned the latter instrument, creating "an instrument of expediency, he calls the Chromolodian [sic]."[10] Cage responded to the instrument's creation by mentioning it at the end of an article in *Modern Music*, writing that "Harry Partch, who has been wandering around and between two continents for the last twenty years, always with only one idea in mind, has finally succeeded in Chicago in getting his Chromolodian constructed.... The Chromolodian gives a welcome definiteness to his work."[11]

Partch eagerly put his new instrument to the test in a series of concerts around the city in early 1942. For these concerts he rewrote three of his works—*Barstow*, a few *Li Po* settings, and the *Two Psalms*, "By the Rivers of Babylon" and "The Lord Is My Shepherd"—to accommodate the Chromelodeon. On January 20, 1942, at the University of Chicago, he presented a program consisting of some of the *Li Po* settings and an early version of his setting of Yeats's "King Oedipus" to the Harriet Monroe Poetry Group of the Friends of the Library. A month later, on February 26, he gave a concert at Fullerton Hall in the Chicago Art Institute for the Conference of Club Presidents and Program Chairmen in honor of "Art Day." For these concerts, Partch had his first collaborators since he left for Europe in 1934: Gilman Chase, music director of the First Unitarian Church, performed on the newly-completed Chromelodeon, and George Bishop, a singer Partch had befriended, intoned the tenor line.[12] The three continued giving concerts in schools and studios around the city throughout the late winter and early spring. Bishop helped Partch in another way during those early months of 1942: always the nomadic hobo, Partch would have had no place to escape the harsh Chicago winter had Bishop not provided him with quarters.[13]

Even with the support of two able musicians, a new instrument to demonstrate, and a series of concerts, Partch could not attract the amount or kind of attention he desired. No matter how much he worked, his situation resembled what he had left in California: a few encouraging supporters from the modern music crowd, but no notice from the broader music community. Looking back fifteen years later, Partch related: "You are probably very right about the provincialism of the two coasts, though I think the east coast is worse than the west. Chicago is certainly less so, although my experience there in 1941–42 indicated that people with the power of money behind them were just as reluctant as those around San Francisco to stand up and be counted, unless New York press agents could be seen out of the corners of their eyes."[14] He decided that since everyone in Chicago was looking to New York for validation, it was time to move that way.

In February, Partch began applying to spend the summer at the Yaddo arts colony outside of Saratoga Springs, thinking that it would be a good intermediary step between Chicago and New York City. He proposed to spend his time there in "the continuation of creative work in music." With a working keyboard instrument in hand, Partch felt that he had finally satisfied his personal requirements for a musical arsenal of instruments with which to compose, and so his application mentioned plans to continue work on setting Yeats's "King Oedipus" drama and a few other short lyrical texts.[15] Yet his plans did not stop at the composition of new works. Since adopting just intonation, Partch had been at work on a theoretical treatise. He knew he was bucking two centuries of musical practice by abandoning equal temperament, so he needed to show both the roots of just intonation, stretching back to Greco-Roman times, and the tuning system's utility. It was a massive undertaking, one that had occupied his thoughts on and off over the course of twenty years. So when University of Chicago Press editor W. K. Jordon approached Partch after a concert in Chicago, the composer had a proposal to make: a book, whose title he had recently changed from *Exposition of Monophony* to *Patterns of Music*. Evidently Jordon was impressed by Partch's performance, which usually included an explanation of his unique tuning system, and assured him that were his book in an academic format, the Press would give it "serious and sympathetic consideration."[16] This was all the encouragement that Partch needed to return his attention to his treatise; he indicated his plans to work on it concurrently with his compositions at Yaddo. Beyond his plans for work while at Yaddo, Partch listed five references in support of his application: Henry

Allen Moe, who had been unflagging in his interest; Bertha Knisely, who had a sustained enthusiasm for Partch and his music in the early 1930s; Dudley Crafts Watson, who had helped arrange concerts for Partch; Philip Manuel and Gavin Williamson, who had provided the melodeon Partch first experimented on when constructing his first Chromelodeon; and the composer Otto Luening.

Partch was extremely presumptuous in placing Luening's name on his list of references, for he had not been in touch with the composer for so long that he had to ask Henry Allen Moe to forward a letter for him.[17] Partch's apparent comfort in making such an assumption shows the respect the two men had for each other, despite a rocky beginning to their acquaintance. Almost a decade before, in September of 1933, Partch had attended a new music festival held at Yaddo at the invitation of Bertha Knisely, then his patron. At the festival, he sought out a performance of Luening's 1924 *First Sonata for Cello Solo*, as he had recently begun a correspondence with the young composer. Upon returning to New York after the festival, Partch eagerly wrote Luening, excited that he had seen in the cello sonata what he believed to be confirmation that they shared a common goal of working "toward an individual, unhazardous, linear expression, and away from the complex, and to me more artificial symphony and choral forms."[18] In other words, Partch saw Monophonic elements in the sonata. As Knisely had first suggested he contact Luening, Partch asked his patron to write Luening on his behalf and deliver a copy of his *Exposition of Monophony*. Knisely did just that, and Luening responded by assuring her that "I shall do what I can to get him a Guggenheim Fellowship."[19]

Luening did as he promised, even though he and Partch exchanged several heated letters toward the end of 1933. First, Partch did not want to put Luening to too much trouble trying to understand the exposition. Then he suggested that he could find composers who might write less sympathetic but more timely recommendations. Partch finally settled down after Luening shot back that the other composers would not write as strong a recommendation as he and that he would get the job done.[20] The dialogue was prickly enough, in Luening's mind, that nine years later he recommended Partch to Virgil Thomson with the caveat "he is a left-handed customer who doesn't know how to talk to people anyhow."[21]

Luening's interest in Partch, evident from the beginning of their correspondence, is not terribly surprising. He had been experimenting since 1918 with alternative tunings, and especially with the way changing acoustical parameters altered musical perception.[22] He was also fascinated by folk music and American culture and believed that by combining the two, the composition faculty could break the stranglehold of European music on university education. In 1936, Luening wrote an article for *Modern Music* discussing the musical situation in Arizona, where he was then teaching. He remarked that "the problem was simply to emphasize to the young musicians the validity of their own background and the impossibility of absorbing the entire musical culture of Europe in four years." When that was done, composers were able "to be themselves with the result that a significant number of individual styles emerged. Indian, Mexican, jazz, hillbilly, cowboy and other strains were represented. The new composers reflected the different localities of Arizona where they had lived."[23] When Partch reappeared in Luening's life in 1942 with a trunk full of music based on his past experience as an acoustically-learned hobo, Luening must have seen him as a kindred spirit and so was ready and willing to support his work.

Luening's twin interests in regenerating Western music and in being true to the American folk past kept him a Partch supporter throughout his life.[24] Luening demonstrated those interests in his autobiography, where he emphasized the import of Partch's hobo experiences to the composer's music. He told how the press could hardly believe that Partch had been a hobo or that he had created a musical system that facilitated his speech-music. He even characterized Partch's unsettled existence over the final three decades of his life as "hitchhiking."[25] Those interests can also be seen in the foreword Luening wrote for the first edition of Partch's treatise, published under the title *Genesis of a Music*—an introduction not retained in the second edition. In it, he eloquently called Partch's voice the voice of his time and the future, and suggested that his expansion of musical parameters offered an escape from the well-worn principles of Western music and pointed toward a new, vital musical age. Then, in two paragraphs, he explained how Partch's years of hobo wandering had unfolded the soul of the American people for him. "In certain of his compositions," Luening continued, "he has given voice to their life, and has become in a moving way a poet and singer of these wandering Americans—perhaps of all wanderers and of all the spiritually isolated."[26]

Chicago and a Return to Hoboing: Spring 1942–Summer 1942

Although plagued by bad health and busy with concerts around Chicago throughout March 1942, Partch redoubled his efforts toward his theoretical writings. He decided that he could reach a wider audience more effectively if he also had promotional material written in laymen's terms, so he put together a ten-page pamphlet describing "A Modern Renascence of the most ancient of civilized Musical Ideals—SPEECH-MUSIC."[27] This small pamphlet richly details how Partch presented himself to Chicago audiences. It is divided into two sections, the first on his musical theories, the second on the music that he had composed to that point.

Believing that an audience could more easily accept his music if it knew the theoretical basis first, Partch was at pains to demonstrate the forty-three-tone scale's historical foundation and the limitations of equal temperament. He explained the fallacy of the circle of fifths and replaced it with the tonality diamond as a visual representation of tonal relationships. He provided his own biographical background as well as the background of his instruments. This first section of the pamphlet is bursting with precise information. The second section is strangely nebulous. Just one page out of the ten lists the various settings of texts he had made, including *Bitter Music*, *Barstow*, and *U.S. Highball*, the last of which he had not even musically sketched at this point, to showcase the variety of texts Monophony could set; he omitted any mention of the music itself.

This lack of information on his music was not the only omission; indeed, the pamphlet is almost more useful for what it does not show. While in Chicago, Partch seems to have focused his self-promotion on the image of a theoretical innovator. The hobo image that he would carefully cultivate in coming years is missing, even though the pamphlet's music section focuses on his hobo-inspired texts. He seemed to know that the hobo image would be useful, but the experiences were too fresh, too raw, for him to exploit easily. So he continued his California habit of focusing on his theoretical language, but soon realized that the image was not carrying him as far as he wished. He began to change it as he moved toward New York City.

Wanting something aural to accompany the pamphlet's production, Partch went to a recording studio that same month. With Gilman Chase playing the Chromelodeon, George Bishop intoning the texts, and himself on Adapted Viola and Adapted Guitar, he recorded most of his compositions on three records. The first contained the *Two Psalms*, "The Lord is My Shepherd (Psalm 23)" for voice and Chromelodeon and "By the Rivers of Babylon (Psalm 137)" for voice, Chromelodeon, and Adapted Viola; the second held six of his *Li Po* settings for voice and Adapted Viola; the final record contained *Barstow* in the new version for two voices, Chromelodeon, and Adapted Guitar. Although Partch was not completely satisfied with the session's outcome because he was unable to experiment with microphone placement in relation to the instruments, he felt that the records were at least a good introduction to his musical principles.

By mid-April, Partch had grown restless again. Tired of imposing on friends and feeling that his progress had stagnated, he decided to make his way to New York in order finally to meet Otto Luening, to make contacts suggested to him by Luening, Moe, and Clara Shanafelt, and to travel to Yaddo to support his application there. Luening, then teaching at Bennington College in Vermont, had invited Partch to stop by the next time he was in the area. While Partch's route did not take him to Vermont, he was fortunate that Luening was in New York during this short trip and they managed to meet, thereby solidifying an important contact. The two composers hit it off immediately, and Luening invited Partch to attend a concert that evening and to lecture at Bennington in the fall.

Partch readily agreed to both propositions and returned to his room to rest before the concert, but, to his horror, he experienced a minor hemorrhage. In spite of the bleeding, he managed to make it to the end of the recital where he was thunderstruck by Ethel Luening's performance of several Ernest Bacon songs. He did not stay to talk with Luening after the concert; although minor, Partch's hemorrhage did lay him up for several days.

Writing a few days later to Luening, Partch remarked on Ethel's wonderful voice and asked if he might write something for her. He had never written expressly for anyone's voice other than his own, and therefore had no experience with the high voice and its unique "auditory sensation area."[28] Ethel's voice haunted him over the next two years until he realized his ambitions and set sections of *Finnegans Wake* for her, the only non-American text in his Monophonic Cycle (discussed below). The oddity of his inclusion of *Finnegans Wake* in this cycle is a testament both to her voice and to his impressions of her.

Once his hemorrhage had cleared up, Partch began following up on the New York contacts he had been given. He met with Richard Lauterbach, an editor at *Life Magazine*, to whom he played his freshly-minted records and showed pictures of the instruments, impressing Lauterbach enough to secure a further interview with another editor, Tom Prideaux. The magazine was interested in a pictorial story and asked Partch to come back when next he was in the city. He also wrote Howard Hanson for the first time to inquire about the possibility of a lecture-demonstration at Eastman similar to the one that Luening proposed for Bennington.[29]

When he had recovered enough to attempt the arduous hitchhiking journey back to Chicago by way of Yaddo, Partch set out. He called ahead to Yaddo to arrange an appointment to drum up support for his application and a Mrs. Ames agreed to see him at 2:30 that afternoon—although, she assured him, the arts colony did not consider interviews when making decisions. Unfortunately, Mrs. Ames neglected to provide Partch with directions to their meeting place. He began walking to Yaddo in time to reach the grounds before 2:30, but once there was unsure where he should go. The only person he could find to ask for directions was a gardener who spoke no English. He wandered the campus for two hours before finally calling Mrs. Ames, only to be informed that she was no longer available. Distraught, he returned to Albany and set out on the five-day, five-night hitchhike trip back to Chicago.[30] Yaddo ultimately rejected his application.

Partch returned to Chicago in April more determined than ever to succeed in New York. He moved in with R. W. Lotz and increased his petitions to Henry Allen Moe for a Guggenheim. In early May, Partch sent copies of the records he had made to Moe, asking that he listen to *Barstow* last, as it was his best and most recent work.[31] With this comment, Partch was not only succumbing to the common trap of thinking one's most recent work the best, but also recognizing the shifting ideological winds and starting to align himself with the dominant musical trend toward Anglo-American folk cultures. At month's end, he forwarded six copies of his pamphlet to be distributed as Moe saw fit.[32] And on June 19, as the climax of this promotional crescendo, he wrote Moe of his decision to reapply for a Guggenheim Fellowship. He mentioned that he had waited to do so until he had overwhelming evidence of progress since his last application which, because of the encouragement of two friends, he now believed that he had.[33]

The Harry Partch who reapplied for a Guggenheim grant in 1942 was a different person and a different composer, advocating his ideas in a much different world. His application demonstrated his growing acumen in the ways artistic foundations operate and his assurance that he could realize his goals. His proposal's focus remained musical composition, but instead of asking the Foundation to support anticipated work as he had a decade earlier, Partch showed evidence of having begun composition on his planned "Monophonic Cycle" with the completion of *Barstow* that year.[34] The Monophonic Cycle was to be a seven-part work that would fill an evening's program of an hour and a half. In addition to *Barstow*, it was to contain, in order, *Variations on a Theme* ("Yankee Doodle"), *San Francisco, Dark Brother* (a setting of Thomas Wolfe's essay "God's Lonely Man"), *God, She* (a satire Partch wrote concerning women's corrupting influence on America's musical life), excerpts from *Finnegans Wake*, and finally *U.S. Highball*.[35] He further showed his readiness to complete the tasks he set down by describing his instrumentarium.

In both previous applications from 1933 and 1934, Partch had declared that he would compose proposed works on proposed instruments.

As George Antheil had remarked in his critique, the lack of a ready base of instruments to play his scale beyond the Adapted Viola had hurt Partch's chances in 1934. But by 1942, his ability to orchestrate the Monophonic Cycle was no longer in doubt, and he wanted to assure the Foundation of that reality: "The fact which I want most to emphasize in these 'Plans for Work' is that I am not hampered by lack of instruments for these particular compositions."[36] In addition to the Adapted Viola, he had completed the Adapted Guitar, the Kithara, and the Chromelodeon, and his proposal went into great detail on the instruments' bases, construction, and utility.

Beyond these preparations, Partch's application indicates that he recognized the need to demonstrate his place in the musical community in order to attract the attention of powerful people. He did this first by assuring the Foundation and the composers with whom he shared his plans for work that "I hold no wish for the obsolescence of the present widely heard instruments and music. My devotion to our musical heritage is great—and critical." Once that rather surprising notion was established, Partch was free to show that he wished simply to build a richer, more inclusive view of music. He wrote that "I feel that more ferment is necessary to a healthy musical culture. I am endeavoring to instil [sic] more ferment."[37] Quite cannily, and truthfully, Partch trumpeted his allegiance to Western music while expressing his profound desire to place it back on the path from which it had strayed.

Partch's proposal contained another point of congruence with New York's musical world, one even more central to his acceptance than his claim of fidelity to Western musical values. At the bottom of the first page of his "Plans for Work," right after introducing the Monophonic Cycle, he pointed out that four of the pieces were based on his recent experience, "which is wholly American." One was based on an American folk tune (*Variations on a Theme*), the text of another was by a prominent American writer ("God's Lonely Man"), and only one "could be labeled 'not American'" (*Finnegans Wake*).[38] While he averred that the overt American theme was unplanned, he still took the space expressly to illuminate this nationalistic foundation to his work. Furthermore, Partch related that those texts were crying out to him to be set and would effectively reveal the possibilities of his speech-music system.[39] In other words, in an age when composers were attempting to discover the American voice in music, Harry Partch planned to use texts born from the American vernacular that could demonstrate that voice. During a time when American intellectuals and the general populace were fascinated by "the folk" and stirred by increased patriotism from the war effort, Partch had a music that brought these American voices into a musical system predicated on Western musical values.

Following his decision to apply for a Guggenheim, Partch's spirits and situation drastically worsened. He felt unable to compose because of distractions, his health, and the semi-permanent residence of the Chromelodeon across town, in a friend's basement. Soon after arriving back in the Windy City, Partch wrote to Luening outlining the causes of his depression and his plans. Luening had evidently been playing his copy of Partch's recent recordings to great acclaim and wanted more, but Partch was not able to produce copies for interested parties.[40] The engineer who had recorded the session was no longer with the record company and apparently no one else had access to the masters. Even the copies he did have were about to run out, and Carlos Chávez, to whom he had sent one by way of introduction, had not sent his back as promised.

Beyond these setbacks to his career, the fact that hurt the worst and dampened Partch's spirits the most was his return to menial labor, to the hobo existence he thought he had left behind after his transcontinental trip. Unable to support himself any other way, he had been surviving by washing dishes ten hours a day for two and a half dollars and a meal. It was a blow to realize that, as in 1933, he could not survive solely by demonstrating his musical theories. Yet he could not, and would not, pursue another career. He wrote Luening that "because I am ill equipped for, and ill adjusted to, this factory-office building civilization the only work I can land, apparently, is that which no one but an itinerant would contemplate."[41] Unable to endure Chicago with "pot-wallopin'" as his only prospect, Partch once again struck out on the hobo trail and left the city, traveling north to work in the fruit and grain harvests through the remainder of the summer.

Partch's readoption of his hobo lifestyle, even for two months, profoundly affected his perception of both himself and his work. By the time he left the hobo's harvest-following world for the last time in September, he knew that although his theories were sound and he could never abandon them, he would have to alter the way he presented himself and prove that he was a composer first and foremost. When he decided to focus his energies on composing, the texts at hand were those based on his hobo experiences. With that decision, the die was finally cast; Harry Partch began presenting himself as a hobo composer. Although he continued to lecture on the freedoms offered by the forty-three-tone speech-music system, and although his theoretical work was still of utmost importance to him, his demonstrations and promotional materials over the next two years focused more on the music itself and its basis in American vernacular culture.

New York City: Fall 1942–Winter 1943

Partch left the grain harvest in September and traveled to Chappaqua, thirty miles north of New York City, to stay with his friends, the Flanders. Since he had never performed for them, Partch demonstrated his ideas and shared his hobo experiences with the family in those early fall months. The Flanders greatly supported his work and both father Donald and son Peter were extremely interested in and influenced by Partch's theories.[42] It was a perfect place for Partch to resume his work, and he attacked it with gusto. By the end of the first week of September, he had completed his Guggenheim application and sent it to several supporters and interested parties, including Howard Hanson. Hanson was extremely impressed with Partch's plans for work; he offered the composer a lecture-demonstration at Eastman and wrote of his own volition to Henry Allen Moe recommending Partch's "unusual creative mind." His letter continued, "I have always been a great admirer of your vision in being willing to undertake projects which are not in the immediate conservative path! But I do think that this young fellow 'has something' and I should like to see him get a chance to work it out."[43] In addition to completing his Guggenheim application, Partch tentatively began composing again, but a dark cloud hung over his future plans—the Selective Service Local Board had sent him notice that it might call him up for military induction.[44]

In early October, Partch received word that he was due for induction on November 1, but he received a release to postpone his enlistment until the end of the month's second week. He reported as ordered, but was not judged proper military material. The experience ended up being one of his more humorous episodes that fall, and Partch related the story to Luening with typical dry panache:

> The army doesn't want me. Reason, among others: "emotional instability." This conclusion was reached after the following conversation:
>
> 1st Psychiatrist: Do you think you would fit into the army?
> A. I think I am adaptable. But I can't see myself toting a gun. I have a horror of violence.
> 2nd Psychiatrist: Did you ever have any nervous trouble?
> A. I have had nervous collapses as the result of too strenuous work with my music and insecurity shock.
> 2nd Psychiatrist: I don't think you belong in the army. Do you?

> If these answers indicate emotional instability, I'm a monkey's grandmother. But I'm not inclined to argue. We went through like boards in a lumber mill, and the above conversations were the longest I had with anyone.[45]

Freed from the specter of military service, Partch resumed work toward obtaining a Guggenheim Fellowship. Moe informed him that he needed references other than Luening and Hanson, and so, at Luening's suggestion, Partch wrote to Virgil Thomson.[46]

Luening's recommendation of Thomson as a good prospect was a perceptive one. Of all the influential composers and critics in New York at the time, Thomson was most likely to be interested in Partch's music. After evoking the Midwest through the music for Pare Lorentz's films *The Plow that Broke the Plains* (1936) and *The River* (1937), Thomson continued to use American themes through the 1940s up to his final opera with Gertrude Stein, *The Mother of Us All* (1947), which explores Susan B. Anthony's lasting impact and was even premiered by Luening. With his interest in Dust Bowl Americana and close ties with the documentary imagination, Thomson aligned with Partch thematically, but the two composers shared musical ideals as well. Like Partch's compositions, Thomson's music grew from a basis in American speech-rhythms. *The Mother of Us All*, which contains snatches of popular waltzes and Southern Baptist hymns much like Partch's *Bitter Music*, began with Thomson's notion that the speech-rhythms of American political oratory could form an opera. Like Partch, Thomson was extremely interested in and careful about setting his country's vernacular; he simply used diatonic means to accomplish the same goal that Partch sought through microtonality. This similarity in conception pushed Thomson's music toward Partch's in terms of its use of Anglo-American folk culture, but Thomson's Neoclassical training kept him from leaving Western formal structures completely behind.

Luening must have mentioned Thomson's interest in properly declaiming American English when he suggested the composer as a likely ally because when Partch initially wrote Thomson in early October he emphasized that aspect of his approach: "My work is directed toward uncovering, again, the infinite musical possibilities of multi-tonal scales, relationships, and chordal structures. Further, it encompasses a synthesis of such an investigation with the musicalization of speech tones and inflections—a medium I call Speech-Music."[47] Along with the letter, Partch included the "Plans for Work" section from his Guggenheim application and a copy of the pamphlet that he had produced in Chicago. Apologizing for supplying so much reading material, Partch concluded, "I hope you are not uninterested in the path of my endeavors. I would prefer outright antagonism, which I have found it possible to penetrate and dispel. This is almost never a possibility with uninterest."[48]

Evidently Thomson was extremely interested indeed in Partch's speech-music; he responded by the end of the month, inviting the composer to visit. Partch was about to leave New York City for a series of presentations, but he wrote back promising Thomson that he would stop by when he returned in November.[49] He made good on his promise, and in early November the two men finally met. Thomson, chief music critic of the *New York Herald Tribune* since 1940, evidently spent much of their meeting critiquing both Partch's music and the texts that he had written. Although he appreciated the subject matter and Partch's attempts to capture hobo speech accurately in *Barstow*, he was concerned about Partch's violation of common musical syntax. Still, Thomson was complimentary on the whole, agreeing to write to the Guggenheim Foundation on Partch's behalf. He was also intrigued enough after their short meeting to request that Partch loan him the one copy of his treatise *Patterns of Music*. Partch, slightly stung by the criticism, fired back the next week that he violated good usage only when necessary, and that "violation is stronger than conformity."[50] As he was still lecturing and needed his treatise to do so, he also wrote that he could not loan it to Thomson immediately. Thomson persisted, responding that he would take the utmost care of the manuscript and return it whenever Partch needed.[51] Partch relented and left his exposition at Thomson's apartment building for the composer to read over the coming holidays.

During these exchanges Partch was actively lecturing, giving recitals, and contacting other composers as possible references. On October 22 and 23, he was with Luening giving two long-planned lecture-demonstrations at Bennington College. A week and a half later, on November 3, he repeated the program at the Eastman School of Music's Kilbourn Hall, meeting with theory and graduate students for a separate demonstration.[52] Fortuitously, the performance at Eastman was recorded in its entirety and provides a revealing glimpse into how Partch adapted and presented his hobo persona, deftly playing into the expectations of an American composer pillaging the vernacular for musical material.

Partch divided his time in the lecture-demonstration into roughly three parts. As his theoretical innovations were still of utmost importance, he opened with an explanation of how his music differed from "the usual music." Using the Chromelodeon, he audibly contrasted just intonation with equal temperament, showing the reasonings behind and the possibilities of his forty-three-tone scale. After a thorough explication of his musical theory, Partch moved into a discussion of his musical aesthetic. Alternately using the Chromelodeon and the Adapted Viola, he discussed Monophony, explaining that music had wrongly been divorced from words. He used excerpts from the *Seventeen Lyrics by Li Po* and *Two Psalms* to illustrate how he recaptured music's power by relating it closely to words. Finally, Partch combined these discussions into a bravura solo performance of the recently-completed *Barstow* for Adapted Guitar.

The event's indelible image was that of an erudite composer, obviously knowledgeable in the inner workings of music, performing as a hobo. It was an image very much in line with Woody Guthrie's demeanor. Throughout the lecture-demonstration, Partch was charming and funny, working hard to win over his young audience—and succeeding. He performed passages too quickly, playing for laughs while poking fun at his own history, yet he remained serious and earnest about music's future and his ideas for it. His presentation style was vastly different from and more congenial than that of the better-known irascible Partch of the 1960s and 1970s. Listening to this revealing glimpse into history, it is easy to see why Partch convinced so many of his work's importance, and why so many were willing to do so much to aid him.[53]

Partch was heartened by the response from faculty and students at Bennington and Eastman. He wrote to Luening, "The response and warmth of Bennington's reception were almost a shock to me. I have become so accustomed to being forced into breaking apathy and inertia that I was a little bewildered in the absence of negation."[54] Partch was so overwhelmed that he decided to find a portable reed organ (similar to those used by "sidewalk evangelists") to adapt like the Chromelodeon. With such a device, he could incorporate the sound into his lecture-demonstrations and even record *Barstow* with some of the interested Bennington students.[55] Already he was seeing the benefits of promoting himself as a composer of speech-music drawn from the dust of migrant and hobo life. Those benefits only increased when Howard Hanson mentioned in passing that he was fairly certain that Partch would receive a Guggenheim.[56]

In addition to these lecture-demonstrations, Partch was busy finding other references for his Guggenheim application.[57] Howard Hanson wrote on his behalf to six colleges in the Midwest, encouraging them to give fair hearing to Partch's theories and to consider inviting him for a demonstration. At Virgil Thomson's suggestion, Partch contacted Paul Hindemith at Yale to arrange for a presentation, although nothing ever came of the inquiry.[58] Partch also introduced himself to Douglas Moore at the urging of

Otto Luening and Mrs. Louise Dunn, Moore's aunt in San Diego, who had been enthusiastic about Partch's ideas.[59] It was a fortuitous suggestion, as Moore became Partch's most influential and steadfast supporter over the following fifteen years.

Even before meeting him personally, Harry Partch knew Douglas Moore artistically. Following Mrs Dunn's recommendation, he had secured copies of Moore's music. Upon playing through it, Partch seems to have felt that he had found another kindred spirit, someone whose songs evidenced an innate understanding of Monophony. He was so struck by Moore's music that in the spring of 1942, seven months before he first contacted the composer, Partch included a recording of George Bishop singing Moore's setting "Come Away Death" on the reverse side of his Chicago recording of "By the Rivers of Babylon."[60] Partch never revealed why he included this one song by another composer in a recording of his own works, but it obviously had a lasting impact. In December 1942, Partch wrote his own arrangement of the text, possibly as homage to the man he had just contacted, but never had it published. And in perhaps the highest compliment Partch could grant, at the decade's end, he wrote in *Genesis of a Music* that "corporeality is present beneath the Abstract habiliments of many other compositions. Douglas Moore's unaccompanied song 'Come Away Death,' truly a Monophonic concept even though its words are not treated as spoken words, is an example."[61]

Moore arguably had the most influence on getting Partch's music noticed and performed in New York City. He arranged for both of Partch's major recitals in the spring of 1944 and worked tirelessly in 1943 and again in 1952 to engineer a collaboration between Partch and dancer Martha Graham, almost succeeding on his second attempt.[62] He convinced Gilbert Chase to include a section on Harry Partch in his 1955 book on American music, one of the first of its kind.[63] From 1944, a little over a year after he had first met Partch, he began devoting an entire day's lesson to the composer in first his "20th-Century Music" class and later his "Modern Music" class at Columbia. Copland and Ives were the only other American composers afforded this distinction.[64] As Jacqueline Onslow-Ford later exclaimed to Partch upon hearing of Moore's efforts, "Now there is a man who knows how to get your music heard."[65]

There is little in Moore's music to suggest that he would naturally have been sympathetic to Partch's theories. Moore primarily composed large-scale symphonies and operas, genres that appalled Partch. He worked within the academic system throughout his life and was well-recognized and rewarded for his service. Yet the two men were both interested in several of the same themes, especially during this period. Most of Moore's work during the time focused on American stories and legends, including his operas *The Headless Horseman* (1936) and *The Devil and Daniel Webster* (1938). Furthermore, much of his work employed Anglo-American folk tunes, although he used them in a decidedly decorative fashion.

Even beyond this surface thematic similarity, both Partch and Moore shared an abiding artistic sensibility, no matter the genre or scale in which they composed. When asked by Marion Bauer in 1943 what made his music "essentially American," Moore responded, "I suppose there may be a special American blend but it won't be effective unless the music can stand on its own feet as music, and will be only a by-product of the composer's aim to write as good music as he can."[66] Partch felt much the same way, attempting always to write expressive music, with the forty-three-tone scale being merely the means to achieve his aim. The problems inherent in setting American speech also intrigued both composers, and they both felt that an American music might arise from proper declamation. In the same letter to Bauer, Moore wrote, "There is really flavor to American speech and if it is faithfully set, the music is bound to catch some of it."[67] In Partch's music, Moore saw a musician attempting to capture this flavor in an artistic manner. "Ever since I have known Partch and his music," he wrote in the 1950s, "I have been very much interested in the music which he has written because it is not the work of a scientific theorist but of a sensitive creator who was impelled toward this type of composition because of his artistic needs rather than by the wish to be novel."[68] That ideology of focusing on artistic expression is something Partch found lacking in the ultra-modern and later experimental communities and is why friendships with composers like Moore were so important to him.

With the support of composers like Moore, Thomson, and Luening, Partch's time in New York from late 1942 through January of 1943 proved to be extremely successful. He had quickly managed to find sympathetic ears among the musical elite for both his music and his theories. He had been able to present his ideas at Bennington College and the Eastman School of Music and had one more presentation planned, at the American Music Center on January 16, sponsored by Douglas Moore. And he had learned of the fascination of his hobo persona through reactions to his *Barstow* performances. But as important as this period of proselytizing was for Partch, he knew he needed new music to present if he were to gain even more momentum. On January 10, he wrote inviting Virgil Thomson to what would be his last presentation in New York for some time, and asking for the return of his manuscript.[69] Despite having had *Exposition of*

Monophony for over a month, Thomson still had not read it, but he agreed to bring it to the event provided that he could have it back immediately following the program. Partch good-naturedly acquiesced, but set a firm date at month's end for its final return, as he planned to visit friends in Ithaca.[70]

This visit was not Partch's sole reason for his trip north. After a flurry of lectures, demonstrations, and recitals, and with a firm foundation in the esteem of several influential composers, he had decided that it was time to compose again. For that, he needed the charts that accompanied his exposition. He had made initial forays back to composing at the end of the previous year, finishing a song cycle called *December, 1942* for Adapted Guitar and voice that included his version of "Come Away Death," from *Twelfth Night*; "The Heron," a poem by Japanese poet Tsurayuki; and "The Rose," by Ella Young.[71] Unsatisfied with them musically, he destroyed the songs a few years later; but they served as a good warm-up for compositions to come. On January 28, he left for Ithaca and embarked on one of his most prolific compositional periods.

Ithaca: Spring 1943–Summer 1943

Partch initially intended to spend only a short visit with his friends in Ithaca before moving on, but he seems to have decided quickly that the surroundings were ideal for sustained compositional activity. By his second week, he had found a part-time bookkeeping job with a scrap-iron company and had rented a room with his small wage at 329 West Seneca Street.[72] The landscape's beauty and the serenity of his situation calmed Partch's mind and provided his first positive outlook in many years. In a reflective mood engendered by his isolation, he wrote to Henry Allen Moe:

> The years 1934–35 I gave to researches in theory, and in the period 1935 to 1942 most of my creative energies were directed toward the building of new instruments. If I seem to be repeating myself, it is because I want to emphasize that I felt an impelling necessity to broaden my base for composition beyond only one viola. As the result of my work through 1935–42 I have that expanded base; a new period of creative or compositional work is opening up for me, of which *Barstow* is the beginning.[73]

Partch recognized that with *Barstow* he had inaugurated a different path, one that was finding acceptance. Recognizing the applicability of his hobo past on his contemplated future works, he began composing *U.S. Highball* on February 14.

Ithaca's calm and beautiful surroundings were not all that impelled Partch's compositional activity. Another precipitant appeared in the form of news for which he had waited a decade. On March 23, Henry Allen Moe wrote to Partch before official notification was given that Partch had been appointed to a Guggenheim Fellowship carrying a stipend of $1,800 for one year.[74] Many factors played into Partch's finally receiving a Fellowship, not the least of which was Moe's friendship and championing of his music and the recent death of Thomas Whitney Surette, in 1941. Aaron Copland took over the role of music adviser to the Guggenheim following Surette and although he had not been positive toward Partch's application in 1934, his taste was much more catholic and his hand not as heavy as Surette's.[75] Overcome by this award, Partch immediately wrote to his references, first praising Luening for the composer's work on his behalf, then thanking Thomson for his help and expressing regret that he had been unable to read the exposition. Partch also related his desire to stay in Ithaca composing, as he had been in a "creative fever," and his plan for completing the first draft of his Monophonic Cycle.[76] On April 5, official notice of the award finally arrived, announcing in formal language that "the terms of his appointment require him to devote himself during this period to creative work in musical composition based on a system of music, instruments and notation having 43 tones to the octave."[77] Partch found those terms easy to keep.

Ithaca's surroundings and his good news compelled Partch into a whirlwind of compositional activity over the following eight months. When he began *U.S. Highball*, he did so without the benefit of his instruments, as they were still stored in Chappaqua following his move from Chicago. But by April, as he began to contemplate the work's second draft, he realized that he needed them in order to proceed. Deciding to stay in Ithaca for the foreseeable future, Partch had his instruments moved there for forty dollars.[78] With that accomplished, he was ready to resume work on *U.S. Highball* and to begin the other hobo-inspired compositions that would make up the Monophonic Cycle.[79] On May 1, he began the second draft of *U.S. Highball*, which he completed five months later on October 1. By June 21, he had completed the fourth piece in the cycle, *Dark Brother*, a setting of Thomas Wolfe's essay "God's Lonely Man." On July 1, he completed the cycle's third work, *San Francisco*. By that week's end, he had also finished work on an addition to the cycle, *Letter from Hobo Pablo*, for voice, Adapted Guitar, and Kithara (see chapter 6). While writing these pieces, he also adapted older works for his new instruments, adding Kithara parts to both *Barstow* and his *Two Psalms*. Much-needed instrument repairs consumed the rest of the summer.[80] Galvanized by interest shown in his work, by season's end he had produced more compositions in a shorter time than at any other point in his career and had created a cycle of works for which he is still known today.

The first work Partch composed during this period, *U.S. Highball*, was the centerpiece of his compositional efforts, and in the following years he promoted it as his definitive piece. His reasons for this emerge in two letters written during the summer of 1943. The first, sent in June to Otto Luening, expressed his hope for *U.S. Highball* as a sequel to *Barstow*. The latter work had become standard in his lecture-demonstrations, and he probably hoped to build on its success.[81] The second letter, written in July, was to Douglas Moore. Moore had evidently been struck by the motivations behind and the possibilities for *U.S. Highball* after reading through Partch's "Plans for Work" section from the Guggenheim application. Accordingly, he had suggested that the composer concentrate his attention on that work. Partch had taken that suggestion and wrote Moore to thank him for it and to offer a copy of the score.[82] Leuning and Moore, his two most ardent supporters, had respectively encouraged him to follow along the lines of *Barstow* and to begin with another hobo-inspired work, and Partch followed their advice.

By summer's end, Partch became restless in Ithaca and started considering how he could form an ensemble to perform his new works and where they might be welcome. He wrote to P. J. Weaver, head of the Cornell Music Department, and received a positive response, including the possibility of having departmental members play the instruments. Partch wrote Luening about visiting Bennington again to renew friendships there and see people at the Estey Organ Company about constructing another Chromelodeon.[83] He was also anxious to display his progress and to continue making inroads into the New York musical community. So, on Thursday, October 28, he left his home of almost eight months and set out for Rochester, New York, en route to Bennington and Boston. He planned to arrive in New York by November 10 to present the fruits of his compositional labors to Moe and the Guggenheim Foundation.[84]

Boston: Fall 1943–Winter 1944

After visiting Ethel and Otto Luening at Bennington (and apologizing profusely to Ethel for having no work done on his *Finnegans Wake* setting for her) Partch made his way to Boston, where Quincy Porter had invited him to give a presentation at the New England Conservatory of Music on November 4. His lecture-demonstration there went extremely well and, reminiscent of the response at Bennington, the student review in the "NEC Bulletin" the following month gushed that "the originality of his settings and his performance aroused spontaneous enthusiasm. His talk injected a vitalizing current that will be remembered."[85] The students even requested that Partch play recordings of his other works in the orientation class and talk to the theory classes.

Partch also impressed Porter, a respect that was altogether mutual. Porter arranged a gathering at his house the Friday night after Partch's presentations and convinced Nicolas Slonimsky to attend. Partch and Slonimsky had met once before at a party given by Henry Cowell in California in 1931. Slonimsky had dismissed Partch's work then as insubstantial, but hearing the composer perform *U.S. Highball* and *Barstow* on Adapted Guitar energized him. He spent the evening making elaborate plans for Partch, even deciding that *Barstow* should be published immediately, whether or not anyone could read Partch's arcane and idiosyncratic notation.[86] This startling about face was common among those who encountered Partch in the early 1930s, forgot about him, and then became reacquainted with him as a hobo composer. The new texts he was setting and the American images they evoked through their rough vernacular captivated those acquaintances. Slonimsky was so taken that he remained enthralled by the works throughout his life, writing to Partch in the 1960s that he wanted to include Partch's American-themed works in his book *Music Since 1900*.[87] Porter was another supporter and promoter in the vein of Luening and Moore. He was interested in Partch's entire output and attempted to entice him to stay on in Boston. Partch agreed to return at the conclusion of his business in New York.

The following week Partch returned briefly as planned to New York City and began renewing his contacts there. He met with Henry Allen Moe and proposed an application to renew his Guggenheim for 1944. Moe favored the notion but warned that there might be stiff opposition and suggested that he discuss the matter with Porter when he returned to Boston. Virgil Thomson was likewise encouraging and, tenaciously clinging to the importance of Partch's exposition, mentioned that it should form a large part of his application. It was a suggestion that surely warmed Partch's heart as he continued around New York the following days, pursuing new contacts for his music and his Guggenheim application.

Oddly enough, the one composer who might have been supposed to have been most sympathetic to Partch's work during this time was decidedly cool toward it. Henry Cowell supported numerous West Coast composers during the early 1930s when Partch was active in San Francisco and Los Angeles, and the younger man had even performed in one of Cowell's New Music Society concerts in 1933. But Cowell missed that particular concert and, like Slonimsky, found Partch's theories inconsequential. He never threw his weight behind Partch, which in turn made Partch suspicious of the man and convinced him that ultra-modern composers were perverting music by ignoring its expressive basis. In many ways, Partch's reaction to Cowell was similar to his reaction to John Cage in Chicago—he expected support and held a grudge when that support did not materialize. Still, understanding Henry Cowell's influence in modern music circles and desiring at least a cordial dialogue with him, Partch phoned the composer during that short jaunt into New York City and offered to show his recent work. The two dined together and Partch performed *U.S. Highball* for him. Cowell was much more sympathetic than he had been in the 1930s, especially as his own work was moving into themes similar to the ones Partch was already exploring.[88] It was a small détente but a rare one for Partch, as he tended to burn his bridges. The composer also performed the work for Martha Graham, who was so impressed that she discussed plans with him to translate it into a dance the following summer.[89] All in all, it was an extraordinarily productive visit. The only disappointment was that Partch failed to see his brother Paul, who had enlisted with the navy and was scheduled to sail into New York harbor. Harry made plans to spend the afternoon with Paul, but his brother's ship was quarantined, and Partch was forced to return to Boston without visiting with him.[90]

An unexpected telegram awaited Partch upon his return to Boston on November 23. Douglas Moore had sent a message the day before asking "can you audition *U.S. Highball*, League of Composers on Monday, November 29 at 9pm, Town Hall Club?"[91] Unbeknownst to Partch, Moore had been working silently in the background, circulating the materials that Partch had sent him and convincing his prominent friends that this young composer held a key to music's future development. Concerts of the League of Composers were arguably the most prestigious for modern music in New York at the time, and a successful audition would mean citywide exposure and reviews in all major newspapers.

Partch eagerly accepted the audition offer and, at the Guggenheim Foundation's expense, quickly retraced his steps to the city. At his audition the following week for the League's executive committee, he performed parts of *U.S. Highball*, in its first version for Adapted Guitar and voice, along with other selections. The works were well-received and the response overwhelmingly positive: despite the League's conservative reputation, the committee offered Partch a League-sponsored concert that season. The key to Partch's success was not only Moore's effective championing, but also the music's close connection to the dominant trend toward "plain folks" Americana. The League stipulated that the second half of Partch's concert would feature *U.S. Highball*. Satisfied, and grateful for the sudden surge of interest in his work (particularly *U.S. Highball*), Partch returned to Boston to begin the groundwork necessary for a concert, including drafting individual parts and repairing instruments.[92]

Immediately upon his return, Partch performed *U.S. Highball* for an eager Howard Hanson, who was in Boston to conduct his fourth symphony. The work pleased Hanson, who declared it the composer's best to date. A bout of the flu and inability to find quarters for himself or his instruments anywhere in the city barred Partch from savoring the accolades. He remained in this miserable condition for almost two weeks until the Boston Conservatory offered a studio and interested musicians. That offer unexpectedly fell through, but Partch did ultimately find a home in a "large, old-fashioned room at 23 Hancock Street on Beacon Hill."[93]

In his drafty room, Partch planned for the coming months.[94] He consulted the conservatory organ technician for recommendations on strengthening the Chromelodeon. He organized an ensemble at the conservatory to record *U.S. Highball* beginning on January 3. And, after talking with Quincy Porter, he crystallized his thoughts concerning a Guggenheim renewal. Encouraged by the reaction that *U.S. Highball* received everywhere he performed it, Partch decided to focus his energies for the remainder of his Fellowship year on copying parts for the League of Composers concert. If he were awarded a second Guggenheim, Partch proposed expanding *U.S. Highball* and completing two compositions from the Monophonic Cycle, *Variations on a Theme* and the *Excerpts from Finnegans Wake* that he had promised Ethel Luening. Much of his music had never been performed by its full complement of instruments, so he wanted to arrange more hearings of his work, such as the planned League concert. Finally, since musicians seemed to be recognizing the importance of his work in general, and since Virgil Thomson had expressed such a strong affinity for the exposition, Partch wanted to return to his theoretical treatise and complete it, so long as that work did not interfere with his other goals. He outlined these objectives in a letter to Moe, adding that, despite his delight at devoting himself to composition over the past year, it was now time to focus on the other roles he was forced to fill: those of theorist, instrument builder, teacher, performer, and promoter.[95]

As the year-end holidays faded to memory, Partch turned to those last two roles. He remembered the impact that his Chicago recordings of *Barstow* had made when Luening and Moe first began circulating them and elected to do the same for *U.S. Highball*. He arranged for a masters student in organ at the Boston Conservatory to learn the Chromelodeon and another music student to play the Kithara. He delivered parts to these two in late December in preparation for a recording session the week of January 17.[96] However, the students lacked the interest and dedication of his Chicago collaborators Gilman Chase and George Bishop; by the first week of January they had resigned from Partch's ensemble, and he was left to record alone.

At Quincy Porter's suggestion, and using Porter's equipment and house for the project, Partch committed *U.S. Highball* to five twelve-inch records by himself. Over a period of a week, Partch executed all four instrumental parts on the recording. He first recorded the voice and Adapted Guitar parts, then successively added the Chromelodeon and finally the Kithara. It was a less than ideal situation, Partch later confided to Moe, because with each addition the parts suffered in resonance and quality. In addition, there was an infrequent but loud "b-r-r-r" marring the sound, a noise caused by a small buzz on the Kithara that was transferred to the microphone through vibrations in the floor and then amplified on the recording. In spite of these defects, he felt that the recording conveyed the piece's character well enough. At the end of January, he asked Porter to deliver copies of the record, along with manuscripts of the completed movements of the Monophonic Cycle, to Moe, in order to show his progress and support his next Guggenheim application.[97]

New York City: Spring 1944

Partch had originally planned to stay in Boston until the League of Composers concert. Transporting his instruments was always a hassle, and he had believed that with Porter's assistance he could find and train an ensemble of students to present his works in New York as well as in Boston and other major cities. By the first of February, however, he had accepted that his vision of dedicated student performers would never materialize. Frustrated by this failure, he returned to New York City and found room for himself and his instruments at 38 West Ninety-Second Street. With only two and a half months left until the League concert, Partch needed to finish the last two movements of the Monophonic Cycle and find musicians that he could train rapidly.

Wondering where he could possibly find musicians willing to give their time and energy freely, Partch happened to remember a young composer named Henry Brant, whom he had met at Douglas Moore's apartment in November the week he auditioned for the League of Composers.[98] At the time, Brant was a freelance commercial musician writing big band jazz arrangements and background music for radio. He was also a composer fascinated with timbres, and many of his early works experimented with sounds from unusual objects or unusual sounds from common objects. His *Music for a Five and Dime* was scored for clarinet, piano, and kitchen hardware, while in his flute concerto *Angels and Devils* he combined different layers of a similar timbre, scoring it for three piccolos, five flutes, and two alto flutes.

Moore had known of these interests and invited Brant to meet Partch. The two had spent the evening in rapt discussion over new instruments, tuning systems, and the harmonic series. When Partch contacted Brant in February about possibly performing in the concert, in the absence of other pressing concerns Brant agreed to take part. He even found another musician to play the Kithara, one who coincidentally knew Calista Rogers, Partch's 1933 Pasadena collaborator. As a viola da gambist, Alix Young Maruchess was familiar with both alternative tuning systems and string instruments, a perfect fit for the Kithara.[99]

The three, along with Ethel Luening on occasion, began rehearsing immediately (see fig. 7.1). By the time of the concert, just over two months later, they had practiced together over forty times. Of course, through all these rehearsals, the musicians were never paid. Even in the final two weeks prior to the concert, when they were practicing fifteen to twenty hours a week, there was never any mention of money. As Partch related right before the concert, their "jobs were little less than heroic."[100] They rehearsed and performed for the love of the music and out of dedication to Partch. It was a dedication he would inspire in performers throughout his life, one none of them could ever fully explain.

Even during this period of intense rehearsal, Partch continued to compose. He was determined to complete the two remaining movements of the Monophonic Cycle. The members of his new ensemble helped hone both of these works, although only one was presented to the League of Composers. Partch had long envisioned a set of variations on the tune "Yankee Doodle." Perhaps inspired by the knowledge of Brant's virtuosity on the tin whistle and the composer's work *The Marx Brothers*, which he scored for tin whistle and chamber ensemble, Partch arranged his variations for soprano, two tin flutes (which Brant had obtained at Woolworth's), Chromelodeon,

Figure 7.1. Harry Partch, Ethel Luening, and Alix Maruchess rehearsing for his League of Composers concert in April 1944. Partch is seated at the Chromelodeon and the Adapted Guitar rests in his lap. Photograph by Larry Gordon. Courtesy of the Harry Partch Estate Archive, San Diego.

Flex-a-tone (a small toy noisemaker similar to a musical saw), and tin oboe (a tin whistle played with an oboe reed and mouthpiece). He wrote the work quickly, between March 25 and 30, and christened it *Y.D. Fantasy*. The text was based largely on the original tune's text as recorded by Oscar Sonneck, with important alterations. Throughout his life, Partch loved satire, and as *Y.D. Fantasy* was to be the last piece performed on the concert, he inserted himself into the text, satirizing the American hobo image he had cultivated and his musical theories by ending the work with these lines:

> Doodle doodle do mama!
> Doodle doodle do papa!
> In forty-three tones to the octave.
>
> Yankee doodle keep it up
> Yankee doodle dandy
> Mind the music and the step
> And with the girls be handy.[101]

He was the American Dandy, riding into town on forty-three tones to the octave, sharing his notions of speech-music based on American hoboes.

Partch did not finish the other work, his long-projected setting of *Finnegans Wake*, in time for the League concert, but he did complete it before a follow-up concert at Columbia University. The ensemble only performed one of the two settings written expressly for Ethel Luening's voice and finished in early May, "Isobel," at Columbia. "Isobel" is scored for soprano, Kithara, and double flageolet; Henry Brant's expertise again helped determine the work's performing forces, as he had a double flageolet on loan from his cousin. The flageolet is a Baroque instrument with four front finger holes and two thumb holes; its double is simply two bodies of the instrument played with a single mouthpiece. The way Partch wrote for the instrument, as well as for the tin whistles, was consistent with his later experiments with traditional instruments in microtonal tunings. He measured the notes precisely against the Chromelodeon and then wrote out the part in his own notational system.[102]

While working toward the League concert, Partch also received unexpected good news from the Guggenheim Foundation. Considering the progress that he had already demonstrated and the stamp of approval given by his achieving a League of Composers concert, the Foundation's board decided that they should continue funding for another year to allow Partch the time to finish his projects. As he had a year earlier, Partch responded quickly to Moe's announcement and accepted the Foundation's generous offer. He also wrote those closest to him thanking them for their support. As he had just completed the *Y.D. Fantasy* in which Ethel Luening was to sing, Partch wrote her husband letting him know about the timing of the concert, set for April 22, and informed him about his most recent composition. Partch was glad to have it finished and felt that the piece reflected his good mood during this time. He knew that it was silly business, but felt that it was "a justified but momentary escape from profundity."[103]

Partch's official New York debut at the League of Composers concert was held in the Carnegie Chamber Music Hall on a Saturday afternoon at 5:00. The rather lengthy program consisted of *Barstow*, followed by *U.S. Highball* bearing its fresh dedication to Henry Allen Moe and the John Simon Guggenheim Memorial Foundation, *San Francisco*, and *Y.D. Fantasy*. As the four musicians took the stage, Partch, wearing black pants and a white shirt, carried with him a hammer, a screwdriver, and a glue pot. Throughout the concert, he fixed the instruments as problems developed, always with the utmost aplomb.[104]

Reaction to the concert was mixed. Many composers in the audience, while genuinely interested in Partch's ideas, were skeptical about the result and dismissive of Partch as a composer because of his lack of professional training and the simplicity of his rhythmic structures. Henry Brant recalled the indignation that met the program:

> It was looked upon as a cheap fraud that somehow Partch, in a sneaky but clever way, had gotten past the learned and solid people who ran the League of Composers and had perpetrated this horrible fraud or else somebody had done it as a spoof. Nobody could quite believe that this was a serious expression. I got comments like this: "How could you waste your time?" "You've been taken in." "It must be something mesmeric about Harry Partch."[105]

Although the concert's music certainly upset many, most reactions to the works' thematic basis were positive. The *New York Times* and the *New York Herald Tribune* sent reviewers, and both men focused on the works' literary aspect rather than the music. The *New York Times* reviewer found that "the value of this sort of thing is almost exclusively literary. The ideas and the words used in their presentation are the center of interest. The instruments add atmosphere and do it admirably, but the music—so-called—is of entirely secondary importance."[106] Paul Bowles, writing for the *Herald Tribune*, related that hearing the words was "absolutely essential to the sustaining of interest, since continuity and planned variety did not appear in the musical accompaniment."[107]

Partch set the stage for such reactions. Although he carefully explained the texts before the performance of each work, the only explanation of his tuning system was a paragraph at the bottom of the program. In the two years since his Chicago concerts he had completely reversed his performing strategy. Instead of exhaustively describing just intonation and his use of the system, Partch presumed that the Americana theme and his sculpturally appealing instruments would ensure a positive reception as they had in schools throughout the Northeast and among his new supporters. Without an explanation of his tuning system, composers and reviewers seemed unable to critique Partch's musical ideas beyond the texture and so naturally focused on the words. As those words came from hoboes and men affected by the Dust Bowl, they held an inherent fascination upon which the reviewers commented favorably. The irony was that this focus on words unwittingly proved Partch's Monophonic concept. By primarily reviewing the text and its intonation, these writers concluded that delivery of the text was key and the music only a means to that end.

The reviews did not end immediately following the concert. *Modern Music* published a review by Lou Harrison in its May-June issue. Although he would later become one of Partch's few close composer friends (after Virgil Thomson gave him a copy of *Genesis of a Music* and he delved into microtonal theories in his own music), Harrison's review was chiding. He perceptively linked Partch's music with that of Ives, as both grew from the rich soil of the American experience, used American tunes in unique ways, and were almost bardic in execution. But he felt that Partch's music lacked the transcendence of Ives's, finding that the instrumental combinations merely decorated a simple melodic line, and that the pieces were much too long. Yet Harrison recognized what remains the most impressive achievement of these works: their ability to conjure a time and place and transport the listener there, as though he or she were riding a boxcar or suffering Dust Bowl deprivations. This was the review in which Harrison wrote about becoming homesick upon hearing *San Francisco*.[108]

For many, it seemed, the sheen had worn off Partch. Once his music was heard with the full ensemble and the extent of his microtonal experiments made plain, many who had been fascinated by the idea of Partch's music lost interest. His hobo evocations earned his music a first hearing, and when that hearing revealed a bardic rendition with guitar much like Woody Guthrie's ballads, it further piqued their curiosity. Partch seemed, on the face of things, a Guthrie for the cultivated music tradition, a composer toeing the decoratively exotic line by appropriating Anglo-American folk culture. But those impressions could not sustain interest beyond a night's entertainment. By April 1944, the country was moving on, past Dust Bowl problems and curiosity about that particular "folk." Only those truly intrigued by Partch's solution to the search for an American musical speech idiom applauded his efforts, though applaud they did. After the last performance of *Y.D. Fantasy* the audience cried out for it to be repeated, which the performers graciously did.

Unfortunately, several Partch supporters did not attend the League concert. Virgil Thomson heard the last rehearsal since he was going to miss the actual concert.[109] The absence of Henry Allen Moe was more surprising: in a grievous oversight, Moe never received an invitation. Partch was understandably appalled and apologetic.[110] Moe and others got a second chance to hear the concert when it was repeated a month later, on May 22, 1944, in the Brander Matthews Theater at Columbia University. The program was the same, except for the addition of Partch's setting of "Isobel" from *Finnegans Wake*. In reviewing this concert, the *New Yorker* voiced concerns similar to those in the New York daily newspapers, but followed up with a Partch interview. The reviewer observed that "he believes that with his forty-three-tone scale he can duplicate the tones of human conversation. He made a pretty good stab at this, we thought."[111] These concert successes buoyed Partch's confidence and he moved on, certain of his trajectory. *U.S. Highball* is one of the few Partch compositions to enjoy near-universal acceptance at its premiere. Every reviewer singled it out and described appreciatively its speech-song aspect and its hobo theme, even while judging it too long and amorphous. *U.S. Highball*'s favored place among Partch's oeuvre probably emerged from a combination of success after so many trials, enthusiastic support from the Guggenheim Foundation and myriad composers, an appreciative segment of an audience that intuitively grasped his concepts, and a confirmation of his compositional path.

In the audience at Partch's League of Composer's concert was Gunnar Johansen, a pianist on faculty at the University of Wisconsin, Madison. Partch's music and its possibilities completely captivated Johansen who, immediately upon arriving home, began making arrangements to get Partch to Wisconsin and find support for the research and publication of *Patterns of Music*. He even arranged for his dean to inquire of Moe the state of Partch's funding. Moe evidently believed that Wisconsin would be a profitable experience for Partch following his New York stint and asked Douglas Moore to convince Partch to grab this opportunity.[112] Moore agreed that the move would be a good one for Partch, so, at the two men's urging, Partch traveled to Wisconsin in early June. The University Research Committee there gave him a grant for the academic year beginning that fall. Convinced that the move was "highly advantageous," Partch left New York to spend the summer in California before heading to Wisconsin.[113]

When Partch first hopped a train into New York City in the spring of 1942, he was unsure and slightly fearful of conservatory-trained composers' reactions to his music. After all, he had long promoted himself as a theoretical innovator and so was as slow to take on the hobo persona professionally as he had been personally. But by the time he applied to the Guggenheim Foundation that fall, Partch had realized the attraction of his music based on those experiences and was prepared to exploit it. He began presenting himself as a composer chronicling in music the plight and culture of a people who, because of the images presented by Lange, Steinbeck, Guthrie, and others, were in the center of a storm of controversy. His lecture-demonstrations around New England introduced to the ears of his audiences the words of a class of people they had never met, wrapped in microtonal theories that promised music's salvation. It was a potent mix, and one successful enough that by the decade's end, as the media moved past Depression-inspired images, Partch was ready to move on as well. Looking forward to his long-awaited completion of Yeats's "King Oedipus," he wrote to Lucie and Larry Marshall that he had grown touchy about all the criticism he had received for his "hobo music."[114]

Nonetheless, the image had been good to Partch. It was so successful in fact that the image has remained tied to his name ever since. That "hobo music" sustained him from 1942 until 1944 and allowed him to win two consecutive Guggenheim Fellowships. It brought him the support of men like Otto Luening, Douglas Moore, and, to a limited extent, Virgil Thomson, all of whom were interested in the questions of what made American music special and different from European music and what directions might assure its future viability. Partch even won over Howard Hanson, a composer with little interest in musical Americana, who believed that Partch's hobo music was an important new direction. When Partch ran out of time in his Eastman lecture, Hanson proclaimed, "Well, we have to hear the hitchhiker song, even if it means canceling all classes this afternoon."[115] Partch's hobo image even carved out a niche for him within New York's musical society. His unique situation of being one of "the folk" that so attracted intellectuals during the Depression and Second World War, but also a member of the intellectual elite by way of his musical/theoretical knowledge and Guggenheim support, allowed him to bridge the gap between the two groups. Unlike Woody Guthrie, who was regarded as a firm member of "the folk," Partch crafted a cultivated music in response to a pressing social fascination. Through this dynamic, he made a profound contribution to the question of what makes an American composer, or an American music. But his musical theories of what made true American speech-music, the conceptually exotic manner in which he engaged his sources, and the question of which of his myriad hobo experiences (old-time hobo, transient, or Dust Bowl migrant) best described him, played a greater role than merely ensuring his acceptance into New York society. They also set the stage for his reception throughout the rest of his life. Upon arriving in New York in 1942, Partch left his years of actual hoboing behind him. He received aid from a variety of sources and left the city two years later to embark on a life supported by universities and foundations. But through his decisions of how to promote himself and on what texts to focus his music during that crucial period, the hobo came to define all his future projects. He may have decided to leave the hobo behind, but it would prove a hard image to shake.

CHAPTER EIGHT

THE STRANGEST KIND OF HOBO

When Harry Partch set out on his journeyman's adventure of securing a Guggenheim Fellowship, completing his proposed catalog of Depression-inspired works, and airing the results in the heady atmosphere of New York City, he carried the weight of his experiences scraping together a living through odd jobs across the western United States. His life as a hobo during the Depression consumed his plans and hopes for the future, but it also gave new direction to the thematic bases of his works and sparked a new, and even greater, period of creative success than he had enjoyed with his first Monophonic songs. From his journal *Bitter Music*, begun as he descended into the hobo jungles in 1935, to *U.S. Highball*, completed as he received salvation in the form of a Guggenheim in 1943, Partch made the characters he met and the words they spoke the centerpieces of his creative aspirations. He allied himself, through life and work, with a group that was fascinating to the broader American culture, one that was searching for the truth of its situation through media such as the documentary expressions of Dorothea Lange's photographs and *The Grapes of Wrath*.

This cultural fascination played a definitive role in Partch's acceptance in New York and his winning the Guggenheims that gave him time to compose, but how did his appropriation of the hobo image shape his subsequent career? This chapter completes the story of Harry Partch and the hobo by taking three passes through the composer's life, from his time in New York City to his death in 1974, in order to discern the figure in three distinct areas. It begins by tracing the hobo and outsider labels through various writings about Partch to see why authors in the 1950s and 1960s so persistently applied these terms when discussing the composer and his music. It then demonstrates how Partch modulated presentations of his music in those decades first to capitalize on the continuing hobo fascination before minimizing the hobo in favor of a more general outsider mystique. And finally, it mines the composer's musical theatre works from the 1950s and 1960s and their cultural milieu, uncovering traces of the hobo in order to determine ways in which he was defined and confined by the hobo throughout his life.

A Hobo in Name

In beginning to ascertain how authors adopted the hobo and outsider labels, it is essential to note that Partch's engagement with the hobo did not end when he arrived in Madison to work under a University of Wisconsin grant in the spring of 1944. Whether or not he intended it, by casting himself as a hobo composer during his sojourn in New York and its environs, he had assumed a label that would be permanently attached to scholarly and popular assessment of his life and work.[1] Glimmers of this label appear in reviews of his work at Wisconsin, where William Kay Archer, writing for the student newspaper the *Daily Cardinal*, remarked that "Mr. Partch, a fellow in music at the university, has radically departed from the accepted channels of musical form."[2] The *Wisconsin State Journal* also focused on Partch's status as a composer looking for "a third ingredient. That third ingredient is something that is to come from experimenting with sound and new instruments, from a probing into 'the adventure of sound association with common experience, such as the sounds of speech.'"[3]

Although rarely explicitly applied in these late 1940s reviews, the hobo label that lurked beneath the proper prose quickly came to define Partch and his music. Most often, the attitudes and impressions associated with the hobo rear their head in reviews and articles through the label "outsider," a common substitution for the figure; in contemporaneous reviews of Woody Guthrie's work, writers regularly used the same label because they wanted to invoke a person beyond society's edge, but were unsure of the currency of the term "hobo."[4] Many reviews of Partch's work in the 1960s and 1970s, when the composer was next in the national spotlight, contain the word "outsider" as their primary descriptor. Consider a 1963 *Time* magazine story on Partch's performance in the ballroom of San Francisco's Sheraton-Palace Hotel. Squeezed in between descriptions of his instruments and their sounds, and surrounded by commonplace comments on the audience's incredulity, was this terse summation of his career: "Partch's galloping whimsy—the very thing that has made him an admirably tireless pioneer—has also kept him a hopeless, penniless outsider all his life."[5] Neatly tied together in one sentence are the sentiments that fifty years earlier had been reduced to one word—hobo.

Reviewers and critics were not the only ones to apply the "outsider" label; it also appeared in the earliest scholarship concerning Partch. On November 26, 1963, Wilfrid Mellers gave a lengthy paper to the Royal Music Association. In it, he outlined the state of American music among those considered avant-garde and played recorded examples to support his thesis that composition in the United States was withdrawing from European influence. He chose the recently-completed *Windsong* and *The Bewitched* as examples of Partch's musical language and commented particularly on the mannerisms of Partch's performers: "So the musicians are also clowns, divine fools, and outsiders, bums, hoboes—like Partch himself, who for eight years lived by riding the rails."[6] Strikingly, Mellers crafted a list containing hobo and bum, one that might also have included tramp, migrant, transient, and newsboy, following the various subcultures on which Partch drew. Mellers looked at the whole and assumed that as Partch had lived outside society for so long, he had no problem adopting a tuning system outside Western musical practices and asking his performers to act like hoboes.

Sometimes scholars chose to detail the various ways in which Partch was an outsider. In his review of the second edition of *Genesis of a Music* for the *Journal of Music Theory*, Richard Wernick claimed that "Partch was a man out of step, out of place, and out of time in relation to the musical values and attitudes that constituted his cultural environment."[7] If Partch seemed to have no place in civilized musical society, he was still important to it: like the hobo, he may have brought to light the uncomfortable notion that something was amiss in a culture, but you would not like to have him around at dinner parties.

Scholarship since Partch's death has likewise framed the composer's life and music as those of consummate outsider, an incorrigible hobo. In 1997 and 1998 two biographies appeared, the first a chronological collection of letters, reviews, writings, and photographs from Partch's personal scrapbooks, called *Enclosure 3*, and the second a more traditional prose biography. In his summation essay at the end of *Enclosure 3*, Philip Blackburn explicitly referenced Partch's hobo mystique: "In thinking of Partch as hobo, we might be forgiven for thinking that he was some savage who dusted himself off one day and became an artist, free from all influences of civilised society. . . . Throughout his life he treated his role of social and musical outcast with both relish and gripe."[8] Bob Gilmore approached the outsider paradigm from a different angle, linking Partch with several American musical traditions (including the experimental tradition, microtonalists, and purveyors of new instruments) but concluding that, "no matter where music historians locate him, Partch remains a true American original."[9]

Gilmore's conception of Partch's outcast nature being a corollary to the traditional, self-reliant American one is perhaps the most common current usage of the outsider label and appears to date from the last years of Partch's life. Larry Stempel, writing in the *Saturday Review* in the early 1970s, said that "the most profound innovators in American music seem to have inherited the sign of Cain that has kept them apart from the musical mainstream," before going on to mention Charles Ives, Edgard Varèse, and Carl Ruggles in relation to Harry Partch. This notion of what in today's marketing is often termed the "American Maverick" denies the interrelationship of the composers grouped under that term and the impact of composers like Partch on contemporary composition, no matter their perceived outsider status.

The idea of Partch as outsider hobo permeates his reception history. It joins a catalogue of his instruments and a quick primer on his forty-three-tone scale to form the triad of features always mentioned in reviews and discussions of his music. Because it is such a pervasive feature of his reception, it raises the question of whether other biographical elements conspired to keep the outsider label fresh once Partch was no longer demonstrably a hobo. Perhaps the clearest explication of why Partch's outsider nature continues to fascinate even in these days when hoboes are rare, and why it became such an overwhelming feature in discourses on his life and work, was given by Ben Johnston, a noted microtonal composer who studied with Partch and actively promoted his music in the 1950s. In an article published ten years after Partch's death, Johnston attempted to position Partch as an important figure with great impact on contemporary composition and so confronted this label head on. He began his discussion of Partch's character by observing that "Partch's sympathies were always with what much later would be called counter-cultures,"[10] before proceeding to describe the ways in which he was an outcast. Johnston's list so penetrates the composer's character, and so usefully defines features that kept the hobo figure at the forefront of his reception, that it bears dissection here.[11]

Johnson first observed that Partch refused to participate in the traditional concert music world, not even that of what has been variously called "modern" or "new music." Apart from a 1932 concert for Henry Cowell's New Music Society and his League of Composers concert in 1944, Partch gave no concerts for the primary composer organizations of his day.[12] Indeed, unlike most of his contemporaries, he never even belonged to a professional society, ignoring the pull that drew composers in the 1920s and 1930s into the Franco-American Musical Society (later renamed Pro Musica), the International Composers' Guild, the League of Composers, and the Pan-American Association of Composers. Partch eschewed the musical superstructure of symphonies, opera houses, and choral societies because he only composed for his own instruments. He relied on contacts at universities to arrange concerts and demonstrations and performed at music festivals held at the various schools with which he was associated. As a result, the concert-going public was largely unaware of his few performances.

In addition to ignoring the concert music scene, Partch also refused all trappings of mid-century commercial music. He greatly respected the vitality of American commercial music, but recoiled from its production modes because they could alter a musician's output for nothing more than money.[13] He demanded complete creative control, and so throughout his life recorded, produced, promoted, and distributed his own recordings. The practice began in Chicago in 1942, when he recorded, with help from George Bishop, *Two Psalms*, *Six Lyrics by Li Po*, and *Barstow*, and continued through his January 1944 recording of *U.S. Highball* and the series of recordings he made with Warren Gilson at Wisconsin between 1945 and 1947 (*Two Settings from James Joyce's Finnegans Wake*, *By the Rivers of Babylon*, *Y.D. Fantasy*, *Dark Brother*, *Barstow*, *San Francisco*, and *U.S. Highball*).[14] The Gate 5 recordings made throughout the 1950s are the epitome of this trend: a series of twelve recordings that Partch produced, enclosed in packaging of his own design, and marketed through the mail, pocketing all the proceeds.[15]

Although most experienced Partch's music through records, he had only five commercial recordings in his lifetime, on two labels: CRI's *From the Music of Harry Partch* (a 1964 release containing *Castor and Pollux*, *The Letter*, *Windsong*, and "Scene 10" and the "Epilogue" from *The Bewitched*), *And on the Seventh Day Petals Fell in Petaluma* (1968), and *The Bewitched* (a 1973 reissue of Partch's 1957 recording); and Columbia Records's *The Music of Harry Partch* (a recording of *Barstow*, *Castor and Pollux*, and *Daphne of the Dunes* produced following a concert given at the Whitney Museum in 1968) and *Delusion of the Fury* (1971). Commercial recordings stimulated awareness of Partch's music but lacked the marketing of more mainstream releases and garnered him limited income.

In addition to steadfastly maintaining his independence from concert-giving organizations and the commercial world, Partch refused any permanent association with a college or university. In some respects this side of his hobo spirit was easiest to nurture, as most colleges and universities did not want him. His first university post was at Madison, where the music faculty so belligerently opposed Partch's appointment that the administration ultimately housed him in the physics department.[16] His other long-term university association, with the University of Illinois at Urbana-Champaign, was similarly supported by outside grants and the university's Graduate School and Department of Speech and Theatre, while the university housed his instruments off campus.[17] His only direct employment by a university music department, as a Regents' Professor at the University of California, San Diego in the fall of 1967, provided housing for his instruments. However, the one series of seminars he taught on his own music there sapped his creative energies and terrified many students.[18] He never repeated the course. All other academic associations guaranteed either performances, such as the 1969 premiere of *Delusion of the Fury* at UCLA, or lectures, such as his 1971 address at the University of Hawaii. His periodic screeds against musical training in the United States certainly did not strengthen his relationship with musical academia. In "Show Horses in the Concert Ring," a satire he wrote while at the University of Wisconsin, Partch urged students away from schools of music: "He will get no help from the music schools in this attitude [of critical questioning]; after all, they are music schools only because they are virtually impervious to individualism. Ritual of classroom double-talk and creed of safety-deposit-box dogma have vested the high priests of the musical academy with a calcification the envy of every other bone of human endeavor."[19]

Johnston isolated one other aspect contributing to the hobo image Partch cultivated—his financial situation. In the United States, concert music of European derivation has long been associated with wealth, power, prestige, and social position. Partch refused those connections by remaining poor, powerless, and in a low social stratum for most of his life. Although he did accept funding, he scrutinized its origin, seeking out individuals who believed in his work and taking assistance from them. In the 1930s he cultivated Henry Allen Moe, who in turn worked on Partch's behalf to secure the Carnegie grant that allowed him to travel to Europe and his two successive Guggenheim grants in the 1940s. During that decade, Partch also nourished a friendship with Bertha McCord Knisely, music critic for the Los Angeles paper *Saturday Night* and a wealthy widow, who established a fund to support Partch in those early years.[20] This pattern continued until his final years, when Betty Freeman became his primary benefactor, providing an annual income, helping establish the Harry Partch Foundation, and commissioning works and films to support him.[21]

All these characteristics became legendary, endlessly repeated by writers in the short biographical sketches that inevitably accompanied articles about him. This repetition confirmed Partch as one of the original outsiders in American music, willing to sacrifice health and security to stay true to his musical ideology. Unfortunately, the hobo and outsider labels obscure as much as they enlighten, for Partch was willing to shift vision, especially in the 1930s and early 1940s, to further his aims.

A Hobo When Necessary

As Harry Partch was finding his way in the musical communities of California and New York in the 1930s and 1940s, he altered how he presented his music and theories based on his sense of the prevailing winds of artistic taste. For our second pass through Partch's life, it is useful to explore how Partch used, and ultimately ignored, the hobo label. This shifting presentation can be seen in how he framed all the compositions based on his eight years of wandering, including *Barstow*, *San Francisco*, and *The Letter*, but is clearest in *U.S. Highball* and *Bitter Music*, the works that chronologically and thematically bookend his years on society's wayward side. Both contain hobo elements, including the casting of transient men desiring work as principal characters and the slang in which they converse. Several sharp differences nevertheless point to divergent conceptions that 1940s audiences would have held and the reasons Partch might have modified his use of the hobo and migrant labels in regards to these works. *U.S. Highball* easily fits into the hobo mold. Its characters have nicknames like "Mac" and "Slim," the piece's action includes encountering railroad police and jumping on and off trains, and its moods reflect the joys and travails of the itinerant hobo lifestyle. *Bitter Music* does not fit that mold as neatly. Its California setting among federal camps lends the journal shadings of *The Grapes of Wrath*. Furthermore, the shame Partch felt, and the antipathy that California residents exhibited toward him and all those receiving aid from the New Deal's Federal Emergency Relief Administration and California's State Emergency Relief Administration, owe much to American reactions to migrants. Therefore *Bitter Music* best fits into migrant traditions and *U.S. Highball* into hobo ones.

The categories are pivotal for tracing how Partch shifted his presentation of *Bitter Music* and *U.S. Highball*, particularly in his 1943 Guggenheim application. Unlike his 1933 and 1934 proposals, Partch's successful 1943 application downplayed his feelings about the use of equal temperament and the abstract nature of music performance in the United States in favor of highlighting a hobo/Americana theme—the music that a decade later coalesced into *The Wayward*. However, *Bitter Music* and *The Letter* are notably absent from the Guggenheim application. The composer carefully brought out the American aspect of his compositions, but did not mention *Bitter Music*, the work in which he first claimed to find the voice of America and which he had promoted so diligently (even sending it to Henry Allen Moe in 1936). It is easiest to assume that Partch did not include any migrant works because they were already completed: after all, the proposal is a "Plans for Work" to be undertaken. But of the seven proposed works, he admitted that three were already complete: *Barstow*, which he had finished earlier that year, and *San Francisco* and *Dark Brother*, both of which existed as rough drafts. While we might assume that he had not considered setting *The Letter* at this point, in fact he wrote that work and *San Francisco* back-to-back; as with *God, She* and *U.S. Highball*, he had the text ready and waiting for a setting. We might even think that the seven proposed works, lacking thematic cohesion (in particular, the text and character of *Dark Brother*, his setting of Wolfe's "God's Lonely Man," are very different from the works of *The Wayward*, though its descriptions of loneliness and isolation, and the pleasures found in those states, are similar to those found in *U.S. Highball*), pointed to a plan to finish work he found most pressing.[22] However, the best assumption is that by the time he was working on that application in the fall of 1942, Partch had astutely realized that the migrant image might be detrimental to his acceptance among the musical establishment, and he had begun working to obscure its role in his music.

Divided reactions to Partch's early experiences during the Great Depression bear out the wisdom of his decision to downplay the transient image as well as that of the migrant. Harry Hopkins, writing about his own successes and failures during the Federal Emergency Relief Administration's tumultuous tenure, best summarized this split when he remarked, "To the stay-at-home, confronted with unescapable problems of his own, the life of a transient, free from the responsibilities of settled life, frequently appeared at once glamorous, and reprehensible."[23] Hopkins could almost have been writing about Partch, who benefited from FERA's initiatives and relished the freedoms of his transient existence, but tired of the way musical society and the larger culture treated him and his ideas. None of his migrant- or transient-based works enjoyed the acceptance and support that *Barstow* and *U.S. Highball* did, so he later recast *The Letter* as a hobo missive and began to view *Bitter Music* as an anomaly, an off-shoot of his speech-inspired works as it used the piano's equally tempered scale instead of his justly-tuned one. He recognized *Bitter Music*'s importance as a piece of documentary art and as history, but was unsure what to do with it, and ultimately believed it a dead end. While his time among California's migrants and transients remained pivotal in his self-perception, a fact born out by his keeping *Bitter Music* on his list of works throughout the 1940s, its importance receded in his musical persona and even his autobiography.[24]

Even taking into account the wisdom of Partch's decision to highlight the hobo over the migrant and transient in his application, it is still surprising to see how he was willing to modify the presentation of his music to win funding from a corporation. It is a portrait of the composer that clashes with his prevailing image. Partch is typically understood as a recalcitrant musician, unwilling to move from his stated positions or change his music for any reason. But his actions in the early 1940s highlight not only his adoption of the hobo image for acceptance, but also his downplaying of the transient, a figure to which he had equal claim. In order to win acceptance he purposefully foregrounded an outsider figure, crafting the image that dogged him for the rest of his life.

Still, the popular conception of Partch as contumacious is based on his temperament, an inclination that would not allow him to follow this path toward acceptance for long. As he prepared for his League of Composers concert, Partch began complaining about being asked to compromise his principles, to give up just intonation and the relationship of music and the human body, in order to continue winning respect and accolades. He accused friends of betraying his vision. He steadfastly refused to compromise. And he alienated those working hardest to support him. He ultimately left New York for the University of Wisconsin, initiating a self-destructive cycle of winning support and then burning his bridges that haunted him the rest of his career.

By 1950, Partch had resolved to put the images of the transient and the migrant behind him for good. At that decade's beginning, a little over a month after he had written his friend Lauriston Marshall about his FERA and WPA experiences, he wrote again with five pages of specifications on the instrument they were building together. But the memories dredged up by that earlier letter had not settled, and he added a postscript: "Do you have my *Bitter Music* ms. I am sure you do not want it, and I intend to destroy it. Of course, I want to have the satisfaction of doing it."[25] Marshall, who had been microfilming all Partch's manuscripts, returned the document and, reminiscent of his adolescent auto-da-fé, Partch destroyed it.[26] For fifteen years he had been the man in *Bitter Music*, and he was ready to be someone else.

Two decades later, when revising *Genesis of a Music* for its second edition, Partch wrote about his destruction of *Bitter Music* as something he did without regret. The transient and migrant images had served their purpose. But perhaps Partch overstated his feelings toward the journal. After commenting that he had destroyed it and never looked back, he also tipped his hand for the only time in his life about the connection between *Bitter Music* and *U.S. Highball*. In the section describing the background of his major hobo work, Partch noted that *Bitter Music* "had given me a large and already faintly delineated canvas for the collection of ideas that I later called *The Wayward*, of which *U.S. Highball* is part."[27] That canvas is available for viewing thanks to Marshall's microfilming, but Partch also did not destroy parts of the journal, no matter his grand statements. He squirreled away many of the drawings that create such a large part of its impact, leaving them to be found among his documents upon his death.[28] He carried them with him through forty years of rootless existence, tenacious evidence that *Bitter Music* retained some hold on his psyche, even if the rest of the country had moved on.

A Hobo by Any Other Name

When Partch began suppressing his migrant and transient experiences in the early 1940s, he simultaneously began promoting his hobo ones. But his use of the hobo image ended roughly when he destroyed *Bitter Music*. Five years after leaving New York City, where he plied his hobo works the hardest, Partch wanted to abandon the "hobo composer" label. On December 31, 1949, a little over a month before he asked Lauriston Marshall to return *Bitter Music*, he wrote Marshall and his wife Lucie about his intentions to record *The Letter* for the first time. In describing the work, Partch mentioned, "It's never been performed, or even rehearsed. It's on a hobo theme, and I began to get touchy over so much criticism of my hobo music."[29]

Partch's destruction of *Bitter Music* seems a logical outcome for a composer who frequently engulfed his past in flames so it would not come, as he said, "screaming back at me."[30] Destroying a label that not only profited him but also inspired so many compositions seems less logical for a composer who clung tenaciously to his ideas of what music was and could be. Still, he was in earnest when he wrote the Marshalls. In early 1950, when Partch returned to *The Letter* and rewrote it for his expanded instrumental ensemble, he changed the title, dropping the "from Hobo Pablo" portion of the title. He had originally inserted the designation "hobo" to delineate his experiences from those of migrants, but by the 1950s, he no longer wanted the association with the hobo either. Comprehension of what the hobo as inspiration and personification meant to Partch throughout his life requires asking why he abandoned that image in the late 1940s and early 1950s.

The first reason emerges in the work that occupied Partch's time in Wisconsin: completion and publication of his treatise *Genesis of a Music*. As Partch altered the presentation of his music and theories to fit World War II–era New York, he also altered his musical thought. Partch's chief concern had been with Monophony, the notion that all music generated from one note and that the purest form of music was presented by the One Voice. But his experiences in hobo jungles and migrant work camps had clearly shown him another component of music—the bodily. Hobo folklore, especially that created and perpetuated by the IWW, was often preoccupied with the hobo's body, with how healthy and courageous and masculine he was.[31] This focus on the corporeal aspect of life as a hobo surely remained amongst the hoboes Partch encountered and influenced the way he viewed that culture's musical products. Partch came to believe that music was essentially of the body, but that Western art music as practiced severed all connection with the body to create an abstract music. He wanted to revive the link between music and the body and began adding a new term to his lexicon: Corporeal.

In the 1949 edition of *Genesis of a Music*, Monophony and Corporeality came into their final form, the form that guided his compositions throughout his remaining thirty years. Partch defined Monophony as the "organization of musical materials based upon the faculty of the human ear to perceive all intervals and to deduce all principles of musical relationship as an expansion from unity."[32] Monophony retained its definition from the 1930s as music arising from a single tone, the 1/1, but Partch transferred to his new term, Corporeality, its use, showing that music arose from the speech of a single voice.

Genesis of a Music opens with Partch's idiosyncratic musical history that traces the idea of the One Voice by separating all music into that which is "abstract" and that which is "corporeal." According to Partch, abstract music concerns form and interplay of sound; it is more about interpretation than creation. Corporeal music, on the other hand, is "the essentially vocal and verbal music of the individual"; it is personal invention. But Corporeality goes farther than a simple connection with the intoning voice. Partch traces the tradition of Corporeal music through ancient civilizations in China, Greece, India, and the Middle East, "in all of which music was physically allied with poetry or the dance."[33] Partch's musical thought moved beyond the bardic tradition of a single performer to a larger conception of music as intertwined with drama, visual art, dance, and literature—a veritable *Gesamtkunstwerk*.

All of Partch's hobo works were Monophonic conceptions: *Barstow* and *U.S. Highball* were both originally conceived as solo works for voice and Adapted Guitar and initially performed in those versions. Although he later rewrote each piece of *The Wayward* for an expanded instrumental palate and began considering them stage works (something he did not do for any other Monophonic work), their origin was still in his earlier musical conception. As he groped toward a new vision of music and a reconceived musical output in the late 1940s and early 1950s, Partch briefly wavered on what to do with these Monophonic hobo works. That he returned to them speaks to their hold on his creative mind, but they were links to a musical system that he had evolved beyond, and he was touchy about them.

As Partch's notions of what constituted music changed, the types of stories he wished to tell changed as well. Those new stories comprise the second reason he abandoned the hobo image. When he was composing and subsequently promoting *U.S. Highball*, Partch recognized the work's documentary aspects, and even stated that it was a documentary of sorts. But looking back while he was at work on *Genesis of a Music*, he also saw the piece rising above documentary to become art, in the manner of Steinbeck's migrant ode *The Grapes of Wrath*. "It is art," he proclaimed, "in an art form, but it is an art that surges up and out of the strictly literal, the experienced narrative, even out of the abysmal. And because it is art, the strictly literal time and place of its concept form merely the flight deck for what follows."[34] He was no longer interested in the mundane, in solely capturing the accents, the rhythms, the essence of a person's speech. He no longer wrote about the work that, "*U.S. Highball* is no saga. It is common experience, the account of Slim's hobo trip from Carmel, California, to Chicago, Illinois."[35] Instead, he wished to go beyond simple recreation. Instead, he wrote, "*U.S. Highball* is not essentially a piece of Americana, a documentary. If it were only this I would not minimize it. But it rises, in fact, beyond the documentary, to several levels of consciousness and communication."[36] This radical shift in understanding the work partly comes from his shift in musical conception to Corporeality, but it also emanates from his use of exotic elements in his music theatre works.

As previous chapters have argued, Partch was interested in a deeper engagement with musical exoticism than the purely decorative—a conceptually exotic approach where patterns of another culture are embedded in a new artistic product (evident in his use of the monika song as a structural basis for *U.S. Highball*). The new forms of documentary he saw during the Depression attracted him for this very reason, as they attempted to describe reality on a conceptual rather than superficial level. But even works like Lange and Taylor's photo-documentary book *An American Exodus* contained a sense of Othering that Partch wanted to avoid. After all, he was part of hobo culture, a fact he went to lengths to demonstrate in the early 1940s, and wanted to provide his audiences a visceral encounter with that culture, not a polite view from a remove.

Partch's desire to go beyond presenting to representing only intensified as he began writing for the stage. Each of his music theatre works combines multiple cultural influences in music, story, dance, costuming, props, and even stage design to form a referential smorgasbord. From the use of Cantonese operatic styles and a Cahuilla chant in *The Bewitched* to marching band and gospel hymn references in *Revelation in the Courthouse Park* to the African folk-tale and Noh-based plot and use of the koto in *Delusion of the Fury*, Partch freely combined ideas from any and all cultures that seemed to him Corporeal. Lou Harrison later called this type of exoticism "transethnicism" because of the way it moved beyond the single appropriations of earlier composers' use to encompass deep understanding of and respect for different musical traditions and attempted to bring them together.[37] In these works, Partch could not have fallen back on the documentary impulse. His grasp was too wide. He had new stories to tell. The hobo-inspired works, with their deep focus on a single culture, seem to come from a different composer, though the conceptually exotic approach remains consistent.

A Hobo in 1950s American Culture

The move to Corporeality originated in changes to Partch's compositional language and his ideas of what constituted music, but several social and cultural factors weighed more heavily than his evolving aesthetic on his response to criticism of his hobo music. The notion of who hoboes were, and Americans' feelings toward them, dramatically transformed again following World War II. As postwar prosperity redefined the American landscape and society equated material accumulation with success, being poor and homeless once again became "the naked stuff of failure."[38] Visions of the hobo as an ignoble dropout from society resurfaced for a short time, and allying one's image with that of the hobo had real consequences. Nels Anderson, the first sociologist to study hoboes in depth, took pains, like Partch, to show that his knowledge was first-hand and therefore trustworthy. In his study of the early Chicago School monographs, Roger Salerno explored Anderson's life after the publication of his landmark study *The Hobo: The Sociology of the Homeless Man*. Summarizing Anderson's scholarly output and job prospects in academia, Salerno concluded that "while [Anderson] helped to strengthen the validity of ethnographic research in sociology, his venture into the marginal areas of the city, into its dark alleys and hobo jungles, put his reputation as a legitimate scholar at risk."[39] Although he sought work all the years following *The Hobo*'s publication in 1923, Anderson did not receive a full-time academic appointment until the fall of 1963, when he was seventy-four years old. Partch could not have waited as long; he died when only seventy-three.

In addition to being seen as a social deviant, the hobo in the late 1940s reemerged as a sexual deviant. The appearance of the hobo as a cultural figure during the 1920s coincided with a changing view of masculinity in middle-class America. Victorian society required men to be honest and industrious, to live virtuous lives and work diligently to care for their families. Conformity was not just expected, but required. By the 1920s, society began to redefine masculinity as individuality. Frontier figures became emblems of masculinity—true individuals who lived by their wit and their strength and bent society to their ideals.[40] The hobo was certainly such a figure and turn-of-the-century worries about hobo sexual mores vanished as he became an icon. Partch carried this view of the hobo with him into New York in the 1940s, championing this view in his music in place of that of the victimized migrant and transient. The hobo symbolized masculine romance of the road, and Partch could thus walk a fine line in his works of the period.[41] Although never demonstrative in his homosexuality, the sexual freedoms he enjoyed on the road would have been considered obviously gay by early moralists—but changing perceptions enabled him to label that lifestyle as masculine.

As it did with views of the hobo's rootless, penniless wandering, the pendulum on hobo sexuality began to swing back after World War II. Certainly, American society at mid-century considered the hobo a rebel on the edge of society, a masculine figure, but the image had an undercurrent of sexual rebellion as well. Those who struck out on the road left behind the nuclear family and were free in their sexual encounters.[42] Partch had no problem with sexual freedom. In *Bitter Music*, he told Pablo that "real love is apt to fluctuate over the whole idea of sex, and beyond too."[43] Bob Gilmore has even postulated that Partch did not believe that anyone had a fixed sexual identity, whether heterosexual, homosexual, or bisexual.[44] No matter his personal views, generational reticence made Partch wary of discussing his sexuality in public or referencing it in his work. He found the idea of having sexuality influence artistic pursuits and decisions ridiculous and made it the point of some of his harshest satire. In his pointed remark from *Bitter Music*'s "December? 1935" entry, the artist, who might be Partch himself since the text is in quotes, bluntly assesses the musical scene he finds: "He is an artist of unusual ideas, he gets financial backing from many patronesses, and he is best hung of any man I ever saw. Considering the constitution of our society I feel that an artist might as well give up who isn't blessed either with a substantial dependable income or a substantial dependable ring dang doo."[45] Partch believed that society should neither base artistic success on sexuality, a personal and private matter, nor on the amount of money an artist earned. He felt neither assessed true creativity. In fact, the work that most publicly dealt with his homosexuality, *Bitter Music*, he confined to the fire.[46]

Of all the musical, societal, and cultural factors affecting Partch's decision to reevaluate the hobo image in relation to his work in the late 1940s and 1950s, the most profound was the writing of the Beat generation, particularly that of Jack Kerouac. Kerouac named the circle of writers that clustered around him and Allen Ginsberg "the Beats" to show their allegiance to mimicking in words the improvisational creative explosion of Bebop jazz and their general weariness with inherited forms and conventions—their "beatness."[47] By challenging the cultural status quo, the Beats helped found the counter-culture movement of the 1950s and 1960s in which America's youth loudly questioned the societal status quo.

Of all the Beats' work, none was more iconically representational of their youthful rebellion than Kerouac's *On the Road*.[48] Kerouac wrote his novel in the late 1940s as one of his first experiments in creating what he termed "spontaneous bop prosody." In style, he attempted to write as fluidly and freely as he believed Bebop musicians played. But he did not write without a plan; on the contrary, he outlined and largely plotted the novel beforehand. But the actual writing only took six days, and he committed the book to a single roll of teletype paper, creating a continuous, unpunctuated 120-foot paragraph. For its 1957 publication, Kerouac added traditional paragraphs and punctuation, but maintained that the original form was a necessary step in freeing his prose from standard linearity.[49]

Sal Paradise, a thinly-veiled stand-in for Kerouac himself, narrates *On the Road*, which chronicles the friendship between Paradise and Dean Moriarty and their three years of bus-riding and hitchhiking across the western United States and into Mexico. At first, Dean and the carefree, reckless abandon with which he lives his life fascinate Sal. He describes Dean's restlessness as a virtue, as rebellion against authority and dominant cultural norms, and writes that he sees Dean "crossing and recrossing the country every year, south in the winter and north in the summer, and only because he had no place he could stay in without getting tired of it and because there was nowhere to go but everywhere, keep rolling under the stars, generally the Western stars."[50] With this kind of spirit, Sal reveals that Dean's father had been a hobo and the two embark on an ultimately fruitless attempt to find Dean Moriarty Senior.

Throughout the novel, Kerouac presents the hobo as a saintly figure, a guide for the wanderer forced to take to the open road to find himself. For Kerouac, the hobo is the frontier figure who knows America best and can unlock its true potential.[51] While his view echoes that of 1920s society, which celebrated the hobo's rugged individualism, it goes beyond the earlier formulation of the hobo as a man persisting in spite of a system that shuns him. In *On the Road*, the hobo no longer rebels against the industrial order and simply survives; he rebels against the entire cultural order and thrives. Kerouac's great success in reshaping the hobo image is in fostering a worshipful attitude toward a man previously admired but rarely emulated. The hobo becomes a pattern for younger men remaking their lives outside standard societal roles.

Although Harry Partch was in San Francisco during the early 1950s when the Beats congregated at Lawrence Ferlinghetti's City Lights Bookstore and transformed American poetry and writing, he never thought of his work as part of their scene—or of any other artistic tradition that was fermenting during the San Francisco Renaissance. In fact, Partch was highly critical of Beat writers. His friend, poet and artist Gerd Stern, was a part of that San Francisco circle and remembered that "Harry had no use for the Beat Generation."[52] Such a stance seems odd for an artist who lived his entire life as the kind of outsider celebrated by the Beats and who would have been sympathetic to Kerouac's new perception of the hobo. But casting off older conventions in search of the new was an artistic view antithetical to

Partch's. Like the 1920s hobo, Partch was antimodern, a stance that expressed itself in his wanting to return music to its ancient form. He never desired novelty for its own sake. As he told Peter Garland when asked about John Cage, "I laugh and say, come again? What?—tickling a big brass gong with a toothpick? Drinking carrot juice with an amplified gullet? Prepared piano? ... Zen Buddhism? (a gimmick that has contributed substantially to a couple of careers.) Showmanship? Fine. Innovation? Not for me."[53]

In spite of Partch's attitude toward Kerouac's prose, he certainly profited from Kerouac's use of the hobo. After *On the Road*'s publication, almost every article published on Partch's work that included a biography mentioned the composer in relation to the novelist, and most positioned Partch as an earlier Kerouac. The formulation appears earliest in Wilfrid Mellers's 1963 article "An American Aboriginal" where he combined the two conceptions of Partch by writing, "For a period of eight years, he in fact lived by 'riding the rails,' identified with the outcast and the Beat Generation."[54] Similarly, Eric Salzman, writing for *Stereo Review* in the early 1970s, told his readers that "Partch spent the years of the Depression literally on the road—long before the Beats and the Hippies got there. Indeed, until recently, he has spent his whole life moving from place to place seeking the means to realize his extraordinary ideals."[55] Other writers linked Kerouac's vision of the hobo with specific pieces, giving a counter-cultural spin on their reception: "Before World War II he was a kind of early Jack Kerouac figure, travelling about as a hobo—some of their scrawled messages gave him the basis for pieces such as *Barstow* of 1941."[56] And still others used Kerouac's assured place in the pantheon of American artists to argue for Partch's inclusion as well. Joel Mandelbaum, eulogizing the composer in *Perspectives of New Music*, opined that "Harry Partch was ahead of his time.... His masterpiece, *U.S. Highball*, ceremonializing a long distance hobo ride on the freights, substantially antedates Kerouac."[57]

In spite of these laudatory remarks, and the positive enticement to do so, Partch never directly compared his work with Kerouac's. As with the shifts he made in his musical aesthetics and larger changes in cultural attitudes, as the 1950s dawned Partch seems to have viewed the Beats as one more reason to downplay the hobo in his music. However, this position did not last long and it certainly lacked the impact on his career that the hobo had a decade earlier. In many ways, because of the Beats the hobo came to define his life and reception even more in his final two decades of life than it had in the previous three.

A Hobo in Musical Practice

How and why others applied the hobo label, and the cultural situation in which Partch found himself following World War II, is less significant than how Partch chose to use or suppress the hobo. For our final pass through Partch's last three decades, it is time to focus on the hobo in his musical compositions. When Partch left New York for his position in Wisconsin, it seemed as though his days of homeless wandering and exploiting the hobo image in his music were over. He was finally settled in an institution that provided space for his instruments, even though that space came from the physics department, and he only occasionally referenced his hobo years during his three years at Madison.[58] But the country's fascination with the hobo lingered over him as he moved about campus. Lee Hoiby, a noted composer who was a student at Wisconsin and played in Partch's ensemble, found little intrinsic musical value in Partch's compositions, but found *U.S. Highball* in particular to be an enticing idea and subject. He also saw the hobo in Partch's daily attitude, remarking that the composer's blaming the musical world for his misfortunes was typical hobo behavior.[59] However, Partch was already leaving the hobo behind and instead, in what was surely the final factor in his touchiness over his hobo compositions, was seeking academic legitimacy by completing his theoretical exposition.[60]

With the publication of *Genesis of a Music* in 1949, most critical attention shifted from Partch's compositions: contemporary reviews rarely mentioned his hobo years and instead discussed his musical instruments, originality in scale and tuning, and his scathing repudiation of Western music's foundational tenets. Charles Warren Fox's review in *Music Library Association Notes* was a typical example: it opened, "About twenty-five years ago, Harry Partch began to worry about problems of musical intonation; he was then a composer and is still a composer. In this quarter century he has gradually evolved a scale with forty-three tones within an octave, has built instruments with this tuning, has learned to play these instruments and has composed for them." Fox then continued, "The book represents a rare combination of autobiographical seriousness, agile wit and enthusiasm, technical thought, and a refreshing lack of dogmatism."[61] No mention of Partch's hobo years appears, nor does any detail about his compositions. Tuning and aesthetics dominate the piece.

Despite generally favorable critical reception of his book, the year of its publication marked Partch's second without career prospects and found him living in an abandoned smithy on Gunnar Johansen's ranch in

Gualala, California.⁶² This severe turnaround in fortunes from having a steady university-based income to living month-by-month and hand-to-mouth established the dominant pattern in Partch's life for the next twenty years. He would come up with a theatrical scenario, write a libretto, and then compose the music. Getting that work performed, more often than not at a university and usually supported by grant money and individual donations, would consume the following few years. Afterward, Partch would retreat into near-homelessness and start the process again. He found work, finished it, and then moved on, only vaguely claiming Northern California as his home. His formative experiences had been colored by that landscape, and it was to those hills and beaches that he continually returned. Over the course of his lifetime, Partch moved more than fifty-five times, mostly in the second half of his life. He wandered from university to university and from ramshackle house to borrowed ranch. He became an institutional hobo.

Partch's nomadic lifestyle worked its way into his compositions after 1950, though the specific hobo references that filled the works of the 1940s were largely absent. Instead, as in the writings about him, Partch simply used the persona of the outsider in place of the hobo in his music. It is as if, subconsciously, Partch could not relinquish the hobo.

The first musical theatre work that Partch finished after declaring that he was tired of the hobo was his long-planned setting of W. B. Yeats's translation of Sophocles's "King Oedipus." The story of the titular character, who murders his father and marries his mother before putting out his own eyes and going into exile, seems like a far remove from the western American hobo, but Partch continually found resonances between Oedipus's situation and his own. Discussing the work a year after its 1952 premiere, he remarked that *Oedipus* was the story of an outsider, "of a man who is destroyed simply because he is who he is."⁶³ Having suffered misunderstandings of, confusion about, and outright hostility to his ideas, Partch seems to have recognized a bit of himself in the persecuted Oedipus, though he never acknowledged the connection between his own unwillingness to compromise and Oedipus's headstrong nature—and the ostracism both suffered as a result.

Partch also saw denied potential in Oedipus's story and equated the king's ultimate isolation with the artistic specialization of the modern age. *King Oedipus* was the first fully Corporeal work to demonstrate the aesthetic condition laid out in *Genesis of a Music*, so Partch wrote an essay to explain briefly his combination of artistic pursuits. "No Barriers," published in San Francisco's *Impulse* magazine in the summer of 1952, opens by calling for collaboration among the various artistic realms in order to engage the whole person. It then details the advantages of this pursuit, noting that "if understanding is a valuable personal asset, it is desirable for each participant in such a work to be aware of the total potential of any human involvement. The musician as dancer, the dancer as ditchdigger, the ditchdigger as physicist, the physicist as hobo, the hobo as messiah, the messiah as criminal, or any other conceivable metamorphosis."[64] Only two years after revealing how tired he was of criticism of the hobo in his works he provocatively juxtaposes hobo with messiah, puts the Little Tramp next to Jesus Christ, showing that those viewed as the lowest sometimes bring ultimate truth and salvation. Again he uses the hobo as he had ten years earlier to carry the truth of just intonation to the masses, if only they would believe. For this son of missionary parents, it is a striking evocation.

Partch's next theatrical work was the dance-satire *The Bewitched*. In it, he attempted to return modern society to its roots in ritual and ceremony, and to find a place for those he called "lost musicians," musicians who "did not feel really at home in either musical world, either the serious or the not-so-serious."[65] Each scenario in the dance-drama features the "unwitching" of a group blinded by the prejudices of the present age. The main character, the Witch, "is an omniscient soul, all-perceptive, with that wonderful power to make other people see also, when she feels so inclined."[66] She dances around three undergraduates who learn to appreciate non-Western music; she weaves her spell around a basketball team so that they learn how life is about experience and imagination, not winning and losing; and she helps a politician live peacefully among constituents whom he cannot convince to vote for him. There is no sign of the hobo anywhere in the ten scenes, the prologue, or the epilogue. The characters treated in *The Bewitched* are common but powerful figures in 1950s America and therefore open to Partch's satire. He has something to say to them, sees something each needs to change. The hobo, on the other hand, has always represented true American life, a person unwilling to compromise and therefore willing to step out on his or her own. For Partch, such a person has no need for unwitching.

This reading of *The Bewitched* is supported by an essay Partch wrote while preparing a new production of the dance-drama at Columbia University in 1959 (following what he considered the disastrous 1957 premiere at the University of Illinois at Urbana-Champaign) and published in *Music Journal* that summer. Unlike "No Barriers," which attempted to frame *King Oedipus* in terms of his aesthetic stance, "The Ancient Magic" attempted to connect his theatrical ideas with those of older civilizations. It is a more direct statement of the principles behind the satire of *The Bewitched*. The essay opens by lamenting the age of "scientific magic" and the ways in which dependence on technology has closed off humanity from insight. Partch bemoans composers who express their era through music and proclaims that the highest goal of any artist is to "transcend his age." He then brings in a hobo, though not by name, to make a pointed comparison:

> The loss of values through the magic of science is at least lessened when we are aware of, and instinctively try to regain contact with, simpler ancient sources. The miracle button, the airplane, the automobile, have all taken their toll. I have walked through a section of country with a pack on my back, preoccupied constantly with all manner of petty personal problems, yet now and then I was aware of the magic of small growing things, the magic of a running stream where I threw down my pack, the magic of a fire by its side.[67]

Although unwilling to call his time wandering with a pack on his back a time of hoboing, he uses the same imagery he conjured for Vivian Perlis in the interview given months before his death and quoted in this study's opening pages. This truer, more down-to-earth hobo existence is one closer to the "ancient magic" he wants to recapture in his music. Living free of material possessions and desires enabled a person to see the beauty in organic materials and rediscover one's body, one's corporeal essence. Hoboing gave Partch a template of how music could be, it gave him direction. And, although he still did not want to identify himself with the hobo two years after *On the Road*'s publication, he was beginning to reach toward a rapprochement with his experiences and the hobo label.

This change in feeling had been percolating for several years. In 1955, immediately after finishing the first version of *The Bewitched*, Partch spent the summer reworking *U.S. Highball*, *San Francisco*, and *The Letter* for his expanded instrumentarium (he had rescored *Barstow* the previous November) and grouped the four hobo-inspired works for the first time, as *The Wayward*.[68] Then, the summer before writing "The Ancient Magic," he and Madeline Tourtelot, a Chicago-based filmmaker with whom he worked extensively in the late 1950s and early 1960s, produced a filmed version of *U.S. Highball*. Between 1943 and 1954, Partch did not work on or record these works with the exception of *The Letter*, which he rewrote in 1950, excising the hobo reference from the title. For over ten years, he had pursued other projects and had avoided the hobo label. By the end of the 1950s, he was coming back around to the compositions and beginning, once again, to accept and even celebrate his outsider status.

Rekindling old memories through recomposition of these works seems to have sparked a need in the composer to look back over his almost sixty years, to deal with issues arising from his difficult, precarious existence, and to explore them through his earlier music. Danlee Mitchell is one of many who regard *Revelation in the Courthouse Park*, begun the August after he wrote "The Ancient Magic," as Harry Partch's personal allegory about his relationship with his mother.[69] *Revelation* is an updating of Euripides's *The Bacchae*, set side-by-side and scene-for-scene as a contemporary parable in a small, middle-America town, the story retold through modern counterparts.

Partch kept the two dramas, American and Greek, apart musically, but held them together by having the three main characters assume dual identities: Dionysus becomes Dion, a modern movie and rock star; Bacchae leader Agave becomes a Mom in thrall to Dion; and Pentheus, king of Thebes and Agave's son, becomes Sonny. Although not explicit, an extremely important musical connection points to Partch as Pentheus/Sonny and his mother, Jennie, as Agave/Mom in this constellation of characters. Partch destroyed *Bitter Music* in 1950, but fragments of it kept reappearing in his music for the rest of his life. The most obvious appropriation of the journal is *The Letter*, where he transformed a transient experience into that of a hobo, taking it from a pessimistic, dependent view to one of choice and independence. But *Bitter Music* also resurfaced in *Revelation in the Courthouse Park*.

In the August 15, 1935, entry, Partch set the following personal reflection: "The gentlest breeze loosens them from their pods. A few of them brush against my cheeks, and fewer still touch my lips, ever so softly, as they fall. They hardly stop at all, and in the briefest moment they are away." The intonation set in this *Bitter Music* entry is from Partch's own voice, but Chorus Four of *Revelation* takes the end of that phrase and gives it to the sleepwalking Mom, using the same vocal line. Likewise, in Chorus Two, Partch gives Sonny the words and vocal line of his own reciting in the July 20, 1935, entry of a short fragment of Lao-tzu: "I am drifted about as on the sea. I am carried by the wind—As if I had nowhere to rest."[70] Nine years after he had burned the journal, its music still rang in his ears and defined the way he saw his past. Partch seems finally to have accepted that he could not escape his eight years of "personal Great Depression," and resolved to embrace their impact on his life and work.

In 1965, six years after beginning *Revelation in the Courthouse Park*, Partch was at work on a new music theatre work, *Delusion of the Fury*. He had recently made the acquaintance of Betty Freeman, one of the most important and influential patrons for American composers in the latter half of the twentieth century, and she wrote to offer a small annual income. Partch responded to her generosity by describing himself in terms of a character he was then crafting for the second act of what would be his last music theatre work: "For over twenty years I have been the strangest kind of hobo—a hobo with over two tons of 'weird' instruments to take, wherever."[71]

In many ways, *Delusion of the Fury* is, as Danlee Mitchell put it, Partch's "reconciliation with the world."[72] Its story is broken into two acts. The first is based on a Japanese Noh drama titled *Atsumori*, translated by Arthur Waley, which is a "portrayal of release from the wheel of life and death." In it, a young warrior, who killed a samurai in battle, seeks forgiveness at the samurai's shrine on the same day that the samurai's son arrives seeking a vision of his father's face. The samurai's ghost appears and is first spurred to revenge by the sight of his slayer and his son, but soon realizes the pointlessness of his anger and grants forgiveness.

The second act, which recasts an Ethiopian folk tale entitled "Justice," "involves a reconciliation with life."[73] In it, a deaf hobo has a quarrel with an old woman over a young goat, and the two go before a deaf and near-sighted Justice of the Peace. The judge misunderstands the squabble and tells the two, thinking that they are a married couple, to go home with their charming child. In response, assembled villagers all sing "Oh, how did we ever get by without justice?"

The theme running through both acts is the "delusion of fury," the common fallacy that anger and fighting can solve the world's injustices. In both stories, anger, whether justified or not, is powerless to resolve disputes or to bring healing. Coming from a composer known to rail against the world's injustices toward him, this message can be seen not only as one of acceptance of his own position, but also as an admonition to learn from his mistakes.

Even more remarkable than Partch's rapprochement with the world through this work is the lack of any written explanation of its meaning or tactics. Partch almost always wrote an introduction to his works either in the form of an essay or as prefatory matter in the libretto. For *Delusion*, however, he pointedly wrote, "These introductory pages consist largely of technical data. They contain no argument, no exposition. I feel that the only investigation which has genuine integrity is the seen and heard performance."[74] His work stood on its own and he wanted audiences to experience the drama rather than read about it.

How, then, are we to understand the astonishing return of the hobo as a character in his works, after an absence of over twenty years? The original Ethiopian folk tale obviously does not feature a hobo as its primary character, but shades of Partch's reasoning appear in an interview he gave Stephen Pouliot in preparation for the film *The Dreamer That Remains*. He remarked,

> Hobo life, or let's say living as a complete individualist, away from the sickening, sycophantic city place, did influence me. Because in one sense my music, or my musical ideas, are not music in the pure sense of the word.... But what it did was almost force me into drawing from my own experience, and everything I've done since then, such as *Revelation*, which was based on the *Bacchae* of Euripides, I have transformed into something I could have experienced. And this was true of *Delusion of the Fury*. Even though it's a Noh play and a farce out of Africa, I did this always in American terms that I knew.[75]

If we accept Danlee Mitchell's assumption that *Delusion* was Partch's attempt to reconcile with the world, and take into consideration Partch's contention that he fit the stories of his music theatre works into his personal, American experiences because of his hoboing years and their perspective, then the relation of the hobo in *Delusion* to the work's overarching theme opens up. Partch regularly threaded autobiographical meaning through his dramatic works and often obliquely identified himself with a single character, as he did with Sonny in *Revelation* and with Oedipus. If Partch is the deaf-to-the-world hobo in *Delusion*'s second act, then the character's acceptance of the world's inability to provide true justice becomes Partch's release of any lingering anger over his years of hoboing, his reception, and the discrimination he had suffered through all his life at the hands of a myopic and hard-of-hearing musical community, as well as his own previous dismissal of his past. In a remarkable act of transference, Partch reclaims the hobo label for himself. Through a cathartic, artistic purging of thirty years worth of wrestling with that label, he was able to accept his situation and even describe himself to Betty Freeman as "the strangest kind of hobo."

A Hobo to the End

Even if Harry Partch did not consciously write the action with this meaning, the aftermath bears out the conclusion. In the nine years remaining to him after completing *Delusion of the Fury*, Partch began openly to discuss his hoboing experiences again with reporters, scholars, and friends and use them to make larger points about music. Articles and reviews written about his work cued off his recollections and his compositions in making such statements as, "So, from a hobo jungle emerged one of the most creative and eccentric musicians the world has known—a unique composer."[76] Scholarly articles discussed how he mixed "unsung heroes, American folklore (particularly society's outcasts—such as himself), African and Oriental elements, mystical (particularly pre-Christian) thought, and magic, together with strong dashes of parody, satire, studied naivete, and irony."[77] In interviews with Stephen Pouliot and Vivian Perlis,[78] in letters to Meiron Bowen and the Rockefeller Foundation,[79] and in his revisions to *Genesis of a Music*,[80] he consistently talked about the freedoms he felt being a hobo, the inspirations he had gleaned from living that life, and the hardships he had endured. Always colored as an outsider, his portrait reacquired hobo hues. He also ruminated on the importance of composers going outside themselves, their situations, and their expectations, connecting this need with the hobo's ability to throw down his pack whenever he felt so led. In the preface to *Genesis of a Music*'s second edition, he recorded an inscription he discovered in 1969: "Once upon a time / There was a little boy / And he went outside."[81] It was an apt epitaph.

By the end of his life Partch also looked more favorably, and with more than a touch of nostalgia, back on his hobo compositions. In 1972 he returned to *The Letter*, which had shifted in labeling more than any other work of *The Wayward*, and reworked it for possible inclusion in *The Dreamer That Remains*. In doing so, he returned to the original manuscript from 1943 and added an annotation to the document's end: "In retrospect, I think this is a better version than the re-writing, summer 1955 (?)."[82] The full title of *Letter from Hobo Pablo* had been dropped in revisions and the work had moved away from its original Monophonic conception with the addition of Corporeal dimensions. It had become less about the migrant and the transient and the hobo and more universally about the delight in reading an unexpected letter. Yet here, in this brief sentence, we hear Partch longing just a little for his earlier, more simple and direct, view. It was another step in reconciling with his past.

Following Partch's death, Ben Johnston published a moving eulogy and call to action in *Perspectives of New Music*. In it, he addressed the fragility of Partch's legacy, particularly given that only one set of instruments existed to play his compositions and that none of his music had been published. But he also explored what Partch had gained in being a musical outsider. He pointed to Partch's years of hobo wandering as the key to understanding the composer's psyche, noting that as hard as those years were on him physically, emotionally, and psychologically, they also marked him by removing any lingering fear he might have had of other's opinions of himself and his music by allowing him to operate with little regard for societal strictures. Johnston ended that section by observing that by being a hobo, "in large part he had won his freedom."[83]

Ultimately, Johnson's keen insight hits at the heart of what the hobo meant to Partch throughout his life. Early in his career, Partch attempted to modulate his activities to suit the particular audience he was addressing. In his Guggenheim applications, he attempted to gauge what was expected to gain acceptance. But after he adopted the hobo as both a musical and metaphorical figure, he seems to have altered his approach. As understood in the early 1940s, the hobo was a masculine, independent character who followed his path no matter the personal, societal, or cultural consequences. He was a figure of strength in the face of overwhelming adversity. As Partch moved on from his period in the New York area, the hobo served as a template for what the composer hoped to accomplish with his musical reforms. Having settled on a justly tuned scale of forty-three tones and a Monophonic and Corporeal vision of music's possibilities, Harry Partch never looked back. He refused to take any job that would dissuade him from his compositional and instrument-building activities. He went wherever his music was accepted. And he crafted a legacy that remains as distinctly American as that of the hobo.

Perhaps the final words on the relationship between his life's work and its reception should be ones that Partch chose himself. In the last pages of *Bitter Music*, as he was coming to terms with his musical apostasy through the grand musical quodlibet, Partch perfectly captured his life as both hobo and composer when he quoted these lines from Everett Ruess's "Wilderness Song": "Say that I starved, that I was cold and weary. That I was burned and blinded by the desert suns . . . but that I kept my dream."[84]

EPILOGUE

To Be American

In many ways, Harry Partch's hobo music could have faded away after his death in the early morning of September 3, 1974. His music was so intimately connected with his persona (and he secured most of his performances through sheer force of will) that performances could have stopped. He had turned to recordings early in his career as a workable solution for dissemination of his music, but through those albums, the One Voice most associated with the sound of his music was Partch's own. Attempts to perform without his voice could have failed, as the recordings make it sound as though the compositions all arose from his own inflections and cadences. As the coming of the automobile signaled the decline of hobo culture, Partch's death could have marked the decline of his music. As Ben Johnston wrote a few months later, after surveying the fragility of Partch's legacy, "The problem staggers conception."[1]

However, Partch's hobo music endured. The fascination it held for students, composers, and audience members in the early 1940s continued as the decades rolled by. In the late 1940s while Partch was at Wisconsin, reviews of *U.S. Highball* marked it as a musically "startling journey," one of "the best in newer music."[2] In the early 1960s, jazz pianist Gil Evans approached Partch because he wanted to perform and record *U.S. Highball* for the new Verve label.[3] In 1965, Partch's friend and colleague Larry Marshall sent a recording of *U.S. Highball* to be included in the Westinghouse Time Capsule that was buried at the New York World's Fair. Marshall chose *U.S. Highball* for inclusion because, "after conferring with a number of those who have worked intimately with Partch, [*U.S. Highball*] appears to be regarded as one of his most definitive works and representative of an era."[4]

U.S. Highball now sits buried in the time capsule alongside Benjamin Britten's *War Requiem*, Francis Poulenc's *Dialogues des Carmelites*, the complete works of Anton Webern, Gian Carlo Menotti's *The Consul*, Douglas Moore's *Wings of the Dove*, and a selection of electronic music by Otto Luening and Vladimir Ussachevsky.[5] In 1982, Tom Waits attended a performance given by the Harry Partch Ensemble, and Partch's hobo music is credited as a central influence on Waits's reinvention of his sound with *Swordfishtrombones* of 1983.[6] In 1991, Dean Drummond led Newband in a performance of *The Wayward* at the four-year-old Bang on a Can Festival in New York City, igniting a new passion for Partch's music among a younger generation of composers who reached musical maturity after Partch was gone.[7] Both during and after Harry Partch's life, *U.S. Highball* and the other works of *The Wayward* have followed a curious route through American musical history, touching surprising cultural moments.

The ripples through American culture caused by Harry Partch's use of the hobo image in his music probably would have surprised no one more than the composer himself. Although this study shows how he turned the hobo's cultural cachet to his advantage, hoboing was not all adventure for Partch. It was more than throwing down his pack where he wanted and drinking clear water from fresh springs. It was also "more or less constant hunger, loss of sleep, filth, and a good deal of petty apprehension and danger."[8] Throughout *Bitter Music*, he wrote not only of his loneliness but also of the toll the time took on his health: "This morning (October 16), in spite of trench mouth, poison oak, and an aching back, carryover from my ten hours of work four days ago, I get up with every intention of asking for a job at the free state employment office."[9] Never particularly healthy, Partch admitted that hoboing further damaged his fragile constitution. He developed hypertension, always felt that his lack of nutrition weakened his immune system, and at some point even contracted syphilis, receiving treatment in Monterey in April 1941.[10] He felt cursed by his aimlessness and resented his lack of achievement during those first years of hoboing. By the time he was writing *Barstow*, he was urgently searching for a way back into the musical society he had left. Hoboing was often a miserable existence he undertook out of necessity, which is why he saw his Guggenheim award as a form of salvation.

Although the hobo is firmly ensconced in Partch's legend, why should his hobo compositions have caused such far-ranging ripples across the surface of American music? The foremost reason must be how deeply embedded the hobo has been and continues to be in the American psyche. In the early parts of the century, the hobo came to represent American individualism and tenacity in the face of obstacles. He was a "knight of the road," a friend of common folk who was able to live free, live according to his own rules. He retained that image through the 1950s as the Beat Generation, through Jack Kerouac in particular, added a frisson of rebellion to his image. The hobo became a figure that knew America truly and sought to return to its roots, free of modern technocratic trappings. These are romantic and nostalgic images of breaking free from the daily grind and finding oneself on the other side of the horizon. Movement as salvation and life is a common theme in American art, and the hobo fits that theme perfectly. He is another emblem of the American desire for unrestrained mobility.

In many ways, the hobo became one figure through which the United States could see itself more clearly. He embodied the *homo viator* and the outsider, someone whose marginality allowed him "continually to reassess his own culture and to relativize the very perceptions of the world and habits of thought that he has inherited from it."[11] Perhaps this combination is why, even in our modern age of instant information and virtual experience, hoboes still ply the railroads, using websites to communicate rather than signs charcoaled on telegraph poles. In 1993, as the internet was in its infancy, hobo Duffy Littlejohn published his *Hopping Freight Trains in America*, a book successful enough to be revised and expanded in 2000.[12] The book offers practical advice on how to get on trains undetected, gear that might be needed, and even what to wear. Young adventurers quickly appropriated and touted the book on their personal websites. Many of those websites, such as Wes Modes's "A No-Bull Guide to Freight-Hoppers On and Off the Web," continue to act as clearinghouses of information on how to hobo safely in the twenty-first century.[13] The Hobo Foundation, which runs the annual Hobo Convention the second weekend of each August in Britt, Iowa, also has a web presence that not only touts the next convention, but offers a list of the best routes to hobo for the scenery and a brief compendium of the rights of all United States citizens in case of arrest.[14]

Hoboes appear with regularity in modern popular culture as well. John Hodgman compiled a list of seven hundred hobo names (including Boxcar Tim, Boxcar Mick, and Boxcar Aldous Huxley) amid his idiosyncratic history of hoboes in *The Areas of My Expertise*.[15] Standup comedian Patton Oswalt toured in 2007 with a segment he called "Historical Hobo Song," in which, after calling on all Harry Partch fans in the room to join him, he sang supposed hobo songs from the 1920s. The songs pushed stories of hobo sexuality and poverty to their limits, playing on the audience's expectations of hoboes being outsiders to American culture.[16] In August 2008, Scott Adams worked the hobo into several days of his *Dilbert* comic, a strip that satirizes the absurdities of contemporary office life. In the first strip of the series, his boss tasks Dilbert with finding a "photogenic hobo" so that they can give him money to improve the company's charitable reputation. Dilbert diligently goes to the street, finds two unshaven homeless men, and offers them a million dollars if they are hoboes. Their response? "Sorry, we're tramps."

This currency explains why although the Kronos Quartet's 2003 release of *U.S. Highball* on Nonesuch features a sepia-toned picture of a train and the performer's names on its cover, the rest of the booklet features obscure charcoal-drawn symbols, reproductions of turn-of-the-century hobo codes that were themselves press fabrications. To sell papers, newspapers promoted the notion that hoboes communicated with each other through elaborate signs and codes, marks left on sidewalks, walls, and freight car doors. They then published a lexicon of the codes so unsuspecting homeowners could protect themselves and their belongings by finding and deciphering the marks around their abodes. Although there was a degree truth in the story, the use of hobo signs was not widespread; homeowners had no need to be on the lookout for signs pointing to their houses. In fact, the codes, as presented in the newspapers, were so complex that hoboes themselves would have needed a lexicon just to remember them all![17] Since their society was not cohesive, hoboes actually used very few signs, but the idea was so appealing that the public devoured publications devoted to it during the 1910s and 1920s, and continues to do so today. The mythology surrounding hoboes continues to work in stories, in humor, and even in advertising.

Clearly, the interest with which Americans viewed hoboes a hundred years ago resonates today with a new middle-class set of rail-riders wanting to live off the grid and with a "home guard" curious about the lifestyle. While that fascination helps explain some of *The Wayward*'s ripples, a simple recounting of hobo adventures would lack its staying power. Like *The Grapes of Wrath* and other documentary-based works from the period, Partch's hobo works move beyond representation into art. Yet the manner in which Partch accomplished this transformation is of particular importance to American musical development through the twentieth century. Using patterns of hobo cultural products as his basis, Partch created music that rises out of its origins to become something new. The compositions are, as Ben Johnston saw, "like folk music in many respects," but unlike folk music in crucial ways.[18] Alan Lomax seems to have realized this distinction when he expressed interest in *Barstow*, but forwarded information on to Charles Seeger, thinking it fit more with Seeger's compositional interests than his own folk music ones.[19]

Each part of *The Wayward* has elements that sound as though Partch lifted hobo songs and used them as compositional fodder, but they lack the readily identifiable melodies of many contemporaneous Americana works.

They walk the fine line of all conceptually exotic composition: *U.S. Highball* traces an actual journey Partch took and captures the voices of the people with whom he rode, but the piece's emotional journey from the exhilaration of movement to the despair of being stranded to the expectancy of arrival portrays complex human—not just hobo—responses. *San Francisco* uses few words but a rich musical vocabulary to tug at our natural nostalgia for a bygone era. *The Letter* features a text that could only have been written from one transient to another; Partch's having lived Pablo's life with him resulted in a document that is profoundly associated with the California migrant experience, but speaks musically to the joy and humor of receiving and reading an unexpected letter from an old friend. *Barstow* collects inscriptions that most people ignored, stringing them together in a frame that transforms them into poetry. In all cases, Partch acted as a documentarian by using materials that were already present. But by remaining true to the people he exoticized in his music, he created music that used the hobo as a foundation, not merely as a decoration.

Finally, the mythology that grew up around these compositions begs consideration. In its background and the ways in which Partch discussed the collection, *The Wayward* plays into the mythos of a pure music. In an interview with Stephen Pouliot, given in preparation for the film *The Dreamer That Remains*, Partch ruminated on the connection between his hobo years and his music:

> It was one of the greatest experiences to be very tired of carrying a pack and then throw it down by a nice beautiful brush, which you don't find in Southern California, alas, but you do in a lot of other places in the country. And find sticks for a fire, and build a fire, being careful not to start a fire that you don't want, of course. And falling face down in the stream and getting something to drink and washing, and taking off all your clothes and stripping. I've done this so many times with rivers and creeks, oceans, everywhere. And then I think in contrast to this, the machines, the juke boxes, the silly machines that are constantly . . . and the tuning of instruments, the tuning of the piano . . . The difference is: here we have a beautiful, bubbling stream and here we have a faucet and sink. On the one side we have the real music you make by cutting up a piece of wood and hitting it, and on the other, the kind of music you get by calling in a piano tuner to tune a totally false scale.[20]

His unadulterated music avoided technology that sought to contain and control its power. In many ways, Partch's later view of his hoboing was equivalent to his view of just intonation—both were ways to get out from under domineering systems, social on the one hand and musical on the other, that threated to destroy all that was natural and good and right in the world.

Contemporary observers of the music scene adopted Partch's representation of his music as somehow more natural and pure than most music produced mid-century. Composer R. Murray Schafer wrote about *U.S. Highball* for the *Canadian Music Journal* early in his career, proclaiming, "Here is a man who can 'bum' his way from San Fran to Chicago, and, when he gets there, can sit down and compose his experiences. There is something wholesomely clean and naturopathic about so unbookish a quest for the muse."[21] Advertisements for Columbia Records's 1969 *The World of Harry Partch* in the young *Rolling Stone* proudly proclaimed "This album will probably make a lot of rock musicians feel insecure." The reason for that insecurity? The music is "more creative and more fluid" than rock music and "richer sounding and more subtle than anything you've ever heard." That sound was the result of Partch's making his own instruments, a fact highlighted by the ad's final dig: "Field that one, Frank Zappa" (see fig. E.1). Then known for his intricate studio editing and production design, Frank Zappa and his band The Mothers of Invention was one of the faces of the counterculture. By juxtaposing Partch with Zappa, Columbia was highlighting Partch's countercultural cachet, showing that he achieved strange sounds outside the mainstream by physically building them, not simply manipulating tape. It was also making a none-too-subtle dig: Zappa had turned down a recording deal with Columbia.[22] As technology creeps into every corner of life and makes it hard to separate the real from the digitally created, Partch's music continues to speak to a desire for homegrown, do-it-yourself musical ingenuity outside mass-produced society. His music is tactile, "Corporeal" in his terminology, and speaks of truth in its rawness.

While all of these reasons factor into *The Wayward*'s cultural position, ultimately that position rests in the fickleness of artistic reception. There is no magic formula by which artistic creation speaks and to whom it speaks and when. But by living the hobo life, turning those dreadful years into transcendent encounters, and then sharing the musical results with the rest of us, Harry Partch created art both of his time and beyond it. Instead of following the well-worn path of decorative exoticism that finds a melody or a rhythm that could represent American life and uses it in a symphony or opera, Partch lived a hobo life and used the patterns of hobo cultural products to create something distinct and true. It is perhaps his conceptually exotic approach that argues most forcefully for the continued power of his hobo-inspired works. Not only did Partch forge an art that sounded American, it was American.

Figure E.1. Columbia Records, advertisement for *The World of Harry Partch*, *Rolling Stone*, July 12, 1969, p. 31.

One last cultural ripple stands out among the ever-expanding rings of influence that surround *U.S. Highball* and Partch's hobo music and mark them as distinctly American. In 2000, Congress passed and the President signed Public Law 106-474, better known as the National Recording Preservation Act of 2000. The law sought "to establish the National Recording Registry in the Library of Congress to maintain and preserve sound recordings and collections of sound recordings that are culturally, historically, or aesthetically significant, and for other purposes."[23] The first registry of significant recordings was made in 2002; two years later, Partch's 1946 recording of *U.S. Highball* was among the fifty recordings inducted to the registry, sandwiched between Sister Rosetta Tharpe's version of "Down by the Riverside" and a 1947 recording of Virgil Thomson's *Four Saints in Three Acts*. During his life and in the years following, Harry Partch's hobo music has continued to elucidate an American icon, draw in new audiences with its subtle harmonies and delightful texts, and weave itself into our national fabric. The works are cultural treasures, and they touch the personal as well as the national psyche.

GLOSSARY OF INSTRUMENTS AND HOBO SLANG

Instruments Used by Partch in His Hobo Compositions

Adapted Viola — Originally called the Monophone, the Adapted Viola featured a viola's soundbox attached to a cello fingerboard with cello strings and frets that mark the ratios of Partch's scale. The instrument's range rests between that of the cello and viola.

Adapted Guitar — A guitar retuned to Partch's scale; the one used originally in *Barstow* and *U.S. Highball* featured new stainless-steel frets.

Chromelodeon — An adapted foot-pump reed organ, retuned to Partch's microtonal scale so the keyboard only covers a little over two 2/1s (or "octaves").

Kithara I — Based on the kithara (as depicted on Greek vases), but with seventy-two strings grouped in twelve groups of six strings, each matching Partch's system of hexads, operated by Pyrex rods that act as movable bridges. Kithara I is an alto kithara.

Kithara II — Like Kithara I, but larger and with six sizable resonators to spread the hexads across a wider pitch range and increase the bass sound.

Surrogate Kithara	A set of two box resonators with eight strings each, manipulated by Pyrex rods under the strings and played much like a Japanese koto.
Diamond Marimba	A series of Pernambuco blocks arranged in the shape and tuning of Partch's tonality diamond with resonators crafted out of Brazilian bamboo.
Harmonic Canon II	Based on a monochord, but instead of a single string stretched over a resonator, it features two identical box resonators supporting 44 strings each. Partch distinguished the two Canons by naming them Castor and Pollux.
Cloud-Chamber Bowls	Fourteen sections of twelve-gallon Pyrex carboys originally used in cloud chamber experiments at the Radiation Laboratory of the University of California, Berkeley, hung from a 4x4 redwood frame. Both the tops and bottoms of the carboys are played, creating a percussive and gong-like sound respectively.
Bamboo Marimba	A series of sixty-four sections of bamboo, tuned through tongues cut in the open end, and mounted in six full rows and one smaller half row.
Spoils of War	An aggregation of six percussion instruments: a woodbock, brass shell casings, Cloud-Chamber Bowls, pieces of bamboo, three strips of spring steel, and a guiro.
Bloboy	A contraption of organ bellows hooked up to an automobile exhaust horn and three organ pipes, designed to mimic the sound of a Southern Pacific train whistle.

Terms Used by Partch in His Hobo Compositions

Balling the jack	Speeding, to really get going
'Bos	Hoboes

Bulls	Police employed by the railroad whose job was to keep hoboes off the trains
Chuck horrors	Indigestion
Coffee and sinkers	Coffee and doughnuts
D. and R.G.	Denver and Rio Grande Railroad
Decking a fast train	Successfully making a difficult leap to catch a moving train
Drag	A slow freight train
Empty	An unlocked, open boxcar where hoboes could climb in to ride
Flophouse	A place to sleep in the city for only a few cents
Gondola	A sided but roofless freight car
Highball	To get going; to speed through without stopping
Highball Whistle	Two long whistles
Hoghead	An engineer
Hogs	Engines in trains, so called because they ate so much coal
Holding down a hard train	Staying on a train through bad weather
Hole in	To shift to a siding, allowing a faster train to pass
Home guard	People who live in houses and travel in their own cars
Hotshot	A fast freight train
Jungle	A shanty town where hoboes lived, usually near a division point for easy access to trains. The name comes from the weeds and tall grasses that usually circled such camps
Main stem	The primary street around which hoboes congregated in large cities
Pot-wallopin'	Washing dishes

Prushin	A young boy riding the rails for the first time
Rattler	An individual car
Sally	Hobo nickname for the Salvation Army
Silver-mounted toppin's	Bakery goods (usually doughnuts) with frosting

NOTES

Prologue

1. Alex Ross, "Harry Partch's Oedipus," *New Yorker*, April 18, 2005.
2. Harry Partch, *Genesis of a Music* (Madison: University of Wisconsin Press, 1949), vi–vii.
3. Paul Earls, "Harry Partch: Verses in Preparation for *Delusion of the Fury*," in *Harry Partch: An Anthology of Critical Perspectives*, ed. David Dunn (Amsterdam: Harwood, 2000), 105.
4. Harry Partch, *Genesis of a Music: An Account of a Creative Work, Its Roots and Its Fulfillments*, 2nd ed. (New York: Da Capo, 1974), x. Partch also recalled that his father's actions were in response to his mother's bringing home prostitutes to give them a meal and get them off the streets for an evening.
5. Harry Partch, interview by Vivian Perlis, tape recording, March 1974, San Diego, California, Oral History of American Music, Yale University. Quoted by permission of Danlee Mitchell, Partch's executor and heir, and Vivian Perlis, director of the Oral History Project.
6. Throughout this study I use the pronoun "he" in reference to the hobo, as hoboes were almost always male and almost always Caucasian. In fact, gender discrimination against female hoboes has been well documented in Tim Cresswell, "Embodiment, Power and the Politics of Mobility: The Case of Female Tramps and Hobos," *Transactions of the Institute of British Geographers* 24, no. 2 (1999): 175–92.
7. Roger A. Bruns, *Knights of the Road: A Hobo History* (New York: Methuen, 1980), 6.
8. Michael Nyman, *Experimental Music: Cage and Beyond*, 2nd ed. (Cambridge: Cambridge University Press, 1999), 39.
9. David Nicholls, *American Experimental Music, 1890–1940* (Cambridge: Cambridge University Press, 1990), 1, 219. Nicholls's list also includes Charles Ives, Charles Seeger, Carl Ruggles, Ruth Crawford, Henry Cowell, John Cage, Lou Harrison, Henry Brant, and Conlon Nancarrow. Besides connecting Partch to the

experimental tradition, Nicholls has also profitably explored how the use of non-Western ideologies, as opposed to merely mimicking non-Western sounds (an aspect he termed "transethnicism" after Lou Harrison's use of the word), led to Partch's rejection by the musical establishment: see Nicholls, "Transethnicism and the American Experimental Tradition," *The Musical Quarterly* 80, no. 4 (Winter 1996): 569–94.

10. Michael Broyles, *Mavericks and Other Traditions in American Music* (New Haven: Yale University Press, 2004), 227.

11. See, for instance, Susan Key and Larry Rothe, eds., *American Mavericks: Visionaries, Pioneers, Iconoclasts* (Berkeley: University of California Press, 2001); and http://americanmavericks.org/meet-the-mavericks (accessed March 22, 2013).

12. Lou Harrison, "Four Inscriptions in Books for Friends," quoted in Philip Blackburn, *Enclosure 3* (St Paul, MN: American Composer's Forum, 1997), 452.

13. Ensemble musikFabrik, "Harry Partch: Delusion of the Fury—a Ritual of a Dream," http://musikfabrik.eu/en/projects/stage-works/delusion-of-the-fury.html (accessed January 9, 2014).

14. Bob Gilmore, "The Climate since Harry Partch," *Contemporary Music Review* 22, nos. 1–2 (2003): 17.

15. Harry Partch, *Bitter Music: Collected Journals, Essays, Introductions, and Librettos*, ed. Thomas McGeary (Urbana: University of Illinois Press, 1991), 5.

16. Quoted in Kyle Gann, "What's American about American Music?" *American Mavericks*, http://musicmavericks.publicradio.org/features/essay_gann02.html (accessed March 11, 2013).

17. My notion of decorative exoticism is adapted from John Corbett's fascinating and useful chapter "Experimental Oriental: New Music and Other Others," in *Western Music and Its Others: Difference, Representation, and Appropriation in Music*, ed. Georgina Born and David Hesmondhalgh (Berkeley: University of California Press, 2000), 163–83. Corbett distinguishes between conceptual and decorative orientalism in discussing how experimental music borrows from and attempts to sound like non-Western cultures. Although American composers' use of non-European sources could be considered a form of orientalism, I consider it more a form of exoticism, a use of musical styles to give an accent (in this case an American accent) to the music. I have altered Corbett's terminology and usage accordingly.

18. Antonin Dvořák, "Music in America," *Harper's Magazine* 90 (February 1895): 433.

19. Michael Pisani, "From Hiawatha to Wa-Wan: Musical Boston and the Uses of Native American Lore," *American Music* 19, no. 1 (Spring 2001): 46–47.

20. Arthur Farwell, "Pioneering for American Music," *Modern Music* 12, no. 3 (March–April 1935): 117.

21. Beth Ellen Levy, "Frontier Figures: American Music and the Mythology of the American West, 1895–1945" (PhD diss., University of California, Berkeley,

2002), 36–38. Levy makes the point that Farwell had no contact with any Native American tribe and relied on his personal intuition, mysticism, and immersion in the song to find insight into "the Indian character."

22. Alice Fletcher, *Indian Story and Song from North America* (Boston: Small, Maynard, 1900).

23. Arthur Farwell, *American Indian Melodies for Solo Piano* (Newton Center, MA: Wa-Wan Press, 1901), 1–2.

24. For a comprehensive discussion of the use of Native American themes in Western art music, see Michael Pisani, "Exotic Sounds in the Native Land: Portrayals of North American Indians in Western Music" (PhD diss., Eastman School of Music, 1996). While Pisani examines the desire of American composers to find an exoticism equal to that occurring in Europe at the same time, and even introduce Native American culture to European composers as another possible musical source, Beth Levy has profitably examined the myriad ironies in this situation and the need for exoticism in American music. See Levy, "'In the Glory of the Sunset': Arthur Farwell, Charles Wakefield Cadman, and Indianism in American Music," *Repercussions* 5, nos. 1–2 (Spring–Fall 1996): 128–83.

25. For more on the Boarding School System, see Ward Churchill, *Kill the Indian, Save the Man: The Genocidal Impact of American Indian Residential Schools* (San Francisco: City Lights Publishers, 2004).

26. Barbara A. Zuck, *A History of Musical Americanism* (Ann Arbor, MI: UMI Research Press, 1978), 63.

27. Quoted in Levy, "Frontier Figures," 46.

28. Zuck, *A History of Musical Americanism*, 66–67.

29. Zuck, *A History of Musical Americanism*, 78–80.

30. Quoted in Howard Pollack, *Aaron Copland: The Life and Work of an Uncommon Man* (New York: H. Holt, 1999), 113.

31. Copland took the 1894 Tin Pan Alley song "The Sidewalks of New York," transformed its 3/4 time into an angular 5/8, and used audience knowledge of its lyrics "She first picked up the waltz step on the sidewalks of New York" to poke subtle fun at the decidedly un-waltz-like descending whole-step motive that characterizes the work's "Prologue." Pollack, *Aaron Copland*, 129.

32. Zuck, *A History of Musical Americanism*, 85.

33. Charles C. Alexander, *Nationalism in American Thought, 1930–1945* (Chicago: Rand McNally, 1969), 60.

34. Barbara L. Tischler, *An American Music: The Search for an American Musical Identity* (Oxford: Oxford University Press, 1986), 109.

35. Quoted in Alexander, *Nationalism in American Thought*, 71.

36. Richard A. Reuss and JoAnne C. Reuss, *American Folk Music and Left-Wing Politics, 1927–1957*, American Folk Music and Musicians 4 (Lanham, MD: Scarecrow Press, 2000), 6.

37. Zuck, *A History of Musical Americanism*, 11. This attempt to discover America in music was concurrent with a desire to represent the "common man."

In praising Marc Blitzstein, Aaron Copland wrote that he had found "a voice for all those American regular fellows" who had not been heard before. Copland, *Our New Music: Leading Composers in Europe and America* (New York: McGraw-Hill, 1941), 199.

38. Tischler, *An American Music*, 4, 8.

39. *Folksong Symphony* was showered with awards upon its premiere, winning the National Association of Composers and Conductors' Award of Merit "for outstanding contribution to American Music" and the first award given by the National Committee for Music Appreciation. Dan Stehman, *Roy Harris: A Bio-Bibliography* (Westport, CT: Greenwood, 1991), 79. It also served as a model for composers during World War II; see Malcom D. Robertson, "Roy Harris's Symphonies: An Introduction (I)," *Tempo* 207 (December 1998): 12.

40. Stehman, *Roy Harris*, 76–77.

41. Ralph P. Locke, *Musical Exoticism: Images and Reflections* (Cambridge: Cambridge University Press, 2009), 47.

42. Levy, "Frontier Figures," 176.

43. Levy, "Frontier Figures," 178.

44. "Transcriptions of Indian Songs," series 13: subject files; box 25, folder 3: Southwest Museum, Pasadena, CA, ca. 1930s, Harry Partch Estate Archive, Sousa Archives and Center for American Music, University of Illinois at Urbana-Champaign (hereafter HPEA/UI).

45. For further reading on this subject, see Richard M. Kassel, "Harry Partch in the Field: Native American Influence on His Music," *Canadian Journal of Sound Exploration* 51 (Autumn 1991): 6–15.

46. Partch, *Genesis of a Music*, 2nd ed., 7, 19–20.

47. Partch, *Genesis of a Music*, 2nd ed., 52.

48. Partch, *Genesis of a Music*, 2nd ed., 52.

49. William Stott, *Documentary Expression and Thirties America* (New York: Oxford University Press, 1973), ix.

50. Stott, *Documentary Expression*, 103.

51. Stott, *Documentary Expression*, 119.

52. Charles F. McGovern, "Woody Guthrie's American Century," in *Hard Travelin': The Life and Legacy of Woody Guthrie*, ed. Robert and Emily Davidson Santelli (Hanover, NH: Wesleyan University Press, 1999), 123.

53. Catherine and Jane L. Collins Lutz, *Reading National Geographic* (Chicago: University of Chicago Press, 1993).

54. Virgil Thomson, *Virgil Thomson* (New York: E. P. Dutton, 1966), 259.

55. Claudia Gorbman, *Unheard Melodies: Narrative Film Music* (Bloomington: Indiana University Press, 1987), 73, and Neil William Lerner, "The Classical Documentary Score in American Films of Persuasion: Contexts and Case Studies, 1936–1945" (PhD diss., Duke University, 1997), 14–19.

56. Thomson, *Virgil Thomson*, 259.

57. Lerner, "The Classical Documentary Score," 86–95, 107.

58. Lerner, "The Classical Documentary Score," 153.

59. Neil Lerner persuasively argues for Larkin's book as Thomson's source, even though Thomson examined six other books at the New York Public Library, because all the songs Thomson used appear in the same key in *Singing Cowboy*. Lerner, "The Classical Documentary Score," 68.

60. *Barstow* has been expertly treated in a critical edition. See Partch, *Barstow: Eight Hitchhiker Inscriptions from a Highway Railing at Barstow, California (1968 Version)*, ed. Richard Kassel, Music of the United States of America 9 (Madison, WI: A-R Editions, 2000).

61. Thomas McGeary, biographical introduction to Partch, *Bitter Music*, xxiv.

62. Ralph Locke has helpfully termed this kind of digging the "'All the Music in Full Context' Paradigm." Locke's definition of the paradigm can be found in his article "A Broader View of Musical Exoticism," *Journal of Musicology* 24, no. 4 (Fall 2007): 477–521; it is explicitly laid out in his book *Musical Exoticism*, 59–64, illuminated throughout with case studies.

Chapter One

1. Jack Kerouac, *On the Road* (New York: Penguin, 1957), 134, 138.
2. Partch, *Bitter Music*, 205.
3. Partch, *Genesis of a Music*, 2nd ed., viii.
4. Partch rarely wrote autobiographical pieces, preferring to focus his prose on his theories, both musical and philosophical, and exposés of the problems of modern concert music. The most detailed self-history he wrote can be found in the preface to *Genesis of a Music*, pp. vi–xiii. The following biography is drawn primarily from Partch's recollections in *Genesis of a Music* and Bob Gilmore's *Harry Partch*.
5. For a full discussion of the implications of this claim, and of Chinese music on Partch's music and aesthetic, see S. Andrew Granade, "Rekindling Ancient Values: The Influence of Chinese Music and Aesthetics on Harry Partch," *Journal of the Society for American Music* 4, no. 1 (February 2010): 1–32.
6. Partch, *Genesis of a Music*, 2nd ed., ix.
7. Although we have no record of Partch watching hoboes in this fashion, he did recall being five years old and using his telescope to watch a group of what he called "bad men" hiding out in some rocks nearby. His sympathies were firmly with the outlaws even at that point. Partch, *Genesis of a Music*, 2nd ed., ix.
8. This music affected Partch enough that later in life he recalled, "Into my twenties I could still sing one or two Chinese songs (in Chinese, of course)." Partch, *Genesis of a Music*, 2nd ed., viii.
9. Partch, *Genesis of a Music*, 2nd ed., ix.
10. Partch most likely heard recordings made by German anthropologist Leo Frobenius, who made Edison cylinder recordings in the Congo in 1906, only a

few years before Partch remembered hearing them. The originals are held in the Berliner Phonogramm-Archiv am Museum für Völkerkunde, Staatliche Museen zu Berlin, Stiftung Preußischer Kulturbesitz (Berlin Phonogramm-Archive of the Ethnographical Museum, State Museum at Berlin, Prussian Cultural Heritage Foundation).

11. Bob Gilmore, *Harry Partch: A Biography* (New Haven, CT: Yale University Press, 1998), 34.

12. Letter from Partch to David Bowen, October 3, 1960.

13. Partch, *Genesis of a Music*, 2nd ed., x.

14. Partch, *Genesis of a Music*, 2nd ed., x.

15. Partch, *Genesis of a Music*, 2nd ed., vii.

16. Letter from Partch to Elizabeth Sprague Coolidge, January 13, 1932.

17. Although Partch never mentioned his homosexuality in relationship to these incidents, Danlee Mitchell has often directly related his romantic relationships to his health.

18. Ken Spiker, "Harry Partch," *Earth Magazine* (March 1971): 72.

19. Hermann von Helmholtz, *On the Sensations of Tone as a Physiological Basis for the Theory of Music*, trans. Alexander J. Ellis (London: Longmans, Green, 1885), 1.

20. Partch, 1933 Guggenheim Fellowship Application, 4, folder 3, Harry Partch Collection, John Simon Guggenheim Memorial Foundation, University of Illinois at Urbana-Champaign (hereafter GMF/UI).

21. In Partch's usage, a "limit" is the highest prime number found in the ratios of the pitches in his system. For his twenty-nine-tone scale, he therefore used intervals that had ratios of 2, 3, 5, 7, and 11.

22. See Gilmore, *Harry Partch*, 63–66, for an excellent discussion of the changing nature of Partch's microtonal scale.

23. Partch, *Genesis of a Music*, 2nd ed., 7.

24. Partch, *Genesis of a Music*, 2nd ed., 5.

25. *Exposition of Monophony*, 44. Individual folders, box 8: PARTCH, HARRY/ *Exposition of Monophony*, HPEA/UI.

26. Partch, 1933 Guggenheim Fellowship Application, 5.

27. For further information, see Cresswell, "Embodiment, Power and the Politics of Mobility."

28. Gilmore, *Harry Partch*, 58.

29. Letter from Partch to David Bowen, October 3, 1960.

30. Partch, interview by Vivian Perlis, March 1974.

31. Harry Partch, interview by Vivian Perlis, March 1974.

32. Gilmore, *Harry Partch*, 57.

33. Partch, *Bitter Music*, 176.

34. Gilmore, *Harry Partch*, 57–58.

35. Partch, *Genesis of a Music*, 2nd ed., x.

36. Partch's "Certificate of Discharge" can be seen in Blackburn, *Enclosure 3*, 7.

37. Gilmore, *Harry Partch*, 71–72.

38. Partch, *Genesis of a Music*, 2nd ed., x.

39. Partch originally considered using C as his scale's fundamental pitch before settling on G. The decision to use G was probably based on Partch's own singing range, as his baritone voice would fit more comfortably within a scale based on G than one based on C. The Adapted Viola's other strings are tuned a 3/2, or justly-tuned fifth, apart. Partch, *Genesis of a Music*, 2nd ed., 198–200.

40. Letter from Partch to Henry Allen Moe, January 29, 1934.

41. Gilmore, *Harry Partch*, 71–72.

42. Harry Partch, "On the Maintenance and Repair of—and the Musical and Attitudinal Techniques for—Some Putative Musical Instruments," 5, Harry Partch Estate Archive, Montclair State University.

43. Partch, "On the Maintenance and Repair of . . . Some Putative Musical Instruments," 2.

44. Henry Cowell, *New Musical Resources* (Cambridge: Cambridge University Press, 1996), x–xi.

45. The tonality diamond was Partch's arrangement of ratios in a diamond pattern with the Otonalities proceeding diagonally up from a given ratio and the Utonalities going downward, each to the 11th limit. He arranged them into a diamond pattern to demonstrate conclusively the dual identity of each ratio. A Utonality in Partch's lexicon is a tonality expressed by focusing its identity on the number in the denominators; the identity of the Otonality is based on the number in the numerator. In essence they are the overtone series projected over and under the fundamental pitch. Many theorists of just intonation consider the tonality diamond Partch's greatest contribution to microtonal theory. For more information see Partch, *Genesis of a Music*, 1st ed., 74–75, 110, and 159; and Partch, *Genesis of a Music*, 2nd ed., 88–90 and 158–61.

46. 1957 film script, writings, folder 46, HPEA/UI.

47. Partch, *Bitter Music*, 60.

48. Partch, *Bitter Music*, 8.

49. Partch listed Mrs. Irene Clabaugh, his only sister, as his nearest kin. His letters from July of 1932 list her house as his return address, so she was the family member with whom he had most recently stayed. He remained close to both siblings throughout their lives.

50. Partch, 1933 Guggenheim Fellowship Application, 1.

51. Partch's scale at this time consisted of fifty-five tones to the octave. Partch, 1933 Guggenheim Fellowship Application, 6.

52. Partch, 1933 Guggenheim Fellowship Application, 5.

53. Partch, 1933 Guggenheim Fellowship Application, 8.

54. Partch, 1933 Guggenheim Fellowship Application, 8. The remaining four references were Partch's former piano teacher Olga Steeb, George Davis (program director of Sherman, Clay, and Co.), pianist, quarter-tone composer, and teacher Mildred Couper, and pianist Lester Donahue.

55. Richard Buhlig, "Report on Candidate for Fellowship," John Simon Guggenheim Memorial Foundation Archives, Offices of the Guggenheim Foundation, New York (hereafter GMF/NY). See the collected reports on Partch's 1933 Guggenheim application.

56. Partch, *Bitter Music*, 62.

57. Gilmore, *Harry Partch*, 99–103.

58. Partch, 1934 Guggenheim Fellowship Application, folder 4, GMF/UI.

59. Letter from W. B. Yeats to Harry Partch, January 6, 1934.

60. Gilmore, *Harry Partch*, 102.

61. George Antheil, "Report on Candidate for Fellowship," GMF/NY.

62. See collected reports on Partch's 1934 Guggenheim application, GMF/NY.

63. Luening, *The Odyssey of an American Composer* (New York: Charles Scribner's Sons, 1980), 342.

64. Partch, *Genesis of a Music*, 2nd ed., 323.

Interlude One

1. Todd DePastino, *Citizen Hobo: How a Century of Homelessness Shaped America* (Chicago: University of Chicago Press, 2003), 175–76.

2. DePastino, *Citizen Hobo*, 178.

3. Nels Anderson, *Men on the Move* (Chicago: Chicago University Press, 1940), 3. See also Anderson's comments when toward the end of his life he looked back on this period. Anderson, *The American Hobo* (Leiden: Brill, 1975), intro.

4. Kenneth L. Kusmer, *Down and Out, on the Road: The Homeless in American History* (Oxford: Oxford University Press, 2002), 203.

5. Anderson, *The American Hobo*, 181. The problem of so many unmarried men wandering the countryside, although exacerbated by the Depression's onset, was similarly prevalent in earlier decades. See the two-part article by Don D. Lescohier, "Hands and Tools of the Wheat Harvest," *Survey* 50 (July 1923): 376–82, 409–11; and "Harvesters and Hoboes in the Wheat Fields," *Survey* 50 (August 1923): 482–87 for a full account of the problem, together with Percy Walton Whitaker, "Fruit Tramps," *Century Magazine* 3 (March 1929): 599–606, for a discussion of harvest migrants in California, specifically among the fruit orchards, a circuit that Partch traveled many times.

6. Kingsley Davis, *Youth in the Depression* (Chicago: University of Chicago Press, 1935), 5.

7. The decrease in the numbers of hoboes was so great that Nels Anderson could not update his classic study *The Hobo*; the transitory migrant had almost completely replaced the culture.

8. Christie Photinos, "Villainous Vagrants, Hard-Travelin' Hoboes, and Sisters of the Road: The Figure of the Tramp in American Literature" (PhD diss., University of California, San Diego, 2000), 194.

9. Kusmer, *Down and Out, on the Road*, 204–8. Nels Anderson first announced the disappearance of hobo culture in *The Hobo*, but later writers equated the highway's rise with the hobo's death, from Thomas F. Healy, "The Hobo Hits the Highroad," *American Mercury* 8 (July 1926): 445–50, to B. A. Botkin and Alvin F. Harlow, eds., *A Treasury of Railroad Folklore: The Stories, Tall Tales, Traditions, Ballads and Songs of the American Railroad Men* (New York: Bonanza Books, 1953), 224.

10. John Dos Passos, *U.S.A.* (New York: The Modern Library, 1937), 559.

11. Walter J. Stein, *California and the Dust Bowl Migration* (Westport, CT: Greenwood, 1973), 141.

12. Nancy E. Rose, *Put to Work: Relief Programs in the Great Depression* (New York: Monthly Review Press, 1994), 39.

13. Katie Louchheim, ed., *The Making of the New Deal: The Insiders Speak* (Cambridge, MA: Harvard University Press, 1983), 188.

14. Harry Hopkins, *Spending to Save: The Complete Story of Relief* (New York: W. W. Norton, 1936), 129.

15. Doris Carothers, *Chronology of the Federal Emergency Relief Administration, May 12, 1933 to December 31, 1935*, Works Progress Administration Research Monograph (Washington: US Government Printing Office, 1937), 3. The distinction among resident, transient, and homeless unemployed was made to help state agencies speedily construct avenues for relief. Resident homeless were state residents able to work at odd jobs who often followed the growing season north and south, moving from harvest to harvest. Transient homeless were in the same category as resident homeless, but were citizens of another state who traveled to work. Bums were often euphemistically called unemployed. Their primary means of support was usually begging.

16. James N. Gregory, *American Exodus: The Dust Bowl Migration and Okie Culture in California* (Oxford: Oxford University Press, 1989), 96.

17. Louchheim, *The Making of the New Deal*, 185.

18. Carothers, *Chronology of the Federal Emergency Relief Administration*, 14.

19. In his 1935 State of the Union address, Roosevelt distinguished between 1.5 million "unemployables," whom local governments should support, and 3.5 million "employables," who needed federal support as victims "of a nationwide depression caused by conditions which were not local but national." Robert H. Bremner, "The New Deal and Social Welfare," in *Fifty Years Later: The New Deal Evaluated*, ed. Harvard Sitkoff (New York: Knopf, 1985), 73.

20. Anderson, *Men on the Move*, 91.

21. All statistics culled from Anderson, *Men on the Move*, 69.

22. Rose, *Put to Work*, 38–39. Camp overcrowding became a sufficiently serious problem to cause FERA to limit camp populations to 250 men as of February 7, 1935. Carothers, *Chronology of the Federal Emergency Relief Administration*, 72–73.

23. FERA Rules and Regulations No. 8, released in November of that year, listed administration expectations for states that continued to receive federal grants

for transient care. Those expectations included promotion of a variety of work projects that developed useful skills, implementation of educational and recreation activities for shelter and camp residents, and creation of rehabilitation programs. Carothers, *Chronology of the Federal Emergency Relief Administration*, 25–26, 34.

24. Jeff Singleton, *The American Dole: Unemployment Relief and the Welfare State in the Great Depression* (Westport, CT: Greenwood, 2000), 114–15.

25. The camps provided rest for many, even if only for a short while before the road summonded them again. For an account of a hobo in a federal transient camp, see J. Benton, "Rest for Weary Willie: Life in a Federal Transient Camp," *Saturday Evening Post* 209 (September 5, 1936): 5–6.

26. Bremner, "The New Deal and Social Welfare," 83.

27. Rose, *Put to Work*, 62.

28. Louchheim, *The Making of the New Deal: The Insiders Speak*, 179.

29. Rose, *Put to Work*, 39.

30. Rose, *Put to Work*, 74.

31. Carothers, *Chronology of the Federal Emergency Relief Administration*, 87.

32. Anderson, *Men on the Move*, 303.

33. M. H. Lewis, *Transients in California*, Special Surveys and Studies (San Francisco: State Relief Administration of California, 1936), 25.

34. Bremner, "The New Deal and Social Welfare," 84.

35. Bremner, "The New Deal and Social Welfare," 85, 89.

36. It would be easy to assume that *The Grapes of Wrath* sparked those studies, but both works were published prior to Steinbeck's novel. The California studies were both conducted or supported, ironically, by the WPA and SERA: Lewis, *Transients in California*, and William T. and Dorothy E. Cross, *Newcomers and Nomads in California* (Stanford: Stanford University Press, 1937). Crouse, *The Homeless Transient in the Great Depression* is the only other state study to date.

37. Watkins, *Great Depression*, 198. This statistic is based on the percentage of California's population that participated in migratory labor.

38. Anderson, *Men on the Move*, 28.

39. Anderson, *Men on the Move*, 253.

40. Edward Ainsworth Williams, *Federal Aid for Relief* (New York: Columbia University Press, 1939), 148.

41. Cross, *Newcomers and Nomads in California*, 30.

42. Cross, *Newcomers and Nomads in California*, 63.

43. This message was driven home further when the SERA publicized FERA T-12 (493), which said that transients should no longer be allowed free rail travel as of December 1933, and FERA T-19 (808) a month later, which discouraged hitchhiking. The Transient program was attempting to limit homeless wanderers' movements, keeping them in the same place for lengthy periods. Cross, *Newcomers and Nomads in California*, 65.

44. Anderson, *Men on the Move*, 255.

45. Stein, *California and the Dust Bowl Migration*, 80–81. This one slip and the resulting propaganda were certainly not solely responsible for Sinclair's failed gubernatorial bid, but they did have significant impact. Likewise, although migrant families from the plains had already begun arriving in California by 1934, the flow did not reach high tide until four years later, so Sinclair's campaign was not a serious impetus for the later migration.

46. Gregory, *American Exodus*, 81.

47. Paul S. Taylor, "Again the Covered Wagon," *Survey Geographic* 24 (July 1935): 349.

48. On February 15, 1935, the Transient program was caring for 38,815 transients in California (in thirteen city processing centers, sixteen shelters, forty-three federal camps, and twenty-six state camps) and by the time the Transient Bureau stopped taking new men in September, the number had reached 70,000, or about 14 percent of the transient population. Lewis, *Transients in California*, 3.

49. Gregory, *American Exodus*, 80.

50. The Los Angeles Committee on Indigent Alien Transients established the following definition, which Chief Davis and his police officers used at the borders: a transient was someone "entering the state of California without visible means of support and whose legal residence is foreign to the state of California." Lewis, *Transients in California*, 245.

51. The full story of the bum blockade, including detailed descriptions of the various actions taken at each border crossing, can be found in Lewis, *Transients in California*, 245–66.

52. Walter Davenport, "California, Here We Come," *Collier's* 96 (August 10, 1935): 49.

53. Stein, *California and the Dust Bowl Migration*, 16–22.

54. Gregory, *American Exodus*, 21.

55. Himmelberg, *The Great Depression and the New Deal* (Westport, CT: Greenwood, 2001), 75–76, noted that what he characterized as the "tremendously active" mass consumption of movies during the Depression was evidence that Americans longed to return to the consumer-oriented society that had been established during the 1920s. That much of the fare was escapist in nature was understandable, given the country's condition, and shows either a desire for a return to the past, or, at the least, a movement away from the present on the assumption that anything else would be better.

56. Gregory, *American Exodus*, 22.

57. Carey McWilliams, *Factories in the Field: The Story of Migratory Farm Labor in California* (Boston: Little, Brown, 1939).

58. Stein, *California and the Dust Bowl Migration*, 32, 44.

59. Quoted in Stein, *California and the Dust Bowl Migration*, 61.

60. Walter Goldschmidt, *As You Sow* (New York: Harcourt, Brace, 1947), 61.

61. Gregory, *American Exodus*, 108.

62. Stuart M. Jamieson, "A Settlement of Rural Migrant Families in the Sacramento Valley," *Rural Sociology* 7 (March 1942): 50.

63. Studs Terkel, *Hard Times: An Oral History of the Great Depression* (New York: Pantheon Books, 1970), 243.

64. R. Douglas Hurt, *Dust Bowl: An Agricultural and Social History* (Chicago: Nelson Hall, 1981), 3.

65. "These Pictures Prove Facts in *Grapes of Wrath*," *Life* 8 (February 19, 1940): 10–12.

66. Stein, *California and the Dust Bowl Migration*, 209.

67. Gregory, *American Exodus*, xiv.

68. Alan Brinkley's *Culture and Politics in the Great Depression* (Waco, TX: Markham Press Fund, 1999) persuasively argues that the Depression was seen as an attack on this newly-formed American Dream. To understand the era's culture, Brinkley wrote, it is important to realize that a fundamental uncertainty in the future replaced what many believed to be the nation's foundation.

69. Gregory, *American Exodus*, 110.

Chapter Two

1. This period has been painstakingly reconstructed in Gilmore, *Harry Partch*, 71–112, but Partch also included a first person account of his European studies in Partch, *Bitter Music*, 22–36.

2. Gilmore, *Harry Partch*, 114.

3. Partch, *Genesis of a Music*, 2nd ed., 323.

4. Partch, *Bitter Music*, 6.

5. Partch, *Bitter Music*, 9.

6. Partch, *Bitter Music*, 14.

7. Cross, *Newcomers and Nomads in California*, 79.

8. Cross, *Newcomers and Nomads in California*, 89–91.

9. Cross, *Newcomers and Nomads in California*, 82.

10. Anderson, *Men on the Move*, 91.

11. Partch, *Bitter Music*, 37.

12. Work camps had stringent guidelines for behavior and regulated every aspect of men's lives. Meal, work, and recreation times were all set and anyone caught breaking the rules was subject to immediate forced removal. Cross, *Newcomers and Nomads in California*, 77–89.

13. Partch, *Bitter Music*, 17.

14. Partch, *Bitter Music*, 18–19.

15. Cross, *Newcomers and Nomads in California*, 91.

16. Partch, *Bitter Music*, 45.

17. Partch, *Bitter Music*, 64.

18. Partch, *Bitter Music*, 73.

19. Partch, *Bitter Music*, 76.

20. Watkins, *Great Depression*, 11.

21. Karin Becker Ohrn, *Dorothea Lange and the Documentary Tradition* (Baton Rouge: Louisiana State University Press, 1980), 6.

22. Studs Terkel, *Hard Times*, 261–62.

23. Andrea Fisher, *Let Us Now Praise Famous Women: Women Photographers for the U.S. Government 1935 to 1944* (New York: Pandora Press, 1987), 134.

24. Ohrn, *Dorothea Lange and the Documentary Tradition*, 35.

25. Lange, quoted in Ohrn, *Dorothea Lange and the Documentary Tradition*, 103.

26. Lange's working method, one of her most distinctive traits as a photographer, is detailed in almost every academic work about her. This description is largely based on Ohrn, *Dorothea Lange and the Documentary Tradition*, 61–65.

27. Ohrn, *Dorothea Lange and the Documentary Tradition*, 50.

28. This recollection is taken principally from Dorothea Lange, "The Assignment I'll Never Forget," *Popular Photography* 46, no. 2 (February 1960): 42, 128. Surprisingly, Lange did not ask the woman's name, so the "migrant mother" remained anonymous until 1983, when Florence Thompson's children used the photograph to raise money for her medical care. Charles J. Shindo, *Dust Bowl Migrants in the American Imagination* (Lawrence: University of Kansas Press, 1997), 228n43.

29. Shindo, *Dust Bowl Migrants in the American Imagination*, 39.

30. Pierre Borhan, ed., *Dorothea Lange: The Heart and Mind of a Photographer* (Boston: Little, Brown, 2002), 19.

31. Shindo, *Dust Bowl Migrants in the American Imagination*, 53. Since then, "Migrant Mother" has continued to be used to represent victimization and suffering. It has been rephotographed, redrawn, and adapted to any number of media, from the Latin-American periodical *Bohemia*, which had the image drawn in color with one of the children facing the viewer, to the Oakland Black Panther paper, where the family was rendered as African-American. Ohrn, *Dorothea Lange and the Documentary Tradition*, 250n56.

32. William Stott devotes an entire chapter of his study to an examination of various photo-documentary books. Stott, *Documentary Expression and Thirties America*, 211–37.

33. Shindo, *Dust Bowl Migrants in the American Imagination*, 47.

34. Paul Taylor and Dorothea Lange, *An American Exodus: A Record of Human Erosion* (New York: Reynal and Hitchcock, 1939), 6.

35. Coleman, "Dust in the Wind: The Legacy of Dorothea Lange and Paul Schuster Taylor's *An American Exodus*," 160.

36. Paul Taylor and Dorothea Lange, *An American Exodus*, 6.

37. John Steinbeck, *Working Days: The Journals of "The Grapes of Wrath,"* ed. Robert DeMott (New York: Viking, 1989).

38. This opinion was first espoused by documentary filmmaker Pare Lorentz in his 1941 essay "Dorothea Lange: Camera with a Purpose," in *U.S. Camera, 1941*, ed. T. J. Maloney (New York: Duell, Sloan, and Pearce, 1941), 94.

39. Alexander, *Nationalism in American Thought*, 202.

40. Shindo, *Dust Bowl Migrants in the American Imagination*, 2.

41. Stein, *California and the Dust Bowl Migration*, 204.

42. Gregory, *American Exodus*, 97.

43. Robert Murray Davis, "The World of John Steinbeck's Joads," in *The Critical Response to John Steinbeck's "The Grapes of Wrath,"* ed. Barbara A. Heavilin (Westport, CT: Greenwood, 2000), 167.

44. Heavilin, "Introduction" to *The Critical Response to John Steinbeck's "The Grapes of Wrath,"* 27.

45. Warren Susman, *Culture and Commitment, 1929–1945* (New York: G. Braziller, 1973), 21.

46. Joe Klein, *Woody Guthrie: A Life* (New York: Delta, 1980), 146.

47. Klein, *Woody Guthrie*, 147. Klein notes that this concert, the first folk music concert before a large, mainstream audience, was the turning point in Guthrie's career, changing his life and the landscape of American music.

48. Partch, lecture given on November 3, 1942, Kilbourn Hall, Archive of Recorded Sound at the Sibley Music Library, University of Rochester, Eastman School of Music. Partch's performance of *Barstow* in this lecture is full of the "talking blues" style of singing for which Guthrie was known. Partch also jokes and goads his audience in a manner reminiscent of recorded Guthrie performances.

49. Woody Guthrie, *Bound for Glory* (New York: E. P. Dutton, 1943), 1–2.

50. Partch, *Bitter Music*, 8–9.

51. Much like Partch, and, indeed, like most hoboes in the 1930s, Woody Guthrie hated riding the rails because of the noise and dirt and much preferred finding a ride along the highway. Shindo, *Dust Bowl Migrants in the American Imagination*, 170.

52. Klein, *Woody Guthrie*, 126.

53. Partch, *Bitter Music*, 5.

54. Gregory, *American Exodus*, 232.

55. McGovern, "Woody Guthrie's American Century," 117.

56. Bryan K. Garman, *A Race of Singers: Whitman's Working Class Hero from Guthrie to Springsteen* (Chapel Hill: University of North Carolina Press, 2000), 94–95.

57. Janelle Yates, *Woody Guthrie: American Balladeer* (New York: Ward Hill Press, 1995), 75.

58. Klein, *Woody Guthrie*, 164–65.

59. This theme helps explain the presence of "Pretty Boy Floyd" on the album. In the song, Guthrie presents the Oklahoma outlaw as a Robin Hood figure, aiding people devastated by the Dust Bowl and justly stealing from businesses that

refused aid. As he sings, "I've seen lots of funny men / Some will rob you with a six-gun / Some with a fountain pen."

60. John R. Gold, "From 'Dust Storm Disaster' to 'Pastures of Plenty': Woody Guthrie and Landscapes of the American Depression," in *The Place of Music*, ed. Andrew Leyshon and David Matless (New York: The Guilford Press, 1998), 263.

61. Guthrie often changed his songs, dialogue, and manner to fit and play to his crowd, in this case people who saw him as the Okies' voice. Steinbeck, who sent fan mail to Guthrie following his first performances of his Dust Bowl songs, strengthened his image as the chronicler of the Okies. Richard A. Reuss, "Woody Guthrie and His Folk Tradition," *Journal of American Folklore* 83, no. 329 (July-September 1970): 292. In fact, Steinbeck went so far as to write, in a review of a Guthrie concert, that "in a way, I suspect he is the people." Quoted in McGovern, "Woody Guthrie's American Century," 120.

62. Woody Guthrie, liner notes to "Dustiest of the Dust Bowlers," *Dust Bowl Ballads*, Folkways Records FA-2011, 1950.

63. Letter from Partch to the Rockefeller Foundation, July 21, 1973.

64. Nicholls, "Transethnicism and the American Experimental Tradition," 570.

65. Alexander, *Nationalism in American Thought*, 29.

Chapter Three

1. Shindo, *Dust Bowl Migrants in the American Imagination*, 174.

2. Todd and Sonkin's collection can currently be accessed via the internet at http://memory.loc.gov/ammem/afctshtml/tshome.html. This online source contains photographs and manuscripts as well as recordings the pair collected during their two trips.

3. Charles Todd and Robert Sonkin, "Ballads of the Okies," *New York Times Magazine*, November 17, 1940, 6. James Gregory wrote that an Oakland journalist went so far as to stress the antiquity of migrant linguistic patterns, saying that they had much in common with old-world English. Gregory, *American Exodus*, 110.

4. Todd and Sonkin were not the only collectors sent to California and supported by the government. Between 1938 and 1940, Sidney Robertson Cowell collected music, drawings, interviews, and photographs from a variety of English- and Spanish-speaking communities in North California under that state's California Works Progress Administration, the Library of Congress, and the University of California, Berkley. Although her collection contains very little from migrant communities in its thirty-five hours of recordings, it is an interesting survey of music being performed in Northern California during the Depression. The collection is currently housed at the Library of Congress and many documents can be reached through the internet at http://lcweb2.loc.gov/ammem/afccchtml/cowhome.html.

5. Partch, *Bitter Music*, 5.

6. Partch, *Bitter Music*, 6. Although Partch often called the piano the "twelve black and white bars in front of musical freedom" (*Bitter Music*, 12), he used it here to give an approximation of the pitches he notated. It could be argued that his later dissatisfaction with the journal stems in part from this compromise.

7. In fact, two of the transcribed fragments of speech-music found in *Bitter Music* resurfaced later in his musical theatre work *Revelation in the Courthouse Park*. The fragments beginning "The gentlest breeze" (*Bitter Music*, 66–67) and "Why wander?" (*Bitter Music*, 81) appear almost unaltered in melodic content in the later work. Richard M. Kassel, "The Evolution of Harry Partch's Monophony" (PhD diss., City University of New York, 1996), 120.

8. Partch, *Bitter Music*, 6.

9. Partch, *Bitter Music*, 5.

10. Tom Kromer, *Waiting for Nothing* (New York: Hill and Wang, 1935).

11. Anderson, *Men on the Move*, 36.

12. Terkel, *Hard Times*, 42.

13. Partch, *Bitter Music*, 60.

14. John N. Webb, *The Migratory-Casual Worker* (Washington, D.C.: Works Progress Administration, 1937), 4.

15. Both Thomas McGeary, in his editor's introduction to Partch, *Bitter Music*, xxv, and Gilmore, *Harry Partch*, 117, highlight *Bitter Music*'s unflinching depiction of, in McGeary's words, "the constant hunger, filth, loneliness, and despair of the transient or hobo," or, as Gilmore has it, the "sordid or degrading aspects of that life."

16. Partch, *Bitter Music*, 40.

17. Partch, *Bitter Music*, 99.

18. Partch, *Bitter Music*, 36.

19. Partch, *Bitter Music*, 20.

20. Partch, *Bitter Music*, 11, 13.

21. Partch, *Bitter Music*, 12.

22. Gilmore, *Harry Partch*, 131.

23. The hymn's music appears six times. On page 8, it opens the journal; on page 43, it ushers Partch alone as he leaves Harrington Ranch; on page 48, it comforts him in jail; on page 73, it appears right before he leaves the SERA camp; on page 87, it ends the recitation of his activities after leaving the SERA camp; and on page 130, it helps him say goodbye to the transient life.

24. Partch, *Bitter Music*, 48.

25. Partch, *Bitter Music*, 86.

26. Partch, *Bitter Music*, 124–28.

27. The settings from Song of Solomon are found on pages 52–57, and are settings of the following verses of the King James Bible: 2:8, 2:5–6, 1:13, 7:2b, 2:16, 5:16, 2:17. Partch originally wrote this setting for his first Ptolemy while in England under the Carnegie Grant.

28. Kassel, "The Evolution of Harry Partch's Monophony," 119.
29. In his 1940 preface Partch thanked his friends for the use of their homes and pianos. Partch, *Bitter Music*, 7.
30. Kassel, "The Evolution of Harry Partch's Monophony," 121.
31. Leta Miller and Catherine Parsons Smith note that in San Francisco alone, forty percent of the Local 6 music union was unable to find work in 1934. "Playing with Politics: Crisis in the San Francisco Federal Music Project," *California History* 86, no. 2 (March 2009): 30.
32. Terkel, *Hard Times*, 20.
33. Partch, *Bitter Music*, 128–32.
34. Partch, *Bitter Music*, 7.
35. Gilmore, *Harry Partch*, 123.
36. Letter from Partch to Henry Allen Moe, December 18, 1936.
37. Kenneth J. Bindas, *All of This Music Belongs to the Nation: The WPA's Federal Music Project and American Society, 1935–1939* (Knoxville: University of Tennessee Press, 1995), xi–x.
38. Gilmore, *Harry Partch*, 123.
39. Partch is listed as an editor of the Arizona guidebook. Writers' Program of the Works Progress Administration, *Arizona: A State Guide* (New York: Hastings House, 1940).
40. Letter from Partch to Henry Allen Moe, December 18, 1936.
41. Bindas, *All of This Music Belongs to the Nation*, 2.
42. Bindas, *All of This Music Belongs to the Nation*, 5.
43. Alan Lawson, "The Cultural Legacy of the New Deal," in *Fifty Years Later: The New Deal Evaluated*, ed. Harvard Sitkoff, 163.
44. Bindas, *All of This Music Belongs to the Nation*, 15.
45. Letter from Partch to Lauriston Marshall, January 10, 1950.
46. Letter from George Cronyn, Washington, D.C., to Partch, June 8, 1937. Cronyn also sent the manuscript to Burton Hoffman of Knight Publications, but there encountered the same difficulties in getting it published—printing the music notation was difficult and costly and few wanted to undertake the task. To Cronyn's credit, he understood the music's importance and recognized that it was integral to the journal. Letter from George Cronyn to Whit Burnett, editor of *Story Magazine*, October 8, 1936.
47. Letter from Partch to Henry Allen Moe, December 18, 1936.
48. Letter from Cronyn to Partch, May 27, 1937.
49. Letter from Cronyn to Partch, June 8, 1937.
50. Lynn Ludlow, "Notes From a Semi-Incompetent Performer on the Surrogate Kithara (1953)," *1/1: The Journal of Just Intonation Network* 8, no. 4 (November 1994): 21. Partch's ideas and work made such an impression on Ludlow that he and his family continued to support Partch financially throughout the composer's life.

Chapter Four

1. Letter from Partch to David Bowen, October 3, 1960.
2. Gilmore, *Harry Partch*, 129.
3. Writers' Program of the Works Progress Administration, *Arizona: A State Guide* (New York: Hastings House, 1940), 270.
4. Partch, Introduction to *Barstow*, in Partch, *Bitter Music*, 201.
5. Letter from Partch to Bowen, October 3, 1960. Bob Gilmore notes that Partch was perhaps confused by the year when he was writing the answers to Bowen's questions. Later in the same letter, he refers to an event that occurred the same year he wrote the songs, one that is known to have taken place in 1929. I have chosen to use Gilmore's dating in this discussion. Gilmore, *Harry Partch*, 419n78.
6. Partch's original words for the song were preserved in his journal *Bitter Music*. Thomas McGeary, *The Music of Harry Partch: A Descriptive Catalog*, I.S.A.M. Monographs 31 (New York: Institute for Studies in American Music, 1991), 78–80.
7. Letter from Partch to Bowen, October 3, 1960.
8. This original, published version can be found in the American Popular Songs microfilm series in the New York Public Library for the Performing Arts, Music Division, catalogue reference # ZB-768.
9. This is the only instance where Partch used the pseudonym. It is unclear what inspired the name, but his older brother, who had served in the navy, was named Paul. Partch enlisted under this name later in 1929 when he served in the Merchant Marines for three weeks. Although Partch says that the lyrics were written by Ted Lewis, they are credited to Larry Yoell, which may also be a pseudonym.
10. Letter from Partch to Bowen, October 3, 1960. Few copies of this song remain; my source was Partch's personal copy, now housed in the HPEA/UI.
11. "Modern Parable I" and "Modern Parable II" are held as typescript carbons in box 1, folder 4, Music and Performing Arts Library Harry Partch Collection, Sousa Archives and Center for American Music, University of Illinois at Urbana-Champaign.
12. "Yankee Doodle" was a favorite tune of Partch's when he wanted to make fun of the musical establishment. In February 1944, he wrote the *Y.D. Fantasy*, a send-up of concert etiquette labeled a "momentary escape from profundity." Letter from Partch to Otto Luening, April 1, 1944.
13. DePastino, *Citizen Hobo*, 68.
14. Letter from Jack Brooks to Partch, August 22, 1939.
15. Letter from Jack Brooks to Partch, August 22, 1939.
16. Letter from Don to Partch, June 17, 1938.
17. Gilmore, *Harry Partch*, 118–19.
18. Anderson also noted that although few hoboes struck out on the road before the age of sixteen, those who did were more likely to engage in homosexual activity to secure the protection of an older and more experienced hobo. Nels

Anderson, "The Juvenile and the Tramp," *Journal of Criminal Law, Criminology, and Police Science* 14, no. 2 (August 1923): 300–303.

19. Kusmer, *Down and Out, on the Road*, 142–43.

20. Although Partch never personally documented that he had caught the disease and his medical records were destroyed upon his death, both Lauriston Marshall and Danlee Mitchell, two of the composer's closest and longest friends, attested to his condition. Gilmore, *Harry Partch*, 125.

21. Letter from Partch to Jimmy, July 28, 1935.

22. Letter from Bill to Partch, December 1, 1935.

23. King Hendricks, "Introduction" to Jack London, *The Road* (Santa Barbara: Peregrine Publishers, Inc., 1970), 1–23.

24. George Witten, "The Open Road: The Autobiography of a Hobo," *Century* 115, no. 1 (1928): 353.

25. Playing to popular expectations, Frank Bunce (an unemployed man better described as a bum than a hobo as he never traveled looking for work) wrote that "I have lost my loyalties to my country, to God, to mankind; that having lived like an animal, I am taking on the ethics of an animal; that I have become, in short, a public menace." Such accounts, common at the time, stoked public fears without offering real analysis or solution to the unemployment problem. Bunce, "I've Got to Take a Chance," *Forum* 89, no. 1 (1933): 108.

26. The siren call this existence exerted can be seen in the popularity of the autobiographies of A-No. 1 (Leon Ray Livingston). America's self-proclaimed most celebrated tramp, he wrote and published twelve books in the first two decades of the twentieth century detailing how he traveled the world for thirty years, covering 526,215 miles for only $7.61. A-No. 1 [Leon Ray Livingston], *Life and Adventures of A-No. 1, America's Most Celebrated Tramp* (Erie, PA: A-No. 1 Publishing Company, 1910), 137. This conception was not limited to popular literature; Anderson also remarked on the attraction of mobility. Nels Anderson, *On Hobos and Homelessness*, Raffaele Rauty, ed. (Chicago: University of Chicago Press, 1998), 26.

27. Hunt, "'Which Way 'Bo?': Literary Impressions of the Hobos' Golden Age, 1880–1930," *Journal of Popular Culture* 4, no. 1 (1970): 23.

28. Gilmore, *Harry Partch*, 125.

29. Partch, *Barstow*, ed. Kassel, xlvi.

30. I am indebted to Richard Kassel's remarkable introduction to *Barstow* for the harmonic analyses that inform this discussion. Partch, *Barstow*, ed. Kassel, li–lii.

31. Letter from Partch to Henry Allen Moe, May 6, 1942.

32. Partch, *Genesis of a Music*, 2nd ed., 31–33.

33. Blackburn, *Enclosure 3*, 65.

34. Warren Burt, *The Music of Harry Partch* (Melbourne: Council of Adult Education, 1982), 24–25.

35. Partch, *Barstow*, ed. Kassel, lxv.

36. *Barstow*, version I, MS score 22, HPEA/UI. This manuscript, upon which this discussion was based, has since been lost. A photocopy of this version still

exists in series 14: musical scores, box 26, folder 4: *Barstow*, 1941 version, Music and Performing Arts Library Harry Partch Collection, Sousa Archives and Center for American Music, University of Illinois at Urbana-Champaign.

37. Partch, lecture given on November 3, 1942, Eastman School of Music.

Interlude Two

1. Jeffrey Scott Brown, "Hoboes and Vagabonds: The Cultural Construction of the American Road Hero" (Master's thesis, SUNY Brockport, 1992), 137.

2. Charles Elmer Fox, *Tales of an American Hobo* (Iowa City: University of Iowa Press, 1989), xvi.

3. Nels Anderson, *The Hobo: The Sociology of the Homeless Man* (Chicago: University of Chicago Press, 1923), xiv–xix. Hobohemia was the nickname Anderson gave to the hobo enclaves he studied because of the Bohemian lifestyle that he felt hoboes enjoyed in them.

4. DePastino, *Citizen Hobo*, xix.

5. Anderson, *The Hobo*, 87.

6. Many commentators, including Gypsy Moon, *Done and Been: Steel Rail Chronicles of American Hobos* (Bloomington: Indiana University Press, 1996), 5, discuss the way hoboes helped industrialize the West through "pioneer labor." See also James Stevens, "The Hobo's Apology," *Century* 109, no. 2 (1925): 464–72.

7. This situation was noted even in the pre–Civil War era, where pro-slavery writings emphasized that Northern states used "wage slaves" in place of slave labor. See the chapter "The Economic Arguments Concerning Slavery" in Mason I. Lowance, *A House Divided: The Antebellum Slavery Debates in America, 1776–1865* (Princeton, NJ: Princeton University Press, 2003).

8. Allan Pinkerton, *Strikers, Communists, Tramps, and Detectives* (New York: G. W. Carleton, 1878), 67.

9. DePastino, *Citizen Hobo*, 18.

10. This view also helps explain both why tramping was seen as such an urgent social problem during the Gilded Age and why people feared that tramps were violent. If tramps were purely masculine, they acted out of their basest instincts no matter the consequences. If all men descended to this point, civilization itself would falter. Although the concept seems far-fetched from our vantage, it was a very real concern at the time. DePastino, *Citizen Hobo*, 26–27.

11. Frank Tobias Higbie, *Indispensable Outcasts: Hobo Workers and Community in the American Midwest, 1880–1930* (Urbana: University of Illinois Press, 2003), 26.

12. Kusmer, *Down and Out, on the Road*, 123. In 1886, the *New York Times* editorialized, "The labor union 'recognizes' the tramp as 'the victim of our present economical [*sic*] system,' instead of recognizing in him, as other people do, the victim of a violent dislike to labor and a violent thirst for rum." "Tramps and 'Labor,'"

New York Times, December 23, 1886. Perhaps the most interesting commentary of the time came from John J. McCook, a priest who corresponded with tramps and took a census of the population in the early 1890s. McCook recognized that economic factors played into the growth of the tramp army, but still identified the root cause as liquor and laziness. John J. McCook, "Increase of Tramping: Cause and Cure," *The Independent* 54 (1902): 622.

13. Kusmer, *Down and Out, on the Road*, 176.

14. Higbie, *Indispensable Outcasts*, 5. Most of these explanations arose years after the term itself, probably dreamed up by hoboes themselves as a sly joke or to highlight their bohemian ways. DePastino, *Citizen Hobo*, 65.

15. The *New York Times Book Review* highlighted the truth of Flynt's tramping experiences by noting that "he did not conceal a pocketful of money and send a trunk full of good clothes from place to place ahead, so that he might be a gentleman on the sly." March 31, 1900, 211.

16. Josiah Flynt, *Tramping with Tramps* (New York: The Century Company, 1899). Flynt's full name was Josiah Flynt Willard, but he did not use his last name in any of his publications, possibly because of his famous aunt, Frances Willard, cofounder of the Women's Christian Temperance Union. Flynt might have reasoned that either his activities would throw a negative light on his aunt's or her name would prejudice his potential audience. Roger A. Salerno, *Sociology Noir: Studies at the University of Chicago in Loneliness, Marginality, and Deviance, 1915–1935* (Jefferson, NC: McFarland and Company, 2007), 96.

17. While the works produced are different, both men used their experiences in similar ways to define their careers. Neither fully left their vagabond days behind, and both combined that lifestyle with a more settled one later in life. Rolf Linder, *The Reportage of Urban Culture: Robert Park and the Chicago School*, translated by Adrian Morris (New York: Cambridge University Press, 1996), 115–17.

18. In his introduction to the work, King Hendricks equates the importance of London's hobo experiences with that of his trip to the Klondike and his sailing on the Pacific to the formation of his art and life. London, *The Road*, v–xi.

19. London, *The Road*, 34.

20. Kusmer, *Down and Out, on the Road*, 179.

21. Frederick Jackson Turner, *The Frontier in American History* (New York: H. Holt, 1920), 38.

22. DePastino, *Citizen Hobo*, 117.

23. Although no one is certain where the name "wobbly" originated, the story most commonly told at the time attributed it to a Chinese restaurant owner in Canada who often served IWW members. When townspeople complained about this practice, the owner supposedly replied "Eye likee Eye Wobbly Wobbly." Stewart H. Holbrook, "Wobbly Talk," *American Mercury* 7 (January 1926): 62. This story underscores the exclusionary nature of hobo culture, where white men were by far the dominant gender and ethnicity.

24. Melvyn Dubofsky, *We Shall Be All: A History of the Industrial Workers of the World* (New York: Quadrangle, 1987), 168.

25. Robert L. Tyler, "The Rise and Fall of an American Radicalism: The I.W.W." *The Historian* 19, no. 1 (1956–57): 49–50, 59.

26. DePastino, *Citizen Hobo*, 119–26. Although it might be thought that Partch's acceptance in New York in the 1940s might have had something to do with the connection between socialism and the hobo, Partch was never accepted by Socialists or Communists during that period. By the 1940s, the IWW had faded to a footnote in history, and the hobo was seen as more connected to American folk culture through migrants than through the Wobblies.

27. Salerno, *Sociology Noir*, 88.

28. T. J. Jackson Lears, *No Place of Grace: Antimodernism and the Transformation of American Culture, 1880–1920* (New York: Pantheon Books, 1981), 4–7.

29. Christie Photinos, "Villainous Vagrants, Hard-Travelin' Hoboes, and Sisters of the Road," 100.

30. Brown, "Hoboes and Vagabonds," 103.

31. Although almost every commentator has noted Dos Passos's relation to Whitman, one of the first to connect his use of the hobo to the poet was Frederick Feied, *No Pie in the Sky: The Hobo as American Cultural Hero in the Works of Jack London, John Dos Passos, and Jack Kerouac* (New York: The Citadel Press, 1964), 55. One of the more interesting and insightful of recent commentaries on this connected was made by Christie Photinos. In her dissertation, Photinos convincingly demonstrates how Dos Passos used Whitman's writings and reputation as a model to construct an antidote to the perceived loss of manhood at the hands of increased femininity. Photinos, "Villainous Vagrants, Hard-Travelin' Hoboes, and Sisters of the Road."

32. Dos Passos, *U.S.A.*, vii.

33. John Lennon, "Interrogating American Subculture: The Hobo Figure and Negotiations of Invisibility" (PhD diss., Lehigh University, 2005), 172.

34. Photinos, "Villainous Vagrants, Hard-Travelin' Hoboes, and Sisters of the Road," 101.

35. DePastino, *Citizen Hobo*, 188–92.

36. David Robinson, *Chaplin: His Life and Art* (London: Collins, 1985), 113–15.

37. Early interviews, especially when Chaplin worked at Keystone, invariably focused on his ability to keep people continually laughing, both on and off screen. Some even remarked on his ability to walk onto the set, burn through a hundred feet of film without a script, and make people laugh the entire time. These early interviews are collected in Kevin J. Haynes, ed., *Charlie Chaplin Interviews* (Jackson: University of Mississippi Press, 2005).

38. "Happy Hooligan" (1902), by Victor Vogel and Bryan Stillman, quoted in Kusmer, *Down and Out, on the Road*, 186.

39. Brown, "Hoboes and Vagabonds," 33.

40. Kusmer, *Down and Out, on the Road*, 189.

41. Brown, "Hoboes and Vagabonds," 46.

42. The line "she's a regular combination" appeared in the first popularly recorded version, that by the Carter family in 1929. But the most popular version, released by Roy Acuff in 1936 and selling more than a million copies in 1942 alone, changed the line to just "the combination." Likewise, Acuff changed the final line, "While she's traveling through the jungle on the *Wabash Cannonball*" to "As we ride the rods and brake-beams of the *Wabash Cannonball*." Norm Cohen, *Long Steel Rail: The Railroad in American Folksong* (Urbana: University of Illinois Press, 2000), 375–77.

43. My information concerning Jimmie Rodgers's impact on country music and his hobo and railroad songs is drawn from Norm Cohen's magisterial work *Long Steel Rail*, 392–95. Anyone interested in hobo and railroad songs and folklore should avail themselves of this collection.

44. Cohen, *Long Steel Rail*, 394.

Chapter Five

1. Danlee Mitchell, personal communication, January 7, 2004.

2. Gilmore, *Harry Partch*, 114.

3. Partch wrote this note to himself on the back of version A of *U.S. Highball*, box 11, folder 8, HPEA/UI. The tone of the note indicates that he might have been considering using it in a prose introduction to the work.

4. 1957 film script, writings, folder 46, HPEA/UI.

5. 1957 film script, writings, folder 46, HPEA/UI.

6. Partch, *Bitter Music*, 204.

7. Charles Elmer Fox, *Tales of an American Hobo*, 136; Bruns, *Knights of the Road*, 18; and Flynt, *Tramping with Tramps*, 155–60, also observed that hoboes went to extraordinary lengths to rid their bodies of grime as it was a sure way to be marked and picked up by the police.

8. Partch, *Bitter Music*, 205–6.

9. Charles Elmer Fox, *Tales of an American Hobo*, 14.

10. The following account is a condensed version of the one Graydon Horath wrote, which was published as H. Roger Grant, "Home by Rail, California to Illinois in 1937: Reminiscences of Graydon Horath," *Railroad History* 172 (Spring 1995): 35–42.

11. Grant, "Home by Rail," 39.

12. Kildahl's account of his journey can be found in Erling Kildahl, "Riding Freights to Jamestown in 1936," in *We Took the Train*, ed. H. Roger Grant (Dekalb: Northern Illinois University Press, 1990), 79–93.

13. Partch, letter to Henry Allen Moe, February 11, 1943, folder 2, GMF/UI.

14. Gilmore, *Harry Partch*, 165.

15. Gilmore, *Harry Partch*, 169.
16. Gilmore, *Harry Partch*, 235.
17. Partch, *Bitter Music*, 204. The emphasis is Partch's own.
18. 1957 film script, writings, folder 46, HPEA/UI.
19. Gilmore, *Harry Partch*, 134.
20. Gilmore, *Harry Partch*, 134.
21. McGeary, *The Music of Harry Partch: A Descriptive Catalog*, 114.
22. See A-No. 1 [Leon Ray Livingston], *Life and Adventures of A-No. 1, America's Most Celebrated Tramp*; William H. Davies, *The Autobiography of a Super-Tramp* (New York: Alfred A. Knopf, 1917); Jim Tully, *Beggars of Life: A Hobo Autobiography* (Garden City, NY: Garden City, 1924); Kromer, *Waiting for Nothing*; Nelson Algren, *Somebody in Boots* (New York: Thunder's Mouth, 1935); Hunt, "'Which Way 'Bo?'"; Anderson, *The American Hobo*; Charles Elmer Fox, *Tales of an American Hobo*; Charles P. "Brownie" Brown and Erling Kildahl, "Riding Freights to Jamestown in 1936" in *We Took the Train*, ed. H. Roger Grant, 74–93; and Moon, *Done and Been*. See also Lynne M. Adrain's introduction to "Reefer Charlie" in Fox, *Tales of an American Hobo*, xv–xxiii.
23. See Fox, *Tales of an American Hobo*, 199–201, and Bruns, *Knights of the Road*, 42, for autobiographical and scholarly accounts respectively of Carr's activities. Carr even makes an appearance in London, *The Road*, 84.
24. Fox, *Tales of an American Hobo*, 202.
25. London, *The Road*, 24–52.
26. Kromer, *Waiting for Nothing*, 136.
27. Warren Huddlestone, "Slow Days," *New Republic* 79 (June 13, 1934): 124–26.
28. Writings, folder 43, HPEA/UI.
29. 1957 film script, writings, folder 46, HPEA/UI.
30. Partch, Guggenheim Fellowship Application, "Plans for Work," 1, folder 6, GMF/UI.
31. Script B, writings, folder 44, HPEA/UI.
32. Hobo literature and lore suggests two interesting parallels to this impromptu lecture. The first is millionaire-hobo James Eads How's International Brotherhood Welfare Association and Hobo College. Eads How established these organizations to educate hoboes, hoping to grant them in turn an entrée into the world of gainful employment. See "'Millionaire Hobo' Is Dead," *The Christian Century* 34 (August 20, 1930): 1020. The second is the "hobo schools" where seasoned hoboes "instructed" impressionable youth and attempted to lure them into the life, usually as that hobo's personal servant. See James Forbes, "Jockers and the Schools They Keep," *Charities* 11 (November 7, 1903): 432–36.
33. Partch, *Bitter Music*, 207.
34. Partch, *Bitter Music*, 211.
35. Partch, Guggenheim Fellowship Application, "Plans for Work," 3, folder 6, GMF/UI.

36. Bob Gilmore, "Harry Partch: The Early Vocal Works 1930–33" (PhD diss., Queen's University of Belfast, 1992), 10.

37. See Partch, *Genesis of a Music*, 2nd ed., 76–85, for Partch's reasoning behind using ratios instead of the arbitrarily assigned letters of common-practice designation. Although initially difficult to understand, once the mathematical principles behind Partch's system become clear, facility with ratios comes fairly quickly and makes the rest of his theory easily understandable. Some scholars argue that comprehending Partch's microtonal theory is not only worthwhile for Partch study, but also an absolute necessity for composers. See Larry Polansky, *New Instrumentation and Orchestration: An Outline for Study* (Oakland, CA: Frog Peak Music, 1986), 72.

38. Version B, scored for voice, Kithara, Chromelodeon, and Adapted Guitar, used the earliest incarnations of a notational system for the first three instruments. The guitar originally used in both *Barstow* and *U.S. Highball* was not used after 1945, and Partch never developed a notational system for it beyond written ratios. Partch, *Genesis of a Music*, 2nd ed., 203–5.

39. Gilmore convincingly found that although Partch's sketches seemed to demonstrate that he thought in a twelve-tone scale while beginning to use a forty-three-tone one, the use of a traditional staff was a shorthand in order to notate the pitches under already-written texts. Gilmore, "Harry Partch: The Early Vocal Works," 86–125.

40. See Partch, *Barstow*, ed. Kassel, and Gilmore, "Harry Partch: The Early Vocal Works" for a detailed study of these two pieces.

41. "Chicago" drafts, writings, folder 45, HPEA/UI.

42. Bruns, *Knights of the Road*, 163.

43. *U.S. Highball*, version A, box 11, folder 8, HPEA/UI.

44. Standard notation is almost an oxymoron for Partch, but this version of the Chromelodeon part utilizes common piano notation, with the Kithara notation set on the spaces of a regular five-line staff. *U.S. Highball*, version B, box 11, folder, HPEA/UI.

45. *U.S. Highball*, version B, 13.

46. Partch, *Genesis of a Music*, 2nd ed., xii–xiii.

47. Partch, *Enclosure 2: Historic Speech-Music Recordings from the Harry Partch Archives*, Innova Recordings 401, 1995.

48. Henry Cowell, "43-Tone Minstrelsy," *Saturday Review* 32, no. 48 (1949): 65.

49. Virgil Thomson, *American Music since 1910* (New York: Holt, Rinehart and Winston, 1970), 165. What is most interesting about Thomson's assertion is that proof of Partch's "intellectual sophistication" lay in the composer's manuscript, which he never read.

50. The paucity of musical training in the Western world was a common theme for Partch at this time and throughout his life. See "Show Horses in the Concert Ring," in Partch, *Bitter Music*, 174–80, for one of his witty and biting essays on the subject.

51. Partch, *Bitter Music*, 205.
52. 1957 film script, writings, folder 46, HPEA/UI.
53. Partch, *Bitter Music*, 212. In the following discussion of *U.S. Highball*, all remarks on form, instrumentation, text, and pitch are in relation to version C. As this was Partch's last statement on the work—he never altered it again, and he released it as both film and recording—I have chosen to use it as the definitive form, recognizing the flexibility and precariousness of that term.
54. Richard Phelps, "Songs of the American Hobo," *Journal of Popular Culture* 17, no. 2 (1983): 2. Phelps' study, while useful, is largely based on Milburn's collection and classification. To date, no other large-scale study has been undertaken.
55. Phelps, "Songs of the American Hobo," 8.
56. Towne Nylander, "Tramps and Hoboes," *Forum* 74, no. 8 (1925): 237.
57. George Milburn, *The Hobo's Hornbook: A Repertory for a Gutter Jongleur* (New York: Ives Washburn, 1930), xi.
58. Also known as monikas, these were the nicknames hoboes gave themselves, usually consisting of their hometown and a distinguishing attribute. Milburn, *The Hobo's Hornbook*, xiii.
59. Milburn, *The Hobo's Hornbook*, xiv. Nels Anderson concurs with this idea, writing that "the poetry most popular among the men on the road are ballads describing some picturesque and tragic incident of the hobo's adventurous life." Anderson, *The Hobo*, 194.
60. Bruns, *Knights of the Road*, 23.
61. Milburn, *The Hobo's Hornbook*, 31.
62. Milburn, *The Hobo's Hornbook*, 33–35.
63. Partch, *Bitter Music*, 204.
64. Moon, *Done and Been*, 64.
65. Harry Partch, *U.S. Highball—A Musical Account of a Transcontinental Hobo Trip*, Gate 5 Ensemble (Evanston). First released on Gate 5 Records, No. 6; rereleased on CRI, CD 752.
66. The Kithara in version B and that of version C are actually two different instruments, labeled Kithara I and Kithara II. While both operate on the same principle of twelve hexachords, Kithara I, used in the first versions of *U.S. Highball*, is an alto instrument that no longer exists in its original form, as Partch redesigned it in 1959; Kithara II is a bass. The tuning on the Kitharas was redone in 1952; they must now be retuned to play version B. See Partch, *Genesis of a Music*, 2nd ed., 220–31 for a full explanation of the differences, along with pictures and charts of notation and tunings.
67. Partch, *Genesis of a Music*, 2nd ed., 249, 251.
68. Dean Drummond, personal communication, September 16, 2003.
69. In discussing the Chromelodeon, I use letter names to indicate a key or distance on the keyboard, for example from C to G. For the actual pitch produced, I use Partch's ratio notation.
70. Danlee Mitchell, personal communication, January 7, 2004.

71. Kromer, *Waiting for Nothing*, 41–58.
72. Fox, *Tales of an American Hobo*, 181.
73. Moon, *Done and Been*, 45. In his oral history, collected in *Done and Been*, Alabama Hobo, who traveled extensively in the 1930s, remarked that hoboes had a choice between missions and the Salvation Army, but at the mission, "You usually had to listen to a sermon every night. Most of the hobos didn't care for that, so they'd go to a Sally. A Sally is just short for Salvation Army."
74. To make extra money for the family, Partch played piano for the Pastime Theatre in Albuquerque while attending high school. On the job he experimented with accompaniments different from the standard ones, such as imitating happy bird calls when a character was shot, killed, and buried. S. Andrew Granade, "When Worlds Collide: Harry Partch's Encounters with Film Music," *Music and the Moving Image* 4, no. 1 (Spring 2011): 9.
75. See Partch, *Genesis of a Music*, 2nd ed., 88–90.
76. Partch, *Genesis of a Music*, 2nd ed., 158–61.
77. Stevens, "The Hobo's Apology," 469.
78. Hunt, "'Which Way 'Bo?,'" 36.
79. Quoted in Bruns, *Knights of the Road*, 8.

Chapter Six

1. Lawrence Stessin, "That Vanishing American, the Hobo," *New York Times Magazine*, August 18, 1940, 11, 18.
2. Partch, forward to *The Wayward*, quoted in Gilmore, *Harry Partch*, 155.
3. The best single overview and in-depth discussion of society's changing perceptions of the newsboy can be found in Vincent DiGirolamo, "Crying the News: Children, Street Work, and the American Press, 1830s–1920s" (PhD diss., Princeton University, 1997).
4. See Elizabeth Johns, *American Genre Painting: The Politics of Everyday Life* (New Haven: Yale University Press, 1991), 184–86.
5. Indeed, selling papers became a common childhood occupation in the second decade of the twentieth century, one that was better than most alternatives. Louis Armstrong, Irving Berlin, George Burns, Frank Capra, Jack Dempsey, the Marx brothers, David Sarnoff, the Warner brothers, and Earl Warren all sold papers as children. See David Nasaw, *Children of the City: At Work and at Play* (New York: Doubleday, 1985), 69.
6. Nasaw, *Children of the City*, 63.
7. Harry Burroughs, *Boys in Men's Shoes: A World of Working Children* (New York: MacMillan, 1944), 271.
8. Nasaw, *Children of the City*, 82.
9. Nasaw, *Children of the City*, 66.
10. DiGirolamo, "Crying the News," 394.

11. Reef, *Working in America*, 211.

12. DiGirolamo, "Crying the News," 5.

13. Song quoted by DiGirolamo, "Newsboy Funerals," 19.

14. The penultimate line of this excerpt is a point of great debate. Multiple versions exist, including some that are more oblique in their reference to homosexuality, such as "To be a homeguard with a lemonade card." Milburn, *The Hobo's Hornbook*, 61–62. The multiple versions are most likely due to publishing conditions which were such that even in 1960, when Alan Lomax collected and published the song, he had to render the line as "To be ----------------------." Lomax, *The Folk Songs of North America in the English Language* (New York: Doubleday, 1960), 411.

15. Lomax, *The Folk Songs of North America*, 410.

16. Hal Rammel, *Nowhere in America: The Big Rock Candy Mountain and Other Comic Utopias* (Urbana: University of Illinois Press, 1990), 26–27.

17. Partch, Guggenheim Fellowship Application, "Plans for Work," 2, folder 6, GMF/UI.

18. *San Francisco: A Setting of the Cries of Two Newsboys on a Foggy Night in the Twenties*, box 11, folder 6, HPEA/UI.

19. Bob Gilmore, liner notes to *The Harry Partch Collection*, vol. 2, CRI Recordings, CD 752, 1997.

20. Lou Harrison, "Season's End, May 1944," *Modern Music* 21, no. 4 (May–June 1944): 236.

21. These recordings, featuring students Christine Charnstrom and Lee Hoiby as well as William Wendlandt and Fralia Hancock, recorded by Warren Gilson, can be found on Partch, *Enclosure 2: Historic Speech-Music Recordings from the Harry Partch Archive*. Partch likewise did not perform *The Letter* in either of the concerts he gave at the university on February 28 and March 7, 1945. Gilmore, *Harry Partch*, 161–62.

22. Letter from Partch to Lucie and Larry Marshall, December 31, 1949.

23. Partch, *Bitter Music*, 14.

24. Higbie, *Indispensable Outcasts*, 5.

25. Grace Eleanor Kimble, *Social Work with Travelers and Transients: A Study of Travelers Aid Work in the United States* (Chicago: University of Chicago Press, 1935), 1–2.

26. Don Mitchell, *The Lie of the Land: Migrant Workers and the California Landscape* (Minneapolis: University of Minnesota Press, 1996), 15.

27. Mitchell, *The Lie of the Land*, 22.

28. Marsha Weisiger, *Land of Plenty: Oklahomans in the Cotton Fields of Arizona, 1933–1942* (Norman: University of Oklahoma Press, 1995), 8.

29. Mitchell, *The Lie of the Land*, 36–40.

30. Mitchell, *The Lie of the Land*, 134.

31. Higbie, *Indispensable Outcasts*, 207.

32. Higbie, *Indispensable Outcasts*, 210.

33. See John Higham, *Strangers in the Land: Patterns of American Nativism, 1860–1925* (New York: Atheneum, 1973), for a detailed account of 1920s nativist ideology that fueled these fears.

34. Mitchell, *The Lie of the Land*, 102–5.

35. Gilmore, "Harry Partch: The Early Vocal Works," 59.

36. In choosing *Barstow* as the subject for his critical edition, Richard Kassel remarked that its accessibility was key. Partch, *Barstow*, ed. Kassel, x.

37. I follow Richard Kassel's distinction between "Tonality" for Partch's use of the word and "tonality" for the common-practice system.

38. Partch, *Genesis of a Music*, 2nd ed., 159.

39. Partch's definitions of these terms and a fuller description of their relationships can be found in Partch, *Genesis of a Music*, 2nd ed., 71–74.

40. Information for this analysis is drawn from the manuscript score of *The Letter*, box 11, folder 6, HPEA/UI.

41. For a full explanation of the organization of the Kithara's strings, see Partch, *Genesis of a Music*, 2nd ed., 230–31.

42. Quoted in Gilmore, liner notes to *The Harry Partch Collection*, vol. 2.

43. Gilmore, liner notes to *The Harry Partch Collection*, vol. 2.

Chapter Seven

1. Danlee Mitchell, personal communication, March 13, 2003. Mitchell went on to explain that he believes that the fine details of Partch's life during this period are lost forever. My presentation here is based on all extant documents currently available.

2. Letter from Partch to Betty Freeman, December 4, 1966.

3. Thomas McGeary, personal communication, March 12, 2003.

4. Partch, *Bitter Music*, 208–9.

5. Partch later remarked that "I had other small jobs, too, but—for some reason—washing dirty dishes is all that I can remember." Partch, *Bitter Music*, 209.

6. Letter from Partch to Alan Lomax, October 16, 1941, folder: Lomax, Alan—Correspondence—1941, Oct., Alan Lomax Collection, American Folklife Center of the Library of Congress.

7. Letter from Partch to Alan Lomax, October 16, 1941, folder: Lomax, Alan—Correspondence—1941, Oct., Alan Lomax Collection, American Folklife Center of the Library of Congress.

8. Concert Program from Chicago School of Design, Harry Partch Personal Scrapbook, HPEA/UI.

9. Partch, *Genesis of a Music*, 1st ed., 199.

10. 1942 Promotional Booklet designed and distributed by Partch, HPEA/UI. Partch originally adopted the spelling Chromelod*ian*, but amended it by the time of his League of Composer's concert.

11. John Cage, "South Winds in Chicago," *Modern Music* 19, no. 4 (May–June 1942): 263.

12. Concert Programs for the Friends of the Library Poetry Group and the Conference of Club Presidents and Program Chairmen, Harry Partch Personal Scrapbook, HPEA/UI.

13. Partch's letters from this time list his return address as c/o G. V. Bishop, 823 E. 46th St., Chicago, Ill.

14. Letter from Partch to Robert Kostka, July 25, 1957.

15. Partch, Yaddo Application, HPEA/UI.

16. Letter from Partch to Henry Allen Moe, February 19, 1942.

17. Letter from Partch to Moe, February 19, 1942.

18. Letter from Partch to Otto Luening, October 7, 1933.

19. Letter from Luening to Bertha Knisely, January 23, 1934.

20. Otto Luening, *The Odyssey of an American Composer*, 341.

21. Letter from Luening to Virgil Thomson, October 12, 1942.

22. Luening, *The Odyssey of an American Composer*, 341.

23. Otto Luening, "Musical Finds in the Southwest," *Modern Music* 13, no. 4 (May–June 1936): 20, 21.

24. In December 1943, a month after Luening introduced Douglas Moore to Harry Partch, Moore called to offer Luening a position at Columbia. Luening accepted, and, in 1959, the two men conspired with Henry Allen Moe to bring Partch's *The Bewitched* to Columbia for a New York performance. Luening, *The Odyssey of an American Composer*, 444. In a very real way, these three men were directly responsible for every major performance Partch gave in New York and for his success there in 1943–44.

25. Luening, *The Odyssey of an American Composer*, 441–44.

26. Partch, *Genesis of a Music*, 1st ed., vii.

27. Partch, Promotional Booklet, 1942, HPEA/UI.

28. Letter from Partch to Luening, April 24, 1942.

29. Letter from Partch to Luening, May 6, 1942.

30. Letter from Partch to Luening, May 6, 1942.

31. Letter from Partch to Moe, May 6, 1942.

32. Letter from Partch to Moe, May 29, 1942.

33. Letter from Partch to Moe, June 19, 1942.

34. As Richard Kassel has shown in his critical edition, *Barstow* went through at least four major revisions to adapt to Partch's changing ensemble. The version he performed in New York for Adapted Guitar, Chromelodeon, and Voice was the work's second version and completed in January, 1942.

35. Partch, Guggenheim Fellowship Application, "Plans for Work," 1, folder 6, GMF/UI.

36. Partch, Guggenheim Fellowship Application, "Plans for Work," 3, folder 6, GMF/UI.

37. Partch, Guggenheim Fellowship Application, "Plans for Work," 3, folder 6, GMF/UI.
38. Partch, Guggenheim Fellowship Application, "Plans for Work," 1, folder 6, GMF/UI.
39. Partch, Guggenheim Fellowship Application, "Plans for Work," 2, folder 6, GMF/UI.
40. One student, Ann E. McMillan, even wrote Partch asking for copies. Letter from Partch to Ann E. McMillan, June 1, 1942.
41. Letter from Partch to Otto Luening, July 11, 1942.
42. Peter Flanders, personal communication, October 14, 2003.
43. Letter from Howard Hanson to Henry Allen Moe, September 17, 1942.
44. Letter from Partch to Moe, September 8, 1942.
45. Letter from Partch to Luening, October 12, 1942.
46. Letter from Partch to Luening, October 5, 1942.
47. Letter from Partch to Virgil Thomson, October 5, 1942.
48. Letter from Partch to Thomson, October 5, 1942.
49. Letter from Partch to Thomson, October 24, 1942.
50. Letter from Partch to Thomson, November 17, 1942.
51. Letter from Thomson to Partch, November 25, 1942.
52. In encouraging his students at Eastman to attend the programs, Howard Hanson wrote "I recommend that all students attend this highly interesting demonstration. It is the first time I have seen an accurate demonstration of the possibilities of a highly complex scale with small variations of pitch. You will also find Mr. Partch's own conception of speech-composition highly interesting and individual." Intramural Correspondence at the Eastman School of Music, October 1942, Harry Partch Personal Scrapbook, HPEA/UI.
53. Partch, Lecture given on November 3, 1942, Eastman School of Music.
54. Letter from Partch to Luening, October 30, 1942.
55. All he would need for a recording, Partch related, would be "a contralto or a good lusty mezzo" to do the diatonic chanting part and a pianist to play the Chromelodeon. Letter from Partch to Luening, October 30, 1942.
56. Letter from Partch to Luening, October 30, 1942.
57. Harry Partch continued to add references to his Guggenheim application up until two weeks before he received notice of his award. In early March, he wrote to Moe asking to add Henry Simon, music critic for *PM* and professor at Columbia, to his reference list. Letter from Partch to Henry Allen Moe, March 4, 1943.
58. Letter from Partch to Luening, November 17, 1942.
59. Letter from Harry Partch to Douglas Moore, November 10, 1942, box 21, folder "20th Century Music," Douglas S. Moore Papers, Columbia University Rare Book and Manuscript Library.
60. Partch, *Enclosure 5*, Innova Recordings 405, 1998.
61. Partch, *Genesis of a Music*, 1st ed., 36.

62. Letter from Douglas Moore to Wilford Leach, December 5, 1952.

63. Letter from Moore to Partch, December 8, 1953. See also Gilbert Chase, *America's Music: From the Pilgrims to the Present* (New York: McGraw-Hill, 1955).

64. Course syllabi for 1944–46, box 21, folder "20th Century Music," Douglas S. Moore Collection, Columbia University Rare Book and Manuscript Library.

65. Letter from Partch to Moore, October 19, 1953.

66. Letter from Moore to Marion Bauer, January 24, 1943.

67. Letter from Moore to Bauer, January 24, 1943.

68. Letter from Moore to Abram Chasins, October 14, 1953.

69. Letter from Partch to Virgil Thomson, January 10, 1943.

70. Letter from Partch to Thomson, January 19, 1943.

71. Gilmore, *Harry Partch*, 145. Although he later destroyed the two versions composed in December 1942, Partch set the texts for both "The Heron" and "The Rose" as two movements of his *Eleven Intrusions*.

72. Letter from Partch to Luening, February 8, 1943.

73. Letter from Partch to Moe, February 11, 1943.

74. Letter from Moe to Partch, March 23, 1943.

75. For more information on Surette's influence, see Denise Von Glahn's work, in particular her presentation "'Meet with Mr. Surette': The Early Years of the John Simon Guggenheim Memorial Foundation Music Composition Awards," presented at the 39th Annual Conference of the Society for American Music, Little Rock, AR, March 7, 2013.

76. Letter from Partch to Luening, March 27, 1943; Letter from Partch to Thomson, March 28, 1943.

77. Letter from Moe to Partch, April 5, 1943.

78. Letter from Partch to Moe, April 1, 1943.

79. In February, soon after beginning work on *U.S. Highball*, Partch wrote to Moe amending his Guggenheim application (letter of February 18, 1943). He had decided to substitute *God, She*, with a new text, *Letters from Sergeant Allen— (A Setting of Excerpts from the Letters of a Man Now Serving in the United States Army)*. Perhaps Partch felt that the time was not right for a satiric view of the very musical establishment that he was attempting to win over, while realizing the timely interest accorded to patriotic American works.

80. Gilmore, *Harry Partch*, 146.

81. Letter from Partch to Luening, June 11, 1943.

82. Letter from Partch to Moore, July 7, 1943.

83. Letter from Partch to Luening, June 11, 1943.

84. Letter from Partch to Moe, October 20, 1943.

85. "NEC Bulletin," December 1943, Harry Partch Personal Scrapbook, HPEA/UI.

86. Letter from Partch to Luening, November 7, 1943.

87. Letter from Nicolas Slonimsky to Partch, February 8, 1965.

88. Right after this meeting, on November 19, 1943, Cowell wrote to the Australian composer Percy Grainger, mentioning that he was working on "a series of things which seem to go back to the feeling of early American folk hymns and fuging tunes."

89. Letter from Partch to Luening, November 15, 1943.

90. Letter from Partch to Moe, November 24, 1943.

91. Telegram from Moore to Partch, November 24, 1943.

92. Letter from Partch to Moe, December 5, 1943.

93. Letter from Partch to Moe, December 21, 1943.

94. Once he found the room, Partch wrote to Luening complaining of the biting cold, saying "I'm a cold-blooded person anyway, and the coldness of it cuts my efficiency to the vanishing point." Letter from Partch to Luening, December 23, 1943.

95. Letter from Partch to Moe, December 21, 1943.

96. Letter from Partch to Luening, December 23, 1943.

97. Letter from Partch to Moe, January 27, 1944.

98. Letter from Partch to Luening, December 23, 1943.

99. Henry Brant, interview by Betty Freeman, December 1, 1985, transcribed by Laura Kuhn, Harry Partch Oral History Project, University of Illinois at Urbana-Champaign.

100. Letter from Partch to Moe, April 25, 1944.

101. Text taken from Partch, liner notes for *Enclosure 2: Historic Speech-Music Recordings from the Harry Partch Archives*.

102. Brant, interview by Freeman, December 1, 1985.

103. Letter from Partch to Luening, April 1, 1944.

104. Brant, interview by Freeman, December 1, 1985.

105. Brant, interview by Freeman, December 1, 1985. What is most interesting is that Partch's concert was not the first one of microtonal music sponsored by the League of Composers. On March 13, 1926, only three years after its founding, the League presented Julin Carillo's *Sonata casi fantasia*, a microtonal piece written for instruments crafted by its composer. David Metzer, "The League of Composers: The Initial Years," *American Music* 15, no. 1 (1997): 55.

106. "Unusual Program by Harry Partch," *New York Times*, April 23, 1944, 40.

107. Paul Bowles, "Harry Partch gives Program of Own Works," *New York Herald Tribune*, April 23, 1944, 38.

108. Harrison, "Season's End, May 1944," 236.

109. Brant, interview by Freeman, December 1, 1985.

110. Letter from Partch to Moe, April 25, 1944.

111. "Kitharist," *New Yorker*, May 27, 1944, 18.

112. Letter from Harold W. Stoke to Henry Allen Moe, May 10, 1944.

113. Telegram from Partch to Moe, June 6, 1944.

114. Letter from Partch to Lucie and Larry Marshall, December 31, 1949.

115. Partch, Lecture given on November 3, 1942, Eastman School of Music.

Chapter Eight

1. In his dissertation on the hobo in American musical culture, Graham Raulerson makes the strong case that the hobo ethos and, in particular, what he terms the hobo's "anarcho-syndicalism," were prevalent themes throughout Partch's career and output. He ultimately, and rightly, concludes that Partch's music has "an essential sonic hobo-ness that could also inhabit the works of other composers." Graham Raulerson, "The Hobo in American Musical Culture" (PhD diss., University of California, Los Angeles, 2011), 96.

2. William Kay Archer, Review of *U.S. Highball*, recording by Harry Partch, the *Daily Cardinal*, October 11, 1946, reprinted as an appendix to Ronald V. Wiecki, "Relieving '12-Tone Paralysis': Harry Partch in Madison, Wisconsin, 1944–1947," *American Music* 9, no. 1 (Spring 1991): 60–61.

3. "Partch Devises 43-Tone Scale and Unique Instruments to Match," *The Wisconsin State Journal*, February 23, 1947.

4. Martin Butler, "'Always On the Go': The Figure of the Hobo in the Songs and Writings of Woody Guthrie," in *The Life, Music and Thought of Woody Guthrie*, ed. John S. Partington (Farnham: Ashgate, 2011), 93.

5. "Harry Isn't Kidding," *Time*, July 5, 1963, 50.

6. Wilfrid Mellers, "The Avant-Garde in America," *Proceedings of the Royal Music Association*, 90th Session (1963–64), 6.

7. Richard Wernick, Review of *Genesis of a Music*, by Harry Partch, *Journal of Music Theory* 20, no. 1 (Spring 1976): 133.

8. Blackburn, *Enclosure 3*, 464.

9. Gilmore, *Harry Partch*, 7.

10. Ben Johnston, "Beyond Harry Partch," *Perspectives of New Music* 22, no. 1–2 (Autumn–Summer 1983–84): 227.

11. Johnston's full list can be found in "Beyond Harry Partch," 228–29.

12. Partch's performance for Cowell's New Music Society was on February 9, 1932, at the Rudolph Schaeffer Studio. It featured Partch on Adapted Viola and Rudolphine Radil intoning "Dialogue from *The Merchant of Venice*," "Potion Scene from *Romeo and Juliet*," seven *Li Po* settings, and the *Two Psalms*. Gilmore, *Harry Partch*, 86–87.

13. "Partch Devises 43-Tone Scale and Unique Instruments," *The Wisconsin State Journal*, February 23, 1947, quotes Partch as saying that popular music "shows the only evidence of real musical ability in the country."

14. Wiecki, "Relieving '12-Tone Paralysis,'" 48.

15. Gilmore, *Harry Partch*, 293–94.

16. Wiecki, "Relieving '12-Tone Paralysis,'" 46.

17. Gilmore, *Harry Partch*, 278.

18. Gilmore, *Harry Partch*, 345–46.

19. Partch, *Bitter Music*, 178.

20. Gilmore, *Harry Partch*, 88.

21. Gilmore, *Harry Partch*, 328–30.
22. See Partch, Guggenheim Fellowship Application, "Plans for Work," folder 6, GMF/UI.
23. Hopkins, *Spending to Save*, 127.
24. Gilmore, *Harry Partch*, 117.
25. Letter from Partch to Lauriston Marshall, February 27, 1950.
26. Marshall returned all the original materials, but Partch destroyed only the text. The drawings and music that he had so painstakingly crafted he retained throughout his life. When Marshall's microfilm collection was donated to the Music Library of the University of Illinois, the journal was discovered and subsequently published, but without most of the sketches and drawings Partch envisioned and completed.
27. Partch, *Genesis of a Music*, 2nd ed., 323.
28. Blackburn, *Enclosure 3*, 474n32.
29. Letter from Partch to Lucie and Larry Marshall, December 31, 1949.
30. Letter from Partch to Betty Freeman, December 4, 1966.
31. DePastino, *Citizen Hobo*, 121.
32. Partch, *Genesis of a Music*, 1st ed., 71.
33. Partch, *Genesis of a Music*, 1st ed., 8.
34. Partch, *Genesis of a Music*, 2nd ed., 322.
35. Partch, *Bitter Music*, 204.
36. Partch, *Bitter Music*, 211.
37. For more information on this term and the American composers who fit under its umbrella, see Nicholls, "Transethnicism and the American Experimental Tradition."
38. John Seelye, "The American Tramp: A Version of the Picaresque," *American Quarterly* 15, no. 4 (Winter 1963): 535.
39. Salerno, *Sociology Noir*, 116–17.
40. Photinos, "Villainous Vagrants, Hard-Travelin' Hoboes, and Sisters of the Road," 10.
41. DePastino, *Citizen Hobo*, 119–26.
42. Tim Cresswell, "Mobility as Resistance: A Geographical Reading of Kerouac's *On the Road*," *Transactions of the Institute of British Geographers* 18, no. 2 (1993): 257.
43. Partch, *Bitter Music*, 18.
44. Gilmore, *Harry Partch*, 378.
45. Partch, *Bitter Music*, 122–24.
46. The only other work to feature homosexual overtones was Partch's last, a musical work for the documentary *The Dreamer That Remains*. Part Two of the work features the line "Even in public parks, where a couple of people want to improve the darkness with a little loving," which is accompanied in the film by an image of two men sitting together on a park bench. *The Dreamer That Remains*, directed by Stephen Pouliot, *Harry Partch: Enclosure 7* (St. Paul, MN: Innova Recordings 407, 2006), DVD recording.

47. Park Honan, ed., *The Beats: An Anthology of Beat Writing* (London: J. M. Dent and Sons, 1987), x.
48. Kerouac, *On the Road*.
49. Cresswell, "Mobility as Resistance," 256.
50. Kerouac, *On the Road*, 28.
51. Seelye, "The American Tramp," 552.
52. Gerd Stern, interview by Thomas McGeary, June 28, 1984. Interview Cassette #64, Oral History Interviews, HPEA/UI.
53. Letter from Partch to Peter Garland, February 29, 1972.
54. Wilfrid Mellers, "An American Aboriginal," *Tempo*, no. 64 (Spring 1963): 3.
55. Eric Salzman, "A Visit with Harry Partch," *Stereo Review*, March 1972, 94.
56. Peter Dickson, Review of *Genesis of a Music*, by Harry Partch, and *Writings About Music*, by Steve Reich, *Tempo*, no. 119 (December 1976): 42.
57. Joel Mandelbaum, "In Memoriam: Harry Partch," *Perspectives of New Music* 13, no. 1 (Autumn–Winter 1974): 239.
58. Gilmore, *Harry Partch*, 160.
59. Lee Hoiby, interview by the author, November 8, 2001.
60. Wiecki, "Relieving '12-Tone Paralysis,'" 50.
61. Charles Warren Fox, Review of *Genesis of a Music*, by Harry Partch, *Music Library Association Notes* 6, no. 4 (September 1949): 621.
62. Gilmore, *Harry Partch*, 187.
63. Partch, *Bitter Music*, 229.
64. Partch, *Bitter Music*, 181.
65. Partch, *Bitter Music*, 243.
66. Partch, *Bitter Music*, 307.
67. Partch, *Bitter Music*, 185.
68. Gilmore, *Harry Partch*, 235.
69. Gilmore, *Harry Partch*, 280.
70. Gilmore, *Harry Partch*, 281.
71. Letter from Harry Partch to Betty Freeman, April 1965.
72. Quoted in Will Salmon, "The Influence of Noh on Harry Partch's *Delusion of the Fury*," *Perspectives of New Music* 22 (1984): 244.
73. All quotations in this section and the plot summary are taken from the libretto as printed in Partch, *Bitter Music*, 445–46.
74. Partch, *Bitter Music*, 445.
75. Partch, interview by Stephen Pouliot for *The Dreamer That Remains*, quoted in Blackburn, *Enclosure 3*, 509n387.
76. Camille Snyder, "Harry Partch: An Innovator," *Los Angeles Herald Examiner*, January 5, 1969, E7.
77. Earls, "Harry Partch: Verses in Preparation for *Delusion of the Fury*," 105–6.
78. Materials from interviews with Pouliot are housed in Music and Performing Arts Library Harry Partch Collection, Sousa Archives and Center for American

Music, University of Illinois at Urbana-Champaign. The March 1974 interview with Perlis is part of the latter's Oral History of American Music, Yale University.

79. Letter from Partch to Meiron Bowen, October 11, 1967, and letter from Partch to the Rockefeller Foundation, July 21, 1973, both housed in the HPEA/UI.

80. Partch, *Genesis of a Music*, 2nd ed., 322-23.

81. Partch, *Genesis of a Music*, 2nd ed., xiii.

82. *San Francisco: A Setting of the Cries of Two Newsboys on a Foggy Night in the Twenties*, box 11, folder 6, HPEA/UI.

83. Ben Johnston, "The Corporealism of Harry Partch," *Perspectives of New Music* 13, no. 2 (Spring–Summer 1975): 87.

84. Partch, *Bitter Music*, 117-18.

Epilogue

1. Johnston, "The Corporealism of Harry Partch," 97.

2. William K. Archer, "Dissonances," *The Daily Cardinal*, Friday, October 11, 1946.

3. Gilmore, *Harry Partch*, 291.

4. Letter from Lauriston C. Marshall to Dr. Allen Kent, Director of the Knowledge Availability Systems Center of the University of Pittsburgh, January 27, 1965, letters folder, Lauriston C. Marshall Collection, HPEA/UI.

5. Westinghouse Press Release concerning the contents of its five-thousand-year time capsule, letters folder, Lauriston C. Marshall Collection, HPEA/UI.

6. Barney Hoskyns, *Lowside of the Road: A Life of Tom Waits* (New York: Broadway, 2009), 279-81.

7. Dean Drummond, "On Newband and the Partch Instruments," *1/1: The Journal of the Just Intonation Network* 8, no. 4 (November 1994): 14-15, 19.

8. Partch, *Genesis of a Music*, 2nd ed., 322.

9. Partch, *Bitter Music*, 85.

10. Gilmore, *Harry Partch*, 125.

11. George Hugo Tucker, *Homo Viator: Itineraries of Exile, Displacement and Writing in Renaissance Europe* (Geneva: Droz, 2003), 279.

12. Duffy Littlejohn, *Hopping Freight Trains in America* (Los Osos, CA: Sand River Press, 1993).

13. Modes's website can be found at http://www.thespoon.com/trainhop/resources.html (accessed May 29, 2012).

14. The Hobo Foundation can be found at http://www.hobo.com (accessed March 11, 2013) and is the best web resource for the practice of modern hoboing. Information on the Britt, Iowa, Hobo Convention, held annually since 1900, is also of particular interest.

15. John Hodgman, *The Areas of My Expertise* (New York: E. F. Dutton, 2005), 97-128.

16. Oswalt later published a version of this routine in *Zombie Spaceship Wasteland* (New York: Scribner, 2011).

17. Kusmer, *Down and Out, on the Road*, 182.

18. Johnston, "The Corporealism of Harry Partch," 92.

19. Letter from Charles Seeger to Alan Lomax, October 30, 1941, folder: Lomax, Alan—Correspondence—1941, Oct., Alan Lomax Collection, American Folklife Center of the Library of Congress.

20. Blackburn, *Enclosure 3*, 54.

21. R. Murray Schafer, "Harry Partch: *U.S. Highball*," *Canadian Music Journal* 3 (Winter 1959): 57.

22. Michael Hicks, "Mass Marketing the American Avant Garde, 1968–1971," paper presented at the 35th Annual Conference of the Society for American Music, Denver, CO, March, 24, 2009. Hicks's fascinating work demonstrates how John McClure and David Behrman at Columbia Masterworks used advertisements to connect rock with the avant garde, a ploy that continues to resonate with modern descriptions of late 1960s and early 1970s musical culture. I am indebted to him for sharing his research.

23. Information on the National Recording Preservation Board of the Library of Congress can be found at its website, http://www.loc.gov/rr/record/nrpb/; the specific listing for Partch can be found at http://www.loc.gov/rr/record/nrpb/registry/nrpb-2004reg.html (accessed February 23, 2013).

BIBLIOGRAPHY

The primary archive of material on and by Harry Partch is the Harry Partch Estate Archive in the Sousa Archives and Center for American Music of the University of Illinois at Urbana-Champaign. The Harry Partch Estate Archive is primarily composed of the materials Partch left to Danlee Mitchell, including Partch's manuscripts, correspondence, recordings, photographs, drawings, writings, and the scrapbooks he kept throughout his life. The Sousa Archives also house the Music and Performing Arts Library Harry Partch Collection which contains the material Ben Johnston and Thomas McGeary began collecting in the late 1970s including the audio tapes that comprise their oral history project. Some additional materials from the archive are housed in San Diego with Mitchell and at Montclair State University, New Jersey, where the late Dean Drummond established the Harry Partch Institute so students could earn a minor in Harry Partch Microtonal Studies. The instruments are currently at Montclair under the care of Charles Corey and are regularly used by Newband to perform and record Partch's works. Materials relating to Partch's Guggenheim applications are held in the Harry Partch Collection, John Simon Guggenheim Memorial Foundation, at the University of Illinois at Urbana-Champaign; further materials, including letters of reference and recommendation, are held in the John Simon Guggenheim Memorial Foundation Archives, Offices of the Guggenheim Foundation, New York.

I have chosen primarily to cite Partch's correspondence using the author's name, the recipient's name, and the date the letter was sent. Partch's letters to Otto Luening are in the Otto Luening Collection at the New York Public Library for the Performing Arts; his letters to Henry Allen Moe are held at the John Simon Guggenheim Memorial Foundation, New York City; his letters to Douglas Moore are in the Douglas S. Moore Papers, Columbia University (boxes 1, 13, 18, and 21); his letters to Virgil Thomson and

Quincy Porter are in the archives of Yale University; and his letters to and from Peter Garland are in the Harry Ransom Humanities Research Center at the University of Texas at Austin. The Harry Partch Estate Archive at the University of Illinois at Urbana-Champaign holds letters from Partch to Bertha Knisely Driscoll, Robert Kostka, Ann McMillan, Lauriston and Lucie Marshall, Charles Moritz, and Quincy Porter. Also held in the Harry Partch Collection at the University of Illinois is correspondence between Partch and George Cronyn, Betty Freeman, Nicolas Slonimsky, and W. B. Yeats.

List of Archives

Alan Lomax Collection. The American Folklife Center of the Library of Congress.
Archive of Recorded Sound, Sibley Music Library. Eastman School of Music. University of Rochester.
Douglas S. Moore Papers. Columbia University Rare Book and Manuscript Library.
Harry Partch Collection. John Simon Guggenheim Memorial Foundation. University of Illinois at Urbana-Champaign. (GMF/UI)
Harry Partch Estate Archive. Montclair State University.
Harry Partch Estate Archive. Sousa Archives and Center for American Music. University of Illinois at Urbana-Champaign. (HPEA/UI)
John Simon Guggenheim Memorial Foundation Archives. Offices of the Guggenheim Foundation, New York. (GMF/NY)
Music and Performing Arts Library Harry Partch Collection. Sousa Archives and Center for American Music. University of Illinois at Urbana-Champaign.
New York Public Library for the Performing Arts. Music Division.
    Henry Cowell Collection
    Otto Luening Collection
    League of Composers Collection
    New Music Papers
Oral History of American Music. Yale University.
Peter Garland Collection. University of Texas at Austin. Harry Ransom Humanities Research Center. Series III. Correspondence, 1968–97; box 36, folder 2: Partch, Harry, 1970–73.
Quincy Porter Papers. Yale University Music Library. Folders 2/19—2/22: Letters from Harry Partch, Douglas Moore, Otto Luening, and Henry Allen Moe.

Published Sources

Alexander, Charles C. *Nationalism in American Thought, 1930–1945*. Chicago: Rand McNally, 1969.

Algren, Nelson. *Somebody in Boots*. New York: Thunder's Mouth, 1935.
Anderson, Nels. *The Hobo: The Sociology of the Homeless Man*. Chicago: University of Chicago Press, 1923.
———. "The Juvenile and the Tramp." *Journal of Criminal Law, Criminology, and Police Science* 14, no. 2 (August 1923): 290–312.
———. *Men on the Move*. Chicago: Chicago University Press, 1940.
———. *The American Hobo*. Leiden: Brill, 1975.
———. *On Hobos and Homelessness*. Edited by Raffaele Rauty. Chicago: University of Chicago Press, 1998.
A-No. 1 [Leon Ray Livingston]. *Life and Adventures of A-No. 1, America's Most Celebrated Tramp*. Erie, PA: A-No. 1 Publishing Company, 1910.
Augustine, Daniel Schuyler. "Four Theories of Music in the United States, 1900–1950: Cowell, Yasser, Partch, Schillinger." PhD diss., University of Texas, Austin, 1979.
Ayers, Lydia. "Exploring Microtonal Tunings: A Kaleidoscope of Extended Just Tunings and their Compositional Applications." DMA diss., University of Illinois at Urbana-Champaign, 1994.
Baldwin, Peter C. "'Nocturnal Habits and Dark Wisdom': The American Response to Children in the Streets at Night, 1880–1930." *Journal of Social History* 35, no. 3 (2002): 593–611.
Barnard, Rita. *The Great Depression and the Culture of Abundance: Kenneth Fearing, Nathanael West, and Mass Culture in the 1930s*. Cambridge: Cambridge University Press, 1995.
Benson, Jackson J. "The Background to the Composition of *The Grapes of Wrath*." In *Critical Essays on Steinbeck's "The Grapes of Wrath,"* edited by John Ditsky, 51–74.
Benton, J. "Rest for Weary Willie: Life in a Federal Transient Camp." *Saturday Evening Post* 209 (September 5, 1936): 5–6.
Bindas, Kenneth J. *All of This Music Belongs to the Nation: The WPA's Federal Music Project and American Society, 1935–1939*. Knoxville: University of Tennessee Press, 1995.
Blackburn, Philip. *Enclosure 3*. St Paul, MN: American Composer's Forum, 1997.
Borhan, Pierre, ed. *Dorothea Lange: The Heart and Mind of a Photographer*. Boston: Little, Brown, 2002.
Botkin, B. A., and Alvin F. Harlow, eds. *A Treasury of Railroad Folklore: The Stories, Tall Tales, Traditions, Ballads and Songs of the American Railroad Men*. New York: Bonanza Books, 1953.
Bremner, Robert H. "The New Deal and Social Welfare." In *Fifty Years Later: The New Deal Evaluated*, edited by Harvard Sitkoff, 69–92.
Brinkley, Alan. *Culture and Politics in the Great Depression*. Waco, TX: Markham Press Fund, 1999.
Broder, Sherri. *Tramps, Unfit Mothers, and Neglected Children: Negotiating the Family in Nineteenth-Century Philadelphia*. Philadelphia: University of Pennsylvania Press, 2002.

Brown, Charles P. "'Brownie.'" In *We Took the Train*, edited by H. Roger Grant, 74–78.
Brown, Jeffrey Scott. "Hoboes and Vagabonds: The Cultural Construction of the American Road Hero." Master's thesis, SUNY Brockport, 1992.
Broyles, Michael. *Mavericks and Other Traditions in American Music*. New Haven, CT: Yale University Press, 2004.
Bruns, Roger A. *Knights of the Road: A Hobo History*. New York: Methuen, 1980.
Bunce, Frank. "I've Got to Take a Chance." *Forum* 89, no. 1 (1933): 108–12.
Burroughs, Harry. *Boys in Men's Shoes: A World of Working Children*. New York: MacMillan, 1944.
Burt, Warren. *The Music of Harry Partch*. Melbourne: Council of Adult Education, 1982.
Butler, Martin. "'Always on the Go': The Figure of the Hobo in the Songs and Writings of Woody Guthrie." In *The Life, Music and Thought of Woody Guthrie*, edited by John S. Partington, 85–98. Farnham: Ashgate, 2011.
Cage, John. "South Winds in Chicago." *Modern Music* 19, no. 4 (May–June 1942): 260–63.
Cameron, Catherine M. *Dialectics in the Arts: The Rise of Experimentalism in American Music*. Westport, CT: Praeger, 1996.
Cameron, Janet Garcia. "Transcriptions of *Seven Li Po Settings* by Harry Partch from 'Eleven poems by Li Po.'" MM thesis, University of Illinois, Urbana-Champaign, 1982.
Carothers, Doris. *Chronology of the Federal Emergency Relief Administration, May 12, 1933 to December 31, 1935*. Works Progress Administration Research Monograph. Washington: US Government Printing Office, 1937.
Chase, Gilbert. *America's Music: From the Pilgrims to the Present*. New York: McGraw-Hill, 1955.
Churchill, Ward. *Kill the Indian, Save the Man: The Genocidal Impact of American Indian Residential Schools*. San Francisco: City Lights, 2004.
Cohen, Norm. *Long Steel Rail: The Railroad in American Folksong*. Urbana: University of Illinois Press, 2000.
Coleman, A. D. "Dust in the Wind: The Legacy of Dorothea Lange and Paul Schuster Taylor's *An American Exodus*." In *Dorothea Lange: The Heart and Mind of a Photographer*, edited by Pierre Borhan, 156–65. Boston: Little, Brown, 2002.
Coles, Robert. *Doing Documentary Work*. New York: Oxford University Press, 1997.
Copland, Aaron. *Our New Music: Leading Composers in Europe and America*. New York: McGraw-Hill, 1941.
Copland, Aaron, and Vivian Perlis. *Copland: 1900 through 1942*. New York: St. Martin's/Marek, 1984.
Cowell, Henry. "43-Tone Minstrelsy." *Saturday Review* 32, no. 48 (1949): 65.
Cresswell, Tim. "Mobility as Resistance: A Geographical Reading of Kerouac's *On the Road*." *Transactions of the Institute of British Geographers* 18, no. 2 (1993): 249–62.

———. "Embodiment, Power and the Politics of Mobility: The Case of Female Tramps and Hobos." *Transactions of the Institute of British Geographers* 24, no. 2 (1999): 175–92.

Cross, William T., and Dorothy E. *Newcomers and Nomads in California*. Stanford: Stanford University Press, 1937.

Crouse, Joan M. *The Homeless Transient in the Great Depression: New York State, 1929–1941*. Albany: State University of New York Press, 1986.

Davenport, Walter. "California, Here We Come." *Collier's* 96 (August 10, 1935): 10–11, 47–49.

Davies, William H. *The Autobiography of a Super-Tramp*. New York: Alfred A. Knopf, 1917.

Davis, Kingsley. *Youth in the Depression*. Chicago: University of Chicago Press, 1935.

Davis, Robert Murray. "The World of John Steinbeck's Joads." In *The Critical Response to John Steinbeck's "The Grapes of Wrath,"* edited by Barbara A. Heavilin, 163–70.

DePastino, Todd. *Citizen Hobo: How a Century of Homelessness Shaped America*. Chicago: University of Chicago Press, 2003.

Dickson, Peter. Review of *Genesis of a Music*, by Harry Partch, and *Writings About Music*, by Steve Reich. *Tempo*, no. 119 (December 1976): 41–43.

DiGirolamo, Vincent. "Crying the News: Children, Street Work, and the American Press, 1830s–1920s." PhD diss., Princeton University, 1997.

———. "Newsboy Funerals: Tales of Sorrow and Solidarity in Urban America." *Journal of Social History* 36, no. 1 (Autumn 2002): 5–30.

Ditsky, John, ed. *Critical Essays on Steinbeck's "The Grapes of Wrath."* Boston: G. K. Hall, 1989.

Dos Passos, John. *U.S.A.* New York: The Modern Library, 1937.

Drummond, Dean. "On Newband and the Partch Instruments." *1/1: The Journal of the Just Intonation Network* 8, no. 4 (November 1994): 14–15, 19.

Dubofsky, Melvyn. *We Shall Be All: A History of the Industrial Workers of the World*. New York: Quadrangle, 1987.

Dupree, Mary Herron. "The Failure of American Music: The Critical View from the 1920s." *Journal of Musicology* 2 (1983): 305–15.

Dvořák, Antonin. "Music in America." *Harper's Magazine* 90 (February 1895): 428–34.

Earls, Paul. "Harry Partch: Verses in Preparation for *Delusion of the Fury*." In *Harry Partch: An Anthology of Critical Perspectives*, edited by David Dunn, 79–106. Amsterdam: Harwood, 2000.

Farwell, Arthur. "Pioneering for American Music." *Modern Music* 12, no. 3 (March–April 1935): 116–22.

Feied, Frederick. *No Pie in the Sky: The Hobo as American Cultural Hero in the Works of Jack London, John Dos Passos, and Jack Kerouac*. New York: The Citadel Press, 1964.

Fisher, Andrea. *Let Us Now Praise Famous Women: Women Photographers for the U.S. Government 1935 to 1944*. New York: Pandora, 1987.
Fletcher, Alice. *Indian Story and Song from North America*. Boston: Small, Maynard, 1900.
Flynt, Josiah. *Tramping with Tramps*. New York: The Century Company, 1899.
Forbes, James. "Jockers and the Schools They Keep." *Charities* 11 (November 7, 1903): 432–36.
Fox, Charles Elmer. *Tales of an American Hobo*. Iowa City: University of Iowa Press, 1989.
Fox, Charles Warren. Review of *Genesis of a Music*, by Harry Partch. *Music Library Association Notes* 6, no. 4 (September 1949): 621–22.
Gann, Kyle. *American Music in the Twentieth Century*. New York: Schirmer Books, 1997.
———. "What's American about American Music?" American Mavericks. Accessed March 28, 2013. http://musicmavericks.publicradio.org/features/essay_gann02.html.
Garland, Peter. *Six American Composers: Partch, Cage, Harrison, Nancarrow, Tenney, Bowles*. Berlin: Merve, 1997.
Garman, Bryan K. *A Race of Singers: Whitman's Working Class Hero from Guthrie to Springsteen*. Chapel Hill: University of North Carolina Press, 2000.
Gilmore, Bob. "The Climate since Harry Partch." *Contemporary Music Review* 22, nos. 1–2 (2003): 15–33.
———. "A European Perspective on Partch." *1/1: The Journal of the Just Intonation Network* 2/1 (Winter 1986): 4–5.
———. "Harry Partch: The Early Vocal Works 1930–33." PhD diss., Queen's University of Belfast, 1992.
———. "'A Soul Tormented': Alwin Nikolais and Harry Partch's *The Bewitched*." *The Musical Quarterly* 79 no. 1 (Spring 1995): 80–107.
———. "Changing the Metaphor: Ratio Models of Musical Pitch in the Work of Harry Partch, Ben Johnston, and James Tenney." *Perspectives of New Music* 33/1–2 (Winter–Summer 1995): 458–503.
———. Liner notes to *The Harry Partch Collection*, Vol. 2. CRI Recordings, CD 752, 1997, compact disc.
———. *Harry Partch: A Biography*. New Haven: Yale University Press, 1998.
Gold, John R. "From 'Dust Storm Disaster' to 'Pastures of Plenty': Woody Guthrie and Landscapes of the American Depression." In *The Place of Music*, edited by Andrew Leyshon and David Matless, 249–64. New York: The Guilford Press, 1998.
Goldschmidt, Walter. *As You Sow*. New York: Harcourt, Brace, 1947.
Gorbman, Claudia. *Unheard Melodies: Narrative Film Music*. Bloomington: Indiana University Press, 1987.
Granade, S. Andrew. "Rekindling Ancient Values: The Influence of Chinese Music and Aesthetics on Harry Partch." *Journal of the Society for American Music* 4, no. 1 (February 2010): 1–32.

———. "When Worlds Collide: Harry Partch's Encounters with Film Music." *Music and the Moving Image* 4, no. 1 (Spring 2011): 9–33.

Grant, H. Roger, ed. *We Took the Train*. Dekalb: Northern Illinois University Press, 1990.

———. "Home by Rail, California to Illinois in 1937: Reminiscences of Graydon Horath." *Railroad History* 172 (Spring 1995): 35–42.

Gregory, James N. *American Exodus: The Dust Bowl Migration and Okie Culture in California*. Oxford: Oxford University Press, 1989.

Guthrie, Woody. *Bound for Glory*. New York: E. P. Dutton, 1943.

———. Liner notes to *Dust Bowl Ballads*. Folkways Records FA-2011, 1950, LP record.

Harlan, Brian Timothy. "One Voice: A Reconciliation of Harry Partch's Disparate Theories." PhD diss., University of Southern California, 2007.

Harrison, Lou. "Season's End, May 1944." *Modern Music* 21, no. 4 (May–June 1944): 230–37.

Hart, James D. *The Popular Book: A History of America's Literary Taste*. New York: Oxford University Press, 1950.

Hayes, Kevin J., ed. *Charlie Chaplin: Interviews*. Jackson: University of Mississippi Press, 2005.

Healy, Thomas F. "The Hobo Hits the Highroad." *American Mercury* 8 (July 1926): 445–50.

Heavilin, Barbara A., ed. *The Critical Response to John Steinbeck's "The Grapes of Wrath."* Westport, CT: Greenwood Press, 2000.

Hecht, Roger. Review of *Folksong Symphony*, by Roy Harris. *American Record Guide* 62 (September–October 1999): 167–68.

Helmholtz, Hermann von. *On the Sensations of Tone as a Physiological Basis for the Theory of Music*. Translated by Alexander J. Ellis. London: Longmans, Green, 1885.

Hicks, Michael. "Mass Marketing the American Avant Garde, 1968–1971." Paper presented at the Thirty-fifth Annual Conference of the Society for American Music, Denver, CO, March 24, 2009.

Higbie, Frank Tobias. *Indispensable Outcasts: Hobo Workers and Community in the American Midwest, 1880–1930*. Urbana: University of Illinois Press, 2003.

Himmelberg, Robert F. *The Great Depression and the New Deal*. Westport, CT: Greenwood, 2001.

Hodgman, John. *The Areas of My Expertise*. New York: E. F. Dutton, 2005.

Holbrook, Stewart H. "Wobbly Talk." *American Mercury* 7 (January 1926): 62.

Honan, Park, ed. *The Beats: An Anthology of Beat Writing*. London: J. M. Dent and Sons, 1987.

Hopkins, Harry. *Spending to Save: The Complete Story of Relief*. New York: W. W. Norton, 1936.

Hoskyns, Barney. *Lowside of the Road: A Life of Tom Waits*. New York: Broadway, 2009.

Huddlestone, Warren. "Slow Days." *New Republic* 79 (June 13, 1934): 124–26.

Hunt, William R. "'Which Way 'Bo?': Literary Impressions of the Hobos' Golden Age, 1880–1930." *Journal of Popular Culture* 4, no. 1 (1970): 22–38.

Hurt, R. Douglas. *Dust Bowl: An Agricultural and Social History*. Chicago: Nelson Hall, 1981.

Ickstadt, Heinz. "The Writing on the Wall: American Painting and the Federal Arts Project." In *The Thirties: Politics and Culture in a Time of Broken Dreams*, edited by Heinz Ickstadt and Rob Kroes, 221–47. Amsterdam: Free University Press, 1987.

Ickstadt, Heinz, and Rob Kroes. *The Thirties: Politics and Culture in a Time of Broken Dreams*. Amsterdam: Free University Press, 1987.

Jamieson, Stuart M. "A Settlement of Rural Migrant Families in the Sacramento Valley." *Rural Sociology* 7 (March 1942): 49–61.

Johns, Elizabeth. *American Genre Painting: The Politics of Everyday Life*. New Haven: Yale University Press, 1991.

Johnston, Ben. "The Corporealism of Harry Partch." *Perspectives of New Music* 13, no. 2 (Spring–Summer 1975): 85–97.

———. "Beyond Harry Partch." *Perspectives of New Music* 22, no. 1–2 (Autumn–Summer 1983–84): 223–32.

Kassel, Richard M. "Harry Partch in the Field: Native American Influence on His Music." *Canadian Journal of Sound Exploration* 51 (Autumn 1991): 6–15.

———. "The Evolution of Harry Partch's Monophony." PhD diss., City University of New York, 1996.

———. See also under Partch

Kerouac, Jack. *On the Road*. New York: Penguin, 1957.

Key, Susan, and Larry Rothe, eds. *American Mavericks: Visionaries, Pioneers, Iconoclasts*. Berkeley: University of California Press, 2001.

Kildahl, Erling. "Riding Freights to Jamestown in 1936." In *We Took the Train*, edited by H. Roger Grant, 79–93.

Kimble, Grace Eleanor. *Social Work with Travelers and Transients: A Study of Travelers Aid Work in the United States*. Chicago: University of Chicago Press, 1935.

Klein, Joe. *Woody Guthrie: A Life*. New York: Delta, 1980.

Kleppinger, Stanley V. "On the Influence of Jazz Rhythm in the Music of Aaron Copland." *American Music* 21, no. 1 (Spring 2003): 74–109.

Kromer, Tom. *Waiting for Nothing*. New York: Hill and Wang, 1935.

Kusmer, Kenneth L. *Down and Out, on the Road: The Homeless in American History*. Oxford: Oxford University Press, 2002.

Lange, Dorothea. "The Assignment I'll Never Forget." *Popular Photography* 46, no. 2 (February 1960): 42–128.

———. See also under Taylor

Lawson, Alan. "The Cultural Legacy of the New Deal." In *Fifty Years Later: The New Deal Evaluated*, edited by Harvard Sitkoff, 69–92.

Lears, T. J. Jackson. *No Place of Grace: Antimodernism and the Transformation of American Culture, 1880–1920*. New York: Pantheon Books, 1981.

Lennon, John. "Interrogating American Subculture: The Hobo Figure and Negotiations of Invisibility." PhD diss., Lehigh University, 2005.

Lerner, Neil William. "The Classical Documentary Score in American Films of Persuasion: Contexts and Case Studies, 1936–1945." PhD diss., Duke University, 1997.

Lescohier, Don D. "Hands and Tools of the Wheat Harvest." *Survey* 50 (July 1923): 376–82, 409–11.

———. "Harvesters and Hoboes in the Wheat Fields." *Survey* 50 (August 1923): 482–87.

Levy, Beth E. "'In the Glory of the Sunset': Arthur Farwell, Charles Wakefield Cadman, and Indianism in American Music." *Repercussions* 5, nos. 1–2 (Spring–Fall 1996): 128–83.

———. "Frontier Figures: American Music and the Mythology of the American West, 1895–1945." PhD diss., University of California, Berkeley, 2002.

———. *Frontier Figures: American Music and the Mythology of the American West*. Berkeley: University of California Press, 2012.

Lewis, M. H. *Transients in California*. Special Surveys and Studies. San Francisco: State Relief Administration of California, 1936.

Linder, Rolf. *The Reportage of Urban Culture: Robert Park and the Chicago School*. Translated by Adrian Morris. New York: Cambridge University Press, 1996.

Littlejohn, Duffy. *Hopping Freight Trains in America*. Los Osos, CA: Sand River Press, 1993.

Locke, Ralph P. "A Broader View of Musical Exoticism." *Journal of Musicology* 24, no. 4 (Fall 2007): 477–521.

———. *Musical Exoticism: Images and Reflections*. Cambridge: Cambridge University Press, 2009.

Lomax, Alan. *The Folk Songs of North America in the English Language*. New York: Doubleday, 1960.

Lomax, Alan, and John Lomax. *American Ballads and Folk Songs*. New York: MacMillan, 1934.

London, Jack. *The Road*. Introduction by King Hendricks. Santa Barbara: Peregrine, 1970.

Lorentz, Pare, "Dorothea Lange: Camera with a Purpose." In *U.S. Camera, 1941*, edited by T. J. Maloney, 93–100, 229. New York: Duell, Sloan, and Pearce, 1941.

Louchheim, Katie, ed. *The Making of the New Deal: The Insiders Speak*. Cambridge, MA: Harvard University Press, 1983.

Lowance, Mason I. *A House Divided: The Antebellum Slavery Debates in America, 1776–1865*. Princeton, NJ: Princeton University Press, 2003.

Ludlow, Lynn. "Notes from a Semi-Incompetent Performer on the Surrogate Kithara (1953)." *1/1: The Journal of the Just Intonation Network* 8, no. 4 (November 1994): 21, 23.

Luening, Otto. "Musical Finds in the Southwest." *Modern Music* 13, no. 4 (May–June 1936): 18–22.

———. *The Odyssey of an American Composer*. New York: Charles Scribner's Sons, 1980.

Lutz, Catherine, and Jane L. Collins. *Reading National Geographic*. Chicago: University of Chicago Press, 1993.

Mandelbaum, Joel. "In Memoriam: Harry Partch." *Perspectives of New Music* 13, no. 1 (Autumn–Winter 1974): 239.

McCook, John J. "Increase of Tramping: Cause and Cure." *The Independent* 54 (1902): 622.

McGeary, Thomas. *The Music of Harry Partch: A Descriptive Catalog*. I.S.A.M. Monographs 31. New York: Institute for Studies in American Music, 1991.

McGovern, Charles F. "Woody Guthrie's American Century." In *Hard Travelin': The Life and Legacy of Woody Guthrie*, edited by Robert and Emily Davidson Santelli, 111–27. Hanover, NH: Wesleyan University Press, 1999.

McWilliams, Carey. *Factories in the Field: The Story of Migratory Farm Labor in California*. Boston: Little, Brown, 1939.

Mellers, Wilfrid. "An American Aboriginal." *Tempo*, no. 64 (Spring 1963): 2–6.

———. "The Avant-Garde in America." In *Proceedings of the Royal Music Association*. 90th Session (1963–64): 1–13.

Metzer, David. "The League of Composers: The Initial Years." *American Music* 15, no. 1 (1997): 45–69.

Milburn, George. *The Hobo's Hornbook: A Repertory for a Gutter Jongleur*. New York: Ives Washburn, 1930.

Miller, Leta, and Catherine Parsons Smith. "Playing with Politics: Crisis in the San Francisco Federal Music Project." *California History* 86, no. 2 (March 2009): 26–47 and 68–71.

"'Millionaire Hobo' Is Dead." *The Christian Century* 34 (August 20, 1930): 1020.

Mitchell, Don. *The Lie of the Land: Migrant Workers and the California Landscape*. Minneapolis: University of Minnesota Press, 1996.

Moon, Gypsy. *Done and Been: Steel Rail Chronicles of American Hobos*. Bloomington: Indiana University Press, 1996.

Nasaw, David. *Children of the City: At Work and at Play*. New York: Doubleday, 1985.

Neal, Joseph C. *Peter Ploddy, and Other Oddities*. Philadelphia: Carey and Hart, 1844.

Nicholls, David. *American Experimental Music, 1890–1940*. Cambridge: Cambridge University Press, 1990.

———. "Transethnicism and the American Experimental Tradition." *The Musical Quarterly* 80, no. 4 (Winter 1996): 569–94.

———. *The Cambridge History of American Music*. Cambridge: Cambridge University Press, 1998.

Nylander, Towne. "Tramps and Hoboes." *Forum* 74, no. 8 (1925): 227–37.

Nyman, Michael. *Experimental Music: Cage and Beyond*. 2nd ed. Cambridge: Cambridge University Press, 1999.
Ohrn, Karin Becker. *Dorothea Lange and the Documentary Tradition*. Baton Rouge: Louisiana State University Press, 1980.
Oswalt, Patton. *Zombie Spaceship Wasteland*. New York: Scribner, 2011.
Partch, Harry. *Genesis of a Music*. Madison, WI: The University of Wisconsin Press, 1949.
———. *Genesis of a Music: An Account of a Creative Work, Its Roots and Its Fulfillments*. 2nd ed. New York: Da Capo, 1974.
———. *Bitter Music: Collected Journals, Essays, Introductions, and Librettos*. Edited by Thomas McGeary. Urbana: University of Illinois Press, 1991.
———. *Enclosure 2: Historic Speech-Music Recordings from the Harry Partch Archives*. Innova Recordings 401, 1995, 4 compact discs.
———. *Harry Partch: Enclosure 5*. Innova Recordings 405, 1998, 3 compact discs.
———. *Barstow: Eight Hitchhiker Inscriptions from a Highway Railing at Barstow, California (1968 Version)*. Edited by Richard Kassel. Music of the United States of America 9. Madison, WI: A–R Editions, 2000.
Phelps, Richard. "Songs of the American Hobo." *Journal of Popular Culture* 17, no. 2 (1983): 1–21.
Photinos, Christie. "Villainous Vagrants, Hard-Travelin' Hoboes, and Sisters of the Road: The Figure of the Tramp in American Literature." PhD diss., University of California, San Diego, 2000.
Pinkerton, Allan. *Strikers, Communists, Tramps, and Detectives*. New York: G. W. Carleton, 1878.
Pisani, Michael. "Exotic Sounds in the Native Land: Portrayals of North American Indians in Western Music." PhD diss., Eastman School of Music, 1996.
———. "From Hiawatha to Wa-Wan: Musical Boston and the Uses of Native American Lore." *American Music* 19, no. 1 (Spring, 2001): 39–50.
Polansky, Larry. *New Instrumentation and Orchestration: An Outline for Study*. Oakland, CA: Frog Peak Music, 1986.
Pollack, Howard. *Aaron Copland: The Life and Work of an Uncommon Man*. New York: H. Holt, 1999.
———. *George Gershwin: His Life and Work*. Berkeley: University of California Press, 2006.
Railton, Stephen. "Pilgrim's Politics: Steinbeck's Art of Conversion." In *New Essays on "The Grapes of Wrath,"* edited by David Wyatt, 27–46.
Rammel, Hal. *Nowhere in America: The Big Rock Candy Mountain and Other Comic Utopias*. Urbana: University of Illinois Press, 1990.
Raulerson, Graham. "The Hobo in American Musical Culture." PhD diss., University of California, Los Angeles, 2011.
Reef, Catherine. *Working in America*. New York: Facts on File, 2000.
Reuss, Richard A. "Woody Guthrie and His Folk Tradition." *Journal of American Folklore* 83, no. 329 (July–September 1970): 273–303.

Reuss, Richard A., and JoAnne C. Reuss. *American Folk Music and Left-Wing Politics, 1927–1957*. American Folk Music and Musicians 4. Lanham, MD: Scarecrow, 2000.
Riis, Jacob. "The New York Newsboy." *The Century Magazine* 85 (December 1912): 247–55.
Robertson, Malcom D. "Roy Harris's Symphonies: An Introduction (I)." *Tempo* 207 (December 1998): 9–14.
Robinson, David. *Chaplin: His Life and Art*. London: Collins, 1985.
Rose, Nancy E. *Put to Work: Relief Programs in the Great Depression*. New York: Monthly Review Press, 1994.
Ross, Alex. "Harry Partch's *Oedipus*." *New Yorker*, April 18, 2005.
Salerno, Roger A. *Sociology Noir: Studies at the University of Chicago in Loneliness, Marginality, and Deviance, 1915–1935*. Jefferson, NC: McFarland, 2007.
Salmon, Will. "The Influence of Noh on Harry Partch's *Delusion of the Fury*." *Perspectives of New Music* 22 (1984): 233–52.
Salzman, Eric. "A Visit with Harry Partch." *Stereo Review* (March 1972): 94.
Sandburg, Carl. *The American Songbag*. New York: Harcourt, Brace, 1927.
Schafer, R. Murray. "Harry Partch: *U.S. Highball*." *Canadian Music Journal* 3 (Winter 1959): 55–58.
Schockley, Martin. "The Reception of *The Grapes of Wrath* in Oklahoma." *American Literature* 14 (1944): 351–61.
Schneider, John. "Bringing Back Barstow." *Guitar Review* 95 (Fall 1993): 1–13.
Seelye, John. "The American Tramp: A Version of the Picaresque." *American Quarterly* 15, no. 4 (Winter 1963): 535–53.
Sheppard, W. Anthony. *Revealing Masks: Exotic Influences and Ritualized Performance in Modernist Music Theater*. Berkeley: University of California Press, 2001.
Shillinglaw, Susan. "California Answers *The Grapes of Wrath*." In *The Critical Response to John Steinbeck's "The Grapes of Wrath,"* edited by Barbara A. Heavilin, 183–200.
Shindo, Charles J. *Dust Bowl Migrants in the American Imagination*. Lawrence: University of Kansas Press, 1997.
Singleton, Jeff. *The American Dole: Unemployment Relief and the Welfare State in the Great Depression*. Westport, CT: Greenwood, 2000.
Sitkoff, Harvard, ed. *Fifty Years Later: The New Deal Evaluated*. New York: Knopf, 1985.
Solomon, William. *Literature, Amusement and Technology in the Great Depression*. Cambridge: Cambridge University Press, 2002.
Spiker, Ken. "Harry Partch," *Earth Magazine* (March 1971): 70–72.
Starr, Larry. "The Voice of Solitary Contemplation: Copland's *Music for the Theatre* Viewed as a Journey of Self-Discovery." *American Music* 20, no. 3 (Fall 2002): 298–316.
Stehman, Dan. *Roy Harris: A Bio-Bibliography*. Westport, CT: Greenwood, 1991.

Stein, Walter J. *California and the Dust Bowl Migration*. Westport, CT: Greenwood, 1973.
Steinbeck, John. *Working Days: The Journals of "The Grapes of Wrath."* Edited by Robert DeMott. New York: Viking, 1989.
Stessin, Lawrence. "That Vanishing American, the Hobo." *New York Times Magazine*, August 18, 1940, 11, 18.
Stevens, James. "The Hobo's Apology." *Century* 109, no. 2 (1925): 464–72.
Stott, William. *Documentary Expression and Thirties America*. New York: Oxford University Press, 1973.
Susman, Warren. *Culture and Commitment, 1929–1945*. New York: G. Braziller, 1973.
Taylor, Paul S. "Again the Covered Wagon." *Survey Geographic* 24 (July 1935): 349.
Taylor, Paul S., and Dorothea Lange. *An American Exodus: A Record of Human Erosion*. New York: Reynal and Hitchcock, 1939.
Terkel, Studs. *Hard Times: An Oral History of the Great Depression*. New York: Pantheon Books, 1970.
Thomson, Virgil. *Virgil Thomson*. New York: E. P. Dutton, 1966.
———. *American Music since 1910*. New York: Holt, Rinehart and Winston, 1970.
Tischler, Barbara L. *An American Music: The Search for an American Musical Identity*. Oxford: Oxford University Press, 1986.
Todd, Charles and Robert Sonkin. "Ballads of the Okies." *New York Times Magazine*, November 17, 1940, 6–7, 18.
Tucker, George Hugo. *Homo Viator: Itineraries of Exile, Displacement and Writing in Renaissance Europe*. Geneva: Droz, 2003.
Tully, Jim. *Beggars of Life: A Hobo Autobiography*. Garden City, NY: Garden City, 1924.
Turner, Frederick Jackson. *The Frontier in American History*. New York: H. Holt, 1920.
Tyler, Robert L. "The Rise and Fall of an American Radicalism: The I.W.W." *The Historian* 19, no. 1 (1956–57): 48–65.
Von Glahn, Denise. "'Meet with Mr. Surette': The Early Years of the John Simon Guggenheim Memorial Foundation Music Composition Awards." Paper presented at the 39th Annual Conference of the Society for American Music, Little Rock, AR, March 7, 2013.
Watkins, T. H. *Great Depression: America in the 1930s*. Boston: Little, Brown, 1993.
Webb, John N. *The Migratory-Casual Worker*. Washington, D.C.: Works Progress Administration, 1937.
Weisiger, Marsha. *Land of Plenty: Oklahomans in the Cotton Fields of Arizona, 1933–1942*. Norman: University of Oklahoma Press, 1995.
Wen-Chung, Chou. "Asian Concepts and Twentieth-Century Composers." *The Musical Quarterly* 57, no. 2 (April 1971): 211–29.
Wernick, Richard. "Review of *Genesis of a Music*, by Harry Partch." *Journal of Music Theory* 20, no. 1 (Spring 1976): 133–37.

Whitaker, Percy Walton. "Fruit Tramps." *Century Magazine* 3 (March 1929): 599–606.
Wiecki, Ronald V. "Relieving '12-Tone Paralysis': Harry Partch in Madison, Wisconsin, 1944–1947." *American Music* 9, no. 1 (Spring 1991): 43–66.
Williams, Edward Ainsworth. *Federal Aid for Relief*. New York: Columbia University Press, 1939.
Witten, George. "The Open Road: The Autobiography of a Hobo." *Century* 115, no. 1 (1928): 351–61.
Wyatt, David. "Introduction." In *New Essays on "The Grapes of Wrath,"* edited by David Wyatt, 1–26.
———, ed. *New Essays on "The Grapes of Wrath."* Cambridge: Cambridge University Press, 1990.
Yang, Mina. "New Directions in California Music, from 1925 to 1945." PhD diss., Yale University, 2001.
Yates, Janelle. *Woody Guthrie: American Balladeer*. New York: Ward Hill, 1995.
Zuck, Barbara A. *A History of Musical Americanism*. Ann Arbor, MI: UMI Research Press, 1978.

Internet Resources

As Harry Partch's works rely upon his unique instrumentarium, many internet sources exist where users can experience his music virtually. Perhaps the most useful and detailed of these websites, hosted by American Public Media, was produced as part of a radio series on the American Mavericks. The site features photographs and archival audio of Partch as well as a virtual instrumentarium built on digital samples taken from the original instruments:

American Mavericks. "Harry Partch's Instruments." Accessed January 20, 2014. http://musicmavericks.publicradio.org/features/feature_partch.html.

The Harry Partch Foundation, the official organization established during Partch's life and currently run by Danlee Mitchell, maintains a website that features most of Partch's libretti, images of his Gate 5 recording releases, and interviews with his associates, among other riches:

The Harry Partch Foundation and Jon Szanto. "Corporeal Meadows." Last updated February 29, 2012. http://www.corporeal.com/cm_main.html.

Newband is the current custodian of Partch's original instruments. They perform on them regularly at their home institution, Montclair State University, and around the region. Their website features upcoming performances as well as a few sound samples of the instruments and an excellent primer on Partch's tuning system:

Newband. "Newband." Accessed January 20, 2014. http://www.newband.org/.

In 2012, Ensemble musikFabrik took on the task of replicating Partch's entire instrumentarium. Their efforts resulted in the first European performance of Partch's *Delusion of the Fury* at the 2013 Ruhrtiennale, and a promise of future performances of Partch's works alongside new compositions for the instruments. They extensively tracked this "Harry Partch Project" at their website and through a youtube channel:

Ensemble musikFabrik. "Harry Partch: Delusion of the Fury—a Ritual of a Dream." Accessed January 20, 2014. http://musikfabrik.eu/en/projects/stage-works/delusion-of-the-fury.html.

Ensemble musicFabrik. "Youtube Channel of the Harry Partch Project." Accessed January 20, 2014. http://www.youtube.com/user/musikFabrikeu?feature=watch.

INDEX

Adams, John Luther, 3
Adapted Guitar, 38, 63, 78, 110, 221, 226, 229, 237, 240, 241, 243, 245, 263, 285, 313n38; in *Barstow*, 124, 126, 234; in *The Letter*, 215–16, 238; in *U.S. Highball*, 144, 149, 150, 151, 159, 161, 170–73, 174, 182, 190–91, 197
Adapted Viola, 38, 110, 207–9, 221, 226, 229, 234, 237, 285, 295n39, 332n12
Agee, James, 19, 73, 110
Agricultural Adjustment Act, 61
American Exodus, An, 75, 92, 108, 264
American Mavericks, 255; concert series of, 3
American Songbag, 178
ancient Greece: musical thought in, 30–32; Partch references to, 14, 29, 65, 87, 196, 263, 273
And on the Seventh Day Petals Fell in Petaluma, 256
Anderson, Laurie, 3
Anderson, Nels, 47, 51, 66, 95, 120, 139, 143, 265, 306n18, 314n59; *The Hobo: The Sociology of the Homeless Man*, 137–38
Antheil, George, 9, 43, 44, 229

Bach, J. S., 123, 125

Baldwin, C. B., 71–72
Bamboo Marimba, 150, 159, 184, 186, 191, 193, 286
Bang on a Can Festival, 279
Barstow, 1, 11–12, 17, 20, 34, 64, 77, 113, 116, 123–28, 144, 145, 147, 149, 150, 151, 159, 165, 169, 170, 181, 189, 194, 198, 204, 209, 213, 219, 221, 226, 228, 233, 234, 236, 237, 239, 240, 243, 247, 256, 258, 259, 260, 263, 268, 272, 279, 281, 285; composition of, 103, 123–24, 166, 217, 222, 238; discovery in inscriptions, 108, 111–13, 282; similarities to Woody Guthrie's work, 79, 84, 302n48. See also *Wayward, The*
Bass Marimba, 150, 159, 184, 186, 191–93
Beat Generation, 266–68, 280
Bennington College, 227, 233, 234, 236, 239, 240
Benton, Thomas Hart, 9–10, 13
Bewitched, The, 13, 254, 256, 264, 271–72, 318n24
"Big Rock Candy Mountain," 142, 205–6
Billings, William, 3
Bishop, George, 222–23, 226, 235, 243, 256

Bitter Music, 1, 17, 18, 20, 33, 40, 52, 54, 64–67, 69, 75, 77–79, 81, 84, 88–109, 110, 124, 127, 163, 210, 216–18, 226, 232, 252, 258–59, 279; destruction of, 260–61, 273; homosexuality in, 67, 120, 266; illustrations in, 79–80, 92–93; microfilm of, 261, 323n26; piano score in, 94–95, 304n6; quotations in, 99–103, 277; structure of, 92–95, 100–103; and the WPA Writer's Project, 104–7
Blackburn, Philip, 254
Bloboy, 182, 184, 188, 192, 286
"Bonus Army," 49–50, 52
Boo. *See* Bamboo Marimba
Bowles, Paul, 247
Brahms, Johannes, 27
Brant, Henry, 244, 246–47, 289n9
British Museum, 42, 45, 63
Brooks, Jack, 119
Broyles, Michael, 3
Buhlig, Richard, 42
bum, 2, 52, 56, 68, 111, 117, 130, 132, 134, 154, 158, 162, 185, 254, 283; definition of, 211, 297n15; in popular song, 143, 180. *See also* "Hallelujah, I'm a Bum"
Bum Blockade, 57, 60, 80, 299n51
"By the Rivers of Babylon." *See Two Psalms*

Cadman, Charles Wakefield, 7–9, 12
Cafferty, James Henry, 200–201, 203
Cage, John, 3, 42, 177, 241, 268; interactions with Partch, 221–22
Cahuilla Indians, 13, 264
Carnegie Corporation of New York, 33, 45, 97, 98, 221, 257
Carr, Jeff, 152
Carroll, Lewis, 112, 158
Castor and Pollux, 159, 183–84, 190, 286. *See also* Harmonic Canons
Castor and Pollux, 256
Cause All Our Sins Are Taken Away, 99, 104, 105, 107–8
Chaplin, Charlie, 129, 140–42, 143, 176
Chase, Gilbert, 235
Chase, Gilman, 222, 226, 243
Chávez, Carlos, 230
Chopin, Frédéric, 27, 101, 102
Chromelodeon, 34, 38, 49, 207–8, 209, 222, 223, 224, 226, 229, 230, 233–34, 239, 242, 243, 244, 245, 246, 285, 314n69; in *U.S. Highball*, 159, 161, 169, 170–72, 174, 183–84, 186, 187–90, 192. *See also* Ptolemy
Cisco, 68, 101
classification of intervals (in Partch's theory), 28–32, 189–90
Cloud-Chamber Bowls, 150, 193, 286
Columbia Records, 256, 283–84, 326n22
Columbia University, 149, 235, 246, 249, 271, 318n24
"Come Away Death," 235, 237
conceptual exoticism, 10, 13, 15, 16–17, 19, 20, 70, 73, 85, 125, 127, 128, 144, 164, 176–78, 219, 251, 264, 282; definition of, 11–12, 290n17. *See also* decorative exoticism
consonance, 28, 188
Copland, Aaron, 8–9, 13, 16, 18, 43, 44, 70, 86, 235, 238
corporeality, 235, 262–64
Couper, Mildred, 40, 42, 44, 68, 295n54
Cowell, Henry, 3, 40, 42, 43, 176, 177, 240–41, 256, 321n88; *New Musical Resources*, 38–39; reactions to Partch's music, 44, 175, 187
Cowell, Sidney Robertson, 303n4
Coxey's Army, 134, 136, 141

Cronyn, George W., 106–8, 305n46

Daphne of the Dunes, 256
Dark Brother, 158, 228, 238, 256, 259
Death on the Desert, 25, 126
Debussy, Claude, 42
December, 1942, 237
decorative exoticism, 7, 9, 11, 13, 14–15, 17, 77, 82, 87, 125, 127, 176, 236, 248, 264, 283; definition of, 5, 290n17. *See also* conceptual exoticism
Delusion of the Fury, 2, 4, 103, 256–57, 264, 273–75
Depression. *See* Great Depression
Diamond Marimba, 38, 150, 159, 184, 185–86, 192–93, 286
Dilbert, 280–81
dissonance, 194
documentary, 31, 61, 92, 95, 100, 108–9, 127, 145, 154, 164, 175, 184, 197, 252, 260, 264, 281, 323n46
documentary imagination, 17–21, 32, 69–71, 91; in Dorothea Lange's work, 71–75; in John Steinbeck's work, 75–77, 263; and Partch, 85–87, 113, 232, 263; in Woody Guthrie's work, 77–85
documentary impulse, 15–17, 20, 62, 86, 98
Dolmetsch, Arnold, 63
Dos Passos, John, 48, 138–39, 142, 153, 176, 310n31
Double Canon. *See* Surrogate Kithara
Dreamer That Remains, The, 217, 275, 276, 282, 323n46
Driscoll, Bertha Knisely. *See* Knisely, Bertha McCord
Drummond, Dean, 279
Dust Bowl, 19, 56, 70, 75, 77, 86, 108, 232, 248–49
Dust Bowl Ballads, 78, 81, 83–85, 249, 303n61; recording of, 83

Dust Bowl migrants, 60, 62, 69, 71, 76, 82, 86, 87, 198, 251
Dust Bowl refugees, 56–58, 81, 104, 199
Dvořák, Antonin, 5–6, 7, 8

Earls, Paul, 2
Eastman School of Music, 127–28, 227, 231, 236; Partch's performance at, 233–34, 250, 203n48, 319n52
Ellis, Alexander J., 28
Enclosure series, 254
equal temperament, 3, 12, 27, 28–29, 32, 30, 123, 190, 223, 226, 233, 259, 260
Evans, Gil, 278
Evans, Walker, 19, 71
exoticism. *See* conceptual exoticism; decorative exoticism
Exposition of Monophony, 29, 31, 32, 41, 223, 224

fabric (in Partch's theory), 30
Factories in the Field, 58–59
Farm Security Administration (FSA), 18, 59–61, 70, 71, 72, 74, 76, 79, 85, 88, 90–91
Farwell, Arthur, 6–8, 9, 12, 290n21
Federal Emergency Relief Administration (FERA), 49–53, 64, 69, 97, 105, 107, 258, 259, 260; California transient camps of, 55–56, 65–66, 68, 297n22, 298n43
Federal Music Project, 105, 106
Federal Transient Bureau, 50–51, 53, 54, 96. *See also* transient
Federal Writers' Project, 105, 108, 220
Field, John, 27
Finnegans Wake, 158, 227, 228, 229, 239, 242, 246, 249, 256
Flanders family, 44, 231
Flex-a-tone, 246

Flynt, Josiah, 133, 134, 135, 152, 309n15, 309n16
forty-three-tone scale, 14, 30, 175, 226, 234, 236, 238, 249, 255, 269, 277
Fox, Charles Elmer, 147
Fox, Charles Warren, 269
Freeman, Betty, 258, 273, 275

Gann, Kyle, 3
Garland, Peter, 268
Gate 5 Records, 183, 256
Genesis of a Music, 26, 30, 33, 150, 254, 261, 276; first edition of, 1, 175, 225, 235, 248, 262–63, 269–70
Gilmore, Bob, 35, 37, 43, 122, 164, 207, 255, 266
Gilson, Warren, 256
Ginsberg, Allen, 266
God, She, 158, 228, 259, 320n79
"God's Lonely Man," 228, 229, 238, 259
Graham, Martha, 16, 235, 241
Grapes of Wrath, The, 18, 58–59, 69, 76–77, 79, 82, 90, 108, 127, 252, 258, 263, 281, 298n36; benefit concert, 78, 83; film version of, 90
Great Depression, 2, 4, 9, 12, 20, 21, 35, 38, 44, 48–49, 51–58, 61–62, 109, 132, 143, 147, 152, 201, 204, 211–13, 296n5, 299n55; and documentary, 15–18, 69–71, 90, 104, 264; impact on artists, 10, 71–79, 127, 250; impact on Partch's life and work, 13, 19, 24, 33–34, 45, 64–65, 85–87, 88, 92, 95–100, 144, 163, 198–200, 220, 252, 259, 268, 273
Guggenheim Foundation, 106, 224, 241, 249; Fellowships to Partch, 34, 238–39, 246–47, 250, 252, 257, 279; Partch's applications to, 29, 41–45, 158, 195, 206, 209, 228–30, 231–34, 240, 242–43, 250, 259, 277
Guthrie, Woody, 20, 77–87, 179, 197, 234, 248, 250, 253; inspiration to Partch, 84, 302n48

Hába, Alois, 3
"Hallelujah, I'm a Bum," 98, 142
Hanson, Howard, 227, 231, 232, 234, 242, 250
Harburg, E. Y., 103
Harmonic Canons, 38, 183–84, 190, 286
harmonic series, 28–30, 38–39, 126, 214, 222, 244; overtones as part of, 12, 41, 295n45
Harrington Ranch, 66, 68, 210, 304n23
Harris, Roy, 18, 42 44, 70, 86, 292n39; as compared to Partch, 10–12
Harrison, Lou, 3, 120, 208–9, 221, 248, 264, 289n9
Helmholtz, Hermann, 28–29; *On the Sensations of Tone*, 28, 36
hitchhiking, 38, 111, 123, 145, 147–48, 151, 154, 157, 158, 161, 166, 184, 196, 209, 220, 225, 227, 228, 250, 267, 298n43
hobo, 46–48, 55, 58, 70–71, 94, 121–22, 137–38, 166–67, 188–89; in American culture, 23–24, 48, 88–91, 101, 135–37, 138–39, 142–43, 152–54, 266–68, 280; in *Barstow*, 111–13, 123–28; definition of, 48, 78, 95, 130, 133, 162, 211–12, 265–66; and food, 120–21; history of, 130–35; influence of on *U.S. Highball*, 194–97, 258; modern hoboing, 280–281; and movement, 119–20; Partch's interactions with and time as, 1–3, 14–15, 24–26, 32–36, 40–41, 63–65, 84, 98, 122–23, 145–49, 184, 209–10, 217–18,

227–30, 252–53; and Partch's reception, 253–58, 282–84; in Partch's writings, 116–18; popular perception of, 23–24, 48, 65, 77–78, 139–42, 163, 176, 213; songs about and by, 113–16, 142–43, 178–82, 205; and Woody Guthrie, 81–84, 253
Hobo's Hornbook, The, 179–80. *See also* Milburn, George
hobohemia, 130, 137, 139, 166, 176, 178, 308n3
Hodgman, John, 280
Hoiby, Lee, 269, 316n21
homosexuality, 265–66, 316n14; among hoboes, 51, 119–20; in transient camps, 67. *See also* Partch, Harry, sexuality of
Hopkins, Harry, 49–50, 105, 259
Horath, Graydon, 147–48
Howells, William Dean, 132, 136
hymnody, 13, 19, 24–25, 87, 94, 126, 142, 232, 264; in *Bitter Music*, 98–101; in *U.S. Highball*, 186, 188–90

Industrial Workers of the World (Wobblies), 98, 136–37, 139, 212, 262, 309n23
Inman, Henry, 200–202
Ives, Charles E., 3, 13–14, 122, 177, 182, 235, 248, 255

Johansen, Gunnar, 249, 269
Johnston, Ben, 3, 220, 255, 257, 276–77, 278, 281
just intonation, 3, 35, 36, 38, 42, 43, 223, 233, 248, 260, 271, 282; definitions of, 28–29; Partch's adoption of, 14, 29–31, 213–14

Kain-tuck, 66, 97, 101, 120
Kassel, Richard, 103, 126

Kerouac, Jack, 129, 139, 280; *On the Road*, 23, 266–68, 272
"King Oedipus" (Yeats), 43, 223, 250
Kithara, 221, 229, 238, 243, 244, 246, 285, 314n66; in *the Letter*, 214–16; in *San Francisco*, 206–9; in *U.S. Highball*, 149, 150, 159, 161, 170–72, 183, 186, 188–91; relationship to Greek original, 38, 123
Knight of the Road, 122–23, 166, 279
Knisely, Bertha McCord, 41, 42, 64, 224, 257
Kronos Quartet, 281

Lange, Dorothea, 18, 19, 20, 56, 69, 71–75, 85–87, 110, 124, 127, 143, 250, 252, 264; photographs of hobos by, 88–92. *See also* documentary imagination; *American Exodus, An*
Lao-tzu, 273
Leadbelly, 78, 84
League of Composers, 8, 241, 242, 244; Partch's concert for, 170, 219, 245, 247, 256, 260
Lee, Russell, 71
Letter, The, 17, 66, 199, 209–18, 256, 272, 273, 276, 282; as hobo composition, 258–60; title change of, 261–62. *See also Wayward, The*
Li Po, 112
limit (in Partch's theory), 30, 214–15, 294n21, 295n45
Lindsay, Vachel, 129, 135
Little Red Songbook, 98
Little Tramp, the. *See* Chaplin, Charlie
Lloyd Campbell Publications, 113, 115
Locke, Ralph, 11, 293n62
"Lord Is My Shepherd, The." *See Two Psalms*
Lomax, Alan, 78, 83, 178, 205, 316n14; correspondence with Partch, 220–21, 281

Lomax, John, 12, 178
London, Jack, 120, 133–35, 143, 153, 162
Los Angeles Philharmonic, 26–27
Lorentz, Pare, 18–19, 61, 232
Ludlow, John E., 108
Luening, Ethel, 227, 242, 244; performance of Partch's music, 245–47
Luening, Otto, 43, 44, 150, 195, 219, 227, 230, 232, 233, 235, 238, 250, 279; preface to *Genesis of a Music*, 1–2; relationship with Partch, 224–25

Mandarin Theater, 28
Manual on the Maintenance and Repair of—and the Musical and Attitudinal Techniques for—Some Putative Musical Instruments, 37–38
Manuel, Philip, 222, 224
Marshall, Lauriston C. (Larry), 250, 260, 262, 278; microfilm of *Bitter Music*, 261, 323n26
Maruchess, Alix Young, 244–45
McClintock, Harry "Mac," 205–6
McGeary, Thomas, 220
meantone tuning, 29
melos, 30–31
Mellers, Wilfrid, 254, 268
MicroFest, 3–4
microtones, 12–14, 164
migrants, 69, 71, 79, 85–87, 94, 95, 104, 110, 113, 179, 196, 210; California's response to, 56–62, 66; as distinct from transients, 51–54; ethnicity of, 59, 141; Partch's use of, 198, 234, 258–61, 262, 265; popular perceptions of, 17–18, 71–77, 78, 90–91, 108–9; and Woody Guthrie, 78–84
"Migrant Mother," 74, 75, 85, 127, 301n28; Lange's taking of, 72–73

Milburn, George, 179, 181
Mitchell, Danlee, 145, 219, 273–75
"Modern Parable I, A," 116–17, 199, 204
"Modern Parable II, A " 117
Modern Times, 141, 142
Moe, Henry Allen, 43–45, 106, 107, 224, 227, 243, 247, 249, 257, 259; and Partch's Guggenheim Fellowships, 44, 228, 232, 238, 240, 246
monika song, 179–80, 196, 314n58; relationship to *U.S. Highball*, 181–82, 264
Monophone, 36–38, 285. *See also* Adapted Viola
Monophonic Cycle, 158, 206, 209, 227–29, 238, 242–44
Monophony, 28–32, 44, 145, 161, 164, 226, 234, 235; definition of, 14, 31, 43, 213, 262
Moore, Douglas, 86, 219, 240, 241, 242, 250, 279, 318n24; "Come Away Death," 235; relationship with Partch, 235–36, 239, 244, 249
Musorgsky, Modest, 125, 164

National Conservatory of Music, 5
National Recording Preservation Act of 2000, 284
Native American music, 6–10, 14; Partch's interactions with, 12–13, 126
New Deal, 33, 60, 61, 64, 85, 90, 95, 109, 134, 258; cultural programs of, 16, 18, 71, 104–7; and transients, 48–53
New England Conservatory of Music, 240
New Music Society, 38, 40, 44, 241, 156, 322n12
Newband, 279

newsboy, 17, 116–17, 198–99, 217–18, 254; in American popular music, 204–6; history of, 200–204; Partch's setting of, 206–9; in visual art, 200–203
Novarro, Ramon, 27
Nyman, Michael, 3

Oedipus (Partch), 1, 173, 222, 270–71, 275
On the Road. *See* Kerouac, Jack
One Voice (Partch's theory), 14, 31, 207, 213, 262, 278
Ontonality, 40, 192–93, 214, 295n45
Oswalt, Patton, 280
overtone series. *See* harmonic series

Pablo (Partch's hobo friend), 66–67, 97, 210, 213, 216–17, 266, 282. *See also Letter, The*
Partch, Harry: American experimental tradition and, 3, 13, 236, 255, 289n9; and army, 231–32; childhood of, 2, 24–26, 126; Christianity and, 24–25, 99–100, 188–90, 271; destroys *Bitter Music*, 260–61, 273; destroys early compositions ("auto-da-fé"), 33, 36, 261; education, 26–32, 60, 176; grants awarded to, 33, 34, 44–45, 238–39, 246–47; instrument building and, 36–38, 63, 110, 123, 149; lecture-demonstrations of own work, 78, 111, 127–28, 227, 231, 233–34, 237, 239, 240, 250, 257; as musical outsider, 2, 4, 252–55, 258, 260, 267, 270, 272, 276, 280; as "Paul Pirate," 36, 116; as proofreader, 28, 33–34, 35–36, 64, 104–5, 122–23; sexuality of, 27, 120, 265–66, 294n17, 323n46; as silent movie pianist, 25; speech-music theories of, 4, 14, 30–32,
37, 42, 79, 94–95, 98, 100, 112, 123–25, 157, 164, 166, 213, 216, 232–33, 249; string quartet of, 36; symphonic tone poem of, 36; theoretical work of, 28–32, 39–40, 164–65, 213–15, 295n45; works for WPA, 104–8, 260; as a writer, 31, 106–8, 116–17, 123, 145, 150–51, 199, 204, 220–21, 257
Partch, Jennie (mother), 24–27, 273
Partch, Paul (brother), 25, 33, 36, 105, 241, 306n9
Partch, Virgil (father), 2, 24–26, 99
Patterns of Music, 223, 233, 249
Perlis, Vivian, 2, 272, 276
Pinkerton, Allan, 131
Plow that Broke the Plains, The, 18–19, 61, 232
Porter, Quincy, 44, 240, 242–43
"Potion Scene" from *Romeo and Juliet*. *See Romeo and Juliet*.
Pouliot, Stephen, 275, 276, 282
Pound, Ezra, 63
Ptolemy, 63, 110, 123, 222
Pythagoras, 28, 30
Pythagorean tuning, 29

Quadrangularis Reversum, 38

Radil, Rudophine, 40
ratios, 28–29, 30, 214, 295n45; as notation for musical intervals, 165–65, 170–71, 189–90
Ratio Keyboard, 41; *See also* Ptolemy
Reich, Steve, 3
Relief Administration, 49, 61
Resolution (in Partch's theory), 188
Revelation in the Courthouse Park, 13, 103, 264, 304n7; relationship to Americana works of, 273, 275
"Rock of Ages," 25, 99–102
Rockefeller Foundation, 84, 276
Rockwell, Norman, 89, 140–43

Rodgers, Jimmie, 142–43
Rogers, Calista, 41, 42, 244
Rolling Stone, 283–84
Romeo and Juliet, "Potion Scene," 37, 43, 94

Roosevelt, Franklin D., 49, 51, 59, 71, 105, 135, 297n19
Ross, Lillian Bos, 123
Ross, Alex, 1
Ruess, Everett, 99, 101, 102, 277
Russell, William, 221

Salvation Army, 132, 189, 288, 315n73
San Francisco, 1, 17, 206–9, 228, 238, 247, 248, 256, 258, 259, 272; as hobo composition, 217–18, 282. See also *Wayward, The*
San Francisco Chronicle, 55–56
San Francisco News, 35–36, 73
Sandburg, Carl, 129, 178–79
Santee, Ross, 105, 107
Schafer, R. Murray, 283
Schlesinger, Kathleen, 63, 123
Schoenberg, Arnold, 31
School of Design, Chicago, 221–22
Schuyten, Ernest, 42
secondary ratios (in Partch's theory), 30
Seeger, Charles, 42, 221, 281
Seeger, Pete, 83
Seventeen Lyrics by Li Po, 37, 43, 164–65, 166, 221, 222, 226, 234, 256
Shahn, Ben, 71
Shakespeare. See *Romeo and Juliet*
Shanafelt, Clara, 43–44, 227
"Show Horses in the Concert Ring," 257, 313n50
Sinclair, Upton, 55–56, 299n45
Slonimsky, Nicolas, 240–41
Sokoloff, Nikolai, 106
Spoils of War, 150, 159, 184, 185, 193, 286
Sonkin, Robert, 90–92, 303n2

Southwest Museum, 12, 41
Stahnke, Manfred, 3
State Emergency Relief Agency (SERA), 50–52, 54–55, 60, 69, 81, 258; Harry Partch's experiences with, 65, 68
Steinbeck, John, 20, 75–77, 78, 82, 108, 124, 250, 263; and California Growers' Association, 58–60; as documentarian, 18, 19, 75, 83, 86, 87, 143. See also documentary imagination; *Grapes of Wrath, The*
Stott, William, 15–17
Surette, Thomas Whitney, 44, 238
Surrogate Kithara, 149–50, 159, 183, 186, 189–90, 191, 186
Susman, Warren, 77

Taylor, Paul, 56–57, 72, 73, 110. See also *American Exodus, An*
Taylor, Noel Heath, 34
Tenney, James, 3
Thomas, Michael Tilson, 3
Thomson, Virgil, 18–19, 236–37, 240, 242, 248, 249, 284; reactions to Partch's theories, 175, 232–33, 250. See also *Plow that Broke the Plains, The*
Todd, Charles, 90–92, 303n2
tonality (in Partch's theory), 126, 213–14
Tonality Diamond, 40, 192, 215–16, 222, 226, 295n45
Tourtelot, Madeline, 150, 272
Transient program. See Federal Transient Bureau
transients, 17, 18, 47–48, 78, 90, 128, 163, 189, 191, 192, 258, 259–61, 265; and *Bitter Music*, 92, 94–100, 108–9; California policies toward, 54–57, 59, 68, 72, 81, 104; definitions of, 60, 61, 199, 297n15; federal policies toward, 48–53,

64–67, 95–96, 107, 299n48; as
  hoboes, 24, 48, 178; and *The Letter*,
  209–13, 217–18, 273, 276, 282
Tully, Jim, 129
Turner, Frederick Jackson, 135–37
Two Psalms, 37, 43, 222, 226, 234, 235,
  238, 256
Two Settings from Lewis Carroll, 158

undertone series, 39–40, 214
University of California, Los Angeles
  (UCLA), 257
University of California, San Diego,
  257
University of California Orchestra, 35
University of Illinois at Urbana-
  Champaign, 257, 271
University of Southern California, 27,
  32, 41, 44
University of Wisconsin, Madison,
  209, 249, 253, 257, 260, 269
University of Wisconsin Press, 262–63
U.S. Highball, 17, 64, 77, 79, 84, 98,
  108, 127, 194–97, 207, 209,
  213, 226, 252, 258, 263–64,
  268–69; composition of, 154–75,
  237–39, 272; film of, 150, 272;
  and Guggenheim applications,
  158, 195, 209, 228, 252, 259; and
  historical record, 152–53, 259–60;
  Overture to, 183–84, 192, 193;
  and Partch's instruments, 186–94;
  performances of, 240, 241, 247,
  278; recordings of, 243, 256,
  278–79, 281, 284; reviews of, 176,
  247–48, 249, 283; sketches of,
  166–70; structure of, 103, 175–86;
  trip that inspired, 34, 145–47,
  220; versions of, 144–45, 149–50,
  158–63; writings about, 150–52,
  194–95. See also *Wayward, The*
US Immigration Service, 24, 212
Utonality, 39–40, 192–93, 214, 295n45
Waits, Tom, 279
Water! Water!, 13
"Wabash Cannonball, The," 142,
  311n42
Wayward, The, 2, 4, 17, 20, 121, 128,
  149, 181, 198–99, 259, 263, 272,
  281, 282–83; and *Barstow*, 126;
  and *The Letter*, 209, 213, 217, 276;
  and *San Francisco*, 116; and *U.S.
  Highball*, 261, 279
Werckmeister III temperament, 29
Wheatland Riot, 212
"While My Heart Keeps Beating Time,"
  101, 102, 113–16, 126
Whitman, Walt, 138, 139, 143
Williamson, Gavin, 222, 224
Windsong, 254, 256
Wolcott, Marion Post, 71
Works Progress Administration
  (WPA), 33, 49, 53, 68, 103, 104–7,
  111, 260

Y.D. Fantasy, 228, 246–47, 249, 256,
  306n12
Yaddo, 223–24, 227–28
Yaqui Indians, 13, 24, 25
Yeats, W. B., 37, 43, 63, 97, 98, 123;
  "King Oedipus," 222, 223, 250, 270
Yoell, Larry, 115, 306n9
Young, Ella, 237

Zappa, Frank, 3, 283–84
Zoller family, 32, 33, 38–39

Harry Partch (1901–74) was one of the most distinctive and influential American composers of the mid-twentieth century. During the Great Depression, Partch rode the railways, following the fruit harvest across the country. Although he is renowned for his immense stage works, such as *Delusion of the Fury*, and his use of highly sophisticated instruments of his own creation, Partch is still regularly called a "hobo composer." Yet few have questioned this label's impact on his musical output, compositional life, and reception.

Focusing on Partch the person alongside the cultural icon he represented, this study examines Partch from historical, cultural, political, and musical perspectives. It outlines the cultural history of the hobo from the mid-1800s through the 1960s, as well as those figures associated with the hobo's image. It explores how Partch's music, which chronicled a disappearing subculture, was received, and how the composer ultimately engaged and frustrated popular conceptions of the hobo. And it follows Partch's later years to question his response to the hobo label and the ways in which others used it to define and contain him for over thirty years.

S. Andrew Granade is associate professor of musicology in the Conservatory of Music and Dance, University of Missouri–Kansas City.

"*Harry Partch, Hobo Composer* is almost epic in its panoramic view of an American subculture as seen through the lens of one artist's life. It should find a ready audience among composers and scholars of American music, not to mention the legions of microtonalists who look to Partch as their primogenitor and patron saint. An important book."
—Michael Hicks, author of *Henry Cowell, Bohemian*

"In *Harry Partch, Hobo Composer*, Andrew Granade invites us to travel at Partch's side, riding the rails, discovering new musical landscapes, and listening with keen ears to the varied inflections of the American vernacular. Partch's hobo compositions, with their rich mix of mythology and autobiography, emerge as works on a par with those of Dorothea Lange, John Steinbeck, Woody Guthrie, Jack Kerouac, and others. Partch's story, in Granade's hands, reminds us of the truth in the notion that not all who wander are lost."
—Beth E. Levy, author of *Frontier Figures: American Music and the Mythology of the American West*